Introduction to Quantitative Macroeconomics Using Julia

From Basic to State-of-the-Art Computational Techniques

Introduction to Quantitative Macroeconomics Using Julia

From Basic to State-of-the-Art Computational Techniques

Petre Caraiani
Institute for Economic Forecasting
Romanian Academy
Bucharest, Romania

ACADEMIC PRESS

An imprint of Elsevier

Academic Press is an imprint of Elsevier
125 London Wall, London EC2Y 5AS, United Kingdom
525 B Street, Suite 1650, San Diego, CA 92101, United States
50 Hampshire Street, 5th Floor, Cambridge, MA 02139, United States
The Boulevard, Langford Lane, Kidlington, Oxford OX5 1GB, United Kingdom

Notices

Knowledge and best practice in this field are constantly changing. As new research and experience broaden our understanding, changes in research methods, professional practices, or medical treatment may become necessary.

Practitioners and researchers must always rely on their own experience and knowledge in evaluating and using any information, methods, compounds, or experiments described herein. In using such information or methods they should be mindful of their own safety and the safety of others, including parties for whom they have a professional responsibility.

To the fullest extent of the law, neither the Publisher nor the authors, contributors, or editors, assume any liability for any injury and/or damage to persons or property as a matter of products liability, negligence or otherwise, or from any use or operation of any methods, products, instructions, or ideas contained in the material herein.

Library of Congress Cataloging-in-Publication Data
A catalog record for this book is available from the Library of Congress

British Library Cataloguing-in-Publication Data
A catalogue record for this book is available from the British Library

ISBN: 978-0-12-812219-8

For information on all Academic Press publications
visit our website at https://www.elsevier.com/books-and-journals

Working together
to grow libraries in
developing countries

www.elsevier.com • www.bookaid.org

Publisher: Candice Janco
Acquisition Editor: Scott J. Bentley
Editorial Project Manager: Susan Ikeda
Production Project Manager: Sujatha Thirugnana Sambandam
Designer: Mark Rogers

Typeset by VTeX

Contents

About the Author

Petre Caraiani is Senior Researcher at the Institute for Economic Forecasting at Romanian Academy in Bucharest. He obtained his Ph.D. in economics from Romanian Academy. He has written more than 40 articles on macroeconomics and economic modeling in various ISI peer-reviewed publications, including (among others) the Economics Letters, Journal of Macroeconomics, Empirical Economics, Economic Modelling, Scottish Journal of Political Economy, International Review of Economics and Finance, Plos One, and Physica A.

Preface

Why a new book?

The reader might ask why I wrote this book when so much on quantitative macroeconomics is already available. Most are familiar with Lucas and Stokey (1989), Acemoglu (2009), Ljungqvist and Sargent (2012), and Miao (2015) who are excellent references for the theoretical side. Other books concentrate on solutions to solve and simulate quantitative macroeconomic models, including Heer and Maussner (2009), Miranda and Falcker (2002), and Stachurski and Judd (2017). Faced by these and other outstanding advanced explorations, I recognized that an introduction that stretches from the basics of computational techniques to frontier methods used in macroeconomic research could make a contribution.

My introduction presents numerical techniques and in specific the techniques used in quantitative macroeconomics: solving deterministic and stochastic systems of equations, log-linearization, simulating DSGE models, dynamic programming, and more advanced computational techniques like perturbation, projection method, and parameterized expectations. It also covers the tools that appear in recent work on heterogeneous agent models.

The greatest strengths of my introduction are the balance between theory (which is more comprehensively covered in the above textbooks) and practical applications. While some of the books I have named have applications, my book introduces the reader to the first steps to doing numerical work using code developed in Julia, the free, open source programming language. By using applications in Julia readers can quickly learn how to solve and implement macroeconomic models while using a language dedicated to scientific computing.

Uses of the book

Introduction to Quantitative Macroeconomics Using Julia can be used in multiple ways in teaching. Its first two chapters can anchor a one-semester computational economics course next to titles like Judd (1998) or Miranda and Falcker (2002). Chapters 3–5 are usable in a first-year graduate macroeconomics course, and Chapters 5–6 lend themselves to specialized macroeconomics courses on advanced computational techniques.

Because it emphasizes applications, Introduction to Quantitative Macroeconomics Using Julia can help those who need an introduction to quantitative macroeconomics or who want to learn about numerical techniques in Julia.

Acknowledgments

I thank Scott Bentley and Susan Ikeda at Elsevier for guidance and support throughout the publishing process, as well as the copyeditor. I am also grateful to all the anonymous referees for carefully reviewing and providing useful feedback that has helped improving the book significantly. A number of people have went through the manuscript and provided very useful feedback. I am also grateful to several people who have let me use their Matlab code and adapt it to Julia, and I would like to thank for this Fabrice Collard, Martin Ellison and George Hall. I am also grateful to a few people who shared very interesting lecture notes material that provided useful references when writing the book. I mention here Fabrice Collard, Klaus Neusser or Martin Ellison. My special thanks to Cristian Bereanu for providing guidance regarding the more abstract topic of measure theory. Jonathan Benchimol has also supported the work and I am thankful for that.

Petre Caraiani
June 30, 2018

Chapter 1

Introduction to Julia

Contents

1.1 OVERVIEW

The aim of this chapter is to offer a background for the following chapters and introduce the reader to Julia. While the chapter will cover the essentials about Julia, the interested reader could find more detailed information in books that focus on the actual programming language. However, the background provided here should be enough to understand the following chapters.

Julia is a very young but promising programming language focused on scientific computing. Its creators and developers had in mind the shortcomings of the current software that is primarily aimed at scientific computing. Julia is only a few years old, however it has already attracted a lot of attention and it is very promising in the eyes of many. Its development began in 2009 while the first version was provided in 2012. Julia is a free and open source programming language with a license provided by MIT.

The main attractiveness of the Julia comes from combining the high level syntax of languages like Python and Matlab with the speed of low level languages like Fortran or C/C++. One of the key features through which it can offer this performance is the use of Just in Time compilation and multiple dispatch.

For economists, the greatest appeal is that Julia has a syntax close to the one of Matlab. Given the widespread use of Matlab among economists, this should surely ease the transition to Julia. Furthermore, for macroeconomists, Fortran is still quite used since it provides a fast solution to computational intensive problems. Julia provides two solutions. First, it can easily embed Fortran (as well as C/C++ code). Second, it also makes possible to write the entire code in Julia, while keeping the execution speed comparable to the ones by Fortran or C/C++.

In spite of having not reached version 1.0, Julia has attracted a lot of interest and we could have seen in the recent years a number of books published on the subject. This chapter draws from what has been written on this topic in the last years. There are not many sources on Julia language. The first source, is, of course, Julia's own manual on its website, https://docs.julialang.org/, see [7]. A few other good resources are [1], [2], [3], [4], [5]. The only source dealing with applications in economics is the excellent set of lecture notes [6].

1.2 JULIA IN A NUTSHELL

1.2.1 Installing Julia

To install Julia, we can download it from the official website: http://julialang.org/downloads/. Currently, Julia can be run under Windows, Linux and OSX. As this book was finished, Julia was at version 0.6.3, while version 0.7 was under development (the pre-release version was available). The developers plan to make version 0.7 equivalent with version 1.0, with the former including depreciation warnings.

To actually run Julia there are a few ways to do it. One can use built-in command line, also known as the REPL (discussed below), in the Julia terminal provided with the installation. While this is a quite direct way to run Julia programs, nevertheless the average user would not feel comfortable with this and would like a rather Matlab like environment that would provide both an interpreter and text editing facilities. And this is what an IDE stands for (i.e. Integrated Development Environments).

At the present moment, one can use the freely-available Juno environment which can be downloaded from: junolab.org. An even better alternative is Julia Computing, available at https://juliacomputing.com/. This is the most complex IDE up to this moment and it integrates the Julia compiler, the most commonly used packages as well as two alternative IDEs. One is the already mentioned Juno, while the second is the Jupyter notebooks. The Jupiter notebooks are an easy way to edit and run Julia code. They can also easily integrate plots. Jupyter can be installed either as a standalone (in this case we have to install both Jupyter and Julia) or it can be installed implicitly when Julia Computing is installed. Jupyter notebooks can also be used through JuliaBox (which allows running Julia from web).

1.2.2 Julia Packages

Once we download and install Julia, we can access the so-called standard library in Julia. Similarly to other free software, like R or Python, Julia allows external contributors to build and make available third party packages. These are available through Git, see https://github.com/. The list of currently available Julia packages can be found at: http://pkg.julialang.org. The baseline Julia installation comes with a built-in package manager called Pkg. We can use this to add any available Julia package. For example, to add the stats package, we can simply write:

```
Julia>Pkg.add("Stats")
```

To start using this package, we can write:

```
julia>using Stats
```

Packages can be easily be updated using the command: Pkg.update().

1.2.3 Understanding REPL

REPL stands for Read/Evaluate/Print/Loop. When we start the Julia command prompt, it will provide a REPL window that is the most direct way to access the above named operations.

To use REPL, we simply type statements and press enter so that Julia can execute them. For example, by writing:

```
Julia> x=0
0
```

We assign the value 0 to the variable x. We can access help, pretty much like in other programming languages, by writing:

```
Julia> ?
```

After accessing the help mode, we can search functions by their names. For example, by writing:

```
Help?> sum
```

We get the full list of functions in Julia containing the word sum. By looking for help for a specific function, say sum!, we get:

```
Help?> sum!
Sum!(r,A)
Sum elements of A over the singleton dimensions of r, and write the results to r.
```

With the command ; we can switch to shell where we can type specific commands. With the command whos() we get information and what is currently installed and loaded in Julia. For example:

```
Julia> whos()
Base                    Module
Compat        21197 KB  Module
```

```
Core                     Module
DataStructures  21369 KB  Module
JuliaPro        1997 bytes Module
Main                     Module
SpecialFunctions 21266 KB  Module
Stats          1152 bytes Module
StatsBase       652 KB    Module
```

Although we are going to review the type of variables and operators more in-depth later, Julia's REPL can be also used a scientific calculator very easily:

```
Julia> 1+5
6
Julia> x=8
8
Julia> y=x+1
9
```

1.2.4   Variables and Operations

Starting with this section, I present the main features of the syntax of Julia. Although Julia is currently only at version 0.6.3, and, by the time it reaches version 1.0, some features might be depreciated, nevertheless Julia should still maintain its main features even after it reaches version 1.0.

One of the key features of Julia language is that of being a typed language. This implies the fact that the programmer can choose the type of variables or the type of arguments specific to a function.

Julia deduces the type of a variable from the way it is initialized. For example, when we initialize a simple variable like this:

```
julia> x=1
1
```

Then Julia will understand that x is an integer. To find the type of a variable in Julia, we can use the function typeof().

```
Typeof(x)   #Int64
```

Another key feature of Julia is that it is also a dynamical-typed language. In other words, even if a variable is initialized with a certain type, later, it can be given another type. To continue the basic example from above, we might write later in program that:

```
julia> x="Hello"
"Hello"
Typeof(x)   #String
```

In the next paragraphs, I discuss the main types of variables one could deal with during his or her work: integers, Boolean, floating, complex numbers and strings.

Integers

There are basically two types of integers one can use in Julia: the signed and the unsigned ones (for positive integers). Signed integers can be Int8, Int32, Int64 and Int128. Int8, for example, takes values from $[-2^7, 2^7 - 1]$. Unsigned integers can similarly be Uint8, Uint16, Uint32, Uint64 and Uint128. Uint8 ranges from 0 to $2^8 - 1$. It is also good to know that Julia also has BigInt type of integer, when there is a need for very high precision outside the range allowed by the above types of integers. When we try to store a number outside the range allowed for its type, say $[-128, 127]$ for Int8, we will get overflow. However, since Julia does not check for overflow automatically, special care needs to be taken when overflow might happen. A potential solution is the use of BigInt type.

Booleans

For this particular variable, Julia has the type Bool. A variable can be assigned the Bool type by attributing it the value true or false or a logical expression. For example, by writing:

```
julia> x=(1>0)
typeof(x)
Bool
```

We assign to the variable x a Bool type.

Floating Point Numbers

Like most programming languages, Julia includes the two basic types of primitive numeric types. Besides the integer types, including here both the signed and unsigned integers, as well as the Booleans, Julia also includes a second primitive numeric type, the floating point numbers. However, in contrast to most programming languages, Julia also allows the programmer to create his own primitives. Similarly to the case of integer numbers, there are few types of floating point numbers: Float16, Float32 and Float64. The number at the end of each type indicates the number of bits. For example, Float32 has 32 bits. Float32 has single precision, while Float64 has double precision. For a high level of precision, Julia has also BigFloat type of floating point number.

Complex Numbers

Julia supports complex numbers too through a special type, the Complex type. The Complex type is built with the help of the primitive numeric types. We can initiate a new variable as a Complex type in two ways in Julia. One way is based on the use of constant *im* which was specially created to represent the square root of -1. Thus, we can write:

```
julia> c=2+3im
2+3im
julia> Typeof(c)
Complex{Int64}
```

A second way to create complex numbers is by the use of the function complex(). For example, we could use:

```
julia> c=complex(2,3)
julia> Typeof(c)
Complex{Int64}
```

Strings

Strings are seen in Julia as succession (or arrays) of characters. Before going into more depth regarding strings, we discuss about characters in Julia. For characters, Julia uses a special type named Char. The simple code below shows how Julia sees characters.

```
julia> y='y'
'y'
julia> typeof(y)
Char
```

Basically, a Char variable stands for a single character. To each character, there is a numeric value associated. To find the numeric value of a character, simply use the function Int():

```
julia> Int('y')
121
```

The mark strings, we use either double quotes or triple quotes. We can initiate strings in Julia the way we initiate any type of numeric variable:

```
julia> str="Hello"
"Hello"
```

We can call a character from the string by appealing to the index. More specifically, we write:

```
julia> str[3]
'l': ASCII/Unicode U+006c (category Ll: Letter, lowercase)
```

It is important to keep in mind that the indexing in Julia starts from 1. The elements of any string can be found by calling the index from 1 to n, where the length of the string is n.

Operators

Arithmetic Operators: The support of arithmetic operators is quite standard. Once we saw how arithmetic operators are implemented in a certain language, be it Matlab or R, we will easily apprehend its implementation in Julia. A few examples below are quite illustrative for the implementation in Julia:

```
Julia> 4+5
9
Julia> 5-4
1
Julia> 2*3
6
Julia> 4/2
2
```

Comparison Operators: We can apply the usual comparison operators, i.e. equality, inequality, less than, greater than for all types of primitive numbers used by Julia. Their use is quite intuitive in Julia:

```
julia> 5==5
True
julia> 5==6
False
julia> 5!=7
True
```

Updating Operators: We can update the value of any variable using updating operators. To do so, we just add the sign '=' after the operator we want to use. For example, we write:

```
Julia> x=2
2
Julia> x+=4
6
```

Mathematical Functions

Given the aim of Julia at becoming a reference programming language for scientific computations, it is not surprising that Julia covers very well the basic mathematical functions. Below, I present some of the most used elementary functions. To round a number to the closest integer, we write:

```
Julia> round (1.2)
1
```

Computing the square root or applying roots and powers is very easy as well:

```
Julia> sqrt(9)
3
Julia> exp(3)
20.08
Julia> log(10)
2.3
```

Trigonometric, hyperbolic and other special functions are well covered too. However, the interested reader might consult the manual if he or she needs to find out more.

1.2.5 Vectors

The type format for a one-dimensional array or vector in Julia is $Array\{Type, N\}(dims)$ where Type stands for the type of variables the array will consist in, while N is the length of the vector and it is determined from dims. There are different ways to create vectors in Julia. First, we can declare its elements, then we can inspect it using the function show() as follows:

```
Julia> v=Array{Float32, 3}
Julia> show(v)
Array{Float32,3}
```

However, this does not necessarily lead to vector containing zero values. To ensure that this indeed happens, we should rather write:

```
Julia> v=Float32[]
0-element Array {Float32,1}
```

There are alternative ways to create vectors which can be very useful in doing computational work. Two functions are quite similar to their Matlab (or R) counterparts, namely zeros and ones, which create vectors of zeros and of ones, respectively:

```
Julia> v1=zeros(5)
5-element Array{Float64,1}:
0.0
0.0
0.0
0.0
0.0
Julia> v2=ones(2)
2-element Array{Float64,1}:
1.0
1.0
```

We can also use the linspace function, with the syntax linspace (start, end, n), which will return a vector of n numbers, equally spaced from the starting number of the last number:

```
Julia> v2=linspace(1,2,5)
1.0:0.25:2.0
```

This can be further put into an array using collect():

```
Julia> v2=collect(v2)
5-element Array{Float64,1}:
1.0
1.25
1.5
1.75
2.0
```

The function rand() can also be used to generate a vector populated with random values:

```
Julia> v=rand(2)
2-element Array{Float64,1}:
0.351085
0.437856
```

Julia has some simple yet effective functions that help working with arrays/vectors. We can concatenate two vectors using the function append. The syntax is append! (v1, v2). Here v1 and v2 are two vectors. The first vector v1 will be appended with v2.

```
Julia> v1=zeros(2)
Julia> v2=ones(2)
Julia> append! (v1,v2)
4-element Array{Float64,1}:
0.0
0.0
1.0
1.0
```

1.2.6 Multidimensional Arrays

Contrary to other programming languages, Julia does not treat arrays differently. To speed up the processing of arrays, Julia focuses on the compiler.

Conceptually, at the most general level, we can think of arrays as being collections of objects memorized using a multidimensional grid. Although Julia can work with arrays that contain any type of objects, the general use of arrays implies using specific numerical types (like floating point numbers of integer numbers).

Julia's way to operate with multidimensional arrays is as intuitive as with the vectors. To declare a vector, we simply write:

```
Julia> v=[1,2,3,4,5];
5-element Array{Int64,1}
```

But to declare a matrix with 1 row and 5 columns, we eliminate the commas:

```
Julia> a=[1 2 3 4 5];
1x5Array{Int64,2}
 1  2  3  4  5
```

In a similar manner, we can also declare an array with multiple rows by using ; to distinguish between rows:

```
Julia> a=[1 2 3 4 5; 6 7 8 9 10];
2x5Array{Int64,2}
1 2 3 4 5
6 7 8 9 10
```

As it was the case of vectors, we can use the functions zeros, ones or rand, or linspace to initiate an array (the latter requires the use of reshape(), explained below). The following examples are quite illustrative:

```
Julia> a=zeros (2,2)
2x2 Array {Float64,2}
Julia> a=ones(2,2)
2x2 Array {Float64,2}
Julia> A=reshape(linspace(0,1,4),2,2)
 0.0        0.666667
0.333333  1.0
Julia> r=randn(2,2)
2x2 Array{Float64,2}:
0.618744  -1.08049
2.07069   -0.107986
```

Besides arrays consisting in values of zero or values of one, we can also create specific arrays, like the identity matrix. This can be done using the function eye(). We can write:

```
Julia> eye(2)
```

And we create a 2x2 identity matrix, or we can use:

```
Julia> eye(2,2)
```

to construct a 2x3 identity matrix.

There are a number of basic functions which greatly enhance working with arrays. A programmer already exposed to the way Matlab treats arrays would quickly apprehend them. To find the number of dimensions of an array, we use the function ndims():

```
Julia> a=zeros(2,2)
2x2 Array {Float64,2}
Julia> ndims(a)
```

To find the dimensions of an array, we use size():

```
Julia> size(a)
2,2
```

While to find the number of columns (or size in a certain direction), we write:

```
Julia> size(a,2)
2
```

We can also learn about what type of elements is stored in the array using eltype().

```
Julia> eltype(a)
Float64
```

A very useful function when dealing with arrays is reshape. We use reshape() to change the dimensions of an existent matrix:

```
Julia> a=[ 1 2 3; 4 5 6]
Julia> b=reshape(a,3,2)
1 5
4 3
2 6
```

To concatenate arrays, the following function is used cat(k,A). This will concatenate an array A along its dimension k. Alternatively, we can use hcat(a,b) to horizontally concatenate two arrays, or vcat(a,b) to vertically concatenate two vectors. A simple example shows how to actually apply them:

```
Julia> a = [1 2 3; 4 5 6]
Julia> v = [6 7 8; 9 10 11]
Julia> hcat(a,v)
1 2 3 6 7 8
4 5 6 9 10 11
```

Many times when working with arrays, we would be interested in calling certain elements of the arrays. To do this, we use the available indexing. In Julia, the indexing of arrays is quite straightforward. If A is an n-dimensional array, we call certain elements by using:

$$X = A[I_1, I_2, ..., I_n]$$

With $I_1, ..., I_n$ taking simple integer values, a range, being : or a colon if we select certain dimensions, an integer vector or even a Boolean vector. Let's see a simple example that illustrates the indexing of arrays in Julia:

```
Julia> a=[1 2 3; 4 5 6]
2x3 Array{Float64}
1 2 3
4 5 6
Julia> a[2]
2
Julia> a[1,:]
1 2 3
```

Once we understand the indexing in Julia, it is very easy to learn assigning values to the cells in an array. The procedure mirrors perfectly calling an entry in an array:

$$A[I_1, I_2, ..., I_n] = X$$

Where $I_1, ..., I_n$ can take values as shown above.

1.2.7 Functions

In Julia, functions are treated as first-class objects. They have a major importance in Julia language since Julia is organized around functions. Functions in Julia are basically objects through which a set of argument values is mapped to a set of return values.

Defining Functions

There are two ways to define functions in Julia: the standard way, and the "assignment" way. The standard approach to define a function is pretty straightforward:

```
Julia> function f(x,y,z)
x+y+z
end
f (generic function with 1 method)
```

The assignment approach is more compact and direct:

```
Julia> f(x,y,z)=x+y+z
f (generic function with 1 method)
```

To call a function, we simply call it using the normal syntax based on brackets:

```
Julia> f(1,2,3)
6
```

The Return Keyword

The role of return keyword in the body of a function is to return the value of the respective function. In Julia, the return will give the value of the last evaluated expression, irrespective of whether there are other expressions following return. A few examples will make things clear.

```
Julia> function g(x,y,z)
return x*y+z
x+y+z
end
```

We can compare now the returned values by the two defined functions, f and g:

```
Julia> f(1,2,3)
6
Julia> g(1,2,3)
5
```

Operators as Functions

As already mentioned, Julia is built around functions. The operators themselves are functions with their own syntax. This is why we can also call them in the way we call functions, using argument lists. Let us see a few examples:

```
Julia> 1*2*3
6
Julia> *(1,2,3)
6
```

Default and Optional Arguments

Until now, we have met functions were all arguments were required. But this is not necessary the case in Julia. We can also use optional arguments when defining a function, under two conditions: first, they are declared after the required arguments, and, second, they must be assigned values. A simple example will illustrate very well this approach:

```
Julia> f(x,y,a=1, b=2)=a*x+b*y
Julia> f(1,1)
3
Julia> f(1,1,2)
4
Julia> f(1,1,2,4)
6
```

The first call of function f, f(1,1), lets the optional arguments a, b at their default value 1 and 2. In the second call of the function, f(1,1,2), the value of the optional argument a is set at 2, while in the third call of the function f, we set the optional arguments a at 2 and b at 4.

Anonymous Functions

Given the nature of functions in Julia as first-class entities or objects, they can also be assigned to variables, used as arguments, and can also be created without giving them a name, that is anonymously. To do so, we can write either:

```
Julia> x->x+1
(::#1) (generic function with 1 method)
```

Or we can write:

```
Julia> function(x)
x+1
end
(::#1) (generic function with 1 method)
```

Both ways are valid ways to create anonymous functions. In this case we have a function without a specific name, although there is actually a name generated by the compiler. In short, this is a generic function with one argument. Anonymous functions are best used as arguments in a standard (with a name) function. A nice example can be provided using the function map(). Its role is to apply a function to each value in an array and return an array with the new values.

```
Julia> map(x->x+1,[1,2])
2-element Array{Int64,1}:
2
3
```

The example above is a typical way to use an anonymous function with one argument and apply it to each of the values of an array using the standard Julia function map.

Multiple Return Values

The way multiple return values are used in Julia is through returning a tuple of values. At the same time, one can also call values within this tuple without the need to call the tuple. Let us create a simple function that returns multiple values:

```
Julia> function fun(a,b,c)
a*b*c, a+b+c
end;
```

In the usual approach, by calling the function with given values, we will get the tuple of values:

```
Julia> fun(1,2,3)
(6,6)
```

But this is not necessary so since we can also "destructure" the tuple and call values from the tuple:

```
Julia> x,y = fun (1,2,3)
Julia> x
6
Julia> y
6
```

The same result, can be obtained by with the help of return:

```
Julia> function fun(a,b,c)
return a+b+c,a*b*c
end
```

Varargs Functions

Functions with a variable number of arguments (hence, the term "varargs") can present serious advantages. They are not unfamiliar to economists, given their usage in Matlab. Defining a varargs function in Julia is straightforward: after the last argument one puts ellipsis. Let us see a basic example:

```
Julia> fun (x,y...) = (x,y)
Fun (generic function with 1 method)
```

In this function, while x is simply the first argument, y is a collection with zero or more values that are passed to the function fun. Calling our basic function fun, we'll help us understand better the usage of varargs functions:

```
Julia> fun(1)
(1,())
Julia> fun (1,2)
(1,(2,))
Julia> fun (1,2,3)
(1,(2,3))
```

We can also consider the iterable collection separately into a function. This time, the ellipsis will be used when calling the function within the list of arguments:

```
Julia> x=(1,2)
(1,2)
Julia> fun(1,x...)
(1,(1,2))
```

Do-Blocks in Julia

We have already met the possibility of using functions as arguments. However, this can turn cumbersome if declaring the function implies a more involved piece of code. This is where Julia helps us through the use of do-blocks. The role of do-blocks is to simplify passing functions as arguments by providing a way to write clean and clear code.

We use again the standard function map() which applies the same function to a tuple of values. The standard use would be:

```
Julia> map(x->x+1,[1,2,3,4])
4-element Array{Int64,1}
2
3
4
5
```

Using the do-block, we can write it as:

```
Julia> map([1,2,3,4]) do x
x+1
end
4-element Array{Int64,1}:
2
3
4
5
```

While the effectiveness and usefulness might not be very obvious from this simpler example, we can still see that it is quite helpful when passing functions as arguments.

1.2.8 Control Flows

Generally speaking, control flows are used in a programming language to direct the order in which instructions and statements are evaluated and executed. Julia has the typical control-flow structures as other high-level programming languages. In the following paragraphs, I will present each of them, providing clear examples at the same time.

Compound Expression

As the name suggests, the role of compound expression is to simplify the declaration/evaluations of expressions by having a single expression instead of multiple ones comprising multiple subexpressions. There are two types of compound expressions in Julia: *begin* and *;* chains. In both cases, the value of the compound expression is the value of last of subexpression. Let us see a few examples. A *;* chain is quite straightforward:

```
Julia> x=(a=5; b=6; a*b)
30
```

We can write the very same thing using the *begin – end* compound expression:

```
Julia> x= begin
a=5
b=6
a*b
end
30
```

Conditional Evaluation

This is a key construction in any programming language. Its role is to tell the compiler whether a certain part of the code should be executed or not. The decision to execute that specific part of the code depends on the evaluation of a Boolean expression which obviously can take the values false or true. The syntax is quite standard using the typical if-elseif-else keywords, such that it should be already familiar to those experienced with Matlab or R.

To get familiarized with the specifics of this control flow construction in Julia, we can see a simple example:

```
Julia> if x>y
x=2
elseif x<y
x=1
else
x=0
end
```

The logic is simple: when the expression $x > y$ is true, the code assigns the value 2 to x. When the reverse is true, i.e. $x < y$, the block x=1 is evaluated. Finally, if neither of the above conditions hold, in other words, $x = y$, then the code assigns to x the value zero.

The code can be easily embedded in a function that would return of the value of x conditional on the evaluation on the expression that compares x and y:

```
Julia> function ineq (x,y)
if x>y
x=2
elseif x<y
x=1
else
x=0
end
end
ineq (generic function with 1 method).
```

To call the function, we write:

```
Julia> ineq(1,2)
1
Julia> ineq(1,1)
0
```

With respect to the actual implementation of the sub-blocks elseif and else, it must be added that they are not necessary but optional since we can also construct a conditional evaluation without using them:

```
julia> if x=y
x=0
end
```

This piece of code simply tests whether x and y are equal. At the same time, we can use as many elseif blocks as we need:

```
Julia> if x=1
x=1
elseif x=2
x=2
elseif x=3
x=3
end
```

It is worth mentioning that the control flow if-else returns a value, which is not typical to many other languages. This is similar to the case of functions, which return that last evaluated expression before the keyword return.

```
Julia> x=1
1
Julia> y=1
1
Julia> if x==y
x=0
end
0
```

Another key difference relative to other known programming languages is that in Julia the conditional expression cannot be anything but a Boolean type, that is, true or false. For example, writing:

```
Julia> if 2
x=1
end
ERROR:TypeError: non-boolean (Int64) used in Boolean context
```

returns a TypeError, i.e. an error related to the type of variables used. The default message already indicates that the conditional evaluation construction requires the use of Boolean type of variables.

Repeated Evaluations: Loops

The loops are another fundamental building block in control flows for any programming language. They essentially consist in one sequence of statements that are kept repeated until a certain condition is met. There are two such loops in Julia, basically common to other known high level languages: the *for* loop and the *while* loop.

```
Julia> j=3;
Julia> while j>0
println(j^2)
j=j-1
end
9
4
1
```

The syntax and use of *while* in Julia is typical for the high programming languages: the *while* loop ensures that the body of the loop (i.e. println (j); j=j-1) will be kept evaluated as long as the condition that $j > 0$ remains true.

The *for* loop performs basically the same thing: it keeps repeating the body of the loop for a number of times. However there is no explicit condition that is evaluated as in the case of while loop. Rather, the condition is implicitly present in the fact that the loop is evaluated for a finite number of times. Let us see a basic example:

```
julia> for j=1:3
println (j^2)
end
1
4
9
```

While this is not typical to Julia, it is important to note that the variable j used in the *for* loop has a local scope only as it is visible only within the for loop but not after the loop is executed. Julia allows for the use of other keywords to declare the range on which the for loop will iterate, unlike Matlab. We can use either the keyword *in* or the keyword $\in$ and produce a neater code:

```
julia> for j in [1,2,3]
println(j)
end
1
2
3
```

If there is a need to stop either the while loop (even before the evaluated condition becomes false) or the for loop before all the range is visited, one can use the break command. Let's see a few clear examples.

```
Julia> for j=1:30
println (j)
if j>=3
break
end
j=j+1
end
1
2
3
```

A similar example can be constructed for the case of the while loop:

```
Julia> j=1
Julia> while j>0
println(j)
If j>=3
end
j=j+1
end
```

Short Circuit Evaluation

As the name suggest, this is another way to perform conditional evaluations. There are two such types of control flows in Julia: && and ||. By using these keywords, we can evaluate a series of expressions. However, for this case of control flows, a minimum number of (sub)expressions is evaluated. For the case of && control flow, for a series of (sub)expressions connected by it: $f_1 \&\& f_2 \&\& f_3 \&\& ... \&\& f_n$ the evaluation will stop the first time a subexpression is evaluated as false. Otherwise, it will evaluate all (sub)expressions. In contrast, for the || construction, if there is again a series of (sub)expressions connected by this, namely: $f_1 || f_2 || f_3 || ... || f_n$ the evaluation will stop when it first gets a true from a subevaluation. If this not happens, it will keep evaluating all the (sub)expressions.

```
julia> ff1=true
julia> ff2=false
julia> ff1 && ff1
True
julia> ff1 && ff2
false
Julia> ff2 && ff1
False
```

We can do the same exercise with the other short circuit evaluator, ||:

```
julia> ff1 || ff1
True
julia> ff1 || ff2
true
Julia> ff2 || ff1
True
Julia> ff2 || ff2
false
```

As already mentioned, the short circuit evaluation can also be used in the place of the if statements, usually when there is a need for short or very short evaluations. To do this, we use the property of the short circuit evaluations constructions that they evaluate iteratively the (sub)expressions until the first is evaluated as false (for &&) or until the first is evaluated as true (||). Keeping this in mind, an if – end block can be replaced by && if we write:

Conditions && instructions (which implies that the instructions will be evaluated only if the conditions are evaluated as true) and

Conditions || instructions (which implies that the instructions will be evaluated only if the conditions are false).

Let us see a very basic example:

```
Julia> function test(x::Int)
x == 0 && return ("x must be positive")
x <= 5 || return 0
end
test (generic function with 1 method)
Julia> test(1)
1
true
Julia> test(6)
0
```

Exception Handling

Julia has its own system of handling exceptions (including here errors). Exceptions occur anytime a function deals with an unexpected condition. In this case, Julia will return a so-called exception handling since the function cannot deal with that particular condition.

Julia includes a number of standard built-in exceptions that deal with specific breaks of the conditions expected by functions. These breaks include type error (whenever the function deals with the inappropriate type of variable), domain error (the variable has a value outside the expected domain) and so on. A list of built-in exceptions can be found in Julia Documentation. We can see how this can happen by looking at a few examples.

```
Julia> if 1 x=0 end
Error: TypeError: non-boolean (Int64) used in Boolean context.
```

The if-end control flow expects a Boolean when checking for the value of the condition which did not happen here. Let us see another example:

```
Julia> sqrt(-4)
Error: DomainError: sqrt will only return a complex value
if called with a complex argument.
```

Using negative numbers with the square root function will return a domain error, unless with specifically tell sqrt() to deal with complex number.

The Function Throw() Julia allows for the manual handling of exceptions, so that we can both create our own "exceptions" or "throw" one. For the latter case, we can use the default function throw(). This is quite simply to be used:

```
julia> f(y)=y>0 ? y+1: throw(DomainError())
f (generic function with 1 method)
julia>f(2)
3
Julia>f(-2)
Error: DomainError in f(::Int64) at .\REPL[9]:1
```

Errors

The role of the function error() is to provide a way to interrupt the regular flow of the program and show an ErrorException. We can use it to stop the execution of the program. The use of the function error() is quite simple. Additionally, it also allows us to write particular error messages that can guide the programmer. To show the use of error function, we can play with the above defined function.

```
julia> f(y)=y>0 ? y+1: error("y must be positive")
f (generic function with 1 method)
julia>f(2)
3
Julia>f(-2)
Error: y must be positive
in f(::Int64) at .\REPL[12]:1
```

The advantage of using the error() function is that whenever the function defined by us is called with an inappropriate value from another function, it will continue the execution, but it will stop and display the error message made by us.

Warnings and Informational Messages

In contrast to exceptions, warnings and informational messages are useful functions that provide the programmers information on unexpected conditions but without interrupting the execution of the statements. These functions are easy to be used as we can see below:

```
Julia> f(x)=x>0 ? x+1: warn("x must be positive")
f (generic function with 1 method)
julia>f(2)
3
Julia>f(-2)
Warning: y must be positive
```

Similarly, for the function info() (information message) we can write:

```
julia> f(x)=x>0 ? x+1: info("x must be positive")
f (generic function with 1 method)
julia>f(2)
3
Julia>f(-2)
Information: y must be positive
```

Before finishing with the way exceptions are handled in Julia, we must also mention the try/catch block. This is a fine way in Julia to test for exceptions. In the examples we had so far, we used errors or warning to handle unexpected conditions for functions. To use again the basic function from above:

```
julia> f(x)=x>0 ? x+1:throw(Domainerror())
f (generic function with 1 method)
julia> g(y) = try
```

```
f(y)
catch
y=0
end
g(generic function with 1 method)
```

This basic example shows that with try/catch we can handle errors in an elegant manner by instructing the program what to do in case of specific errors.

Task (Coroutines)

The first five types of control flows are standard to high level programming languages. Tasks, also known as coroutines, are a typical construction for control flow in Julia. The main role of the tasks is to allow for a body of instructions to be both suspended and resumed according to the needs of the programs. To achieve this in Julia, we define the set of instructions or function(s) as tasks such that we can interrupt them and switch to different tasks and get back later to the initial task. Tasks are not simply function calls because in Julia switching tasks do not consume any space and they can happen in any order. In contrast, functions call consume space, and, on the other hand, a function call must allow for that function to be executed and finished before returning to the calling function.

A typical example where tasks are very useful is the producer-consumer problem. Here, there is a "producer", or a set of instructions generating values, and a "consumer" which consumes these values. Unlike function call, the producer and consumer can run indefinitely, with the producer passing values to the consumer. To implement and solve this kind of problems, Julia uses the functions put!() and take!(). Let us construct a simple example:

```
julia> function test(c::Channel)
put!(c,"begin")
for x=1:2
put!(c,x+1)
end
put!(c,"end")
end;
```

We first constructed a function that uses the function produce() for a set of values. Second, we use Task such that Julia will be able to repeatedly call the function test and consume the generated/produced values:

```
Julia> chnl=Channel(test);
Task (runnable)
Julia> take!(chnl)
"begin"
Julia> take!(chnl)
2
Julia> take!(chnl)
3
Julia> take!(chnl)
"end"
```

The main difference between calling a function and using Task is quite obvious: with Task we can suspend the execution of a function, and return later to it, while with a simple function we would have to finish executing the function.

1.2.9 Random Numbers

Generating random number in Julia is quite easy. As we might be accustomed to other languages, we use seed to set the random number generator. In Julia we use srand() for this:

```
Julia> srand (1234)
```

To actually generate random numbers, we use the function rand() which randomly draws numbers from the uniform distribution [0,1):

```
Julia> rand()
0.5908
```

Not unlike similar high level programming languages, we can fill vectors or arrays with random numbers.

```
Julia> v=rand(5)
5-element Array{Float64,1}
0.76
0.57
0.46
0.79
0.85
```

Similarly, we can create a matrix with:

```
Julia> m = rand(2,2)
2x2-element Array{Float64,2}
0.20 0.24
0.29 0.57
```

While the function rand() is used to generate random numbers from the $(0, 1)$ uniform distribution, we can also use randn() to generate numbers from a standard normal distribution with mean 0 and standard deviation 1:

```
Julia> m = randn(2,2)
2x2 Array{Float64,2}
-0.56 0.12
-0.01 1.85
```

1.2.10 Working With Data

Text Files

To work with text files, Julia provides a few functions, i.e. read(), open() and close(). Their use is quite intuitive, as we can see below.

```
Julia> f=open("example.txt")
```

This statement creates a file handle and f becomes the connection of Julia to the file "example.txt" from the disk. After we process the file the way we want, we must close this connection. To do so, we use:

```
Julia> close(f)
```

This is not the best way to deal with reading file in Julia. Rather, it is better to process the files with the help of do block, as shown below. Basically, we embed the file processing within the do block:

```
open ("example.txt") do f
#instructions
end
```

Working With Pathnames and Filenames

Julia provides a whole range of functions to work with pathnames and filenames. To check the current home directory, we use:

```
Julia> homedir()
"C:\\users"
```

The function pwd() can be used to check the working directory:

```
Julia> pwd()
"C:\\users"
```

To change the current folder, we can use the function cd().

```
Julia> cd("/")
```

To read the contents of the current folder, we use readdir() (we can also specify the path to read the contents of a given path).

Working With Data Files

To read data files, Julia uses the function readlm(). Its syntax is presented below:

```
Readdlm (source, delim:Char, T::Type, sol::Char; opts...)
```

Readdlm is constructed to deal with Delimited File (DLM, hereafter), a generalization of the CSV file. While CSV files are data files where the separator is the comma, the main issue is that when the data contains commas, since CSV files must add commas to deal with them. To overcome these issues, the standard DLM (delimited file) became more widespread.

The syntax above indicates that with readdlm we read from a source (which can be a text file, or a data file). The fields are separated by a specified type of Char, while lines are separated by a specified eol (end of line). Let us see a basic example. We create a vector containing random values and then write this vector to a text file.

```
Julia> vector=rand(5)
5-element Array{Float64,1}:
0.235644
0.195471
0.838713
0.0657537
0.220544
Julia> writedlm ("example.txt", vector)
```

To read from the file, we simply use readdlm and store the values in a new array:

```
Julia> vector_read=readdlm ("example.txt")
5x1 Array{Float64,2}:
0.235644
0.195471
0.838713
0.0657537
0.220544
```

By default, readdlm() assumes a standard end-of-line separator and that the delimitator for the fields is the whitespace. Julia has also special functions that deal with CSV file. The syntax for readcsv():

```
readcsv(source; header=false, skipstart=0, skipblanks=true,
use_mmap, ignore_valid_chars=false, quotes=true, dims,
comments=true, comment_char='char')
```

For header=true, the readcsv function will treat the first row of the file as the header. The option skipstart is used to ignore a preset number of lines, while skipblanks to tell readcsv whether blank lines should be skipped.

```
Use_mmap()
```

is used to speed up the memorization of the file (which is the default option in Windows). When we would like to speed up the reading, especially for large file, we can tell readcsv() the dimensions of the stored data.

1.2.11 Working With Dates

Julia provides functions to work with dates and time in the package included in the base installation Dates. There are two types provided here: one for Date and a second one for DateTime, however they are constructed as subtypes of the type TimeType. The first works with days, while the second works at a precision of milliseconds. Both are stored internally as Int64 values.

To construct Date and DateTime types it is quite easy since we can do it using the Period type (which is basically the way we use to talk about time). A few examples are quite relevant:

```
Julia> DateTime(2016)
2016-01-01T00:00:00
Julia> DateTime(2016,3)
```

```
2016-03-01T00:00:00
Julia> DateTime(2016,3,10)
2016-03-10T00:00:00
Julia>DateTime(2016,3,10,11)
2016-03-10T11:00:00
```

Working with Date is similarly easier:

```
Julia> Date(2015)
2015-01-01
Julia> Date(2015,5)
2015-05-01
```

When needed, we can also modify the format for Date type using raw strings:

```
Julia>date_format = DateFormat("y-m-d")
Julia> d = Date("2016-05-05",date_format)
2016-05-05
```

To compute time duration or compare two Date or DateTime variables is quite straightforward, once we understand that the first will be returns in terms of days while the second in terms of milliseconds.

```
Julia> date_1=Date(2016,1,30)
Julia> date_2=Date(2015,1,30)
Julia> date_1-date_2
365 days
```

While, for the DateTime variable, using the same dates, we get a different in terms of milliseconds:

```
Julia> date_1=DateTime(2016,1,30)
Julia> date_2=DateTime(2015,1,30)
Julia> date_1-date_2
31536000000 milliseconds
```

Although Julia's treatment of time and dates is more comprehensive, it is enough for now to say that we can access the fields included in the two types directly through the so-called accessor functions.

```
Julia> time=Date(2015,2,22)
2015-02-22
Julia> Dates.year(time)
2015
Julia> Dates.month(time)
```

When calling the fields with the uppercase, we get the type Period:

```
Julia>Dates.Year(time)
2014 years
Julia>Dates.Month(time)
2 months
```

Finally, we can get multiple fields at the same time easily too:

```
Julia> Dates.yearmonth(time)
(2015,2)
Julia> Dates.yearmonthday(time)
(2015,2,22)
```

1.2.12 Data Frames

A usual feature of real life datasets is that they can be represented using tables as well as that is might present missing data. Programming languages oriented towards statistics like R have clear ways to deal with such features. To work with tabular data, Julia has a special library called DataFrames. I present its main characteristics following [5]. This package is not part of Julia base, so, to install and use it we write:

```
Julia> Pkg.add("DataFrames")
Julia>using DataFrames
```

DataFrames uses NA to represent missing values. It also uses two types, DataArray and DataFrame. The first allows for a way to store missing values into an array, thus providing an useful alternative for the Array type in Julia. The second can store tabulated data including missing values. Both types are part of the DataFrames, so we must type "using DataFrames" before accessing these types. To create a data array, we use @data:

```
Julia> vector=@data([1, 2, 3, 4, NA])
5-element DataArrays.DataArray{Int64,1}
```

As we can see, we created a data array with 4 observations and one missing value of type Int64. To apply different statistic operations, we can drop NA using the function dropna():

```
Julia> mean(dropna(vector))
2.5
```

We can also substitute the missing values with a certain value. To achieve this, we use:

```
Julia> new_vector=convert(Array,dropna(vector))
4-element Array{Int64,1}:
1
2
3
4
```

While DataArray type is very efficient in handling arrays with missing values, there are many cases in which the data comes in a tabular form. For this type of data, Julia provides a second type, DataFrames, that can handle this particular case. As already mentioned, DataFrames can handle missing value. However, the columns must have equal sizes.

DataFrames can be created by reading data from a file. Alternatively, we can generate a DataFrame using the random numbers generator. In the following example, a Data Frame consisting two columns is created: one containing 10 values between 0 and 1, and another one containing randomly generated numbers:

```
Julia> data=DataFrame (x=linspace(0,1,10),y=randn(10))
102 DataFrames.DataFrame
 Row  x          y

 1    0.0        -0.26101
 2    0.111111   1.20691
 3    0.222222   -0.556195
 4    0.333333   -0.696848
 5    0.444444   -0.650466
 6    0.555556   0.636074
 7    0.666667   -1.04917
 8    0.777778   0.982242
 9    0.888889   0.239035
 10   1.0        0.343151
```

To access a column we can use either use the number of the column or we can use the column name:

```
Julia> data[1,:]
Julia> data[:x]
```

We can easily read data from a datafile using readtable() and write the data to a datafile using the function writetable(). The latter has the following syntax:

```
Writetable(filename, data; opts...)
```

We can apply statistical functions to the data table constructed above. Julia provides the function describe() that bundles together a few key statistics, including the mean and the average:

```
Julia> describe(data)
x
Summary Stats:
Mean:              0.500000
Minimum:           0.000000
1st Quartile:      0.250000
Median:            0.500000
3rd Quartile:      0.750000
Maximum:           1.000000
Length:            10
Type:              Float64
Number Missing:    0
% Missing:         0.000000
```

1.2.13 Plotting in Julia

A common criticism of Julia is the fact that the installation of the basis Julia does not contain graphic commands. While this is technically true, there are a variety of options to plot in Julia through various packages so that in the end there are no limited capabilities in terms of plotting. Following [4], we can classify the possibilities to plot in Julia into three:

- Basic graphics
- Graphic engines
- Web graphics

Basic Graphics

There are a quite a few modules that have the most basic graphic capabilities, like TextPlots, Cairo or Winston.

Text Plotting

As the name suggests, text plotting refers to a self-standing packages that can draw very basic graphs. Its main advantage is that is one of the quickest ways to plot in Julia.

Winston

A more developed package is Winston which is close to what Matlab provides in terms of two-dimensional plots. Winston is a self-standing graphics package. However, I do not cover neither TextPlots, nor Winston, since neither of them of will be used later. On the other hand, their graphics capabilities are actually included in the far more advanced packages that will be presented next.

Graphic Engines

These are well developed graphic packages that cover almost any need if not everything a programmer would need. I focus on two such packages, Pyplot and Gadfly. I also discuss Plots, which is actually a metapackage.

Pyplot

Pyplot uses the Python graphics by exploiting the possibility to call Python (and its graphics package Matplotlib) from Julia using the package PyCall. The main advantage is that the user can send directly the data to Matplotlib for plotting. The installation assumes that the system has already Python installed. Otherwise, Julia will install a very basic version of Python, Conda, for the specific use within Julia. To install it and use it, simply write:

```
Julia> Pkg.add("PyPlot")
Julia> using PyPlot
```

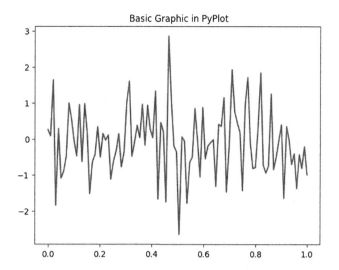

FIGURE 1.1 PyPlot graphic.

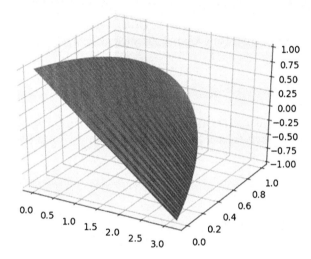

FIGURE 1.2 PyPlot 3D graphic.

This will also add PyCall, so that Julia can call Python, as well as any other libraries the Python basic installation, Conda, needs. We can create a simple graphic by writing (see Fig. 1.1):

```
Julia> x=linspace(0,1,100)
Julia> y=randn(100)
Julia> plot(x,y,color="blue")
Julia> title("Basic Graphic in PyPlot")
```

We can easily change the thickness and the style of the line using the available options for the function plot():

```
Julia>plot(x,y,color="black", linewidth=1.5, linestyles= "--")
```

We can also create 3D plots using functions like bar3D, contour3D, surface, scatter3D (see Fig. 1.2). We would need this time three variables.

```
Julia> x=linspace(0,pi,100)
Julia> y=sin(x)
Julia> z=cos(x)
Julia>surf(x,y,z)
```

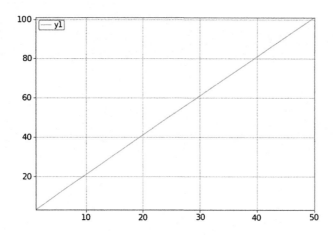

FIGURE 1.3 Simple Plot.

Gadfly

While PyPlot makes use of the graphics capabilities available in Python through matplotlib, Gadfly is a similarly powerful graphics engine, inspired this time from the R package ggplot2. Given the fact that it is inspired from an R package, Gadfly has graphic capabilities that can deal with almost any kind of statistical data, including here dataframes. We install and run Gadlfy like any other Julia package:

```
Julia> Pkg.add("Gadfly")
Julia> using Gadfly
```

We already learned that Gadfly can deal with Dataframes so that the plot() function is extended to take into account this. Thus, the plot() function can deal with arrays (as any plotting function), functions and Dataframes. The basic use of Gadfly with vectors is pretty standard:

```
Julia> x= linspace(0,1,100)
Jula>  y=randn(100)
Julia> plot(x=x,y=y, Geom.line)
```

To plot functions, Gadly uses the following syntax:

```
Plot(f::Function,a,b, elements:: Element...)
```

This syntax takes into account the fact that Julia can deal in a direct way with any function:

```
Julia> plot(sin, 0, 25)
```

This indicates that we simulate the function sin(x) where x takes values from 0 to 0.25 We can plot multiple functions at the same time with the same plot() statement.

```
Julia>plot([sin, cos],0,25)
```

Plots

Finally, Plots is not an actual package but a metapackage that embeds different plotting capabilities under a single API. To install and use it write:

```
Pkg.add("Plots")
using Plots
```

We can create plot based on different individual packages. For example, to create a simple graphic, wr can write:

```
x = 1:50; y = 2x+1
plot(x,y)
```

The result is presented in Fig. 1.3.

1.3 ADVANCED FEATURES

In this section, I discuss several particular features of Julia that can help in both understanding it better (beyond its basic description from the previous section) and write faster code.

1.3.1 Julia's Type System

In terms of type systems, programming languages can be split into two categories, static and dynamic ones. In the case of static type languages, each variable or expression has a definite type before the program or code is executed. For the case of the dynamic type languages, the type of a value is known only at the run time of the program after it is produced. Of course, this is classification is mostly for reference, since in practice, a programming language can mix these types.

Julia has a dynamic type system. However, it also includes features from the static type. For example, one can indicate that a value is of a certain type. This is known to generate faster running code. Another particular feature of Julia's type system is that it allows the programmer to omit types such that the value can be of any type. At the same time, Julia also allows for type annotation, that is, provide information to compiler that a value is of a certain type. To type annotate in Julia, one can use the :: operator. For example, writing:

```
Julia> (2+2)::Int
```

Would return 4, however type annotating with an unexpected type, would produce an error:

```
Julia> (2+2)::Float64
ERROR: TypeError: typeassert: expected Float64, got Int64
```

It is also worth noting that, in Julia, the values have types, and not the variables. Also, since a value has only its actual type at the time of the code's execution, there is no such thing as "compile-time type".

Julia's type system is important because it also allows for multiple dispatch which is the topic of the next section.

1.3.2 Multiple Dispatch

As discussed in the section dedicated to function, see Section 1.2.7, functions in Julia are simply – put objects through which a set of arguments is transformed to a return value. Although this definition seems quite clear, it is less obvious how Julia deals with similar functions. For example, implementing the operation of multiplication for real numbers is different from implementing the operation of multiplication for natural numbers, although both implementations would fall into the more general category of multiplication.

A method is a definition of the behavior of a function for specific arguments. Julia facilitates working with functions that comprise multiple methods. The selection of a particular method within a function to be executed is called a dispatch. Since Julia allows using all of function's arguments in order to select a method, we say that Julia allows for multiple dispatch.

We can define a basic function that constrains the parameters by using :: (see the previous section). We can thus write:

```
Julia> f(x::Float64, y::Int)=x+y-1
f(generic function with 1 method)
```

This function will work only when x is Float64 and y Int, otherwise it would return a method error. But we can also define the same function to include an additional methods, by constraining x and y to be numbers:

```
Julia> f(x::Number, y::Number)=x+y-2
f(generic function with 2 methods)
```

This would still return an error, if any of the arguments would not be numeric. To check the methods associated with the function f, we can type:

```
Julia> methods(f)
f(x::Float64, y::Int) in Main at none:1
f(x::Number, y::Number) in Main at none:1
```

That is, the function would return "x+y-1" when the types are as in the first case and "x+y-2" otherwise. Sometimes, it is possible that there is an ambiguity in the sense that multiple function methods are applicable. In such a particular case, instead of arbitrarily picking-up a function method, Julia will throw an error.

1.3.3 Vectorization

Starting with version 0.6, Julia offers its particular implementation of vectorization. The implementation comes with particular advantages:

1. multiple operations can be put within a simple loop
2. there is no need for additional auxiliary arrays
3. while other programming languages offer vectorization for a limited set of operations, Julia allows it for even types and functions defined by the user

A simple example can illustrate very well the use of vectorization in Julia. Assume a function defined as:

```
Julia> f(x)=x^2-2
```

To apply this to a whole array Y, we can write in Julia in two ways. Let us generate a simple array Y:

```
X=[1, 2, 3, 4, 5]
```

Then we can write either:

```
julia> @. X=f(X)
5-element Array{Int64,1}:
-1
2
7
14
23
```

or:

```
julia> X.=f.(X)
5-element Array{Int64,1}:
-1
2
7
14
23
```

REFERENCES

[1] I. Balbaert, Getting Started with Julia, 1st ed., Packt, Birmingham, UK, 2015.
[2] I. Balbaert, A. Sengupta, M. Sherrington, Julia: High Performance Programming, 1st ed., Packt, Birmingham, UK, 2016.
[3] A. Sengupta, Julia High Performance, 1st ed., Packt, Birmingham, UK, 2016.
[4] M. Sherrington, Mastering Julia, 1st ed., Packt, Birmingham, UK, 2015.
[5] Introducing Julia, https://upload.wikimedia.org/wikipedia/commons/2/2e/Julia.pdf, Wiki Books, 2015.
[6] T. Sargent, J. Stachurski, Quantitative economics with Julia, https://lectures.quantecon.org/, 2017.
[7] Julia documentation, https://docs.julialang.org/en/stable/, The Julia Language, 2017.

Chapter 2

Basic Numerical Techniques

Contents

2.1 OVERVIEW

This chapter deals with an introduction to the main methods used in computational analysis, with a focus on the techniques usually employed in economics. The chapter has two purposes. A first one is to familiarize the reader with main techniques in computational economics, while a second one is the show how to apply them in Julia. The emphasis is not towards the theoretical side. However, the chapter aims at providing sufficient background for the reader to understand the methods presented here such that he or she can apply them in Julia. The chapter follows mainly [1], where the emphasis is rather on the theory, while the book stops short of coding the algorithms, and [2] who provide a much more applied approach with an emphasis on the actual application in Matlab. It also draws from the very good set of lectures with an emphasis on macroeconomics as provided by [3]. Other materials which were proven to be useful for this chapter, though written with an emphasis on other programming languages are [4], who provide a thorough synthesis of numerical methods with an engineering audience in mind using Python, as well as [5], who provide a very good book accompanied by detailed code written in C++.

2.2 LINEAR ALGEBRA

I start the chapter by focus on one of the building blocks in both economics and numerical analysis, i.e. linear equations. Linear equations are ubiquitous in economics, they appear across the various fields in economics, from econometrics to macroeconomics. They are also a building block in computational economics, as they appear both directly and indirectly in more complex numerical problems, for exampling when solving nonlinear models that are decomposed into a number of smaller linear models.

Let us define first a linear equation. A linear equation with n unknowns x_i and n constants a_i, $i = 1..n$, is an equation in the following form:

$$a_1 x_1 + a_2 x_2 + ... + a_n x_n = b \tag{2.1}$$

Here b is a constant. All the variables are up to power 1 and there are no nonlinear functions within in (like the exponential function, for example).

A system of linear equations consists in a set of linear equations and can be written as follows:

$$a_{11} x_1 + a_{12} x_2 + ... + a_{1n} x_n = b_1 \tag{2.2}$$
$$a_{21} x_1 + a_{22} x_2 + ... + a_{2n} x_n = b_2 \tag{2.3}$$
$$... \tag{2.4}$$
$$a_{n1} x_1 + a_{n2} x_2 + ... + a_{nn} x_n = b_n \tag{2.5}$$

In a more simplified manner, we can represent a system of linear equations by writing:

$$Ax = b \tag{2.6}$$

Here A is a matrix of dimensions $n \times n$ containing the coefficients a_{ij}, b is a vector with a length n and x is also a vector of length n.

Given the importance of the systems of linear equations in numerical analysis, there are many methods to deal with them. They generally fall into two categories:

1. Direct methods: they consist in algorithms that apply basic operations to a system to solve it.
2. Iterative methods: they are algorithms that can theoretically iterative infinitely, but are practically bounded to a finite number of iterations, so that the solution is an approximation to the real solution.

2.2.1 Direct Methods

Backward/Forward Substitution

The direct methods lead to exact solutions in the sense that, after taking in account some rounding error, they provide the actual solution to the original equation Ax=b after a number of operations. The most basic direct method is the method of substitution. This can be a forward substitution, if the matrix A is lower triangular, or a backward substitution, if the matrix A is upper triangular.

$$A = \begin{bmatrix} a_{11} & a_{12} & a_{13} \\ 0 & a_{22} & a_{23} \\ 0 & 0 & a_{33} \end{bmatrix}$$

Let us consider an upper triangular matrix 3x3:

We can solve it directly as follows using backward substitution:

$$x_3 = b_3 / a_{33} \tag{2.7}$$
$$x_2 = (b_2 - a_{23} x_3) / a_{22} \tag{2.8}$$
$$x_1 = (b_1 - a_{12} x_2 - a_{13} x_3) / a_{11} \tag{2.9}$$

LU Factorization

While this is quite illustrative for the basic principle of direct methods, its main disadvantage is that we rarely meet in practice triangular matrices. To overcome this issue, the most widely used approach is the L-U algorithm. The name comes from the fact that the matrix A in Eq. (2.6) is decomposed into the product of a lower triangular matrix L and an upper triangular matrix U.

The LU algorithm consists in two distinct phases. In the first phase, we apply the Gaussian elimination (consisting into row and columns operations) to factor the initial matrix A into the upper diagonal matrix U and the lower diagonal matrix L, obtaining: $A = LU$

The next step consists in using the matrices obtained in the previous step to derive the solution. The initial system of equations becomes:

$$Ax = (LU)x = L(Ux) = b \tag{2.10}$$

We use $Ux = y$ and solve for:

$$Ly = b \tag{2.11}$$

And then we solve for:

$$Ux = y. \tag{2.12}$$

The LU factorization is the most widely used method to solve linear equations. Paralleling the Matlab command, Julia uses:

```
\(A,B).
```

This will solve Eq. (2.6), with the implicit use of the LU factorization (provided matrix A is non-triangular). If the matrix A falls into a special case, then Julia will either use a special factorization (see below) or backward/forward substitution.

The LU factorization implies the use of the Gauss elimination. This approach basically consists in the use of two elementary operations that can lead to a factorization of the A=LU while transforming L into a lower triangular matrix and U into an upper triangular one. The two elementary operations, namely interchanging two rows as well as subtracting a row multiplied by a constant from another row, do not change the final solution.

To understand better this method, we can a look at a basic example. Let us consider that the matrix A is given by:

$$A = \begin{bmatrix} 1 & 2 & 3 \\ 0 & 3 & 1 \\ 1 & 4 & 2 \end{bmatrix}$$

while the vector b is:

$$b = \begin{bmatrix} 3 \\ 4 \\ 5 \end{bmatrix}$$

In Julia, the LU factorization can be implemented via the available function in the base installation, within the linear algebra module: lufact(A), where A is the matrix that will be decomposed into L and U.

```
Julia> A=[1 2 3; 0 3 1; 1 4 2]
3x3 Array{Int64}
1  2  3
0  3  1
1  4  2
Julia>f=lufact(A)
Base.LinAlg.LU{Float64,Array{Float64,2}} with factors L and U:
[1.0 0.0 0.0; 0.0 1.0 0.0; 1.0 0.666 1.0]
[1.0 2.0 3.0; 0.0 3.0 1.0; 0.0 0.0 -1.66]
```

We can access the L and U matrices through indexing:

```
Julia> L=f[:L]
Julia> U=f[:U]
```

Once the matrices L and U are obtained, we can solve first for $Ly = b$ by forward substitution and then for $Ux = y$ by backward substitution. The solution can actually be obtained directly by using:

```
Julia>\(A,b)
3x1 Array{Float64,2}:
-0.6
 1.2
 0.4
```

Two major issues must be considered with respect to LU factorization. A first one is the speed and a second one the rounding error. With respect to speed, the LU factorization, implicit in most cases when solving for a system of type $Ax = b$, is the best approach to solving systems of linear equations. However, in practice, especially when dealing with the repeated operations (e.g. the matrix A remains the same, but the vector b differ), a more direct approach is more feasible, i.e. computing the inverse of A, and multiplying it with the vectors b.

As for the rounding error, this can become an issue once the precision of the computer is not accurate enough to distinguish between close numbers, leading to errors in the final result. This can be usually addressed through the technique of pivoting. Given this, the empirical application of the LU factorization in any software includes some pivoting.

The default approach to factorization is based on the LU method. However, this approach can be improved when the matrix of interest has a special structure. For this latter case, alternative methods for factorization are available.

QR Factorization

A matrix A is said to be orthogonal matrices if $A^T A$ is a diagonal matrix. For this special case, one can apply the QR factorization. The QR factorization is given by:

$$A = QR \tag{2.13}$$

Here Q is an orthogonal matrix, while R is upper triangular.

We can solve for the initial equation Ax=b, by taking into account the fact that:

$$Q^T Ax = Q^T b \tag{2.14}$$

Which is equivalent to:

$$Q^T QRx = Q^T b \tag{2.15}$$

Which is further equivalent to:

$$DRx = Q^T b. \tag{2.16}$$

Here, the matrix $D = Q^T Q$ is a diagonal matrix, and, since R is upper triangular, so will DR be. The equation can be easily solved by backward substitution once we obtain the matrices Q and R.

In Julia, the QR factorization is implemented in the linear algebra module of the base installation, using the function:

```
qrfact()
```

To access the matrices Q and R, we can write:

```
Julia> F=qrfact(A)
Julia> F[:Q]
Julia> F[:R]
```

Cholesky Factorization

For symmetric positive definite matrices, one can use the Cholesky factorization. The most common use of Cholesky factorization is within the context of optimization problems where one encounters symmetric positive definite matrices.

We write a Cholesky decomposition as:

$$A = LL^T \tag{2.17}$$

Here, the matrix L is lower triangular. Once the Cholesky decomposition is performed, we can solve the initial system of linear equations as in the LU decomposition. The Cholesky decomposition is much faster than the Gauss elimination and it should be preferred to the later in case the matrix is positive definite.

In Julia, to perform a Cholesky factorization, we can use the function:

```
cholfact()
```

Cramer's Rule

This is a rather straight solution, relying on a mathematical formula using the elements of the matrix A and vector b. Unfortunately, the Cramer's rule is quite slow and it preferable only when there are closed form solutions.

2.2.2 Iterative Methods

The direct methods offer an exact solution to the system Ax=b. In contrast, the iterative methods provide an approximate solution that approaches the true solution as the number of iterations increases. Iterative methods should be used to solve large systems of linear equations and are very efficient when the A matrix in the system above is sparse (it contains many zero entries). The two most known iterative methods are the Gauss-Jacobi and the Gauss-Seidel approaches.

To apply these methods, we can rewrite the initial linear system as:

$$Qx = b + (Q - A)x \tag{2.18}$$

Where Q is chosen such that it can easily be inverted. We can further write the above equation as:

$$x = Q^{-1}b + (I - Q^{-1}A)x \tag{2.19}$$

Using this equation, we can propose a difference equation for x, namely we write:

$$x_{k+1} = Q^{-1}b + (I - Q^{-1}A)x_k \tag{2.20}$$

There are a few things in common for the two methods. First, they both set the matrix Q on the basis of matrix A. For the case of the Gauss-Jacobi method, Q is set as the diagonal matrix containing the diagonal elements of A. For Gauss-Seidel method, Q is formed from the upper triangular elements of A and thus it is set as an upper triangular matrix. Second, both methods have in common the fact that they start from an initial value of the solution (and this is actually a characteristic of iterative methods). The initial guess is either the vector b or a vector consisting in zero values.

These two methods will converge if A is diagonally dominant, i.e. the value of diagonal elements is bigger than the value of the other elements. Formally, this condition would be written as:

$$|A_{ii}| > \sum_{i=1, i \neq j}^{n} |A_{ij}| \tag{2.21}$$

We implement below the Julia code for solving a system of linear equations in Julia. We construct the diagonal matrix of A using the Julia linear algebra function Diagonal(), which is case sensitive. We then proceed to implement the Gauss-Jacobi method:

```
A=[4.0 1.0 -1.0; 2.0 7.0 1.0; 1.0 -3.0 12.0];
d=Diagonal(A);
x=[1.0;1.0;1.0];
b=[3.0;19.0;31.0];
maxit=1000;
dx=[0.0;0.0;0.0]

d=zeros(size(A,1))
diag=Diagonal(A)
for iii=1:size(A,1)
d[iii]=diag[iii,iii]
end

for i=1:maxit
dx=(b-A*x)./d
x=x+dx
if norm(dx)<0.00001
break
end
```

```
x
3-element Array{Float64,1}:
 1.0
 2.0
 3.0
```

The algorithm is a bit more involved than the Matlab solution provided in [2]. The main reason is that there is no equivalent function of diag() from Matlab in Julia, since the function Diagonal() from Julia a matrix that retains only the diagonal from the original matrix.

We can similarly write a code to implement the Gauss-Jacobi iteration. The first part of the code is similar, i.e. setting up the A matrix, the b vector as well as an initial guess solution. This time, instead of using a diagonal matrix d, we construct an upper triangular matrix U from the initial matrix A. In Julia, to construct a lower triangular matrix from a given matrix, we use the function tril(). Apart from this, the algorithm is pretty straightforward when implementing it:

```
Q=tril(A);
for i=1:maxit
dx=\(Q,b-A*x)
x=x+dx
if norm(dx)<0.00001
break
end
end
x
3-element Array{Float64,1}:
 1.0
 2.0
 3.0
```

The Gauss-Seidel algorithm can also include a so-called overrelaxation parameter λ which usually helps speeding up the algorithm, such that the next iteration is computed used $x = x + \lambda * dx$. For values of $\lambda \in (1, 2)$, this can accelerate the algorithm.

2.2.3 Eigenvalues and Eigenvectors

Eigenvalues and eigenvectors arise naturally in dynamic systems and are met when checking for the stability of a dynamic system. They can also be met when doing singular value decomposition. Their importance cannot be underestimated, and, as such, a succinct presentation of how they are implemented in Julia is necessary and it will be useful later when working with dynamic macroeconomic models.

Given a square matrix A, an eigenvector is a nonzero vector v such that the following relationship is verified:

$$Av = \lambda v \tag{2.22}$$

Here, λ is the eigenvalue (characteristic value) of the matrix A. Julia includes functions for eigenvalues and eigenvectors. Let's declare first a 3×3 square matrix:

```
Julia> A=[2 -1 7; 2 5 3; 1 1 1];
```

To determine the eigenvalues, we use the function eigval():

```
Julia> eigvals(A)
3-element Array{Float64,1}:
  6.0
  3.0
 -1.0
```

This returns the vector of eigenvalues containing 3 values. To extract the eigenvectors, we use:

```
Julia>eigvecs(A)
3x3 Array{Float64,2}:
-0.14825    -0.707107     -0.909137
-0.963624   0.707107      0.101015
-0.222375   2.41041e-17   0.404061
```

The same can be performed using a single function, eigfact(), which will return both the eigenvalues and the eigenvectors. This function will return an object F which will contain both the eigenvalues in F[:value] and the eigenvectors in F[:vectors].

```
Julia> F=eigfact(A);
Julia>F[:value]
3-element Array{Float64,1}:
6.0
3.0
-1.0
Julia> F[:vectors]
3x3 Array{Float64,2}:
-0.14825    -0.707107     -0.909137
-0.963624   0.707107      0.101015
-0.222375   2.41041e-17   0.404061
```

In Julia, we can also directly compute the minimum and the maximum eigenvalues using the functions eigmin and eigmax.

```
Julia>eigmin(A)
-1.00
Julia>eigmax(A)
6.00
```

2.3 INTERPOLATION AND CURVE FITTING

Interpolation *per se* is a less discussed topic in computational economics books and is rather treated together within the more general topic of function approximation methods. Here, I treat the two methods in two separate sections, and I focus in this section on the more basic problem, that of interpolation. I also discuss curve fitting, which just another way to look at the same problem of approximation: based on a number of observations, it produces an approximation that is "very close" to the data.

In the most general sense, interpolation is a method through which we find a function that goes through a set of given points. Thus, given the observations (x_i, y_i), through interpolation we construct a function that will pass through all these given points.

The theoretical discussion in this chapter draws from [4] and [5].

2.3.1 Polynomial Interpolation

This is the most basic way to interpolate. Given $n + 1$ different points, we can construct a unique polynomial of degree n that will pass through all the n+1 given points. Two of the most basic methods are Lagrange's and Newton's.

Lagrange's Method

Given any two points (x_0, y_0) and (x_1, y_1), the most basic approach to interpolation would be to derive a straight line between these two points. We can write any straight line as follows:

$$y = cx + d \qquad (2.23)$$

Here c stands for the gradient and d for the intercept. They would be equal to: $c = \frac{y_1 - y_0}{x_1 - x_0}$ and $d = y_0 - cx_0$.

Using these last two equations, we can write the first equation as:

$$y = \frac{y_1 - y_0}{x_1 - x_0}x + \frac{x_1 y_0 - x_0 y_1}{x_1 - x_0} \tag{2.24}$$

The basic idea of Lagrange's approach to interpolation, is to write the above equation such that the two given points are included within it. The linear equation will be written as:

$$P_1(x) = a_0(x - x_1) + a_1(x - x_0) \tag{2.25}$$

Here a_0, a_1 are constants. After applying the equation for points (x_0, y_0) and (x_1, y_1), we can be rewrite the above equation as:

$$P_1(x) = y_0\frac{x - x_1}{x_0 - x_1} + y_1\frac{x - x_0}{x_1 - x_0} \tag{2.26}$$

To achieve interpolation with Lagrange's method for any set of points and a polynomial of degree n, we can use the formula due to Lagrange:

$$P_n(x) = \sum_{i=0}^{n} y_i l_i(x) \tag{2.27}$$

Here, P_n stands for the polynomial, y_i are the datapoints, n is the degree of the polynomial and the function $l_i(x)$ is given by:

$$l_i(x) = \frac{x - x_0}{x_i - x_0}\frac{x - x_1}{x_i - x_1}...\frac{x - x_n}{x_i - x_n} = \prod_{j=0, j\neq i}^{n} \frac{x - x_j}{x_i - x_j} \tag{2.28}$$

For $i \neq j, i = 1, ..., n$. For $n = 2$, the polynomial becomes:

$$P_n(x) = y_0 l_0(x) + y_1 l_1(1) + y_2 l_2(x) \tag{2.29}$$

In this particular case, the functions $l_i(x)$ are given by:

$$l_0(x) = \frac{(x - x_1)(x - x_2)}{(x_0 - x_1)(x_0 - x_2)}, l_1(x) = \frac{(x - x_0)(x - x_2)}{(x_1 - x_0)(x_1 - x_2)}, l_2(x) = \frac{(x - x_0)(x - x_1)}{(x_2 - x_0)(x_2 - x_1)} \tag{2.30}$$

Thus, each function $l_i(x)$ is a polynomial function of degree n that is characterized by the following property:

$$l_i(x_j) = \begin{cases} 0, & i \neq j \\ 1, & i = j \end{cases}$$

Using this function and the definition of Lagrange polynomial, we can easily check that the interpolated polynomial will pass through each of the given points.

Newton's Method

A second approach, due to Newton, is seen as more computationally efficient since the procedure by Lagrange implies many computations when the number of given points is large. The basis of the Newton's method is to write the polynomial of degree n in the following form:

$$P_n(x) = a_0 + a_1(x - x_0) + a_2(x - x_0)(x - x_1) + ... + a_n(x - x_0)(x - x_1)...(x - x_{n-1}) \tag{2.31}$$

It is quite straightforward to evaluate this polynomial. Consider the case of 3 data points, implying the use of a polynomial of degree 2. We write it as $P_2(x)$:

$$P_2(x) = a_0 + a_1(x - x_0) + a_2(x - x_0)(x - x_1) \tag{2.32}$$

Which can be further written as:

$$P_2(x) = a_0 + (x - x_0)(a_1 + a_2(x - x_1)) \tag{2.33}$$

This can be easily evaluated with backward iteration as follows:

$$P_0(x) = a_2 \tag{2.34}$$
$$P_1(x) = a_1 + (x - x_1)P_0 \tag{2.35}$$
$$P_2(x) = a_0 + (x - x_0)P_1 \tag{2.36}$$

There are various ways to evaluate Newton polynomials: divided difference, forward and backward-difference, central-difference. In the following paragraphs, I present the divided difference approach.

By definition, the divided difference $d_{k,i}$ is the i-th divided difference of $f(x)$ at x_i, given by:

$$d_{k,i} = \frac{d_{k-1,i+1} - d_{k-1,i}}{x_k - x_i} \tag{2.37}$$

With the initial values for $d_{0,i}$ given by: $d_{0,i} = y_i$, for $i = 0, 1, ..., n$ and $k = 1, 2, ..., n - 1$. Using the divided difference constants, the Newton polynomial of degree 2 from above will be written as:

$$P_2(x) = d_{0,0} + (x - x_0)d_{1,0} + (x - x_0)(x - x_1)d_{2,0} \tag{2.38}$$

Although polynomial interpolation is useful when working with small data sets, it is preferable to interpolate with other techniques (cubic splines, for example) for larger data sets. The main reason is that a polynomial passing through all the data points will tend to fluctuate in an excessive manner.

2.3.2 Spline Interpolation

Splines are a much better way to perform interpolation due to their very smooth nature. By definition, a spline is a curve which is formed from joining piecewise continuous polynomials of the same degree that pass through a set of given data points. Although a spline consists in joint set of continuous functions, they are smooth not only because they are continuous in all points, but also because they are continuous in their derivatives.

A spline of degree n will be formed using polynomials of degree n. For example, a quadratic spline will consist in polynomials of degree two. Of large practical interest are the cubic splines. Formally, a cubic spline can be written as:

$$s_k(x) = a_k + b_k x + c_k x_k^2 + d_k x_k^3 \tag{2.39}$$

Here, the coefficients a_k, b_k, c_k, d_k are constants that characterize each polynomial k, with $k = 1, ..., n$. The coefficients differ along each of the polynomials.

The m splines are used to interpolate $n + 1$ data points (x_i, y_i). In the following paragraphs, I present one of the methods to compute the coefficients of the piecewise polynomials. Due to the implied property of continuity of the second derivatives in each of the interpolated points k_i, we have the following equations:

$$f''_{i-1,i}(x_i) = f''_{i,i+1}(x_i) = k_i \tag{2.40}$$

The coefficients k_i are unknown at this point, except the endpoints k_0 and k_n which are equal to zero. To compute the coefficients, we can start from the fact that the second derivatives in each interpolated point are linear. If we use the Lagrange's method to interpolate between two points, we can write:

$$f''_{i,i+1}(x_i) = k_i l_i(x) + k_{i+1} l_{i+1}(x) \tag{2.41}$$

Here, the functions l_i are defined as we already know from Lagrange's approach: $l_i(x) = \frac{x - x_{i+1}}{x_i - x_{i+1}}, l_{i+1}(x) = \frac{x - x_i}{x_{i+1} - x_i}$. Thus, we can write the second derivative as:

$$f''_{i,i+1}(x_i) = \frac{k_i(x - x_{i+1}) - k_{i+1}(x - x_i)}{x_i - x_{i+1}} \tag{2.42}$$

This equation can be integrated twice to find $f_{i,i+1}(x+i)$:

$$f_{i,i+1}(x_i) = \frac{k_i(x - x_{i+1})^3 - k_{i+1}(x - x_i)^3}{6(x_i - x_{i+1})} + A(x - x_{i+1}) - B(x - x_i) \tag{2.43}$$

To find the coefficients A and B, we can use the condition $f_{i,i+1}(x_i) = y_i$ above to get:

$$\frac{k_i(x_i - x_{i+1})^3}{6(x_i - x_{i+1})} + A(x_i - x_{i+1}) = y_i \tag{2.44}$$

and from here we can determine A: $A = \frac{y_i}{x_i - x_{i+1}} - \frac{k_i}{6}(x_i - x_{i+1})$.

From $f_{i,i+1}(x_{i+1}) = y_{i+1}$ we get:

$$y_{i+1} = \frac{-k_{i+1}(x_{i+1} - x_i)^3}{6(x_i - x_{i+1})} - B(x_{i+1} - x_i) \tag{2.45}$$

We can also derive the coefficient B as: $B = \frac{y_{i+1}}{x_i - x_{i+1}} - \frac{k_{i+1}}{6}(x_i - x_{i+1})$. We get now the following relationship:

$$f_{i,i+1}(x) = \frac{k_i}{6}\left[\frac{(x - x_{i+1})^3}{x_i - x_{i+1}} - (x - x_{i+1})(x_i - x_{i+1})\right] -$$
$$\frac{k_{i+1}}{6}\left[\frac{(x - x_i)^3}{x_i - x_{i+1}} - (x - x_i)(x_i - x_{i+1})\right] + \frac{y_i(x - x_{i+1}) - y_{i+1}(x - x_i)}{x_i - x_{i+1}} \tag{2.46}$$

For $i = 1, 2, ..., n - 1$.

To solve for the unknown second derivatives k_i's, we use the condition that the first derivatives are continuous in each of the knot point, i.e. $f'_{i-1,i}(x_i) = f'_{i,i+1}(x_i) = k_i$. This leads to the following $n - 1$ equations:

$$k_{i-1}(x_{i-1} - x_i) + 2k_i(x_{i-1} - x_{i+1}) + k_{i+1}(x_i - x_{i+1}) = 6\left(\frac{y_{i-1} - y_i}{x_{i-1} - x_i} - \frac{y_i - y_{i+1}}{x_i - x_{i+1}}\right) \tag{2.47}$$

For $i = 1, 2, ..., n - 1$. To apply the cubic splines, we need to solve for the unknown k_i, given the fact that $k_0 = k_n = 0$. In the second step, we can determine the coefficients of the spline.

2.3.3 B-splines

The B-splines are another very well-performing type of splines that are widely used in empirical applications due to their properties. Their name, i.e. that of B-splines, comes from basis splines, since they are constructed such that they represent a basis for splines. Since the splines can be conceived as a collection of nodes x_i, and coefficients specific for each spline, i.e. a_i, b_i, etc., for $i = 0, ..., n$, we can create a vector space from the space of splines with nodes on a given grid.

Assume a grid of knots $x_{-k} < ... < x_{-1} < x_0 < ... < x_{n+k}$. Splines of order 1 basically consist in step functions. The B-splines of order 0, i.e. B_0-splines, are basis for such splines and they are usually written as:

$$B_i^0(x) = \begin{cases} 0, & x < x_i \\ 1, & x_i \leq x \leq x_{i+1} \\ 0, & x_{i+1} < x_i \end{cases}$$

Here $i = -k, ..., n$.

Splines of order 2 consist in linear functions (polynomials of order 1). The basis for them is given by B_1-splines. The latter are represented as:

$$B_i^1(x) = \begin{cases} 0, & x \leq x_i \text{ or } x \geq x_{i+2} \\ \frac{x - x_i}{x_{i+1} - x_i}, & x_i \leq x \leq x_{i+1} \\ \frac{x_{i+2} - x}{x_{i+2} - x_{i+1}}, & x_{i+1} \leq x_i \leq x_{i+2} \end{cases}$$

To build B-splines of higher-order, we can use the following relationship between splines of order k and of order $k - 1$:

$$B_i^k(x) = \frac{x - x_i}{x_{i+k} - x_i} B_i^{k-1}(x) + \frac{x_{i+k+1} - x}{x_{i+k+1} - x_{i+1}} B_{i+1}^{k-1}(x) \qquad (2.48)$$

We can use this relationship to build any type of splines.

2.3.4 Interpolation in Julia

One of the main packages dealing with interpolation in Julia is Interpolations which replaces the older Grid package. The basic variable type which Interpolations works with is AbstractArray. AbstractArray is the parent type for any Array variable. An AbstractArray is endowed with indexation and iteration.

Let us consider that we already have an object of type AbstractArray. The function used in Interpolations to construct a so-called interpolation object has the following general syntax:

```
Itp=interpolate(A, options...)
```

Here A us the object of interpolation, while with options we control the type of interpolation we want to apply. Once the interpolation was accomplished, we can find the values of the interpolated function for any given two points using:

```
Itp=[x,y,...]
```

Interpolations covers two major methods: bsplines and gridded interpolation. There are a few options that can be chosen for bsplines: degree, grid behavior, grid representation and boundary conditions. For bsplines, i.e. basis splines, Interpolations can apply bsplines from order zero up to order 3. In terms of grid representation, for discrete representations, any data point is associated to a so-called cell. We can consider that the given data points lie on the boundaries on these cells, and we choose the option onGrid, or we may consider that they lie on the half-intervals between cell boundaries, and then we can choose the option onCell. For B-splines of quadratic order (or higher), we also have to specify a so-called boundary condition. This is necessary in order to solve the resulting system of equations. We can selected one of the following boundary conditions: flat, line, free, period, reflect.

Below, I provide a few examples for interpolation using the package Interpolations. The package treats differently the cases of uniformed and non-uniformed spaced data. For the first case, one can use B-splines. But one should also tell the function *interpolate* about the grid, in case one has data in the form *[f(x) for x in A]*, with A a uniformed space vector.

```
#create some data
A_x = 1.:4.:50.
A = [2x for x in A_x]

#use Interpolations
using Interpolations
itp = interpolate(A, BSpline(Cubic(Line())), OnGrid())
sitp = scale(itp, A_x)
sitp[3.] # exactly log(3.)

5.999999999999998
```

For data that is uniformed space, we can alternatively use the Gridded interpolation which is similar to Bspline, except that we don't have the choice of choosing the grid representation, since all are "OnGrid" and we also have to specify coordinates that define the knots.

```
A = rand(20)
A_x = collect(1.0:2.0:40.0)
knots = (A_x,)
itp = interpolate(knots, A, Gridded(Linear()))
itp[2.0]
```

A second package for interpolation is Dierckx. This package actually consists in routines written in Fortran and wrapped within Julia. It is partially overlapping with what Interpolations offer, however it provides a more diverse supply of methods. Apart from B-splines (which are well covered in Interpolations), Diercks also covers splines from first to fifth order, one-dimensional and two-dimensional interpolations, and interpolations on irregular or unstructured grids. In the following paragraphs, I will refer mainly to the capability of Diercks to work with splines.

Considering two vectors of data, x and y, we can fit a one-dimensional spline using the function spline1D(x,y). The general syntax is:

```
Spline1D(x, y; w=ones(length(x)), k=3, bc="nearest", s=0.0)
```

Where x and y are the input vectors, k indicates the order of the splines applied. We can use 1 for linear, 2 for quadratic, 3 for cubic and so on. The default order is 3. The value of the parameter bc indicates how to evaluate the spline outside its support domain. It can take as values: "nearest", "zero", "extrapolate", or "error".

Once an interpolated object has been created, say sp, we use the function evaluate to evaluate the spline at specified points:

```
evaluate(sp,[x_1,y_1,...])
```

Where sp is the interpolated object, while x1, y1 are the new points. For two-dimensional interpolation, the approach is similar. We use the function spline2D, with the general syntax:

```
Spline2D(x, y, z; w=ones(length(x)), kx, ky, s=0.0)
```

Here, x and y must be one-dimensional vector of the same dimension. The variable z can be either one-dimensional, and then it is implicitly assumed we are working with unstructured data, or it might be two-dimensional, and the implicit assumption is that gridded data. Finally, kx indicates the order of the spline for the first dimension and ky the order for the second dimension.

In general, the benchmark tests show that the routines in Dierckx are much faster than the corresponding routines in Interpolations. Thus Dierckx might be preferable in the end when doing interpolation in Julia.

There are other packages in Julia that deal with interpolation. However, although they are worth mentioning, their focus is much more technical and of less use to the usual needs of an economists. The package GridInterpolations deals with multivariate interpolations on a rectilinear grid. A second package, ApproXD, deals with the approximation of function of dimension X. But this will be more discussed when we deal with function approximation.

2.3.5 Curve Fitting

While interpolation is a method that finds a function that passes through a set of given points, the curve fitting approach seeks to find a function that approximates well the given points. I focus on the least square approach, one of the most used approaches in economics, which seeks to minimize sum of the squared errors (i.e. the distance between the given data points and the estimates implied by the function).

In practice, only low order polynomial functions are considered. If the function used is given by:

$$f(x) = f(x; a_0, a_1, a..., a_m) \tag{2.49}$$

Then we use it to approximate the $n + 1$ data points (x_i, y_i) using a function consisting in $m + 1$ variables, where $m < n$. The least square approach tries to find that function $f(x)$ which results in a minimized sum of square errors given by:

$$SSE = \sum_{i=1}^{n} [y_i - f(x_i)]^2 \tag{2.50}$$

In practice, we usually employ lower degree polynomials, like the linear function:

$$f(x) = a_0 + a_1 x \tag{2.51}$$

the quadratic polynomial:

$$f(x) = a_0 + a_1 x + a_2 x^2 \tag{2.52}$$

Or cubic functions:

$$f(x) = a_0 + a_1 x + a_2 x^2 + a_3 x^3 \tag{2.53}$$

Given the ubiquitous presence of linear regression in economics, I succinctly present it. I focus on the simplest case of a univariate linear regression. In terms of specifying the function, we can write: $f(x) = a_0 + a_1 x$.

Fitting this curve amounts to minimizing the sum of squared errors, as the difference between yi the actual observations, and $f(x_i)$ the values of the fitted curve, which is equivalent to minimizing:

$$SSE = \sum_{i=1}^{n}[y_i - f(x_i)]^2 = \sum_{i=0}^{n}[y_i - a_0 - a_1 x_i]^2 \tag{2.54}$$

Since this is an optimization problem, at the optimal values for a_0 and a_1, the first derivatives will be zero.

$$\frac{\partial SSE}{\partial a_0} = \sum_{i=0}^{n} -2(y_i - a_0 - a_1 x_i) = 2[a_0(n+1) + a_1 \sum_{i=0}^{n} x_i - \sum_{i=0}^{n} y_i] = 0 \tag{2.55}$$

$$\frac{\partial SSE}{\partial a_1} = \sum_{i=0}^{n} -2(y_i - a_0 - a_1 x_i)x_i = 2[a_0 \sum_{i=0}^{n} x_i + a_1 \sum_{i=0}^{n} x_i^2 - \sum_{i=0}^{n} x_i y_i] = 0 \tag{2.56}$$

We can denote by $\bar{y}$ the average value of y, with $\bar{y} = \frac{1}{n+1} \sum_{i=0}^{n} y_i$ and by $\bar{x}$ the average value of x, with $\bar{x} = \frac{1}{n+1} \sum_{i=0}^{n} x_i$. Then, dividing by 2(n+1), after some algebra, we can get:

$$\bar{y} = a_0 + a_1 \bar{x} \tag{2.57}$$

and:

$$a_0 \bar{x} + (\frac{1}{n+1} \sum_{i=0}^{n} x_i^2)b = \frac{1}{n+1} \sum_{i=0}^{n} x_i y_i \tag{2.58}$$

We can then solve for a_0 and a_1:

$$a_0 = \frac{\bar{y} \sum x_i^2 - \bar{x} \sum x_i y_i}{\sum x_i^2 - n\bar{x}^2} \tag{2.59}$$

For a_1 we get:

$$a_1 = \frac{\sum x_i y_i - \bar{x} \sum y_i}{\sum x_i^2 - n\bar{x}^2} \tag{2.60}$$

While the simple regression is one of the most widely used methods in curve fitting, there are other approaches that are quite often used. I simply sketch them in the next paragraphs, before turning to the practice of curve fitting in Julia.

The generalization of the simple linear regression is the linear form which combines functions to result in the following specification:

$$f(x) = a_0 f_0(x) + a_1 f_1(x) + \ldots + a_m f_m(x) = \sum_{j=0}^{m} a_j f_j(x) \tag{2.61}$$

Here, each function $f_i(x)$ is predetermined and is known as a basis function. This type of linear form can be easily solved using the least square approach. A particular case of the linear form is the polynomial specification. In this specific case, the basis functions are specified as:

$$f_j(x) = x^j \tag{2.62}$$

for each j, with $j = 0, 1, \ldots, m$.

In certain cases, some weighting of data might be necessary. In such cases, we would work with the weighted residuals and we would write them as:

$$W_i(y_i - f(x_i)) \tag{2.63}$$

The objective function, the sum of squared errors, becomes:

$$SSE = \sum_{i=1}^{n} W_i^2 [y_i - f(x_i)]^2 \tag{2.64}$$

2.3.6 Curve Fitting In Julia

There are two packages covering curve fitting in Julia. One is LsqFit, covering least square fitting, and the second is CurveFit, covering various specifications for curve fitting. While they are not very comprehensive, they still address the most basic needs in terms of curve fitting and least square estimations.

The package LsqFit offers a nonlinear approach to curve fitting. It currently uses the Levenberg-Marquardt algorithm. The two basic functions in LsqFit are curve_fit(), estimate_errors() and estimate_covar(). The function curve_fit has the following general syntax:

```
fit=curve_fit(model,x,y,w,p0; kwargs...)
```

Here fit is a composite type object that will store the degrees of freedom (fit.dof), the best fit parameters (fit.param), the residuals (fit.resid) and the Jacobian (fit.jacobian). The variable x is the independent variable while y is the dependent one. In w we may store a vector or matrix of weights, p_0 are the initial values, while with $kwargs$ we set the parameters specific to the algorithm used in LsqFit, Levenberg-Marquardt.

The function estimate_errors is used to provide the error associated to each fitted parameter. The general syntax for this function is:

```
sigma = estimate_errors(fit, alpha=0.95)
```

Here, fit is the fitted composite object using the function curve_fit(). The parameter alpha provides the confidence limit for the errors. Finally, the function estimate_covar() is also applied to the same fitted object fit. The syntax used:

```
covar = estimate_covar(fit)
```

The result of applying this function is a covariance matrix evaluated at the best fit.

The second package dedicated to curve fitting in Julia is CurveFit. This second package has an expanded capability. The package is based on the least square approach. In contrast to LsqFit, it offers both linear and nonlinear approaches to least square curve fitting.

For linear least square, CurveFit covers most basic needs, offering a variety of functions. For example, for simple linear fit, we can use:

```
linear_fit(x,y)
```

which will estimate the coefficients of a linear regression between y_t as dependent variable and x_t as independent variable.

Similarly, to estimate an exponential equation, we use:

```
exp_fit(x,y)
```

which will fit an exponential model.

CurveFit covers more general specification too, like polynomials. To fit a polynomial regression, we use the function:

```
poly_fit(x,y,n)
```

which estimates a model with the data y as the dependent series and x as the explanatory series, using a polynomial of order n.

When the function is nonlinear with respect to coefficients, CurveFit provides a nonlinear least square approach. In contrast to LsqFit, which uses the Levenberg-Marquardt, the package CurveFit provides the user with a Newton type algorithm. The general syntax for the function based on the nonlinear least squares is:

```
nonlinear_fit(x, fun, a0, eps=1e-7, maxiter=200)
```

Where x are the data points, fun is the specification of function/regression used, a_0 are the initial conditions, eps is the tolerance threshold and maxiter the maximum number of iterations allowed.

To simplify further its use, the package CurveFit offes a general function for curve fitting that covers both linear and nonlinear least squares and each particular specification that might be used. The general syntax for this is:

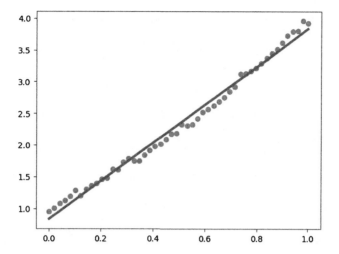

FIGURE 2.1 Curve fitting.

```
fit = curve_fit(::Type{T}, x, y...)
```

Which will fit a regression as specified by the user using a variable of type T with the dependent variable y and the explanatory variable x.

A simple example can illustrate very well its use. Assuming CurveFit was installed using Pkg.add("CurveFit"), we load it first, as well as Pyplot to plot the results (the latter package was presented in the chapter that introduces Julia).

```
using CurveFit
using PyPlot
x = [linspace(0, 1, 50)];
y = 1 .+ 2* x .+ x.*x .+ randn(50)/20
fit = curve_fit(Poly, x, y)
yOb = fit(x)
plot(x, y0, "o", x, yOb, "r-", linewidth=3)
```

The code is quite simple. It starts by created an equally spaced vector x with values between 0 and 1. It then creates a vector y_0 that it is taken as the dependent variable, while x is the explanatory one. I fit a regression on this data using the polynomial specification. The results are stores in the object fit. I further plot both the initial series y_0 and the fitted series y_{0b} in a plot Fig. 2.1 using the graphic package PyPlot.

2.4 FUNCTION APPROXIMATION

As [1] explains, approximation in computational problems can be understood in several senses. In an already discussed sense in the previous section, we use interpolation to find a well-behaving function that passes through a set of given points.

A different problem is that of local approximation. The aim of this type of approximation is to find a "good" approximation of the behavior of a function f near a point x_0, given a function f as well as its derivative at the point x_0.

Yet another type of approximation, the L_p approximation, aims at finding a well-behaving function g close enough to a given function over a given interval and using the L_p norm as a criterion for closeness. However, we should keep in mind that computing the L_p approximation is somehow unrealistic, since it actually needs a full information about the function.

Finally, we also deal with regression. The main characteristic of this approximation technique is the use of m observations to estimate n parameters, where the value of m has to be higher than the value with n.

The presentation draws mainly from [1] and [3].

2.4.1 Local Approximation

Macroeconomists widely use techniques to find local approximations of systems of equations that describe macroeconomic models. There are many advantages of working with linear models, while usually a macroeconomic model leads to a system of nonlinear equations. There are two widespread techniques for local approximation, the Taylor expansions and rational approximations. In macroeconomics we deal usually with the former, and this is the focus of this section.

The idea of Taylor expansion is based on the well-known Taylor's theorem which shows that we can approximate a function that is n-differentiable in the neighborhood of a point x_0 by using a polynomial approximation. We can write a polynomial of degree n as follows:

$$f(x) \doteq f(x_0) + (x - x_0)f'(x_0) + \frac{(x - x_0)^2}{2} f''(x_0) + \dots + \frac{(x - x_0)^n}{n!} f^{(n)}(x_0) \tag{2.65}$$

We can also understand the Taylor expansion as an approximation of the function by using an infinite series. We can understand better when we look at the exponential function, $exp(x)$. Formally, we can write it as:

$$exp(x) = \sum_{i=0}^{\infty} \frac{x^k}{k!} \tag{2.66}$$

This illustrates very well the idea that an infinite series can finely approximate a given function.

The Taylor expansion is very used in macroeconomic practice to linearize the system of nonlinear equations that characterizes the usual macroeconomic models. There are two basic approaches in linearizing economic equations, linearization and log-linearization. We will deal with them in the chapter dedicated to solving and simulating dynamic stochastic general equilibrium models (Chapter 3).

2.4.2 Doing Approximations With Regression

We already dealt with curve fitting in the context of interpolation: finding a function that approximates well a number of given points, in contrast to interpolation, which aims at finding a function that passes through all the points considered. Here we rather look at this as a method of approximating a function and less a problem of fitting of a curve. Thus, although the distinction may seem superfluous, we will see that in the context of numerical analysis it implies a rather particular understanding.

In the most general sense, we use regression as a mean to approximate a function of interest $f(x)$ by using a simpler function g of exogenous variables. Given the observed data points y_i, with $i = 1, \dots, n$, we try to explain them with the help of a number of exogenous variables x_i, with $i = 1, \dots, m$. Using the ordinary least squares, we aim at finding the set of parameters $a_1, \dots, a_m$ that minimizes the sum of squared errors:

$$min_{a_1, a_2, \dots, a_m} = \sum_{i=1}^{n} (a_1 x_1^i + a_2 x_2^i + \dots + a_m x_m^i - y_i)^2 \tag{2.67}$$

Although the problem at hand seems just a typical econometric problem, in numerical analysis there are some sensible choices one has to make with respect to the number of data points, functional forms, etc.

In contrast to econometrics, in numerical analysis we are not constrained to have a set of given points as in econometrics, but rather we can choose over what set of points the estimation is done. Furthermore, the constraint of having more observations than parameters is also relaxed and we can actually fit n parameters by using just n observations. A third essential difference is that in numerical approximations we also control the space over which the estimation is done and focus on the points where the functions behaves in a more complex manner (for example, by displaying kinks).

In terms of functional forms, choosing an adequate function form is key to approximate well the function at hand. While the usual approach implies selecting monomials that increase in degree, i.e. selecting a set of the following form: $1, x^1, x^2, \dots, x^m$, in practice, we should adapt our choice to the problem at hand. To circumvent this problem, one can use orthogonal polynomials, neural networks, etc.

2.4.3 Orthogonal Polynomials

This is a powerful technique that is a building block for other approaches in numerical approximation. As [3] points out, it helps solving the collinearity problem we might encounter when doing least square regression. It also accelerates the implementation of other algorithms for approximation.

The main idea that lies behind orthogonal polynomials is that if we want to build bases for vector spaces so that we can represent functions that result in good approximations, we also need for such polynomials to be orthogonal.

Let us define first weighting functions.

TABLE 2.1 Families of orthogonal polynomial

Family	$w(x)$	$[a, b]$	Definition
Legendre	1	$[-1, 1]$	$P_n(x) = \frac{(-1)^n}{2^n n!} \frac{d^n}{dx^n}[(1 - x^2)^n]$
Chebyshev	$(1 - x^2)^{-1/2}$	$[-1, 1]$	$T_n(x) = cos(ncos^{-1}x)$
Laguerre	e^{-x}	$[0, \infty)$	$L_n(x) = \frac{e^x}{n!} \frac{d^n}{dx^n}(x^n e^{-x})$
Hermite	e^{-x^2}	$(-\infty, \infty)$	$H_n(x) = (-1)^n (e^{x^2}) \frac{d^n}{dx^n}(e^{-x^2})$

Source: [1], [3]

Definition 2.1: A positive function $w(x)$ almost everywhere on an interval $[a, b]$ and having a finite integral on the same interval, is said to be a weighting function on this interval $[a, b]$.

Using the weighting function, we can define the inner product between two functions $f(x)$ and $g(x)$ defined on the same interval $[a, b]$.

Definition 2.2: For two functions $f(x)$ and $g(x)$ defined on the interval $[a, b]$, and giving a weighting function w(x) as defined above, the inner product between the two functions $f(x)$ and $g(x)$, is defined as:

$$< f, g >= \int_a^b f(x)g(x)w(x)dx \tag{2.68}$$

Equipped with these definitions, we are ready to define orthogonal polynomials.

Definition 2.3: We say that a family of polynomials $f_n(x)$ is mutually orthogonal with respect to $w(x)$ if and only if the following conditions holds:

$$< f_i, f_j >= 0 \tag{2.69}$$

for $i \neq j$.

In a similar manner, we can define orthonormal polynomials as:

Definition 2.4: A family of polynomials $f_n(x)$ is mutually orthonormal with respect to $w(x)$ if and only if they are orthogonal and following conditions holds as well:

$$< f_i, f_i >= 1 \tag{2.70}$$

for all i.

The families of orthogonal polynomials used in computational economics are presented in Tables 2.1 and 2.2. I present both their definitions and their recursion formulas.

However, in practice we may find that it is not that simple to apply directly the above formulas. A more efficient approach could consist in applying recursive formulas that are both more intuitive and faster to apply. The second table shows the recursion formula for the families of orthogonal polynomials defined above. Table 2.2 shows first the values of the families of polynomials in 0 and in 1 based on which, using the recursive formulas, then we can find the value of polynomials at any point.

2.4.4 Least Square Orthogonal Polynomials Approximation

We can connect the previously discussed orthogonal polynomials with the ideas of least square approximation in a rather direct way. Consider again a function $f(x)$ on a given interval $[a, b]$. We say that the least square polynomial approximation of f with respect to a weighting function $w(x)$ is the degree polynomial that solves:

$$min_{deg(p) \leq n} \int_b^a (f(x) - g(x))^2 w(x)dx \tag{2.71}$$

TABLE 2.2 Recursive formulas for families of orthogonal polynomial

Family	P_0	P_1	Recursive formulas
Legendre	$P_0(x) = 1$	$P_1(x) = x$	$P_{n+1}(x) = \frac{2n+1}{n+1} x P_n(x) - \frac{n}{n+1} P_{n-1}(x)$
Chebyshev	$T_0(x) = 1$	$T_1(x) = x$	$T_{n+1}(x) = 2x T_n(x) - T_{n-1}(x)$
Laguerre	$L_0(x) = 1$	$L_1(x) = 1 - x$	$L_{n+1}(x) = \frac{2n+1-x}{n+1} L_n(x) - \frac{n}{n+1} L_{n-1}(x)$
Hermite	$H_0(x) = 1$	$H_1(x) = 2x$	$H_{n+1}(x) = 2x H_n(x) - 2n H_{n-1}(x)$

Source: [1], [3]

The role of the weights is to give a subjective importance to the approximation errors. We may also consider the approximation errors as equally important and set the $w(x)$ as equal to 1.

While apparently, the least square approach and the least square polynomial approximation may not seem strongly linked, when solving for the coefficients we get to a solution similar to the least square solution. Assuming the polynomials $g(x)$ are written using orthogonal polynomials:

$$g(x) = \sum_{i=0}^{n} c_i p_i(x) \tag{2.72}$$

Where $p_i(x)_{i=0}^{n}$ is a sequence of orthogonal polynomials. Solving for the coefficients that lead to an optimal solution, we get:

$$c_i = \frac{<f, p_i>}{<p_i, p_i>} \tag{2.73}$$

We can determine now $g(x)$ as:

$$g(x) = \sum_{i=0}^{n} \frac{<f, p_i>}{<p_i, p_i>} p_i(x) \tag{2.74}$$

This is very similar to the solution resulting from running a regression between a function $f(x)$ and n+1 orthogonal regressors given by the orthogonal polynomials $p_i(x)$.

The least square approximation is not the only feasible approach. Since it relies on the L^2 norms, the main limitation is that the convergence in L^2 puts no restriction on the approximation at any individual point. Alternative approaches include:

Uniform Approximation

While in the least square approach we focus on minimizing the total sum of squared errors, in the uniform approximation we rather try to make the approximation close to the original function f at each point. To achieve this, we aim at finding a sequence for which the following equation holds at each x:

$$\lim_{n \to \infty} \max_{x \in [a,b]} |f(x) - p_n(x)| = 0.$$

Minimax Approximation

Whereas in the uniform approximation we aim at finding an approximate of the original function for each point x, in the minimax approximation we aim at finding that function that is the best approximation of the original function in an uniform manner. To do so, we use:

$$\rho_n(f) = \inf_{deg(q) \leq n} \|f - g\|_\infty$$

Where f is the original function, g is the approximation we look for and $\rho_n(f)$ is the infimum of the approximation errors. While in theory such an approximation does exists, see [1], nevertheless it is very hard to find it in practice due to computational complexities.

Chebyshev Economization

Considering a function $f(x)$ which is a m-th degree polynomial, we can write it as a sum of Chebyshev polynomials as follows:

$$f(x) = \sum_{k=0}^{m} a_k T_k(x)$$

Based on this formula, we can derive the n-th degree least square approximation of the original function $f(x)$, provided that $n < m$:

$$p_n(x) = \sum_{k=0}^{n} a_k T_k(x)$$

In this way we can approximate the initial function $f(x)$ through a lower order polynomial $p_n(x)$ which is the n-th degree Chebyshev economization of the function f.

2.4.5 Chebyshev Approximation

We can apply the same idea of approximating through regression this time by using Chebyshev polynomials. This approach embeds the method of Chebyshev economization: to approximate a polynomial of degree m, we use only the first n terms, while dropping the terms $n + 1$ to $m - 1$ which results in a smoother function (since we only drop the higher order polynomials). The second element on which the Chebyshev approximation relies is the fact that the nodes are computed using the zeroes of the n-th degree Chebyshev polynomial.

Below, I provide the basic algorithm to compute a Chebyshev approximation or regression to a given function (f) on an interval $[a, b]$.

We start by computing the m nodes of Chebysev interpolation on an interval $[-1, 1]$, provided that $m \geq n + 1$. We compute them using the formula that gives us the roots of the Chebysev polynomial of degree m:

$$p_k = -cos(\frac{2k - 1}{2m})\pi \tag{2.75}$$

for $k = 1, ..., m$.

Since our interval of interest is [a,b], we recomputed the nodes for this interval using:

$$x_k = (p_k + 1)\frac{b - a}{2} + a \tag{2.76}$$

again, for $k = 1, \ldots m$.

Based on which we can evaluate the function f at these evaluation points: $y_k = f(x_k)$. We can compute now the Chebyshev coefficients using:

$$a_i = \frac{\sum_{k=1}^{m} y_k T_i(p_k)}{\sum_{k=1}^{m} T_i(p_k)^2} \tag{2.77}$$

We can finally now evaluate the approximation of the function f on the given interval [a,b]:

$$\hat{f}(x) = \sum_{i=0}^{n} a_i T_i(2\frac{x - a}{b - a} - 1) \tag{2.78}$$

2.4.6 Shape-Preserving Approximation

While the techniques presented until now for approximation are close enough to the original function f as indicated by a norm we may use, they may lead to some undesired properties in the sense that the approximation might fail to retain the initial properties of the original function. For example, using the minimax approach results in an approximation that, although it is close to the original functions in terms of the norm used, nevertheless it has an oscillation which might not be found in the original function. Whenever we might be interested in keeping some original properties of the shape of the function to be approximated, we may use shape-preserving approximation methods.

Piecewise-Linear Interpolation

This is rather the naïve and the most direct way to apply a shape-preserving approximation. While it has certain attractive properties (for example, it will preserve the concavity of a given function), it is not differentiable due to its piecewise-linear characteristic.

Quadratic Interpolation

This technique preserves some essential features of the shape of the function to be approximated, however it is also differentiable due to being smooth. There are two basic ways to achieve this. One is the Hermit interpolation, while the second uses a method derived from Lagrange's method to interpolate. Both approaches are due to [6].

Hermite Interpolation

The basic assumptions of this approach imply that we know both the level and the slope of the functions that will be approximated. The approximation is done on an interval $[x_1, x_2]$ and it aims at constructing a function g that is both piecewise quadratic and that, given the points y_1, y_2 and z_1, z_2 it verifies that: $g(x_i) = y_i$ and $g'(x_i) = z_i$, with $i = 1, 2$. To find such a function, we can start from the following lemma, due to [6]:

Lemma 2.1: If the following conditions hold, i.e.:

$$\frac{z_1 + z_2}{2} = \frac{y_2 - y_1}{x_2 - x_1} \tag{2.79}$$

the following quadratic form:

$$S(x) = y_1 + z_1(x - x_1) + \frac{z_2 - z_1}{2(x_2 - x_1)}(x - x_1)^2 \tag{2.80}$$

Will satisfy the conditions mentioned above, namely: $S(x_i) = y_i$ and $S'(x_i) = z_i$, with $i = 1, 2$.

Although this lemma is very attractive and seems to find a way to approximate a given function through a polynomial with the desired properties, in reality, the conditions are too strict, that they are rarely met. In order to overcome this, Schumaker proposed a second lemma which uses a supplementary point or node x^*.

Lemma 2.2: Consider a point or node $x^* \in (x_1, x_2)$. Then there exists a unique quadratic spline $S(x)$ that fulfills the following conditions: $S(x_i) = y_i$ and $S'(x_i) = z_i$, with $i = 1, 2$, with the following formula:

$$S(x) = \begin{cases} \alpha_{01} + \alpha_{11}(x - x_1) + \alpha_{21}(x - x_1)^2 & x \in [x_1; x^*] \\ \alpha_{02} + \alpha_{12}(x - x^*) + \alpha_{22}(x - x^*)^2 & x \in [x^*; x_2] \end{cases} \tag{2.81}$$

The coefficients of the spline are determined as follows: $\alpha_{01} = y_1, \alpha_{11} = z_1, \alpha_{21} = \frac{\bar{z} - z_1}{z(x^* - x_1)}, \alpha_{02} = y_1 + \frac{\bar{z} + z_1}{2}(x^* - x_1),$ $\alpha_{12} = \bar{z}, \alpha_{22} = \frac{z_z - \bar{z}}{2(x_2 - x^*)}$. Here, $\bar{z} = \frac{2(y_2 - y_1) - (z_1(x^* - x_1) + z_2(x_2 - x^*))}{x_2 - x_1}$.

Although this lemma seems to give a clear answer to the problem of finding the proper quadratic spline $S(x)$, some uncertainty remains related to the choosing the point x^*. In practice, the point x^* is selected such that the quadratic spline will have the desired properties in terms of the shape.

Lagrange Interpolation Revisited

The second way to perform approximations that preserve the shape is through a modified Lagrange algorithm. This algorithm applies when the basic assumption is that the true slope of the function is unknown. The algorithm assumes that we only know the actual data points (x_i, y_i), where $i = 0, 1, \ldots, n$. This contrasts with the Hermite interpolation when we had information regarding the slope by knowing: $g'(x_i) = z_i$, with $i = 1, 2$.

Here we need a new way to compute the z_i values. To find them, Schumaker proposed to start from:

$$L_i = [(x_{i+1} - x_i)^2 + (y_{i+1} - y_i)^2]^{1/2} \tag{2.82}$$

and from:

$$\Delta_i = \frac{y_{i+1} - y_i}{x_{i+1} - x_i} \tag{2.83}$$

with $i = 1, \ldots, n - 1$.

Using these two expressions we can compute the values for z_i as follows:

$$z_i = \begin{cases} \frac{L_{i-1}\Delta_{i-1} + L_i\Delta_i}{L_{i-1} + L_i}, & \text{if } \Delta_{i-1}\Delta_i > 0 \\ 0, & \text{if } \Delta_{i-1}\Delta_i \leq 0 \end{cases} \tag{2.84}$$

with $i = 2, \ldots n - 1$.

To compute the values of z_i at the end of the intervals, we can use: $z_1 = \frac{3\Delta_1 - z_2}{2}$ and $z_n = \frac{3\Delta_{n-1} - z_{n-1}}{2}$.

Once the values of the z_i are computed, we can apply again the algorithm developed for the Hermite shape preserving approximation.

2.4.7 Multidimensional Approximations

The methods studied until deal with the special case of univariate functions. However, when doing numerical analysis in economics, most likely we are going to meet multivariate functions. Although the extension of algorithms from univariate to multivariate functions might seem straightforward, in reality, dealing with multidimensional approximations leads to potential complications that are not easy to solve.

We can start from the example by [1] to fix these ideas. When we are given a number of data points, say $\{P_1, P_2, P_3, P_4\}$ in $\mathbb{R}^2$, for example, and we are interested to approximate the function $f()$ such that: $f(P_i) = z_i$. If we want to do this through a linear combination as follows: $G(x, y) = a + bx + cy + dxy$ such that $G(x, y)$ is an approximation of the initial function F, that is: $G(x_i, y_i) = z_i$. This would lead us to a linear system which we could not solve since the rank of the matrix is not full. Basically, there are two fundamental problems when generalizing the univariate methods to deal with multivariate methods:

1. Due to the multidimensional case, we might deal with cross-products which implies making difficult choices with respect to the polynomial bases we might use;
2. Of critical importance is also how to select the grid of nodes used for the approximation.

Tensor Product

The simplest way to perform multidimensional approximation is through the use of the tensor product. In this case, the algorithm relies on the use of tensor products of univariate functions.

In this approach, we approximate a given function by using the combinations of the functions (or monomials) employed as a tensor product basis. For the general case, we can define a n-folder tensor product for a function in $\mathbb{R}_n$ with n variables $x_1, x_2, \ldots, x_n$ as follows:

Definition 2.5: The tensor product basis for n functions of the single variable x_i $P_i = \{p_i^k(x_i)\}_{k=0}^{\kappa_i}$ is given by:

$$B = \prod_{k_1=0}^{\kappa_1} \ldots \prod_{k_n=0}^{\kappa_n} p_1^{k_1}(x_1) \ldots p_n^{k_n}(x_n) \tag{2.85}$$

Obviously, the fundamental problem related to the application of this algorithm is the fact that the terms increase exponentially with the number of terms used. If there is a m-dimensional space and we use polynomials of up to order n, we get $(n+1)^m$ terms. The algorithm however is rather efficient for lower order polynomials (e.g. up to order 2).

Complete Polynomials

Despite the obvious simplicity, the tensor product approach suffers from a major drawback, it becomes exponentially difficult to compute as the dimensions increase. In contrast, the approach using complete polynomials leads to a direct proportional increase in complexity as the dimensions of the function approximation increase.

To parallel the definition used for the case of tensor product, for complete polynomials of order κ for a n-dimensional problem, we may write the basis of the approximation as:

Definition 2.6: Given $\kappa \in \mathbb{N}$, and consider n variables, the basis of polynomials is given by:

$$P_k^n = \{x_1^{k_1} \times \ldots \times x_n^{k_n} : k_1, \ldots, k_n \geq 0, \sum_{i=1}^{n} k_i \leq \kappa\} \tag{2.86}$$

This complete set of polynomials actually is used in Taylor's theorem for the multidimensional case. For a Taylor series expansion of order k for a n-variables problems we can write:

$$f(x) \doteq f(x^0) + \sum_{i=1}^{n} \frac{\partial f}{\partial x_i}(x^0)(x_{i_1} - x_{i_1}^0) + \ldots + \frac{1}{k!} \sum_{i_1=1}^{n} \ldots \sum_{i_k=1}^{n} \frac{\partial^k f}{\partial x_{i_1} \ldots \partial x_{i_k}}(x^0)(x_{i_1} - x_{i_1}^0) \ldots (x_{i_k} - x_{i_k}^0) \tag{2.87}$$

For example, a Taylor expansion of order $k = 1$ for a problem in n dimensions would use the terms in the complete set of polynomials given by $P_k^n = \{1, x_1, \ldots, x_n\}$.

The differences in terms of complexity of the basis used for the two approaches are rather obvious. Considering a n-dimensional problem and polynomials of up to order $k = 2$, then the tensor product basis would yield 3^n terms while the complete set of polynomials would imply the use of: $1 + n + \frac{n(n+1)}{2}$ terms.

The Bilinear Approximation

Following the example from [1], we assume that the values of a two-dimensional function f(x,y) are $(x, y) = (\pm 1, \pm 1)$. The basic idea of the bilinear approximation is to interpolate the data in both coordinate directions. To achieve this for the given function, we can use the following four functions that form a cardinal basis for the interval $[-1, 1]^2$:

$$\phi_1(x, y) = \frac{1}{4}(1 - x)(1 - y) \tag{2.88}$$

$$\phi_2(x, y) = \frac{1}{4}(1 + x)(1 - y) \tag{2.89}$$

$$\phi_3(x, y) = \frac{1}{4}(1 + x)(1 + y) \tag{2.90}$$

$$\phi_4(x, y) = \frac{1}{4}(1 - x)(1 + y) \tag{2.91}$$

The original element of the finite element approximation comes into play here: except one point, each of the four functions of the basis have zero entries. Using this basis, we can approximate the original function on the interval $[-1, 1]^2$ using:

$$f(-1, -1)\phi_1(x, y) + f(1, -1)\phi_2(x, y) + f(1, 1)\phi_3(x, y) + f(-1, 1)\phi_4(x, y) \tag{2.92}$$

The Simplicial 2-D Linear Approximation

This is an alternative to the bilinear approximation that is preferred by many due to the use of the simplicial triangular element. Let us start again from the x-y plane specific to the two-dimensional case. Following [1], triangulation in this plane might be achieved by setting three points which can be conveniently defined as: $P_1 = (0, 0)$, $P_2 = (0, 1)$ and $P_3 = (1, 0)$

To form a cardinal interpolation basis, we need to define the functions ϕ which satisfies the following relationship: $\phi_i(P_i) = 1$ and $\phi_i(P_j) = 0$ for $i \neq j$.

We can use the following functions that indeed form a cardinal interpolation basis (and it can be easily verified):

$$\phi_1(x, y) = 1 - x - y \tag{2.93}$$
$$\phi_2(x, y) = y \tag{2.94}$$
$$\phi_3(x, y) = x \tag{2.95}$$

Adding a new point $P_4 = (1, 1)$ we can form a new cardinal interpolation basis for the points P_2, P_3 and P_4:

$$\phi_4(x, y) = 1 - x \tag{2.96}$$
$$\phi_5(x, y) = 1 - y \tag{2.97}$$
$$\phi_6(x, y) = x + y - 1 \tag{2.98}$$

Thus, to approximate the function on the square formed from the points P1, P2, P4, P3 we use the following function:

$$\hat{f}(x, y) = \begin{cases} f(0, 0)(1 - x - y) + f(0, 1)y + f(1, 0)x & x + y \leq 1 \\ f(0, 1)(1 - x) + f(1, 0)(1 - y) + f(1, 1)(x + y - 1) & x + y \geq 1 \end{cases} \tag{2.99}$$

with $i = 2, \ldots n - 1$.

2.4.8 Doing Function Approximations in Julia

There are quite a few packages doing function approximation in Julia. Given the strong relationship between interpolation and function approximation, some of these packages might be able to implement both techniques.

A good starting point if one intends to do function approximation in Julia is the package ChebyshevApprox. Written by an economist, Richard Dennis, it has the advantage of providing key features that any economist would expect, while, at the same time, using a language rather familiar to the economist with a basic training in numerical methods.

As the name suggest, the package can approximate continuous function using Chebyshev polynomials. The package can deal with both univariate and multiple variables function approximation. For the univariate case, there are just a few functions one needs to understand.

A starting point, common to both the univariate and multivariate function approximation, is to create Chebyshev nodes. The function used to create Chebyshev nodes has the following general syntax:

```
Chebyshev_nodes(n, range)
```

Where n is the number of nodes and range is the interval within which the nodes are created. When we don't provide the range, the function will create the nodes within the $[-1.0, 1.0]$ interval.

For the univariate case, there are two further functions used to make the approximation, relying on the already computed Chebyshev nodes. The first, computes the weights associated to these nodes. The general syntax is:

```
chebyshev_weights(y,nodes,order,range)
```

Here by y we denote the function evaluation at the nodes. The variable nodes contains the nodes already created with the function:

```
chebyshev_nodes
```

The variable order gives the order of the polynomial. There is also an alternative version of this function, as shown below:

```
chebyshev_weights(y,poly,order,range)
```

Here, poly is an array that contains a two-dimensional array. Both version of this function will determine the Chebyshev weights using the Chebyshev regression.

The final step in doing the approximation using Chebyshev polynomials is to actually evaluate the function for a certain point x. To achieve this, we use the function *chebyshev_evaluate*, with the following syntax:

```
chebyshev_evaluate(w,[x],order,range)
```

Here, w are the Chebyshev weights which were computed above, x is the point where the function is approximated, while order and range have the meaning and values as explained above. There is an alternative function here too, *clenshaw_evaluate* which uses the same options and variables, but it is based on the Clenshaw's recursion.

To approximate multivariate functions, the approach is rather similar. The first step, that of creating Chebyshev nodes is identical to the case of univariate functions. In the following steps, approximating multivariate functions require the use of functions specially designed to deal with this case. Additionally, we can set the polynomials to be either tensor products or complete polynomials. To compute the Chebyshev weights for a function of two variable, we can use:

```
chebyshev_weights(y,nodes_1,nodes_2,order,range)
chebyshev_weights(y,nodes,order,range)
```

or

```
chebyshev_weights(y,poly,order,range)
```

Thus we can either declare the nodes for each dimension, as in the first case, or declare or the nodes as an array. We evaluate the functions with the same functions and a similar syntax:

```
chebyshev_evaluate(w,x,order,range)
clenshaw_evaluate(w,x,order,range)
```

I present a simple example of function approximation using this package for the univariate case. The example is drawn from the package itself. I start by setting the range and the number of points to be created. Afterwards, I create the Chebyshev nodes using the function described above:

```
using ChebyshevApprox
n = 20
range = [-2.0,2.0]
nodes = chebyshev_nodes(n,range)
```

In the next step, I initialize y as a vector with zero values and I fill this vector with the values of the function $f(x) = (x+2)^{1/2}$ at the nodes:

```
y = zeros(n)
for i = 1:n
y[i] = (nodes[i]+2.0)^(1/2)
end
```

Next, I compute the Chebyshev weights using the Chebyshev regression by using both the tensor product and the complete polynomials (after setting the order of approximation to 5):

```
order = 5
w_tensor   = chebyshev_weights(y,nodes,[order],range)
w_complete = chebyshev_weights(y,nodes,order,range)
```

In the final step, I compute the function approximation at a given point using the alternative approaches which I also compare in the end:

```
point = [1.2]
y_chebyshev_tensor   = chebyshev_evaluate(w_tensor,point,[order],range)
y_chebyshev_complete = chebyshev_evaluate(w_complete,point,order,range)
y_clenshaw_tensor    = clenshaw_evaluate(w_tensor,point,[order],range)
y_clenshaw_complete  = clenshaw_evaluate(w_complete,point,order,range)
y_actual = (point+2.0).^(1/2)
println([y_actual y_chebyshev_tensor y_chebyshev_complete
y_clenshaw_tensor y_clenshaw_complete])
[1.78885 1.79396 1.79396 1.79396 1.79396]
```

There are a few other package dealing with function approximation. One pretty developed package is ApproxFun. A package dealing with computing the nodes and weights in a fast way with Gauss Quadrature is FastGaussQuadrature. Using ApproxFun is quite easy and the package additionally provides functions for computing the root, differentiation, etc.

2.5 NUMERICAL DIFFERENTIATION

Computing the Jacobian and or Hessian matrices is a problem we frequently deal with in economics. This section deals with numerical methods to compute the derivatives of a function.

Surprisingly, in contrast to numerical integration (which is more used in economics), the numerical differentiation is not well covered in classical books on numerical methods in economics, like [1] or [2]. The material here draws mainly from [4] and [3].

As we are going to see, treating numerical differentiation right after the problem of interpolation and approximation is the right order to do so. The problem in numerical differentiation is that given a function $f(x)$ and a point x_k we are interested to find the derivative of order n of the function in the point x_k:

$$\frac{\partial^n f}{\partial x_k^n} \tag{2.100}$$

The link to interpolation becomes clear when we realize that numerically computing the derivate of a function f in a point x_k amounts to locally approximating the function with the means of a polynomial and differentiating this polynomial. Equivalently, we might also use the Taylor expansion to achieve the same result.

2.5.1   Finite Difference

This approach stems from the very definition of the derivative. As we already know, the first order derivative can be computed using:

$$f'(x) = \lim_{h \to 0} \frac{f(x+h) - f(x)}{h} \tag{2.101}$$

We can use this formula to approximate the derivative and the finite difference approach is based on this basic idea. A finite difference approximation can be done by means of a Taylor expansion. In the most basic form, see [2], we can write:

$$f(x+h) = f(x) + f'(x)h + O(h^2) \tag{2.102}$$

Where $O(h^2)$ contains the higher power terms. Comparing the above formula with the definition of the derivative, we can notice that the error of the approximation using the Taylor expansion amounts to: $\frac{O(h^2)}{h} = O(h)$, where $O(h)$ is the error in the derivative. Thus, we can write:

$$f'(x) = \frac{f(x+h) - f(x)}{h} + O(h) \tag{2.103}$$

There are more accurate ways to compute the derivative numerically, but to achieve this, we first have to compute the forward and backward expansions given by:

$$f(x+h) = f(x) + hf'(x) + \frac{h^2}{2!}f''(x) + \frac{h^3}{3!}f'''(x) + \dots \tag{2.104}$$

$$f(x-h) = f(x) - hf'(x) + \frac{h^2}{2!}f''(x) - \frac{h^3}{3!}f'''(x) + \dots \tag{2.105}$$

We can also compute the same backward and forward expressions using $\pm 2h$, as follows:

$$f(x+2h) = f(x) + 2hf'(x) + \frac{(2h)^2}{2!}f''(x) + \frac{(2h)^3}{3!}f'''(x) + \dots \tag{2.106}$$

$$f(x-2h) = f(x) - 2hf'(x) + \frac{(2h)^2}{2!}f''(x) - \frac{(2h)^3}{3!}f'''(x) + \dots \tag{2.107}$$

We can also add and subtract these series, to get:

$$f(x+h) + f(x-h) = 2f(x) + h^2 f''(x) + \dots \tag{2.108}$$

$$f(x+h) - f(x-h) = 2hf'(x) + \frac{h^3}{3}f'''(x) + \dots \tag{2.109}$$

for the first type of expansion, while the formula for the second type of expansion is similar.

Using these expressions, we can apply a few different approaches to numerically compute the derivatives. A first widely used approach is the first noncentral finite difference approximation.

First Central Finite Difference Approximation

We can use the above difference between $f(x+h)$ and $f(x-h)$ to compute the first derivative as:

$$f'(x) = \frac{f(x+h) - f(x-h)}{2h} - \frac{h^2}{6}f'''(x) \tag{2.110}$$

Which can also be rewritten as:

$$f'(x) = \frac{f(x+h) - f(x-h)}{2h} + O(h^2) \tag{2.111}$$

This is basically the formula for the first central difference approximation of the first derivative $f'(x)$, where the last term, $O(h^2)$ is an error term that varies with h^2. In a similar manner, we can also derive the first central approximation of the second derivative, i.e. $f''(x)$:

$$f''(x) = \frac{f(x+h) - 2f(x) + f(x-h)}{h^2} - \frac{h^2}{12} f^{(4)}(x) \tag{2.112}$$

Which can be rewritten too as:

$$f''(x) = \frac{f(x+h) - 2f(x) + f(x-h)}{h^2} - O(h^2) \tag{2.113}$$

In order to express it as depending on an error term as a function of h^2 too.

Finite Noncentral Finite Difference Approximations

An alternative to the first central finite difference approximation is the noncentral finite difference approximation. Its advantage stems from the fact that in certain situations, we might not be able to apply the central finite difference approximation. One standard example is that of having at our disposition only discrete points, $\{x_1, x_2, ..., x_n\}$ such that the standard first central finite difference approximation formula is inapplicable, since we would have to use points on both sides of the endpoints x_1, x_n. In contrast, the noncentral finite difference approximation rather relies on evaluations on one of the sides of the point x.

From the Taylor standard formula, we can derive the first order derivative as follows, using only the forward difference approximation:

$$f'(x) = \frac{f(x+h) - f(x)}{h} - \frac{h}{2!} f''(x) - \frac{h^2}{3!} f'''(x) - ... \tag{2.114}$$

It becomes apparent thus that we can have an approximation of $f'(x)$ which does not rely on points on both sides of the given point x, by using only the terms on the right hand side. The above formula can be made more compact by using the standard notation (including an error term):

$$f'(x) = \frac{f(x+h) - f(x)}{h} + O(h) \tag{2.115}$$

The noncentral finite difference approximation can be computed by using the first backward difference approximation too. This would lead to a similar formula to the one above, i.e.:

$$f'(x) = \frac{f(x) - f(x-h)}{h} + O(h) \tag{2.116}$$

Second Noncentral Finite Difference Approximations

The first central and noncentral finite difference approximations rely on the $O(h)$ error term. However, a different category of finite difference approximations, the second noncentral ones, rely rather on the $O(h^2)$ error terms. The second noncentral finite difference approximations can be both forward and backward. Its name stems from the fact that, in contrast to first finite difference approximation, we also use the second order derivative.

To achieve this for the case of the forward case, we can start from the Taylor expansions using h and $2h$:

$$f(x+h) = f(x) + hf'(x) + \frac{h^2}{2!} f''(x) + \frac{h^3}{3!} f'''(x) + ... \tag{2.117}$$

$$f(x+2h) = f(x) + 2hf'(x) + 2(h)^2 f''(x) + \frac{4(h)^3}{3} f'''(x) + ... \tag{2.118}$$

Instead of simply using either $f(x+h)$ or $f(x+2h)$ as in the first finite difference approximations, here we combine the two by doing eliminating $f''(x)$. To achieve this, we can multiply the first equation by 4 and subtract it from the second, to get:

$$f(x+2h) - 4(f+h) = -3f(x) - 2hf'(x) + \frac{h^4}{2} f^{(4)}(x) + ... \tag{2.119}$$

Based on this, we can approximate the first order derivative using the following expression:

$$f'(x) = \frac{-f(x+2h) + 4f(x+h) - 3f(x)}{2h} + \frac{h^2}{4}f^{(4)}(x) + ... \tag{2.120}$$

Which can be rewritten in the standard format used until now by relying on the error term $O(h^2)$:

$$f'(x) = \frac{-f(x+2h) + 4f(x+h) - 3f(x)}{2h} + O(h^2) \tag{2.121}$$

2.5.2 Richardson Extrapolation

We have already got exposed to the idea that any approximation depends proportionally on one or more parameters. Let us consider that we start from a parameter h and compute an approximation $A(h)$ for a quantity of interest A (which can be a function, its first order derivative, etc.). At the most general level, [3] suggests writing the original function as follows:

$$A = A(h) + \Phi h^k + \Phi' h^{k+1} + \Phi'' h^{k+2} + ... \tag{2.122}$$

With k the order of the error, a parameter that is known, while Φ, Φ', Φ'' are unknown parameters. Using the already familiar notation based on error, we may write it like:

$$A = A(h) + \Phi h^k + O(h^{k+1}) \tag{2.123}$$

Here, the approximation depends on the error term $O(h^{(k+1)})$ which, as the notation suggests, is the sum of terms of order equal to and higher than h^{k+1}. If we eliminate the error term, what we get consists in a difference equation in the unknowns A and Φ, and it turns out that for each value of h, we get a difference equation. Thus, we can write for the $h/2$ similarly:

$$A = A(h/2) + \Phi(h/2)^k + O(h^{k+1}) \tag{2.124}$$

Multiplying this by 2^k and subtracting from it the previous formula, we get:

$$(2^k - 1)A = 2^k A(h/2) - A(h) + O(h^{k+1}) \tag{2.125}$$

Which yields:

$$A = \frac{2^k A(h/2) - A(h)}{2^k - 1} + O(h^{k+1}) \tag{2.126}$$

By denoting with $B(h)$ the first term of the equation, we get:

$$A = B(h) + O(h^{k+1}) \tag{2.127}$$

Thus, by using this approach, we were able to improve the original approximation, $A(h)$ of order k, with a better approximation $B(h)$ of order $k + 1$. This is the basic idea of Richardson extrapolation.

This basic idea can be directly applied to approximating a first order derivative at a point x, see [3]. The first order derivative would amount to:

$$D_0^0(F) = \frac{F(x + h_0) - F(x - h_0)}{2h_0} \tag{2.128}$$

We change the value of h_0 to $h_1 = h_0/2$, such that the first order derivative would be now:

$$D_0^1(F) = \frac{F(x + h_1) - F(x - h_1)}{2h_1} \tag{2.129}$$

Using the previously determined formula, we may write a better approximation of F:

$$D_0^1(F) = \frac{4D_0^1(F) - D_0^0(F)}{3} \tag{2.130}$$

This can be further written in a recursive manner:

$$D_0^1(F) = D_0^1(F) + \frac{D_0^1(F) - D_0^0(F)}{3} \tag{2.131}$$

This allows us to form a recursive relationship on which we can iterate. This can be done by using the above formula:

$$D_j^l(F) = D_{j+1}^{l-1}(F) + \frac{D_{j+1}^{l-1}(F) - D_j^{l-1}(F)}{4^k - 1} \tag{2.132}$$

Here, $D_j^l(F)$ is an approximation for $F'(x)$ with an error given by $h_j^{2(l+1)}$. We iterate on this value until the improvement is smaller than a given threshold ϵ: $|D^m - D_0^{m-1}| < \epsilon$

2.5.3 Using Interpolation to Approximate the Derivatives

We used different interpolation techniques to approximate a function $f(x)$ consisting in discrete points. In a similar manner, we may use the interpolation based approximation to estimate the derivative of the same function $f(x)$. We may use the various techniques proposed to find the approximation through interpolation. For example, for the interpolation using polynomials, we may approximate the function $f(x)$ for $n + 1$ data points through a polynomial of the form: $P_n(x) = a_0 + a_1 x + a_2 x^2 + ... + a_n x^n$.

To numerically approximate the derivative at a point x^*, we may compute the derivative of the polynomial $P_n(x)$ at this given point x^*.

We can approach the numerically differentiation through interpolation by cubic splines too. There are basic advantages when dealing with cubic splines interpolation for numerically differentiation. First, as we previously discussed, the cubic splines are one of the best way to perform interpolation. Second, it is quite straightforward to differentiate the cubic splines.

2.5.4 Numerical Differentiation in Julia

The most basic way to numerically compute the derivative of a function is to use the finite difference approach which is basically just the formula of the first derivative. Practically, we may apply this for any function and a predefined perturbation constant h. The code below, defines first a function that performs the finite forward difference. It then applies it to a specified function, for a given perturbation value:

```
Julia> firstdiff(f,x,h) = (f(x+h)-f(x))/h;
f(x) = x^2;
x = 0.0;
h = 10^(-8.);
Julia> firstdiff(f,x,h)
1.0e-8
```

The value is approximately equal to the exact value of the first order derivative 0. Although this algorithm allows us to compute the first derivative in a simple manner, the algorithm is both inefficient (think of the case of numerically computing the gradient), and it is also an approximation whose precision critically depends on the perturbation constant h.

While this approach covers the most basic needs, there are a few quite comprehensive packages in Julia. One of the best is the package Calculus. While the package provides methods to deal with derivative approximating based on the finite-differencing approach, it also uses the symbolic differentiation to compute exact solutions of the derivatives of simpler functions.

2.6 NUMERICAL INTEGRATION

Computing the integral of a given function f defined on $\mathbb{R}^n$ is an often encountered task in economic research. In the most general form, see [2], the problem we face is to compute the integral for a given weight function, i.e.:

$$\int_I f(x)w(x)dx \tag{2.133}$$

Where I is a given interval part of $\mathbb{R}^n$. How the weight function $w(x)$ is defined depends on the problem at hand. For example, if we are interested to compute the expected value of a continuous random variable, the weight function $w(x)$ would be given by probability density function of the random variable.

The typical way to numerically compute a definite integral is by using a weighted sum of the values of the function, that is, we write:

$$\int_I f(x)w(x)dx \approx \sum_{i=0}^{n} w_i f(x_i) \tag{2.134}$$

Basically, this general formula covers the most used methods to numerically compute an integral. How these methods differ between each other is in the way they define the weight function $w(x)$ or the points x_i. The next sections detail three of the most used methods to numerically compute an integral which differ basically through the way they define the weight: Newton-Cotes methods, Gaussian Quadrature and Monte Carlo Integration. The presentation draws mainly on [1] and [3].

2.6.1   Newton-Cotes Methods

There are few approaches that all are part of the Newton-Cotes methods: the mid-point rule, the trapezoid rule and the Simpson's rule. In this section we deal with univariate Newton-Cotes methods. Essentially, they evaluate the function of interest f at a given number of points over the interval $[a, b]$, and constructs a usually linear interpolation based on these points which is finally integrated.

The Mid-point Rule

This is the simplest approach in dealing with the approximation of an integral. In its most basic form, the approach consists in using the four points at the extremes of the rectangle they form, i.e.: $P_0 = (a, 0)$; $P_1 = (b, 0)$; $P_3 = (a, f(\xi))$; $P_4 = (b, f(\xi))$.

Here, we define ξ as given by the mid-point value of the given interval $[a, b]$ such that, by definition: $\xi = \frac{a+b}{2}$.

The approximation of the integral can be written in this case as:

$$\int_a^b f(x)dx = (b-a)f(\frac{a+b}{2}) + \frac{(b-a)^3}{4!}f''(\xi) \tag{2.135}$$

With $\xi \in [a, b]$ chosen such that the approximate integral is:

$$\hat{I} = (b-a)f(\frac{a+b}{2}) \tag{2.136}$$

Given that this approach uses a very small number of points to provide an approximation of the integral, the approximation provided through it is usually not very accurate. To increase the accuracy, the usual solution is to break the initial interval $[a, b]$ into a number of smaller intervals.

Let us assume that we use n such intervals, each having a size of $h = (b-a)/n$. In this case, we end up using $n + 1$ data points with the values:

$$x_i = a + (i - 1/2)h \tag{2.137}$$

In this particular case, the approximation of the integral is given by:

$$\hat{I} = h \sum_{i=1}^{n} f(x_i) + \frac{h^2(b-a)}{12} f''(\xi) \tag{2.138}$$

Below, I coded the mid-point rule for a given function $f(x) = 2x$ and an integration domain $[0, 1]$. The algorithm follows [3]. The domain is divided into 11 sub-intervals. Of course, for more complex function, the number of subdivisions should be higher.

```
#define the interval [a,b]
a=0.0;
```

```
b=1.0;
#define the number of divisions
n=10.0;
h=(b-a)/n;
v=linspace(1,n,10)';
x=a+(v-1/2)*h;
f(x)=2x;
y=map(f, x)
mid_point_int=h*sum(y)
```

The code returns the following approximation of the integral: 1.0000000000000002.

We might observe that applying a function to a vector can be done through the function $map(f, A)$, where A is an array.

The Trapezoid Rule

This is the most basic type of closed approach to approximate an integral since it is based on the values of the function at the endpoints of the interval, i.e. $f(a)$ and $f(b)$. Its approach relies on the same idea of interpolation which consists now in using a linear approximation of the function whose integral we approximate between the two end points. Using these points, we can define a trapezoid through the points $(a, 0)$, $(a, f(a))$, $(b, f(b))$, $(b, 0)$. We can approximate the integral using the following rule:

$$\int_a^b f(x)dx = (b-a)[f(a) + f(b)] - \frac{(b-a)^3}{12}f''(\xi) \tag{2.139}$$

Where $\xi \in [a, b]$.

Since this approach relies on using a very limited number of points for interpolation, it is advisable to split the initial interval $[a, b]$ similarly as for the mid-point rule. If we consider again n+1 such points, each defined by: $h = \frac{b-a}{n}$, we get n intervals, and we can produce a better approximation of the integral using:

$$\hat{I} = \frac{h}{2}[f(x_0) + 2f(x_1) + \ldots + 2f(x_{n-1}) + f(x_n)] - \frac{h^2(b-a)}{12}f''(\xi) \tag{2.140}$$

Where $x_i = a + ih$, and ξ is a point in the interval $[a, b]$.

Below, I present a code for integrating a simple function f(x)=2x over the interval [0, 1] using the trapezoid rule, following again [3]:

```
#Trapezoid rule
#define the interval [a,b]
a=0.0;
b=1.0;
# define the number of divions
n=10.0;
h=(b-a)/n;
v=linspace(0,n,11)';
x=a+v*h;
f(x)=2x;
y=map(f, x)
trapezoid_int=0.5*h*(2*sum(y[2:length(y)-1])+y[1]+y[length(y)])
```

The algorithm returns: 1.0000000000000002.

This is a similar result for the case of mid-point rule. However, for more complicated functions, the results accuracy for the two methods might differ significantly.

2.6.2 The Simpson Rule

Given the fact that the approximation of an integral using the trapezoid approach relies on the endpoints only, a simple way to improve this approach consists in using an additional point. Simpson's rule improve the trapezoid algorithm by consider the values of the function f at points a, b as well as the mid-point $(b + a)/2$. In contrast to the trapezoid approach,

Simpson's rule also considers a quadratic approximation of the integral. The rule to compute the approximation of the integral is shown below:

$$\int_a^b f(x)dx = \frac{(b-a)}{6}[f(a) + 4f(\frac{a+b}{2}) + f(b)] - \frac{(b-a)^5}{2880} f^{(4)}(\xi) \tag{2.141}$$

Where ξ is a point from the interval $[a, b]$.

As for the other approaches within the Newton-Cotes family, we can improve the accuracy of the integral approximation by splitting the original interval $[a, b]$ into n intervals, each having the same size: $h = (b - a)/n$, resulting in a number of $n + 1$ data points x_i. Each such point is defined by: $x_i = a + ih$.

Where i takes values from 0 to n. Using these $n + 1$ points leads to a composite rule to approximate the integral written as:

$$\hat{I} = \frac{h}{3}[f(x_0) + 4f(x_1) + 2f(x_2) + 4f(x_3) + ... + f(x_n)] - \frac{h^4(b-a)}{180} f^{(4)}(\xi) \tag{2.142}$$

Where, again, ξ is a point from the interval $[a, b]$.

Does the Simpson's algorithm really improve the accuracy relative to the performance of the trapezoid rule? Comparing the errors in each case, we find that the order magnitude of error for the trapezoid rule to be h^2, while for the Simpson's rule it is h^4, indicating a significant improvement when the Simpson's rule is used.

I code the same example of integrating the basic function $f(x) = 2x$ over the same interval $[0, 1]$, this time based on the Simpson's rule. The coding approach is based on [3]. Most of the code is similar except the last line:

```
#Simpson's rule
#define the interval [a,b]
a=0.0;
b=1.0;
# define the number of divisions
n=10.0;
h=(b-a)/n;
v=linspace(0,n,11)';
x=a+v*h;
f(x)=2x;
y=map(f, x)
simpson_int=h/3*(2.0*dot((1+rem.(1:length(y)-2,2)),(y[2:(length(y)-1)])'))
+y[1]+y[length(y)])
```

Applying this algorithm leads to a more accurate approximated integral, with the value of the approximation equal to 1, corresponding precisely to the exact value of the integral.

2.6.3 Infinite Integration

The discussion up to now dealt with approximating an integral over a definite interval $[a, b]$, i.e. approximating the following integral:

$$\int_a^b f(x)dx \tag{2.143}$$

However, there are cases when we need to approximate integrals over infinite domains. To achieve this, we simply have to adapt the above approximation rules to the infinite domains using the change of variable formula.

Before applying any change of variable formula, we need to ensure that the integral defined over the infinite domain (also known as an improper integral) does exist. To define such an improper integral over the interval $[0, \infty)$, we can write:

$$\int_a^\infty f(x)dx = lim_{b \to \infty} \int_a^b f(x)dx \tag{2.144}$$

We say that this improper integral exists, if the limit exists. When dealing with the double infinite integral, we may rewrite it using the limit function for both a and b, as follows:

$$\int_a^\infty f(x)dx = lim_{\substack{b\to\infty \\ a\to\infty}} \int_a^b f(x)dx \tag{2.145}$$

Which, again, will be defined if these limits exist.

A key theoretical result that forms a basis for approximating improper integrals is the change of variables theorem states below.

Theorem 2.1: Change of Variable Theorem: Let us consider a function f, with $f : \mathbb{R} \to \mathbb{R}$, and f continuously differentiable and monotonically increasing on the interval $[a, b]$. The following relationship holds for any integrable function $h(x)$ on the interval $[a, b]$:

$$\int_a^b h(x)dx = \int_{f^{(-1)}(a)}^{f^{(-1)}(b)} h(f(y))f'(y)dy \tag{2.146}$$

In other words, this theorem ensures that, provided that a function f meets certain conditions, we can approximate an integral of a function h with respect to x with an equivalent integral with respect to y where x and y are related through: $x = f(y)$.

There are many ways to convert a difficult integral into one that can be easily approximated using the Newton-Cotes methods. The general principle is to use a change of variable that yields an integral which can be easily approximated using integration methods.

One easy to use change of variable should satisfy the conditions: $x(0) = 0$; $x(1) = \infty$. Then, by the Change of Variable Theorem, we get the following new integral:

$$\int_0^\infty f(x)dx = \int_0^1 f(x(z))x'(z)dz \tag{2.147}$$

This can be approximated using the Newton-Cotes techniques. An example of change of variable that satisfies these conditions is the function: $x(z) = \frac{z}{1-z}$. This function has the following first order derivative: $x'(t) = \frac{1}{(1-z)^2}$.

This leads to the following integral:

$$\int_0^\infty f(x)dx = \int_0^1 f(\frac{z}{1-z})(1-z)^{-2}dz \tag{2.148}$$

Provided that f is chosen such that $f(x(z))x'(z)$ has bounded derivatives, $x(z)$ is a good choice in approximating integrals even when dealing with difficult functions. If the derivatives are not bounded, then the error bounds associated to the approximate integrals will not converge.

To see an example using this change of variable, consider that we want to approximate the integral:

$$\int_0^\infty e^{-t}t^2dt \tag{2.149}$$

By using the transformation: $t = \frac{z}{1-z}$.

We get the following integral as a result of the change of variable transformation:

$$\int_0^1 e^{-z/(1-z)}(\frac{z}{1-z})^2(1-z)^2dz \tag{2.150}$$

2.6.4 Gaussian Quadrature Methods

The Newton-Cotes methods rely on the same basic formula to approximate an integral for a given function $f(x)$:

$$\int_a^b w(x)f(x)dx = \sum^n \omega_i f(x_i) \tag{2.151}$$

Here, x_i are quadrature nodes which are from the interval $[a, b]$ while ω_i are quadrature weights.

The main characteristic of the Newton-Cotes based approach is the use of low-order polynomials on small intervals in order to determine the approximation of the f which is piecewise-polynomial and which is further integrated. Two additional essential characteristics are the fact that the points x_i are picked-up in an arbitrary manner (actually, as we have seen, they are most of the times uniformly spaced on the given interval $[a, b]$) while the weights are set in order to ensure a fine approximation if f is a low degree polynomial.

An alternative approach, the Gaussian one, ensures actually that the approximation is exact for the case of a low order polynomial function f by setting the nodes and weights appropriately. As a general rule, we can write the approximation of the integral using the Gaussian approach by relying on the formula below:

$$\int_a^b f(x)w(x)dx = \sum_{i=1}^n \omega_i f(x_i) + \frac{f^{(2n)}(\xi)}{q_n^2(2n)!} \tag{2.152}$$

Where the x_i are nodes that are from the same interval $[a, b]$ and ω_i are some weights. The main advantage of the Gaussian approach is the fact that if f is a polynomial of degree $2n - 1$, then it can be proved that the approximation provided is exact. The theorem below due to [7] is a key result that supports this claim.

Theorem 2.2: Assume a function $w(x)$ defined on the interval $[a, b]$, and an orthonormal family of polynomials defined with respect to this function $w(x)$, denoted by $\{\phi_k(x)\}_{k=0}^\infty$. Define q_k such that for each polynomial, $\phi_k(x) = q_k x^k + ...$ If x_i are the zeros of the polynomial $\phi_n(x)$, then we have that $a < x_1 < ... < x_n < b$. Given these assumptions, for a function f defined on the interval $[a, b]$ that is $\mathbb{C}^{(2n)}$, the following equation is verified:

$$\int_a^b w(x)f(x)dx = \sum_{i=1}^n \omega_i f(x_i) + \frac{f^{(2n)}(\xi)}{q_n^2(2n)!} \tag{2.153}$$

Where ξ is from the interval $[a, b]$, while the weights ω_i are defined as:

$$\omega_i = -\frac{q_{n+1}/q_n}{\phi_n'(x_i)\phi_{n+1}(x_i)} > 0 \tag{2.154}$$

This theorem ensures two key properties. On one hand, by using the zeros of the orthogonal polynomials, it implies that the values x_i are in the interval $[a, b]$. On the other hand, the weights, according to the above formula, are always positive. This avoids the problems associated to using higher order formulas of the Newton-Cotes family.

In practice however, one does not use this formula directly, but rather relies on standard Gaussian formulas that provide exact solutions for the nodes and weights. We discuss a few such formulas below.

Gauss-Chebyshev Quadrature

This is applicable to the problems which have the following specification:

$$\int_{-1}^1 f(x)(1 - x^2)^{-1/2}dx \tag{2.155}$$

In this particular case, the weights are given by: $(1 - x^2)^{-1/2}$, which correspond to the weights in the Chebyshev polynomials.

For this type of integrals, we can use the following formula for approximation:

$$\int_{-1}^1 f(x)(1 - x^2)^{-1/2}dx = \frac{\pi}{n}\sum_{i=1}^n f(x_i) + \frac{\pi}{2^{2n-1}}\frac{f^{(2n)}(\xi)}{(2n)!} \tag{2.156}$$

Here, ξ is value in the interval $[-1, 1]$, while the nodes are defined as: $x_i = cos(\frac{2i-1}{2n}\pi)$, where $i = 1, \ldots m$.

There are two basic advantages for using the Gauss-Chebyshev formula: the weights are constant across the nodes (since they are equal to π/n), and, at the same time, the formula can be applied with no difficulty.

Gauss-Legendre Quadrature

For the same interval $[-1, 1]$, we could alternatively use the standard weighting function for which $w(x) = 1$. This leads to the Gauss-Legendre quadrature which is written below:

$$\int_{-1}^{1} f(x)dx = \sum_{i=1}^{n} \omega_i f(x_i) + \frac{2^{2n+1}(n!)^4}{(2n+1)!(2n)!} \frac{f^{(2n)}(\xi)}{(2n!)} \tag{2.157}$$

As before, ξ is a point from the interval $[-1, 1]$.

Gauss-Hermite Quadrature

This quadrature applies very well to the case of computing the expectations of normal random variables. The Gauss-Hermite quadrature applies to problems where one needs to evaluate expressions in the form:

$$\int_{-\infty}^{\infty} f(x)e^{-x^2}dx \tag{2.158}$$

By using n points.

The Gauss-Hermite quadrature relies on the following formula:

$$\int_{-\infty}^{\infty} f(x)e^{-x^2}dx = \sum_{i=1}^{n} \omega_i f(x_i) + \frac{n!\sqrt{\pi}}{2^n} \frac{f^{(2n)}(\xi)}{(2n!)} \tag{2.159}$$

Here, the point ξ is from the interval $[-\infty, \infty]$.

In the context of normal random variables, assuming that a variable y is normally distributed following $N(\mu, \sigma^2)$, where μ is the mean, while σ is the standard deviation, we can approximate the expectation of the variable y as follows:

$$E\{f(y)\} = (2\pi\sigma^2)^{-1/2} \int_{-\infty}^{\infty} f(y)e^{-(y-\mu)^2/2\sigma^2}dy \tag{2.160}$$

Before actually applying the Gauss-Hermite quadrature, we need to use a change of variable formula as shown below: $x = (y - \mu)/\sqrt{2}\sigma$. This allows us to write the expectation of a normal variable as:

$$E\{f(y)\} = (2\pi\sigma^2)^{-1/2} \int_{-\infty}^{\infty} f(y)e^{-(y-\mu)^2/2\sigma^2}dy \doteq \pi^{-1/2} \sum_{i=1}^{n} \omega_i f(\sqrt{2}\sigma x_i + \mu) \tag{2.161}$$

Where we also took into account the following identity:

$$\int_{-\infty}^{\infty} f(y)e^{-(y-\mu)^2/2\sigma^2}dy = \int_{-\infty}^{\infty} f(\sqrt{2}\sigma x + \mu)e^{-x^2}\sqrt{2}\sigma dx \tag{2.162}$$

Gauss-Laguerre Quadrature

While the Gauss-Hermite quadrature applies naturally to the case of normal random variables, the Gauss-Laguerre formula fits rather very well the case of exponentially discounted sums (which is often encountered in macroeconomics). This quadrature applies to integrals having the following specification:

$$\int_{0}^{\infty} f(x)e^{-x}dx \tag{2.163}$$

In this particular case, the weighting function is given by: $w(x) = e^{-x}$. The formula to approximate using this quadrature has the following form:

$$\int_{0}^{\infty} f(x)e^{-x}dx = \sum_{i=1}^{n} \omega_i f(x_i) + (n!)^2 \frac{f^{2n}(\xi)}{2n!} \tag{2.164}$$

The point ξ is from the interval $[0, \infty)$. In macroeconomics, one would often have to approximate an integral of the form:

$$\int_a^\infty f(y)e^{-ry}dy \tag{2.165}$$

To apply the Gauss-Laguerre method, we have to use a change of variable formula, with $x = r(y - a)$, such that the approximation of the initial integral becomes:

$$\int_a^\infty f(y)e^{-ry}dy \doteq \frac{e^{-ra}}{r}\sum_{i=1}^n \omega_i f(\frac{x_i}{r} + a) \tag{2.166}$$

2.6.5 Multivariate Integration

Multivariate integration arises naturally in the context of macroeconomic models due to the presence of stochastic shocks. Below I discuss two non-Monte Carlo approaches, the product rule and the monomial approaches, while the discussion of Monte Carlo methods is postponed to the following section.

Product Rules

A multivariate integral for a function $f : \mathbb{R}^s \to \mathbb{R}$ and given a weighting function w_k has the following general form:

$$\int_{a_1}^{b_1} ... \int_{a_s}^{b_s} f(x_1, x_2, ..., x_s)w_1(x_1)...w_s(x_s)dx_1...dx_s \tag{2.167}$$

The product rule is a straight extension of the univariate integration techniques. Assume that we obtained the nodes x_i^k and the weights ω_i^k through one of the methods previously described, which would either based on a Newton-Cotes formula or a Gaussian quadrature.

The approximation of the product rule is given by a multiple sum that generalizes the individual approximation by using multiple sums as follows:

$$\sum_{i_1=1}^{n_1} ... \sum_{i_s=1}^{n_s} \omega_{i_1}^1...\omega_{i_s}^s f(x_{x_{i_1}}^1, ..., x_{x_{i_s}}^s) \tag{2.168}$$

Despite its simplicity and apparent easiness in applying it, the algorithm suffers from a major deficiency: namely, the computational costs increase exponentially as the number of dimensions increase. This is known as the "curse of dimensionality" and it typically refers to the exponential increase in complexity as the number of dimensions increases.

Below, I describe a typical use of this approach, following [3]. Assume that we would like to integrate a two-dimensional function $f(x_1, x_2)$, where x_1 and x_2 are normally distributed. Formally, we write that:

$$\begin{pmatrix} x_1 \\ x_2 \end{pmatrix} \sim N \left[\begin{pmatrix} \mu_1 \\ \mu_2 \end{pmatrix}, \begin{pmatrix} \sigma_{11} & \sigma_{12} \\ \sigma_{12} & \sigma_{22} \end{pmatrix} \right]$$

The integral that we are going to approximate is written as follows:

$$|\Sigma|^{-1/2}(2\pi)^{-1}\int_{-\infty}^\infty \int_{-\infty}^\infty f(x_1, x_2)exp((-1/2)(x - \mu)'\Sigma^{-1}(x - \mu))dx_1 dx_2 \tag{2.169}$$

The following notations were used above: $x = (x_1, x_2)'$, $\mu = (\mu_1, \mu_2)'$,

$$\Sigma = \begin{pmatrix} \sigma_{11} & \sigma_{12} \\ \sigma_{12} & \sigma_{22} \end{pmatrix}$$

If we denote by Φ the Cholesky decomposition of Σ, i.e. $\Sigma = \Phi\Phi'$ and use the change of variable: $y = \Phi^{-1}(x - \mu)/\sqrt{2}$, which is equivalent to rewriting the x variable as: $x = \sqrt{2}\Phi y + \mu$, then, we can put the original integral in the following form:

$$\pi^{-1} \int_{-\infty}^{\infty} \int_{-\infty}^{\infty} f(\sqrt{2}\Phi y + \mu) exp(-\sum_{i=1}^{s} y_i^2) dy_1 dy_2 \tag{2.170}$$

This integral can be approximate pretty much directly with the help of the product rule based on the Gauss-Hermite formula:

$$\frac{1}{\pi} \sum_{i_1=1}^{n_1} \sum_{i_2=1}^{n_2} \omega_{i_1}^1 \omega_{i_2}^2 f(\sqrt{2}\phi_{11}y_1 + \mu_1, \sqrt{2}(\phi_{21}y_1 + \phi_{22}y_2) + \mu_2) \tag{2.171}$$

Monomial Formulas

Product formulas lead to the curse of dimensionality due to the specific approach they use: the exact integration of tensor product of bases. As we have already seen in the case of doing multivariate approximations, complete polynomials, as compared to tensor products, are both a solid alternative and one that does not suffer from the curse of dimensionality.

The monomial rules combine the Gaussian approach to integrate polynomials with the idea of complete polynomials leading to a perfectly viable alternative to product rules. For a generic monomial of degree l over a set $D \subset \mathbb{R}^d$, we can approximate each polynomial $p(x)$ of degree l with the help of N points x_i and their associated weights ω_i over the same set D such that we can write:

$$\sum_{i=1}^{N} \omega_i p(x_i) = \int_D p(x) dx \tag{2.172}$$

We say that this formula is complete for the degree 1. To be more specific, when $l = 2$, we will deal with a system of equations consisting in sums of monomials for each polynomial of degree 0, 1 and 2 as follows:

$$\sum_{i=1}^{N} \omega_i = \int_D 1 dx \tag{2.173}$$

with $j = 1, ..., d$.

$$\sum_{i=1}^{N} \omega_i x_j^i = \int_D x_j dx \tag{2.174}$$

with $j = 1, ..., d$.

$$\sum_{i=1}^{N} \omega_i x_j^i x_k^i = \int_D x_j x_k dx \tag{2.175}$$

with $j, k = 1, ..., d$.

These system of monomials will consist in a number of $1 + d + 1/2d(d + 1)$ equations, with a number of $(d + 1)N$ unknowns which consist in the N weights ω_i, as well as the N nodes x_i, however each node having d components. As [1] explains, the system is theoretically solvable when the number of equations exceeds that of unknowns, although there might be many solutions, however, the solutions become more involved as the dimensionality increases due to the nonlinear character of the system.

Following the contribution by [8], despite the complexity in applying this approach, we can nevertheless use it with considerable efficiency. A first condition is to restrain the focus to symmetric domains and impose some form of symmetry restrictions. Starting from here, we should choose a set of quadrature nodes that follows certain symmetry. The next step is to choose the weights such that we can have exact integration for important classes of functions.

2.6.6 Monte Carlo Integration

The basic principle underlying the Monte Carlo approach to integration is the Law of Large Numbers from probability. Since this approach is a probability based method, its approximation will consist in random variables which follow a specific distribution. However, there is also a serious advantage which consists in improving the accuracy of approximation by increasing the sample size.

Let us assume a random variable x and a number of independent realizations of this variable. For a continuous function f, given an interval $[a, b]$, the expectation can be computed as:

$$\int_a^b f(x)dx = (b-a)Ef(x) \tag{2.176}$$

According to the Monte Carlo integration method, we can approximate the above integral by using:

$$\int_a^b f(x)dx = \frac{(b-a)}{n} \sum_{i=1}^n f(x_i) \tag{2.177}$$

To produce an approximation of an integration, the Monte Carlo method relies on the Law of Large Numbers.

Theorem 2.3: Law of Large Numbers: Consider that x_i is a collection of random variables that are independent and identically distributed with a density $\mu(x)$. Then, we can write that:

$$lim_{n \to \infty} \frac{1}{N} \sum_{i=1}^N x_i = \int x\mu(x)dx \tag{2.178}$$

in an almost-sure sense.

The main difficulty in doing a Monte Carlo approximation is that it is based on the random numbers generated by a computer. However, the random numbers generated by a computer are not random numbers in a true sense, but are actually pseudo-deterministic numbers. Rather, the algorithms used to generate with a computer random numbers are actually deterministic algorithms that produce numbers that seem random.

Improvements in the algorithms to approximate an integral can be made in several ways. I present several methods that improve the accuracy of Monte Carlo approach to integration.

1. **Antithetic variable** This applies to the case of monotonically increasing f functions, implying a negative correlation between $f(x)$ and $f(1-x)$. An improved approximation of the integral will be given by:

$$\frac{1}{2N} \sum_{i=1}^N (f(x_i) + f(1-x_i)) \tag{2.179}$$

This new approximation is not only unbiased, but it also provides a lower variance for this approximation.

2. **Stratified Sampling** This approach exploits the idea that the variance for a subinterval within $[0, 1]$ is lower than the variance of the whole interval $[0, 1]$. Basically, this approach consists in splitting the $[0, 1]$ intervals into smaller intervals and visit each of these intervals when approximating the integral.

   The algorithm is very simple: we pick up a value ϵ within the interval $(0, 1)$. We draw points over the intervals $[0, \epsilon]$ and $[\epsilon; 1]$. From the first interval, we draw a number of $N_a = \epsilon N$, while from the second we draw $N_b = (1-\epsilon)N$ points. The new approximation of the integral will be given by:

$$\frac{1}{N_a} \sum_{i=1}^{N_a} f(x_i^a) + \frac{1}{N_b} \sum_{i=1}^{N_b} f(x_i^b) \tag{2.180}$$

   The points x_i^a are drawn from the interval $[0, \epsilon]$, while the points x_i^b are drawn from the interval $[\epsilon, 1]$.

3. **Control Variables** In this approach, we try to use a function that has two attractive properties: it is a good approximation of the function whose integrate we would like to compute and it is also easy to integrate. Let us denote this function by $\phi(x)$. Then, we can restate the problem as:

$$\int f(x)dx = \int (f(x) - \phi(x))dx + \int \phi(x)dx \tag{2.181}$$

Such that, since the integral of $\phi(x)$ is easy to compute, the initial problem resides now in approximating the integral:

$$\int (f(x) - \phi(x))dx \qquad (2.182)$$

4. **Importance Sampling** In the original approach, the Monte Carlo integration method consists in drawing numbers from a uniform distribution over the interval $[0, 1]$. However, there is an essential problem linked to this approach: while in some cases it might be desirable to draw points uniformly from the interval $[0, 1]$, in many cases this solution is not optimal.

Importance Sampling exploits this deficiency of the standard Monte Carlo approach to integration and restates the problem as follows. Assume that we want to integrate the original function over a given set M:

$$\int_M f(x)dx \qquad (2.183)$$

We also assume that there exists a function g such that $h = f/g$ is almost constant over the interval of interest M. The original problem will be restated as:

$$\int_M \frac{f(x)}{g(x)}g(x)dx = \int_M h(x)g(x)dx \qquad (2.184)$$

To produce an approximation of the original integral, we sample h over a non-uniform density $g(x)dx$. The new approximation will be given by:

$$\frac{1}{N}\sum_{i=1}^{N}\frac{f(x_i)}{g(x_i)} \qquad (2.185)$$

2.6.7 Quasi Monte Carlo Integration

We might be tempted to think that the Quasi Monte Carlo approach is a generalization of the Monte Carlo method. However, the two methods rely on different principles. While the Monte Carlo approach relies on probability theory, and especially on the Law of Large Numbers, the Quasi Monte Carlo methods are based on number theory.

The Quasi Monte Carlo approach is founded on equi-distributed sequences. To build up the intuition, we can start the one-dimensional case of sequences. Assume a sequence $\{x_i\}_{i=1}^{\infty}$ included in $\mathbb{R}$. We say that such a sequence is equi-distributed if, given a function that is integrable in the Riemann sense, it holds that:

$$\lim_{N\to\infty}\frac{b-a}{N}\sum_{i=1}^{N}f(x_i) = \int_a^b f(x)dx \qquad (2.186)$$

The uni-dimensional equi-distributed sequences can be generalized to case of sequences in $\mathbb{R}^n$ as follows:

We say that a series $\{x_i\}_{i=1}^{\infty}$ included in $D \subset \mathbb{R}^d$ is equi-distributed over the set D if the following condition is verified:

$$\lim_{N\to\infty}\frac{\mu(D)}{N}\sum_{i=1}^{N}f(x_i) = \int_D f(x)dx \qquad (2.187)$$

Where $\mu(D)$ is the Lebesgue measure of the set D, while the function f is again Riemann-integrable. What this approach practically does is to deliver an approximation of the uniform distribution which, given the properties of the equi-distributed points, is quite efficient. Since the Quasi Monte Carlo approach is based on number theory, we can select the way the points are distributed and avoid issues specific to Monte Carlo integration method (for example, the tendency towards clustering).

[1] has a full chapter dedicated to Quasi Monte Carlo methods, however, in this section, I strictly focus on the use of this approach to approximate integrations. There are various methods to generate equi-distant sequences:

1. The Weyl method: $(k\sqrt{p_1}, ..., k\sqrt{p_n})$
2. The Haber approach: $(\frac{k(k+1)}{2}\sqrt{p_1}, ..., \frac{k(k+1)}{2}\sqrt{p_n})$

3. The Niederreiter method: $(k2^{1/(1+n)}, ..., k2^{n/(1+n)})$

4. The Baker approach: $(ke^{r_1}, ..., k2^{r_n})$

In the latter case, the numbers r_i, for $i = 1, ..., n$, are rational and distinct. For all cases, n is the dimension of space. Furthermore, all the different sequences use the same difference equation for generation: $x_{k+1} = (x_k + \theta) mod\, 1$.

2.6.8 Numerical Integration in Julia

In the previous sections, I have detailed the most used to numerically approximate an integral in Julia. I also implemented in Julia a few simple approaches that numerically compute an integral. In this section, I focus on the package based implementations of numerical integration in Julia.

There are several packages developed in Julia that deal with numerical integration. The first of these, quadgk, was initially included in the base installation of Julia. However, starting with the version 0.6 of Julia, quadgk (renamed QuadGK) has become an independent package. There are three available functions that can be used for numerical integration: QuadGK.quadgk(), QuadGK.gauss() and QuadGK.kronrod().

The general syntax of the function QuadGK.quadgk() used to numerically integrate is given below:

```
QuadGK.quadgk(f, a, b, c...;reltol=sqrt(eps), abstol=0, maxevals=10^7,
 order=7, norm=vecnor)
```

Here, the function of interest is f. The values a and b are used to express the definite integral of the function f between a and b. Adding other values (c, and so on), we can evaluate the integral also between b and c. This is very useful when the function of interest has a known discontinuity at a certain point x, such that we divide the interval $[a, b]$ over which we integrate into $[a, x]$ and $[x, b]$ and we write:

```
QuadGK.quadgk(f, a, x, b)
```

The syntax additionally allows for declaring the relative error tolerance which is set, by default, to sqrt(eps), the absolute error tolerance, the maximum number of function evaluations and the order of the integration rule.

To increase the precision, we may increase the precision of endpoints (using for example floating-points). For smooth integrands, we may increase the precision by relying on higher order of integration. The function is actually designed to work well with smooth functions within the defined intervals.

The main disadvantage of the quadgk function is that it can be used only with one-dimensional functions. For multidimensional problems, anyway the algorithm is not optimal and should and could rely on external packages, as discussed below. The algorithm used by quadgk function is the adaptative Gauss-Kronrod method. The algorithm relies on the Kronrod rule (that is, on a number of 2*order+1 points, with order being the order of integration), while the error is estimated with a Gauss rule. If for a given interval, the error tolerance is not achieved, this interval can be further split into two smaller intervals on which we can compute the integral.

The function quadgk will return a pair of the form (I, E), where I is the numerically computed integral while E is the upper bound on the absolute error. Let us try a simple example using the function quadgk:

```
f(x)=2*x;
quadgk(f, 0,1)
(1.0,0.0)
```

The returned pair (1.0, 0.0) indicates that the numerically approximation of the integral is 1.0, while the absolute error is 0.0.

Besides the package QuadGK, we can also use two additional packages: Cubature and Cuba.

Cubature is pretty well developed package that can deal with both one-dimensional and multidimensional integration problems. Additionally, Cubature allows for parallelization as well as vector-valued integration. The main characteristic of the underlying algorithm for integration in Cubature is the use of adaptative integration. The idea of adaptative integration is deceptively simple: we use an increasing number of points until we get convergence in terms of tolerance error. Cubature uses two basic approaches which differ only in the way they achieve convergence, h-adaptivity and p-adaptativity. Each of these two approaches can use two different routines, quadrature and cubature.

Although the two procedures for integration, h-adaptive and p-adaptive, are similar, they address different types of needs. As the package makers suggest, the h-adaptive approach should be applied when there is little prior information about the function that will be integrated. In contrast, the p-adaptative integration should be used rather for smooth functions for a small number of dimensions (lower than 2).

The algorithms behind the two approaches, although both adaptative, also differ in some points which makes them being applicable in specific situations as detailed above. In the h-adaptative approach we divide the domain for integration in a recursive manner into sub-regions that are smaller and smaller until the error estimate is within the tolerance limit. Each integration is done based on the same number of points. The reason that this approach works well with functions we know little about (and especially when they have peaks or kinks) is that the algorithm is able to add more points into these specific intervals that may pose difficulties. The h-adaptative integration uses a similar algorithm as the function quadgk in the default installation of Julia for one-dimensional problems, i.e. Gauss-Kronrod. However, as already mentioned, this is not suitable for higher dimension problem where the algorithm used is the Genz-Malik one.

The way the p-adaptative integration is built does not help it dealing with problematic zones like kinks and peaks: the algorithm consists in doubling the points for the whole domain and using increasingly higher order polynomials. This is why the p-adaptative integration works well with smooth functions.

The syntax for these functions in Cubature is similar to the syntax of the built-in quadgk function. The syntax is identical irrespective whether we use the h-adaptative or the p-adaptative approach. As for the quadgk function, the function returns a pair of two values consisting in the approximated value of the integration and the absolute error of it. Thus, if we use h-adaptative integration we can write:

```
(val,err) = hquadrature(f::Function, xmin::Real, xmax::Real;
reltol=1e-8, abstol=0, maxevals=0)
```

While switching to p-adaptative integration implies writing:

```
(val,err) = pquadrature(f::Function, xmin::Real, xmax::Real;
 reltol=1e-8, abstol=0, maxevals=0)
```

Here, f is a function type taking as argument real variables and returning real variables. The interval over which the integral is defined is set by the values x_{min} and x_{max}. The remaining parameters define the relative error tolerance, the absolute error tolerance (this is used by the adaptative algorithm to check the convergence), and maxevals specifying the number of function evaluations.

Below, I integrate the same function $f(x) = 2x$ on the interval [0, 1], to parallel the earlier example using the function quadgk. I use both hquadrature and pquadrature.

```
using Cubature;
f(x)=2*x;
hquadrature(f, 0,1)
```

which returns:

```
(1.0,1.1102230246251565e-14)
```

Alternatively, we could also use pquadrature (f,0,1) and we get:

```
f(x)=2*x;
pquadrature(f, 0,1)
```

which returns:

```
(1.0,0.0)
```

Dealing with multi-value integrals is quite easy in terms of syntax and parameters, once we got familiar with the univariate approach in Cubature. Multidimensional integration in Cubature consists in integrating a uni-dimensional function f(x) over a multidimensional box. The function will take now a vector as argument, while x_{min} and x_{max} are also vectors having the same dimensions. The functions used in Cubature will integrate the function f with respect to each coordinate $x[i]$ for a set defined by $[x_{min}[i], x_{max}[i]]$.

Cuba is another well-developed Julia package for numerical integration. Cuba also allows handling the numerical computation of integrals, for both uni and multidimensional cases. However, there is little overlap between Cuba and Cubature since the algorithms used are different. While Cubature uses various types of algorithms from the family of adaptive integration, the package Cuba relies mostly on various versions of Monte Carlo integration.

There are four different algorithms used in Cuba which I sketch below. The principles of Monte Carlo integration were covered earlier, and so were a few improvements of it (importance sampling or stratified sampling, see above). The following algorithms are used in Cuba:

1. Vegas (Monte Carlo integration using variance reduction with importance sampling)
2. Suave (Monte Carlo integration using variance reduction with globally adaptive subdivision and importance sampling)
3. Divonne (Monte Carlo integration or deterministic where the variance reduction is achieved using stratified sampling)
4. Cuhre (deterministic integration with the variance reduction achieved using globally adaptive subdivision)

By default, all the described algorithm above will integrate a function the n-dimensional unit hypercube $[0, 1]^n$. Integrating over a different interval requires rescaling to achieve the equivalent integral on $[0, 1]^n$.

For each of the algorithms enumerated above, there is a corresponding function in Cuba. However, the syntax is similar in each case:

```
vegas(integrand, ndim, ncomp[; keywords...])
suave(integrand, ndim, ncomp[; keywords...])
divonne(integrand, ndim, ncomp[; keywords...])
cuhre(integrand, ndim, ncomp[; keywords...])
```

There are three mandatory arguments here, the function to be integrated (the integrand), as well as the number of dimensions of the integration domain (the default value is 1) and the number of components of the integrand (again, the default value is 1). I apply these four functions to the same simple example of integrating the function f(x)=2x (which is integrated over the default domain [0,1]):

```
using Cuba
f(x)=2*x;
Vegas((x,f)->f[1]=2*x[1], 1, 1)
```

Which returns a 6 tuple:

```
([1.0],[9.93926e-5],[2.55963e-5],232000,0,0)
```

We can also use suave, by writing:

```
Suave((x,f)->f[1]=2*x[1], 1, 1)
```

Which will return:

```
([1.00463],[0.00016954],[1.0],1000000,1,1000)
```

To use divonne, we can write:

```
divonne((x,f)->f[1]=2*x[1], 1, 1)
```

This will return:

```
([1.0],[9.78826e-5],[0.0],5669,0,16)
```

Finally, to use cuhre, we similarly write down:

```
cuhre((x,f)->f[1]=2*x[1], 1, 1)
```

to get:

```
([1.0],[8.58392e-15],[0.0],195,0,2)
```

As we have seen, all four functions return a 6-tuple which contains the following variables:

```
(integral, error, probability, neval, fail, nregions)
```

Although we had above a simple uni-dimensional integration, still the first three values are actually arrays with a length equal to the length of the variable ncomp (i.e., the number of dimensions). With small differences, all four algorithms return the about the same numerically approximated integral at 1.0. The other values are scalar, irrespective the value of the variable ncomp.

2.7 ROOT FINDING AND NONLINEAR EQUATIONS

Root finding is one of the fundamental issues in numerical analysis. In economics, we meet this when doing optimization, which actually implies that the first derivative is equal to zero (a root finding problem). We also encounter the root finding problem whenever we deal with a system of nonlinear equations, a typical situation in macroeconomics. This section draws mainly from [1], [2] and [3].

Root finding consisting in finding a vector x of dimension n (the root of a given function f), for which the following relationship holds: $f(x) = 0$.

However, the root finding problem may arise in a different but equivalent form. A second way is when we deal with a fixed point problem. In this case, we look for a vector x of dimension n, called this time the root of the function, for which: $x = g(x)$. Actually, the two formulations are identical if we set $g(x)$ as: $g(x) = x - f(x)$.

Furthermore, see [2], one can see the root/fixed-point problems as special case of the so-called complementarity problems, where one looks for the n-dimensional vector x such that, given two vectors a and b for which the property $a < b$ holds, and a function f, the following conditions are verified:

$$x_i > a_i \text{ implies } f_i(x) > 0, \text{ for each } i = 1, ..., n$$
$$x_i < b_i \text{ implies } f_i(x) \leq 0, \text{ for each } i = 1, ..., n$$

It can be easily seen that the finding a root is just a particular application of the complementarity problems when we consider that $a_i = -\infty$ and $b_i = \infty$ for all i.

As we will see, the modern approaches usually consider hybrid solutions to root finding that improve on the standard methods. However, from a pedagogical point of view, and since the more complex methods rely on the same basic ideas, it is better to start from the simplest methods.

2.7.1 The Bisection Method

From the Intermediate Value Theorem, we know that if a continuous function f takes two distinct values, then it will also take the values from the interval between the former values. More precisely, if a function f is continuous, and it has distinct signs at the ends of an interval, $[a, b]$, the function, according to the Intermediate Value Theorem, must also have a root within the $[a, b]$ interval.

To code the bisection method, I follow the approach in [2]. The value of the function at the boundaries of the interval must have opposite signs. I consider a basic function: $f(x) = x^2 - 3$ for which I give an initial interval of $[1, 2]$. I set the error (tolerance) at 1e-9.

```
f(x)=x^2-3;
s=sign(f(a));
a=1;
b=2;
err=0.000000001;
x=(a+b)/2;
d=(b-a)/2;
while d>err
d=d/2
if s==sign(f(x))
x=x+d;
else
x=x-d;
end
end
```

The code starts from a guess value x, taken as the mean of the interval. It then computes the distance from x to the boundaries of the interval. In each iteration, it compares $f(x)$ and $f(a)$. In case they have the same sign, x becomes $x + d$ and moves towards b. Otherwise, x becomes $x - d$ and moves towards a. The main rationale behind this iterative procedure is that in doing this, the algorithm ensures that will eventually isolate the root with a certain precision.

The package Roots offers a "bracketing" method that is based on the bisection algorithm (although the name of the function does not explicitly say so). This is rather a special feature of Roots that differentiates the algorithm applied through the way the syntax of the functions used is declared. For this particular case of the bisection method, the Roots package uses the functions:

```
fzero(f,a::Real, b::Real) and fzero(f, bracket::Vector)
```

which are actually identical, since it is the same thing declaring the interval $[a, b]$ by declaring a and b or a bracket as a vector. Using this function, will call the find-zero algorithm through the function fzero() within the bracket $[a, b]$. The code below shows the application of this method using the Roots functions.

```
Julia> using Roots
Julia>x = fzero(f, [1, 2]);
Julia>x, f(x)
(1.7320508075688774,4.440892098500626e-16)
```

This is also the main argument in its favor, namely that, despite its simplicity, the bisection method is very robust since it guarantees that it will find the root with a given precision, provided one gives a valid interval. At the same time, the bisection method is slower than other methods (it needs more iterations), and it is limited to only one-dimensional root finding problems. In practice, the bisection method is not that much used *per se*, but rather in combination with more advanced methods. Many times, one uses the bisection method to get a first approximation of the unit root and a second more complex method to get a very accurate solution for the unit root.

2.7.2 Newton's Method

As already mentioned, despite its robustness, the bisection method is rarely used in direct applications by itself to find the root of a function. However, many times it is used in conjunction with other methods. The preferred approach in practice is the Newton's method (or variations of it). The main principle behind this method is that of successive linearizations which implies that the initial nonlinear problem is replaced by linear problems which eventually converge to the solution of the initial problem which was nonlinear.

The algorithm of the Newton's method is pretty straightforward as the linearization is done using the Taylor expansion. Assume a function f and an initial guess of the root given by x_0. We create an iteration equation on x^{k+1} given x^k using a Taylor approximation of order one to replace $f(x)$:

$$f(x) \approx f(x^k) + f'(x^k)(x - x^k) = 0 \qquad (2.188)$$

Which can be rewritten to yield an iteration equation:

$$x^{k+1} = x^k - (f'(x^k))^{-1} f(x^k) \qquad (2.189)$$

The package Roots includes the Newton's method among its solutions to root finding problems rather for historical and pedagogical reasons, although the modern approaches are rather derivations of this classical method. The syntax for Newton's method is:

```
newton(f,fp,x0)
```

where f is the function, fp is the first derivative and x_0 is the guess of the initial solution. The code is straightforward:

```
Julia> f(x)=x^2-3;
Julia> fp(x) = 2x
Julia> x = newton(f, fp, 2)
Julia> x, f(x)
(1.7320508075688774,4.440892098500626e-16)
```

As we can see, the solution reported is similar to the solution reported using the bisection method. However, there is no 100 percent guarantee that the algorithm will produce a correct solution. The solution provided by the Newton's method converges depending on a two factors: f must be continuously differentiable and the initial solution must be close enough to a root of f at which the f^{-1} is also invertible. The fact that f behaves "well" or not also makes the Newton's algorithm more or less sensitive to the initial condition.

One of the main issues associated to the Newton's algorithm is the need to provide the first derivative. This is also a potential source for coding error and can potentially lead to a wrong solution. To alleviate these problems and eliminate any source of coding errors, we can use automated differentiation. Julia's package ForwardDiff can perform the automatic differentiation of a function and can be used in combination with other functions, including when solving for roots.

```
Julia>Pkg.add("ForwardDiff");
Julia> using ForwardDiff;
Julia> newton(f, D(f), 2);
1.7320508075688772
```

While for the previously coded problem it may not matter, however, for more complex functions and when many iterations are involved, there is a faster way to declare anonymous functions in Julia. This could be done in earlier version of Julia using the package FastAnonymous. However, starting with version 0.5, Julia language includes now the possibility of working with anonymous functions. The code below implements the Newton method using anonymous functions:

```
fa = x -> x^2 - 3
newton(fa,D(fa),2)
```

2.7.3 Function Iteration

As already stated, root finding and function iteration are the two ways to express the same problem. Solving for the root $f(x) = 0$ is mathematically equivalent to looking for a fixed point for which $x = g(x)$ when we rewrite the problem as: $x = x - f(x)$. To apply the function iteration, we need a starting point which must be reasonably close to the root of $f(x)$. One way to set the initial value is to find an interval $[a, b]$ such that $f(a)f(b) < 0$ and to set x equal to a or to b.

Given that we rewrote the root finding problem as a fixed-point problem, we get the following iteration equation:

$$x^{k+1} = g(x^k) \tag{2.190}$$

where $k = 0, 1, ...$

Finding the fixed-point is ensured provided the following condition is met:

$$||g'(x_i)|| \leq 1 \tag{2.191}$$

It is not difficult to code this in Julia. I start by providing a maximum number of iterations (maxit variable), an error (tol) and an initial solution ($x = 0.7$). I also define a very simple function: $f(x) = x^{1/2}$. The code will iterate on the function, each time assigning x the last value of the function following the iteration equation above. The code stops when either the maximum number of iterations is reached or the function is very close to the fixed point.

```
maxit=1000;
tol=0.000000001;
x=0.7;
f(x)=x^0.5;
for it=1:maxit
if norm(f(x)-x)<tol
return
end
x = f(x);
end
```

2.7.4 Quasi-Newton Methods

As the name suggests, the Quasi-Newton (also known as free derivative) methods are derived from the classical Newton's method to solve for a root. They keep the same principle of successive linearizations, however they address one of the major shortcomings of the classical Newton's method: the necessity of providing the Jacobian. Instead, they rely on simple numerical methods to approximate the Jacobian without deriving it. I focus on two of the most widely used Quasi-Newton methods: the secant and Broyden method.

The secant method is also a univariate method. The essential difference relative to the classical Newton's method is the use of an approximation for the derivative of the function f based on the previous two values:

$$f'(x^k) = \frac{f(x^k) - f(x^{k-1})}{x^k - x^{k-1}} \tag{2.192}$$

Based on this approximation, we can derive an iteration equation for x^{k+1}:

$$x^{k+1} = x^k - \frac{x^k - x^{k-1}}{f(x^k) - f(x^{k-1})} f(x^k) \tag{2.193}$$

I implement below the secant method in Julia. Since the approximation of the derivative depends on the previous two iterations, the algorithm asks for two initial points, x_1 and x_2. It is necessary that they are chosen such that they fulfill the following condition: $f(x_1)f(x_2) < 0$, ensuring that the root lies within these two points.

```
tol=0.00000001;
f(x)=x^2-3;
x0=1.0;
x1=2.0;
err=1.0;
while err>0
d=-f(x1)*(x1-x0)/(f(x1)-f(x0))
x=x1+d;
err=abs(x-x1)-tol*(1+abs(x));
x0=x1;
x1=x;
end
x,f(x)
(1.7320508075688772,-4.440892098500626e-16)
```

I used the same function $x^2 - 3$ as before and choose the initial points in order to ensure that the root lies in it, i.e. $[1, 2]$. I also set the tolerance for identifying the root to be very close to zero.

The secant method is an univariate method and it cannot deal with multivariate root finding problems which are quite frequent in economics (for example, when dealing with a system of nonlinear equations). A direct generalization of the secant method within the multivariate context is the Broyden method. I discuss the multivariate Newton and Broyden methods in next section.

2.7.5 Multivariate Methods

Instead of solving for the univariate root x such that: $f(x) = 0$, in the case of multivariate root finding we deal with multiple equations. Assume there are n such equations written as:

$$f_1(x_1, x_2, ..., x_n) = 0 \tag{2.194}$$
$$f_2(x_1, x_2, ..., x_n) = 0 \tag{2.195}$$
$$... \tag{2.196}$$
$$f_n(x_1, x_2, ..., x_n) = 0 \tag{2.197}$$

We look for that vector x of dimension $n \times 1$ that solves for the above system. I discuss two such methods, both extensions of their univariate counterparts. To understand them, we need to reformulate the Taylor expansion in the multivariate setting:

$$f(x^*) \cong f(x_k) + \nabla f(x_k)(x^* - x_k) \tag{2.198}$$

We know however that x^* is a root of a function such that $f(x^*) = 0$. We rewrite the above equation as:

$$f(x_k) + \nabla f(x_k)(x^* - x_k) = 0 \tag{2.199}$$

From which we can derive a recursive equation for x_{k+1} in terms of x_k:

$$x_{k+1} = x_k + (\nabla f(x_k))^{-1} f(x_k) \tag{2.200}$$

To apply the Newton multivariate algorithm, we set a vector of initial values, and values for termination criteria. I use simple functions since the purpose is just to illustrate the method. The code can be however easily expanded for more complex functions.

```
#Newton multivariate method
maxit=1000;
tol=0.00000001;
function f(x,y)
x^2+y-3,x*y-2
end;
x0=[1.0; 1.0];
y0= reshape(collect(f(x0[1], x0[2])),2,1);

#computation of the Jacobian
using Calculus
gr1 = Calculus.gradient(x -> x[1]^2+x[2]-3, x0);
gr2 = Calculus.gradient(x -> x[1]*x[2]-2, x0);
dy0 =  [gr1'; gr2']
err=1.0;

while err>0
d0=-\(dy0,y0);
x=x0+d0;
y= reshape(collect(f(x[1], x[2])),2,1);
err=norm(x-x0,2)-tol*(1+norm(x,2));
x0=x;
y0=reshape(collect(f(x0[1], x0[2])),2,1)
end
```

The solution provided solves the system of equations:

```
2x1 Array{Float64,2}:
2.0
1.0
```

Two observations are worth mentioning with respect to coding in Julia. The function collect() is used to transform a simple tuple as returned by $f(x, y)$ into an array. The function reshape() is used to arrange this array into a 2×1 dimensional array. We also note the use of matrix divisions

```
\
```

which pretty much corresponds to the matrix division operator in Matlab.

```
\(A,B)
```

provides the solution to the linear system: $Ax = B$.

Instead of relying on the Jacobian matrix $\nabla F(x_k)$, the Broyden multivariate method replaces it with an approximation matrix S_k at the corresponding iteration k. Thus, instead of solving for:

$$f(x_k) + \nabla f(x_k)(x^* - x_k) = 0 \tag{2.201}$$

We solve now for:

$$f(x_k) + S_k(x^* - x_k) = 0 \tag{2.202}$$

such that we get now:

$$x_{k+1} = x_k + \delta_k \tag{2.203}$$

To solve for S_k, we need to remember that this is just the multivariate generalization of the univariate secant method. Since S_k is an approximation of the actual Jacobian, it should be close to secant, i.e.:

$$S_{k+1}\delta_k = f(x_{k+1}) - f(x_k) \tag{2.204}$$

This implies that we can predict the change in $f()$ for a given direction δ_k. To do the same for other directions, in the Broyden algorithm, we assume that the predicted change in $f()$ for directions orthogonal to δ_k remains the same, i.e. for $z'\delta_k = 0$, then we have: $S_{k+1}z = S_k z$, based on which we can finally derive an iteration equation for S_k:

$$S_{k+1} = S_k + \frac{(f(x_{k+1}) - f(x_k) - S_k\delta_k)\delta_k'}{\delta_k'\delta_k} \tag{2.205}$$

```
#Broyden method
maxit=1000;
tol=0.00000001;
function f(x,y)
x^2+y-3,x*y-2
end;
x0=[1.0; 1.0];
S = eye(size(x0,1));
y0= reshape(collect(f(x0[1], x0[2])),2,1);
err=1.0;
while err>0
d=-\(S,y0);
x=x0+d;
y= reshape(collect(f(x[1], x[2])),2,1);
S=S+((y-y0)-S*d)*transpose(d)/(transpose(d)*d);
err=norm(x-x0,2)-tol*(1+norm(x,2));
x0=x;
y0=reshape(collect(f(x0[1], x0[2])),2,1)
end
x
```

The code returns the following vector:

```
2x1 Array{Float64,2}:
2.0
1.0
```

Which solves the nonlinear system of equations. The main advantage of this approach is that it does not rely on computing the Jacobian, and it might be faster for larger systems of equations. However, when the system of equations is highly nonlinear, the Jacobian might change in a significant manner and the approximation used here (relying on the secant approach) might lead to bad results.

2.7.6 Comparing Methods to Solve for Roots

There is no perfect method to solve for the root of a function. The bisection method, although robust and it guarantees the reach of a solution, is rather slow and it deals only with univariate problems. The secant problem can be generalized to deal with multivariate root finding problems. However, although it can be fast and it can normally provide accurate solutions, it is well known that it can have problems when applied to highly nonlinear system since the Jacobian can change drastically, making the approximation of it using the secant method highly unreliable.

Newton's and Newton based methods are basically the most widely used in practice, although they have they own shortcomings too. There are three major shortcomings: coding the Jacobian, choosing the initial guess and ill-conditioned Jacobian at the root. It is quite obvious that one should program carefully the Jacobian and errors can be made easily.

There are various ways to prevent making errors here: using approximations of the derivative (like in the secant/Broyden method), computing the Jacobian automatically. In the last case, Julia offers packages like Calculus that allow for automatic computing of the Jacobian and thus can prevent any error in coding the Jacobian manually.

A second major shortcoming is that of badly chosen initial values. This shortcoming can be alleviated with the use of backstepping technique. This consists in repeating a step dx whenever the step does not produce a consistent improvement over the iteration x. Practically, one can "step back" and repeat the dx step but at half of its value or keep halving it until the new step $x + dx$ offers a real improvement.

Finally, the last type of shortcoming is that of ill-conditioned Jacobian at the root and can lead to a lack of accuracy in the solution provided. Although this happens in reality less often, it is quite important to prevent it. One of the major sources for the emergence of such behavior is a high variation in the scale of the variables from the function/linear system.

2.7.7 Solving for Roots of Polynomials

In this small section, we present how polynomials are treated in Julia and how to find their roots. At the moment this book is written, there is a special package dealing with polynomials, called Polynomials (which replaces the older Polynomial package). The package allows for constructing polynomials, applying basic arithmetic operations to them, integrating and differentiating them as well as root finding. We add the package Polynomials like any other package and load it before using it:

```
Julia> Pkg.add("Polynomials")
Julia> using Polynomials
```

To declare a polynomial, we can use its coefficients writing:

```
Julia> Poly([0,1,2,0])
To get:
Poly(x + 2x^2)
```

Alternatively, we can construct a polynomial from its roots. By declaring its roots:

```
Julia> poly([0,1,2])
And we get:
Poly(2x - 3x^2 + x^3)
```

Assume that we already have a polynomial. We can find the roots using the function fzeros from Roots. This can be applied either to a function or a polynomial. Below, I apply this to a function f.

```
Julia> f(x)=2x - 3x^2 + x^3
Julia> fzeros(f,-1,4)
3-element Array{Real,1}:
0
1
2
```

But the same can be easily done with a polynomial.

```
Julia> x = poly([0]);
Julia> fzeros(2x - 3x^2 + x^3,-1,4)
3-element Array{Number,1}:
0//1
1//1
2//1
```

2.7.8 Complementarity Problems in Julia

In this section, I discuss separately complementarity problems. Although, not confined to the economics discipline, they are very often met in quantitative economics. As already discussed in the introduction, complementarity problems are a more general cases of root finding and fixed point problems. Considering two vectors of length n, $a < b$, as well as a function f, the complementary problem consist in finding a vector x with the same length confined to the interval $[a, b]$, for which:

$$x_i > a_i \Rightarrow f_i(x) \geq 0, \forall i = 1, ...n \tag{2.206}$$
$$x_i < b_i \Rightarrow f_i(x) \leq 0, \forall i = 1, ...n \tag{2.207}$$

Although when solving for the complementarity problem, we also implicitly solve for the root, since one of the complementarity conditions is that $f_i(x) = 0$ for $a_i < x_i < b_i$, we may also have nonzero $f_i(x)$ as solutions to the complementarity problem when x_i falls on any of the bounds.

While the complementarity problem can be seen as a more general case of root finding of fixed points problems, at the same time, we can recast the complementarity problem as a root finding problem when we write it as:

$$\hat{f}(x) = min(max(f(x), a - x), b - x) = 0 \tag{2.208}$$

In this minmax formulation, the operators min and max are applied along the rows.

Usually, the books written on numerical methods when discussing root finding (and fixed points) problems do not cover complementarity problems. A reasonable explanation would be that they usually address an audience with science/engineering background. While there is a package dealing with roots in Julia, i.e. the package Roots, it does not cover complementarity problems. An alternative package, written with an economics audience in mind, addresses this type of problem.

The package NLsolve (from NonLinear solve) is designed to deal with both the classical root finding and the complementarity problems more specific to economics. To solve for complementarity problems, NLsolve offers the function mcpsolve (multi-complementarity problems solve). The syntax for mcpsolve is the following:

```
mcpsolve(f, x0, a,b, reformulation, autodiff)
```

Here f is the function of interest (or the declared functions, if there is a multivariate function), x_0 is the vector of initial values, a and b are the vectors containing the intervals for each functions. Finally, there is also an option on the type of algorithm used as indicated by the value of reformulation. There are two options available in NLsolve, smooth (which uses a smooth approach based on the Fischer function) and minmax (which reformulates in the way discussed above the problem in terms of a min-max problem).

To understand how to apply it, let's consider a simple case of a multivariate complementarity problem. We first load the package NLsolve and declare the functions:

```
using NLsolve
function f!(x, fvec)
fvec[1]=4*x[1]^2+3*x[1]*x[2]+2*x[2]^2+x[3]
fvec[2]=x[1]*x[2]+2*x[2]^2+3*x[3]+5
fvec[3]=x[1]^2+x[2]*x[3]+2*x[3]^2-4
end
```

We solve this complementarity problem using the function mcpsolve with a declared vector of initial values and 0 and infinite as intervals. The algorithm used is the smooth algorithm.

```
r = mcpsolve(f!, [0., 0., 0.], [Inf, Inf, Inf],
[1.0, 1.0, 1.0], reformulation = :smooth, autodiff = true);
Results of Nonlinear Solver Algorithm
* Algorithm: Trust-region with dogleg and autoscaling
* Starting Point: [1.0,1.0,1.0]
* Zero: [3.45189e-17,8.26168e-16,1.41421]
* Inf-norm of residuals: 0.000000
* Iterations: 6
* Convergence: true
* |x - x'| < 0.0e+00: false
* |f(x)| < 1.0e-08: true
* Function Calls (f): 7
* Jacobian Calls (df/dx): 7
```

The object r will store the solution. By calling r.zero we get:

```
3-element Array{Float64,1}:
3.45189e-17
8.26168e-16
1.41421
```

This shows that the first and second components of the solution hit the zero bound. The function will have positive values for these first two components:

```
fvec = similar(r.zero);
f!(r.zero, fvec);
fvec
3-element Array{Float64,1}:
1.41421
9.24264
-4.44089e-16
```

2.7.9 Solving for Roots in Julia

In this section, I review the main libraries that deal with solving for roots and fixed points in Julia. Although the language is still young, the interested user can find many packages that cover most of the potential problems in terms of root finding, fixed points and complementarity problems.

There are two dedicated packages that deal with roots: Roots and NLsolve. Roots is the more comprehensive one and contains the algorithms one would usually need. As mentioned before, the modern approaches are derivations of Newton and Quasi-Newton methods. The package Roots uses a baseline function to solve for roots, i.e. fzero, but the different options used imply the use of different algorithms – bracketing, derivative free, and so on. For historical and pedagogical reasons, the package includes standard methods, including Newton's method, or the secant method.

The package NLsolve was written with an economics audience in mind and thus it is not dedicated to just solve for roots, but also to complementarity problems which are often met in economics. The package uses a function nlsolve to find the roots of a functions (although it was designed with the purpose of dealing with nonlinear systems of equations) and the user can choose from two available algorithms, the trust region method and the line search Newton method. At the same time, NLsolve allows for quite a few ways to deal with the Jacobian: approximating it with finite differencing, automatic differentiation, or simply declaring the Jacobian.

There is an additional (meta-)package ValidatedNumerics that provides (through the package IntervalRootfinding) a function that applies the Newton approach in solving for roots. It also supplies an function, the Krawczyk method, which however applies only to multivariate problems. However, the coverage of root finding problems in this package is limited.

Nevertheless, there is also a package that provides an indirect approach to root finding problems, and this is JuMP. In essence, this is a package that deals with mathematical optimization and it can solve a variety of such problems: linear, non-linear, semidefinite. The solution provided by JuMp to the root finding problems consists in reformulating the optimization problem with nonlinear constraint such that the equations are used as constraints and the value 1 as the objective function.

2.8 OPTIMIZATION

In economics, the fundamental characteristic of the behavior of the agents (whether firms or households) is optimization under a given set of constraints. The essential role of optimization in economics gives it a fundamental place in numerical methods for economics.

Although the optimization might consist in either maximization or minimization, it is preferable to present the general optimization problem from the perspective of minimization. There are two basic reasons for doing this: first, most optimization software is built with a views towards minimization, and second, and not unrelated to the first point, in applied sciences (like engineering) it is usually the minimization problem where the focus lies (and thus the literature from these fields has this feature). At the same time, maximizing a function f is equivalent to the minimization of $-f$.

Any optimization problem comprises an objective function f. We assume here that: $f : \mathbb{R}^n \to \mathbb{R}$. An optimization problem might also be characterized by a set of equality constraints as well as a set of inequality constraints defined as follows:

1. A vector g of m equality constraints, with $g : \mathbb{R}^n \to \mathbb{R}^m$;
2. A vector h of l inequality constraints, with $h : \mathbb{R}^n \to \mathbb{R}^l$.

In this chapter, it is assumed that the functions f, g, h are continuous. Thus, the problem at hand may be generally defined as:

$$
\min_{x \in \mathbb{R}^n} f(x)
$$
$$
\text{s.t. } g(x) = 0 \tag{2.209}
$$
$$
h(x) \leq 0
$$

There are various ways to present the various techniques of numerical optimization. Some authors, see [2] for example, present them according to the algorithm used. Alternatively, [1] starts from unconstrained uni-dimensional optimization problem and then moves to unconstrained multidimensional optimization to finally treat constrained optimization problems. It is the latter approach that I follow. However, the presentation is based on both sources, [1] and [2].

2.8.1 One-Dimensional Optimization

This is the simplest possible optimization problem where there aren't any constraints. In its minimization specification, we can write it as:

$$
\min_{x \in \mathbb{R}} f(x) \tag{2.210}
$$

With the function f defined as $f : \mathbb{R} \to \mathbb{R}$.

The Golden Search Algorithm

Similarly to the root finding problem, we can find the local minimum by relying on a progressively smaller interval around it. These type of algorithms are derivative free since they not compute the first derivative of the function f. In this section I cover the golden search algorithm, the most widely applied bracketing (or derivative-free) algorithm to find the local optimum.

We start from an interval $[a, b]$ and select two numbers x_1 and x_2, with the property that: $x_2 > x_1$. The function is evaluated at these two points and a new interval is selected conditional on these evaluations:

- $[a, x_2]$, provided that $f(x_2) > f(x_1)$
- $[x_1, b]$, if $f(x_1) > f(x_2)$

The algorithm ensures that, in each iteration, the newer smaller interval will contain the local minimum since the new interval contains a point at which the evaluated function has a smaller value then the value of the function at the endpoints. In order to selected the interior points each time a new interval is determined, two basic criteria are used:

- Whenever a new interval is set, its length should be independent of whether we fix a new value for the lower end or for the upper end;
- To speed up the process, we should keep one point in the new interval and thus evaluate the function only once in each iteration.

The practical way to set the interior points is to use the following relationship in each recursion: $x_i = a + \alpha_i(b - a)$, where we use the following relationships to determine α_1 and α_2:

$$
\alpha_1 = \frac{3 - \sqrt{5}}{2} \tag{2.211}
$$

$$
\alpha_2 = \frac{\sqrt{5} - 1}{2} \tag{2.212}
$$

I code the golden search method for minimization in Julia below. I use the function $f(x) = x^3 - 2 * x - 5$ with the interval $[a, b] = [0, 3]$ and follow the approach in [2].

```
#golden search method:
#set the interval
a=0;
b=3;
#accuracy
```

```
epsilon=0.000001;

#coefficients
alfa1=(3-sqrt(5))/2;
alfa2=(sqrt(5)-1)/2;

#define the function
f(x)=-(x^3-2*x-5);

#set interior points
x1=a+alfa1*(b-a);
x2=a+alfa2*(b-a);

#the value of the function in x1 and x2
f_x1=f(x1);
f_x2=f(x2);
d=alfa1*alfa2*(b-a)

while d>epsilon
d=d*alfa2;
if(f_x1<f_x2)
x2=x1;
x1=x1-d;

f_x2=f_x1;
f_x1=f(x1);

else
x1=x2;
x2=x2+d;

f_x1=f_x2;
f_x2=f(x2);
end

end
if(f_x2<f_x1)
x=x2;
else
x=x1;
end
```

The code starts from setting the interval, the function and then it iterates on increasingly smaller interval until it identifies the local minimum at $x = 0.8164$.

The Newton-Raphson Algorithm

Given the fact that root finding and identifying the local optimum are essentially equivalent problems, it is no wonder that the Newton-Raphson algorithm for finding the optimal point is similar to the Newton approach for root finding.

The Newton-Raphson algorithm consists in starting from an initial guess x_0 for the local optimum and then iterating on a rule based on the a Taylor approximation. In each iteration, the new value x_{k+1} is obtained using the value x_k from the previous iteration. To obtain this rule, we use a second order Taylor approximation for the function f at the point x written as:

$$f(x) \approx f(x_k) + f'(x_k)(x - x_k) + \frac{1}{2}(x - x_k)^T f''(x_k)(x - x_k) \tag{2.213}$$

Which leads to the following first order condition with respect to $x - x_k$:

$$f'(x_k) + f''(x_k)(x - x_k) = 0 \tag{2.214}$$

This allows us to derive an iteration rule as follows:

$$x_{k+1} = x_k - [f''(x_k)]^{-1} f'(x_k) \tag{2.215}$$

The effectiveness of the Newton-Raphson method depends on several issues:

- The initial point x_0 must be reasonable close to the local optimum point (be it a minimum or maximum);
- The function f is twice continuously differentiable;
- The Hessian is positive (negative) definite in order to reach a minimum (maximum).

However, if the initial point is not close enough to the optimal point and/or the function is not globally concave (for maximum points)/convex (for minimum points), the Newton-Raphson approach might not function that well. Furthermore, the Newton-Raphson algorithm is also more computationally involved since it implies computing both first and second order derivatives of the function f. If the initial guess is a good one, the Newton-Raphson algorithm might converge rapidly, provided that the other shortcomings are addressed.

Below, I present an implementation of the Newton-Raphson algorithm in Julia. I consider a basic function defined by $f(x) = x^2 - 2x + 1$. I consider the interval where the local minimum is searched for as $[a, b] = [0, 4]$. The initial point is 1.5, close the to the actual local minimum equal to 1.

```
#Newton-Raphson method
x=0.5;
#number of iterations
k=200

#set the function
f(x)=x^2-2x+1;
#set the first derivative
df(x)=2x-2;

for i=1:k
x1=x-(f(x)/df(x));
x=x1;
end
NewtonRaphson_sol=x
0.9999999925494194
```

The algorithm iterates for a given number of iterations (set here to 100) and it returns the last approximation of the optimal point, here a minimum.

2.8.2 Multidimensional Optimization

In the multidimensional case, the unconstrained optimization problem can be written as:

$$\min_{x \in \mathbb{R}^n} f(x) \tag{2.216}$$

With the function f defined as $f : \mathbb{R}^n \to \mathbb{R}^n$.

The Grid Search

This approach is the most direct way to find the optimal point for a given function. It consists in setting within the interval where the minimum is searched a large number of points, be it 500 or 1000. It then evaluates the given function for each of these points. The algorithm finally selects the optimal points by comparing the evaluations.

Given that the algorithm evaluates the function for a large number of points, the algorithm is clearly not very computationally efficient. Despite this obvious disadvantage, the algorithm is very useful for several reasons. First, it can provide a first evaluation for the optimal point which can be used further as in input for more advanced algorithms. Second, the evaluation might also indicate the presence of multiple local optima, or a flat function over a larger interval, suggesting that the problem at hand should be addressed with more complicated approaches.

The Newton Algorithm

The multidimensional version of the Newton algorithm is a straight generalization of the uni-dimensional version. In the multivariate case, we rely on the gradient and Hessian to describe the algorithm.

If x is a column vector of variables, then, the gradient of the function f at x is given by:

$$\nabla f(x) = (\frac{\partial f}{\partial x_1}(x), ..., \frac{\partial f}{\partial x_n}(x)) \tag{2.217}$$

The Hessian of the function f at x can be written as:

$$H(f(x)) = (\frac{\partial^2 f}{\partial x_i \partial x_j}(x))_{i,j=1}^n \tag{2.218}$$

The Newton algorithm for the multidimensional case starts from the multidimensional quadratic approximation of the function f at x_k which will be written as:

$$f(x) = f(x_k) + \nabla f(x_k)(x - x_k) + \frac{1}{2}(x - x_k)^T H(x_k)(x - x_k) \tag{2.219}$$

From here we can derive an iteration relationship for the value of x_{k+1} as follows:

$$x_{k+1} = x_k - H(x_k)^{-1}(\nabla f(x_k))^T \tag{2.220}$$

The Quasi-Newton Algorithm

As in the case of root finding, the Quasi-Newton methods are an adaptation of the Newton approach where the Hessian used in the latter method is replaced with an approximation. This approximation is chosen in such a way that it respects an essential condition: it is positive definite such that it ensures an improvement of the function value in the direction of the Newton step.

All Quasi-Newton methods start from the recursive equation typical to the Newton approach:

$$x_{k+1} = x_k - H(x_k)^{-1}(\nabla f(x_k))^T \tag{2.221}$$

In this approach, the second part of the recursive equation is adapted such that the Hessian is replaced with a positive definite approximation: H_k. We have that:

$$x_{k+1} = x_k + d_k \tag{2.222}$$

Where d_k is the step improvement which is now given by:

$$d_k = -H(x_k)^{-1}(\nabla f(x_k))^T \tag{2.223}$$

Here, H_k is the approximation of the Hessian matrix.

A special feature of the Quasi-Newton methods is that, in contrast to the standard Newton approach, the full step d_k is not necessarily considered, but rather an optimization approach is applied. The optimization consists in taking a step $s > 0$ whose value solves:

$$\min_s f(x_k + sd_k) \tag{2.224}$$

There are several Quasi-Newton methods, however they mostly differ through the way the approximation of the Hessian matrix is set. In the simplest Quasi-Newton approach, the approximation is set as equal to the identity matrix, namely: $H_k = I$. Such that the improvement step becomes:

$$d_k = -(\nabla f(x_k))^T \tag{2.225}$$

In this way, each step leads to the maximum decrease (when the minimum of the function is sought) since each step is equal to the gradient. This is why this basic Quasi-Newton approach is also known as the steepest descent (or the steepest ascent when the problem at hand is one of maximization).

The major shortcoming of the steepest descent approach is that although it might perform very well locally, there is no guarantee that it is also the best approach globally. It is well known that this method converges slowly.

More efficient Quasi-Newton methods try to address the main problem of the steepest descent approach by taking into account information about the curvature of the function. To achieve these, such methods condition the selection of the approximation of the Hessian to respect two properties. The first one simply states that the Hessian approximation must satisfy the Quasi-Newton property, namely that:

$$d_k = -H_k^{-1}(\nabla f(x_k + \delta_k)^T - \nabla f(x_k)^T) \tag{2.226}$$

The second condition states that, similar to the original Hessian matrix, its approximation H_k must also be both symmetric and positive definite (negative definite when maximizing the function). These conditions will ensure that each step will decrease the function in the direction of the Newton step.

There are two widely used methods that satisfy both conditions, Broyden-Fletcher-Goldfarb-Shano (BFGS, hereafter) and Davidson-Fletcher-Powell (DFP, hereafter).

As before, d_k is the improvement step: $d_k = x_{k+1} - x_k$ and by y_k the difference between the improvement in the gradient: $y_k = \nabla f(x_k + \delta_k) - \nabla f(x_k)$. We also use w to denote: $w = y_k - H_k d_k$.

In the BFGS approach, the approximation of the Hessian is updated using the following relationship:

$$H_{k+1} = H_k + \frac{y_k y_k^T}{y_k^T d_k} - \frac{H_k d_k d_k^T H_k}{d_k^T H_k d_k} \tag{2.227}$$

The alternative DFP method uses a similar updating scheme for the approximation of the Hessian, as follows:

$$H_{k+1} = H_k + \frac{(w y_k^T + y_k w^T)}{y_k^T d_k} - \frac{d_k^T w y_k y_k^T}{(y_k^T d_k)^2} \tag{2.228}$$

The two algorithms are quite close to each other, however the literature generally considers that the BFGS approach is superior (but not always).

A known issue related to the Quasi-Newton methods is that the updating formula for the approximation of the Hessian H_k uses the division with $d_k^T y_k$ which however can be too small sometimes, leading to inaccurate results. The usual approach in dealing with this issue is to not update the approximation of the Hessian H_k when this happens. To effectively quantify whether this quantity is too small, [2] propose the use of the following rule:

$$|d_k^T y_k| < \epsilon ||d_k|| ||y_k|| \tag{2.229}$$

2.8.3 The Nonlinear Least Square

Although this problem is also a multivariate optimization problem, nevertheless, its structure presents a few special characteristics that require some changes in the methods presented until now, be it the Newton algorithms, or the Quasi-Newton approaches. Since this problem is often met in economics, this section presents what optimization methods can be used in dealing with it. The presentation draws from [1]. In the most general problem, a nonlinear least square is written as:

$$\min_x \frac{1}{2} \sum_{i=1}^{m} f^i(x)^2 = S(x) \tag{2.230}$$

Here $f^i : \mathbb{R}^n \to R$, for $i = 1, ..., m$.

In an econometric problem, we will deal with a vector β of unknown parameters and data y_i, such that $f^i(x)$ becomes $f(\beta, y^i)$. The latter will usually represent the disturbance corresponding to observation i, while $S(\beta)$ will be the sum of squared residuals.

Theoretically, this problem should be solvable using standard multivariate optimization approaches. However, as we are going to see, we can improve over standard methods by taking into consideration the special structure of this problem.

The Jacobian of the function $f(x) = (f^1(x), ..., f^m(x))^T$ is denoted by $J(x)$. We can also write:

$$f_l^i = \frac{\partial f^i}{\partial x_l} \tag{2.231}$$

$$f_{jl}^i = \frac{\partial^2 f^i}{\partial x_j \partial x_l} \tag{2.232}$$

Furthermore, we can write the gradient of $S(x)$ as $J(x)^T f(x)$ while the Hessian can be written as:

$$J(x)^T J(x) + \sum_{i=1}^{m} f_{jl}^i(x) f^i(x) \tag{2.233}$$

When the second term of the Hessian is not taken into consideration (because $f(x) = 0$), then the Hessian simplifies to $J(x)^T J(x)$. Its computation is simple, since it consists in using only the terms $f_j^i(x)$. When $f(x)$ is close enough to zero, then a good approximation of the Hessian consists in $J(x)^T J(x)$, and it can be efficiently used. Basically, we arrive at a Gauss-Newton algorithm where the approximation of the Hessian is $J(x)^T J(x)$ such that the improvement step in each iteration will be given by:

$$d_k = -(J(x^k)^T J(x^k))^{-1} (\nabla f(x^k))^T \tag{2.234}$$

This approach presents the considerable advantage of a fast computation in each step since it does not compute any second order derivative of the function f. However, this approach is also prone to inaccuracy since it involves the product $J(x)^T J(x)$ which might be poorly conditioned (either because $J(x)$ is poorly conditioned itself, or because this is a square of a matrix). Not at last, the step computed this algorithm might not lead towards the minimum.

An effective alternative to this approach, widely used in empirical applications, is the Levenberg-Marquardt algorithm. This approach replaces $J(x)^T J(x)$ as an approximation of the Hessian with $J(x)^T J(x) + \lambda I$, where λ is a scalar while I is the identity matrix. In this approach, the step becomes:

$$d_k = -(J(x^k)^T J(x^k) + \lambda I)^{-1} (\nabla f(x^k))^T \tag{2.235}$$

There are two essential advantages resulting from this change: the risk for ill-conditioned matrices is reduced, while for a large enough scalar λ, the algorithm ensures that each step is taken in the minimum direction.

Julia implements nonlinear least square in the packages that were already discussed in the Interpolation section (the sub-section on Curve Fitting, to be more precise). Here, I just sketch how one can fit a nonlinear least square model using these packages, with a focus on the actual implementation of this approach.

The package CurveFit applies various models to estimate regressions on data. By default, it deals with linear models. However, when the main function used by CurveFit detects a model that is nonlinear in its coefficients, then CurveFit will apply a Nonlinear Least Square approach. The generic function used in CurveFit has the following syntax:

```
curve_fit(::Type{T}, x, y...)
```

Here, T is the type of the curve/regression to be estimated, x stands for the explanatory variable(s) while the y is the dependent variable. Alternatively, we might declare from the beginning that we deal with a nonlinear regression and use the following function:

```
coefs, converged, iter = nonlinear_fit(x, fun, a0,
eps=1e-7, maxiter=200)
```

Here, x is the dataset with explanatory variables, fun returns the residuals and may also be called using:

```
residual = fun(x, a)
```

With x the dataset and a the estimated coefficients of the regression.

The nonlinear_fit function uses a nonlinear algorithm from the Newton class that it not based on derivatives. Its syntax uses the variable a_0 as the initial guess of the solution, a tolerance for the accuracy of the estimation as given by the variable eps as well as a specified number of iterations.

An alternative package, LsqFit offers functions to estimate both linear and nonlinear regression models. It is worth mentioning that LsqFit has been part of one of the optimization packages in Julia, Optim (which is going to be presented later), which underscores again that Nonlinear Least Squares is a special case of the larger optimization techniques used in economics.

The package LsqFit uses a Levenberg-Marquardt algorithm to estimate nonlinear regression models. As explained above, the Levenberg-Marquardt algorithm is designed to deal specifically with Nonlinear Least Square problems. Its adaptation of the more general multivariate optimization techniques has the advantages of reducing the risk of ill-conditioned matrices and that each step is made in the right descent direction.

The generic function used to fit models using LsqFit is:

```
fit = curve_fit(model, x, y, w, p0; kwargs...):
```

Here model stands for the regression specification. This is a function that will depend on the variable(s) x and a set of parameters (params). By x, we denote the independent variables, while by y we denote the dependent variable. The variable w can be used to weigh the residuals (which can consists either in a vector with a dimension equal to the dimension of the explanatory variables, or into a matrix). Since this is an optimization algorithm, the function will also need an initial point (denoted by p_0), as well as a number of parameters necessary for the Levenberg-Marquardt algorithm (the maximum number of iterations, for example).

2.8.4 Constrained Optimization

This is one of the most widely encountered problems in economics: the agent maximizes or minimizes an objective function by optimally choosing a number of control variables which are subject to a number of constraints.

Keeping the focus on the minimization (for reasons explained at the beginning of this section), the general problem can be written as:

$$\min_{x} f(x) \tag{2.236}$$

With the constraints given by: $g(x) = 0$, $h(x) \leq 0$. Here, it is assumed that the functions f, g and h are $\mathbb{C}^2$ and that $f : \mathbb{R}^n \to \mathbb{R}$, $g : \mathbb{R}^n \to \mathbb{R}^m$ and $h : \mathbb{R}^n \to \mathbb{R}^l$, where n is the number of control variables, m is the number of equality constraints while l is the number of inequality constraints.

Assuming that there is a local minimum point denote by x^* and that a constraint qualification is verified (although the latter is usually neglected in the economics), then according to the Kuhn-Tucker theorem, there exist the multipliers $\lambda^* \in \mathbb{R}^m$ and $\mu^* \in \mathbb{R}^l$, and x^* is a critical point of the Lagrangian function written as:

$$L(x, \lambda, \mu) = f(x) + \lambda^T g(x) + \mu^T h(x) \tag{2.237}$$

For the optimal solution, i.e. for $\lambda = \lambda^*$, $\mu = \mu^*$ and $x = x^*$, the value of the Lagrangian is equal to zero:

$$L_x(x^*, \lambda^*, \mu^*) = 0 \tag{2.238}$$

The solution to this problem involves the following first order conditions:

$$f_x + \lambda^T g_x + \mu^T h_x = 0 \tag{2.239}$$

$$\mu_i h^i(x) = 0, i = 1, ..., l \tag{2.240}$$

$$g(x) = 0 \tag{2.241}$$

$$h(x) \leq 0 \tag{2.242}$$

$$\mu \leq 0 \tag{2.243}$$

There are numerous methods to numerically solve a constrained optimization problem and it is practically impossible to summarize them in a section. The reader might want to consult books that are fully dedicated to this subject, like [9], for example.

Nevertheless, in the following paragraphs I sketch some of the most used approaches to numerically solve for constrained optimization problems, although the reader should be aware that actual implementations of algorithms to solve such problems might involve combinations of some of the below techniques. The discussion follows basically [1].

The Kuhn-Tucker Framework

The constrained optimization problem can be rewritten as a system of nonlinear equation which is solvable through the techniques discussed in the previous chapter. The only caveat is that the presence of binding and non-binding inequality constraints may lead to situations in which there is no solution. In this latter case, comparing over the finite number of solutions that respect the Kuhn-Tucker conditions we may choose the solution which has the associated smallest objective function.

The above solution would be written in this case as follows:

$$f_x + \lambda^T g_x + \mu^T h_x = 0 \tag{2.244}$$

$$g(x) = 0 \tag{2.245}$$

$$h^i(x) = 0 \tag{2.246}$$

$$\mu^j = 0 \tag{2.247}$$

where $i \in \mathcal{P}$, $j \in \{1, 2, ..., l\} - \mathcal{P}$ and $\mathcal{P} \subset \{1, 2, ..., l\}$. Thus we obtained a set of nonlinear equations, with different combinations f binding and non-binding inequality constraints for each $\mathcal{P}$.

Penalty Function Method

The previous approach has the disadvantage that although a minimum might be found, it might not verify all the constraints. In this particular case, one would have to search for all potential solutions that verify the constraints and choose the one leading to the minimal value of the objective function. To circumvent this, a convenient way is to introduce a penalty into the objective function such that the potential solutions that do not respect the constraint significantly affect the objective function.

A typical constrained problem, written as:

$$\min_x f(x) \tag{2.248}$$

With the constraints given by: $g(x) = a$, $h(x) \leq b$, can be rewritten with the help of a penalty function problem as follows:

$$\min_x f(x) + \frac{1}{2} P \left(\sum_i (g^i(x) - a_i)^2 + \sum_j (max[0, h^j(x) - b_j])^2 \right) \tag{2.249}$$

The key parameter here is P, the so-called penalty parameter. Obviously, as P gets larger, the solution of the penalized function converges to the solution of the initial solution.

Sequential Quadratic Method

An alternative to the previous two approaches relies on the fact that there are efficient solutions to quadratic problems (i.e. problems that consist in quadratic objectives and linear constraints).

The sequential quadratic method is an algorithm that consists in updating in each iteration the value of the choice variable x_k in a manner that it is similar to the formerly discussed Newton-like algorithms: $x_{k+1} = x_k + d_k$.

Assuming that the current iteration has associated the values (x_k, λ_k, μ_k), the current iteration consists in solving the following quadratic problem:

$$\min_d (x_k - d_k)^T L_{xx}(x_k, \lambda_k, \mu_k)(x_k - d_k) \tag{2.250}$$

With the constraints given by: $g_x(x_k)(x_k - d_k) = 0$ and $h_x(x)(x_k - d_k) \leq 0$.

Active Set Methods

In spite of offering a viable alternative to the direct Kuhn-Tucker approach, the penalty function involves the computation of the constraints in the penalty function. Both approaches, the direct and the penalized one, are thus not computationally efficient since they involve either evaluating too many combinations (the direct Kuhn-Tucker approach), or computing the constraints although when they do not necessarily bind (in the penalized case).

A more practical approach, the so-called active set methods, which choose the potential solutions in a rational way. The problem is defined as above, namely:

$$\min_x f(x) \tag{2.251}$$

With the constraints given by: $g(x) = 0$, $h^i(x) \leq 0$ with $i \in \mathcal{P}$ defined as before.

The active set method will start by considering a set of constraints and then proceed to numerically solve this problem. In each iteration, the constraints are checked and dropped if they are not binding, while new ones will be added if they are binding. Furthermore, the algorithm will increase in time the penalty parameter. It has been shown that for a sufficiently large number of iterations, the algorithm will converge to the true solution.

2.8.5 Optimization in Julia

While the above section discussed the theory behind some of the most known algorithms to optimization, either constrained or unconstrained, the focus on the actual code in Julia has been weaker. One reason for this is that the included code were rather illustrative since there are already a number of well-developed libraries for optimization in Julia.

The package Optim, although still in development, covers the most basic needs for optimization. The focus lies minimization and generally on unconstrained optimization. Provided that certain conditions are satisfied, the algorithms used will converge to a local minimum. When a global minimum is searched for, the alternative is to use packages that are specifically designed for this, like BlackBoxOptim.

The generic function used in Optim has the following syntax:

```
Optimize(f, x0, algo, options)
```

Here, $f(x)$ is the function that will be optimized. It can take either univariate or multivariate arguments. The variable x_0 represents the initial guess of the solution and its length will be determined by the length of the control variable x. Finally, algo stands for the algorithm used in optimization. The function allows for setting a number of options related to the typical characteristics of a numerical optimization like the tolerance in objective function, tolerance in control variable(s), trace, the number of iterations, or whether automatic differentiation should be used or not.

Optim implements algorithms from a variety of classes. The user can implement derivative-free methods like Nelder-Mead or simulated annealing, Quasi-Newton methods (where the gradient is required but not the Hessian since the latter is approximated) like gradient descent or BFGS, or, finally, Newton type methods (which require both the gradient and the Hessian). Additionally, the package included a number of line search algorithm that were later relegated into a separated package LineSearch that will be discussed later.

Most of the algorithms were discussed before, however the derivative-free methods used here deserve a few words (given that they are widely used in practice). The Nelder-Mead algorithm implemented here is a direct search algorithm that will keep evaluating the function on for a number of points until a minimum is reached using a simplex approach (such that in each iteration, the worse points are replaced by better choices in terms of minimization). The other derivative-free algorithm, Simulated Annealing, uses the Metropolis-Hasting algorithm that is familiar to economists from its use in the Bayesian estimation.

To optimize a univariate function, Optim provides two algorithms: golden section search and Brent's method. After defining a function, we set the interval where the minimum is searched for and the algorithm to be used. The default choice is the Brent's method. Below, I code the minimization of a simple function over the interval $[-2.0, 0.0]$:

```
#Optim
using Optim
#1.Univariate function
f(x)=x^2-2x+1
optimize(f,0.0, 4.0)
```

The results are shown below:

```
Results of Optimization Algorithm
* Algorithm: Brent's Method
* Search Interval: [-1.000000, 4.000000]
* Minimizer: -4.370131e-09
* Minimum: -1.000000e+00
* Iterations: 59
* Convergence: max(|x - x_upper|, |x - x_lower|) <= 2*(1.5e-08*|x|+ 2.2e-16): true
* Objective Function Calls: 60
```

However, for the multivariate case, we rather use the algorithms discussed above. Consider the well-known Rosenbrok's function: $(a-x)^2 + b(y-x^2)^2$ (difficult to minimize for most algorithms). To find the minimum, we use again the function optimize, input a guess value and choose the algorithm. For the case where a gradient is not provided, the default algorithm is Nelder-Mead. We could write:

```
f(x) = (1.0 - x[1])^2 + 100.0 * (x[2] - x[1]^2)^2
optimize(f,[0.0, 0.0])
```

And the result will be:

```
Results of Optimization Algorithm
* Algorithm: Nelder-Mead
* Starting Point: [0.0,0.0]
* Minimizer: [0.0,0.0]
* Minimum: -4.000000e+00
* Iterations: 17
* Convergence: true
*   \sqrt{\sum(y_i-\bar y)^2}/n < 1.0e-08: true
* Reached Maximum Number of Iterations: false
* Objective Function Calls: 21
```

When using a Quasi-Newton method, there are different ways to specify how the gradient will be computed. When using the LBFGS algorithm, we could simply specify the use of this algorithm, and, by default, optimize will rely on a finite differencing method to compute the gradient (see the section on numerical differentiation).

```
optimize(f, [0.0, 0.0], LBFGS())
```

Which leads to these results:

```
Results of Optimization Algorithm
* Algorithm: L-BFGS
* Starting Point: [0.0,0.0]
* Minimizer: [0.9999999929485478,0.9999999859278973]
* Minimum: 4.981785e-17
* Iterations: 21
* Convergence: true
* |x - x'| < 1.0e-32: false
* |f(x) - f(x')| / |f(x)| < 1.0e-32: true
* |g(x)| < 1.0e-08: false
* Reached Maximum Number of Iterations: false
* Objective Function Calls: 157
* Gradient Calls: 157
```

Alternatively, we could either specify ourselves the gradient and pass it to the function optimize, or use call the automatic differentiation capabilities from the package Calculus.

As mentioned before, there is also an additional package, derived from Optim, focusing on the line search algorithms, LineSearches. It includes several types of line search algorithms to perform optimization.

Another smaller package is SimpleOptimizers. Although the creator of the package has designed it with a focus on derivative-free methods, the package also has a few derivative-based methods, including BFGS or conjugate gradient.

The final mention, although is by far the best optimization package in Julia, is the package JuMP (from Julia for Mathematical Optimization). JuMP is more than a simple package and it is described by its creators as a domain-specific language for mathematical optimization. Furthermore, in contrast to the other optimization package, JuMP also relies on third-party (sometimes commercial) solvers such that it covers a much wider range of problems: linear and nonlinear programming, semidefinite programming, etc.

A complete introduction to JuMP is not possible within this section, however a short introduction driven by examples will be done in the following paragraphs. The interested reader might learn more from the well-written documents that accompany the package.

In contrast to the other packages that rely on pre-given functions, JuMP relies on a specific language that allows to formulate any type of optimization problem using specific objects. There are two types of such objects: models and objectives. We create a model by calling specific constructor as follows:

```
m = Model()
```

To further advance with specification the optimization problem, we use the macro @variables to create the variables objects. We can write:

```
@variable(m, x )
```

This will add the variable x to the model m. However, no condition on bounds is specified. To specify lower or upper bounds, we can write:

```
@variable(m, lb <= x <= ub )
```

This adds both lower bounds (lb) and upper bounds (ub) to the variable x. To complete the problem, we also have to specify the objective function. This can be done using the macro @objective:

```
@objective(m, Min, fun)
```

Here m is the model, Min is the type of optimization set (which can be either a maximum or a minimum) and fun is the objective function. We can also specify a number of constraints with the macro @constraints:

```
@constraint(m, constr)
```

Where m is the model and constr is the equality or inequality constraint imposed on the model. Below I present a simple unconstrained optimization problem in Julia that is based on the above elements.

```
using JuMP
using SCS
m = Model(solver=SCSSolver())
@variable(m, 0 <= x <= 4 )
@variable(m, 0 <= y <= 4 )
@objective(m, Min, x+y-2 )

print(m)
status = solve(m)
println("Objective value: ", getobjectivevalue(m))
println("x = ", getvalue(x))
println("y = ", getvalue(y))
```

This returns:

```
Min x + y - 2
Subject to
0 <= x <= 4
0 <= y <= 4
Objective value: -1.999997402003805
x = 1.2989980975862232e-6
y = 1.2989980975862232e-6
```

There are many options in terms of solvers that can be used with JuMP, but I have used here the freely available and easy to install SCS (through SCS.jl).

2.9 COMPUTING THE ACCURACY OF APPROXIMATIONS

Later chapters will deal with methods to approximate solutions to DSGE models. It is thus of high interest to have tools to evaluate these approximations. An excellent presentation on this topic can be found in [3]. The presentation here draws on this material.

The discussion is based on the optimal growth model which is several times in this book. I sketch the model below.

A representative household maximizes the expected discounted life-time utility given by:

$$\max_{c_t} E_t \sum_{t=0}^{\infty} \beta^t \frac{c_t^{1-\sigma} - 1}{1 - \sigma} \tag{2.252}$$

Here, the discount factor $\beta \in (0, 1)$. The representative household faces a typical budget constraint:

$$y_t = c_t + i_t \tag{2.253}$$

Where y_t is the output, while c_t, i_t are consumption and investments. The output is given by:

$$y_t = exp(a_t)k_t^\alpha \tag{2.254}$$

Where the capital stock follows $k_{t+1} = (1 - \delta)k_t + i_t$, while the productivity a_t evolves according to:

$$a_t = \rho a_{t-1} + \epsilon_t \tag{2.255}$$

The parameter δ stands for the depreciation rate and $\rho < 1$ is the autocorrelation of productivity shocks. Such a model can also be put into the following representation (which will prove useful when presenting formal approaches to deal with accuracy):

$$E_t F(y_{t+1}, x_{t+1}, y_t, x_t, \epsilon_{t+1}) \tag{2.256}$$

Here, y_t are the control variables, x_t the state variables while ϵ_t stands for the shocks. The function F is defined as $F : \mathbb{R}^{n_y} \times \mathbb{R}^{n_x} \times \mathbb{R}^{n_y} \times \mathbb{R}^{n_x} \times \mathbb{R}^{n_\epsilon} \to \mathbb{R}^{n_x+n_y}$. It is also assumed that the solution method can be represented as follows:

$$y_t = g(x_t; \theta)$$
$$x_{t+1} = h(x_t, y_t; \epsilon_{t+1}) = h(x_t, g(x_t; \theta); \epsilon_{t+1}) \tag{2.257}$$

There are various ways to evaluate the approximate solutions to the above model which can be basically split into two categories, informal and formal ones. In terms of informal approaches, one could perform quite many types of evaluations:

1. analyze the qualitative features of decision rules;
2. compute the impulse response functions for different approximate solution methods;
3. analyze the qualitative features of the approximation of the model in terms of distributions or moments of key variables;
4. solve the model using different solution methods.

The literature has also proposed several ways to test for the approximate solutions in formal ways. I detail a few such approaches below.

The Difference Criterion

Assuming that we have the true solution of the model, we can compute the accuracy of the approximation by simply calculating how far away are the approximated decision rules from the true decision rule. If the actual solution is denoted by y_t and the approximate solution by $\tilde{y}_t$, then we may compute the difference criterion using the following variables:

$$E_1 = 100 \times E|\frac{y_t - \tilde{y}_t}{y_t}|$$
$$E_\infty = 100 \times max|\frac{y_t - \tilde{y}_t}{y_t}| \tag{2.258}$$

Here, E_1 is the average approximation error, while E_∞ can be interpreted as the maximal relative error of the approximation.

The Euler Equation

This is based on the accuracy of the Euler equation and it has been proposed by [10]. For the case of the optimal growth model presented above, the accuracy error of the Euler equation can be written as:

$$u_t = c_t - [\beta E_t c_{t+1}^{-\sigma}(\alpha exp(a_{t+1})k_{t+1}^{\alpha-1} + 1 - \delta)]^{-\frac{1}{\sigma}} \tag{2.259}$$

We can normalize u_t by consumption and interpret the new variable u_t/c_t as the loss in terms of consumption provided one would use the approximate solution instead of the true solution. We can define a few statistics as follows:

$$E_1 = log_{10}(E|\frac{u_t}{c_t}|)$$

$$E_2 = log_{10}(E\left\|\frac{u_t}{c_t}\right\|^2)$$

$$E_\infty = log_{10}(\max|\frac{u_t}{c_t}|)$$

(2.260)

The D-M Statistic

This has been proposed by [11] and it relies on simulating the model using the Monte Carlo approach. Assume first that the model of interest can be represented as in (2.256), while the solution can be written as in Eq. (2.257). It follows that, if $\tilde{y}_t$ and $\tilde{x}_t$ are the approximate solution, the residuals can be defined as:

$$u_{t+1} = F(\tilde{y}_{t+1}, \tilde{x}_{t+1}, \tilde{y}_t, \tilde{x}_t, \tilde{\epsilon}_{t+1})$$

(2.261)

The test procedure starts from defining a set of simulated instruments that correspond to the variables in the model, either predetermined or exogenous variables, $\tilde{x}_t$. A number of q such instruments are defined and they are denoted by $\tilde{z}_t$. Based on Eq. (2.256), it follows that the residuals u_{t+1} should verify the following $q \times n$ equations:

$$E[u_{t+1} \otimes \tilde{z}_t] = 0$$

(2.262)

The simulated version of this equation can be written as:

$$g_T = \frac{1}{T}\sum_{t=1}^{T} u_{t+1} \otimes \tilde{z}_t$$

(2.263)

For an exact solution, as $T \to \infty$, g_T converges to zero in an almost-sure sense. However, since there are sampling errors, under the hypothesis that the approximation method provides an accurate solution, g_T will be different from zero. To circumvent this issue, [11] introduced a *J-statistic* to test whether g_T is statistically different from zero or not:

$$J_T = T g_T' \Omega_T^{-1} g_T$$

(2.264)

The statistic J_T is asymptotically distributed following a χ^2 with $q \times n$ degrees of freedom.

REFERENCES

[1] K. Judd, Numerical Methods in Economics, MIT Press, 1998.
[2] M.J. Miranda, P. Fackler, Applied Computational Economics and Finance, 3rd, MIT Press, 2002.
[3] F. Collard, Notes on numerical methods, Mimeo, 2015.
[4] J. Kiusalaas, Numerical Methods in Engineering with Python, 3rd, Cambridge University Press, 2010.
[5] S. Salleh, A. Zomaya, S. Bakar, Computing for Numerical Methods Using Visual C++, Wiley-Interscience, 2007.
[6] L. Schumaker, On shape preserving quadratic spline interpolation, SIAM Journal on Numerical Analysis 20 (4) (1982) 854–864.
[7] P.J. Davis, P. Rabinowitz, Methods of Numerical Integration, Academic Press, 1984.
[8] A.H. Stroud, Approximate Calculation of Multiple Integrals, Prentice Hall, 1971.
[9] J. Nocedal, S. Wright, Numerical Optimization, Springer, 2006.
[10] K. Judd, Projection methods for solving aggregate growth models, Journal of Economic Theory 58 (1992) 410–452.
[11] W.J. Den Haan, M. Marcet, Accuracy in simulations, Review of Economic Studies 61 (1994) 3–17.

Chapter 3

Solving and Simulating DSGE Models

Contents

3.1 INTRODUCTION

Modern macroeconomics has a pronounced focus on expectations and hence it tends to focus on stochastic difference equations and stochastic difference systems. It comes as no surprise that few books on modern macroeconomics discuss deterministic difference equations although the latter ones have clearly had a historical role in the development of the macroeconomics and they still play a significant role in specific research topics like deterministic growth models. For example, the older Macroeconomic Theory by Sargent, see [2], was split into two parts, with the first one dealing with deterministic difference equations, while the second introducing and building on stochastic difference equations. However, the newer Recursive Methods in Macroeconomics, see [1], completely eliminates the discussion of deterministic difference equations.

This chapter starts from discussing deterministic difference equations and deterministic dynamic systems. A few illustrative examples are shown. The chapter moves to the case of stochastic counterpart of difference equations and discusses solution method to stochastic dynamic systems in macroeconomics (or rational expectations models or DSGE models). The chapter also illustrates how to solve and simulate standard DSGE models in Julia.

3.2 DETERMINISTIC DIFFERENCE EQUATIONS

There are not too many good resources on the use of deterministic difference equations in economics. Neusser, see [5] provides a good set of lecture notes on difference equations both deterministic and stochastic. Miao, see [3], is among the few recent books on macroeconomics that cover the essentials of difference equations and their use in macroeconomics. Good examples of uses of both deterministic difference equations and deterministic dynamic systems can also be found in [2]. The theoretical presentation in this chapter draws from [3] and [5].

3.2.1 First-Order Linear Equations

The most basic difference equations one could deal with can be written as:

$$x_t = ax_{t-1} + b \tag{3.1}$$

Here x_t is a variable of interest that evolves in time. The equation above simply states that the current value of x_t depends on the past value. To solve it, we can set $x_t = x^*$ for any t and get the solution:

$$x^* = \frac{b}{1-a} \tag{3.2}$$

For this solution, also known as the stationary point (or the steady state) the condition that $a \neq 1$ must hold.

Introduction to Quantitative Macroeconomics Using Julia. https://doi.org/10.1016/B978-0-12-812219-8.00010-0

The general solution to the difference equation in (3.1) is given by:

$$x_t = (x_t - x^*)a^t + x^* \tag{3.3}$$

Using this equation, and based on the values of the coefficient b as well as the initial solution x_0, we can characterize the long run solution to the equation in (3.1). If $|a| < 1$, it can be shown that the general solution for Eq. (3.1) will converge asymptotically to x^* regardless the initial value x_0 (in this case is solution is globally asymptotically stable). At the same time, the solution is indeterminate when x_0 is not given. In other words, any value of x_0 will lead to a solution based on Eq. (3.3).

In the second case $|a| > 1$, except the case $x_0 = x^*$, the solution is said to be explosive. For the particular case when $x_t = x^*$, for all $t \geq 0$, the solution is however stable.

The case discussed above is that of an autonomous difference equation. This type of equation can be simplified by considering that $b = 0$ which leads to the co-called homogeneous equation. However, the more general difference equation is usually written as:

$$x_t = ax_{t-1} + bz_t \tag{3.4}$$

Here, it is assumed that z_t is a sequence that is given and it is assumed to be bounded. This general form is known as the non-autonomous difference equation. This equation can be solved in two ways, depending on whether the initial value x_0 is known or not. Assuming that x_0 is known, the above equation can be solved by backward substitution. We obtain:

$$x_t = b \sum_{j=0}^{t-1} a^j z_{t-1-j} + a^t x_0 \tag{3.5}$$

For $|a| > 1$, the solution diverges. However, when $|a| < 1$, writing the solution in limit, we may get (the second element in the right hand side gets to zero at the limit):

$$\lim_{t \to \infty} x_t = b \lim_{t \to \infty} \sum_{j=0}^{t-1} a^j z_{t-1-j} \tag{3.6}$$

which leads to finite limit.

In the alternative case when the initial value x_0 is not known, we can still solve the equation in a forward manner and get: $x_t = (\frac{1}{a})^T x_{t+T} - \frac{b}{a} \sum_{j=0}^{T-1} (\frac{1}{a})^j z_{t+j}$, with $T \geq 1$. When we impose the so-called no-bubble condition that $\lim_{T \to \infty} (\frac{1}{b})^T x_{t+T} = 0$, we get the forward-looking solution:

$$x_t = -\frac{b}{a} \sum_{j=0}^{\infty} (\frac{1}{a})^j z_{t+j} \tag{3.7}$$

3.2.2 Lag Operator

For higher order linear equations is it very useful to apply the so-called operator lag (or the back-shift operator). Consider a sequence x_t. By definition, the lag operator is given by $Lx_t = x_{t-1}$.

While applying p times the lag operator to the sequence x_t results in:

$$L^p x_t = x_{t-p} \tag{3.8}$$

When applying the lag operator to a constant c, we get: $Lc = c$.

3.2.3 Higher-Order Linear Equations

The generalization of Eq. (3.1) is the difference equation with p lags (of order p). This can be written as:

$$x_t = a_1 x_{t-1} + a_2 x_{t-2} + ... + a_p x_{t-p} \tag{3.9}$$

It can be proven that, in general, the solution to an inhomogeneous difference equation is given by the sum of the general solution to the homogeneous equation and a particular solution to the inhomogeneous solution.

Homogeneous Difference Equation of Order p

The solution to the homogeneous first order difference equation:

$$x_t = a x_{t-1} \tag{3.10}$$

can be simply written as:

$$x_t = c a^t \tag{3.11}$$

Where c is a constant $c \neq 0$. We can assume that the solution to the homogeneous difference equation of order p can be written as: $x_t = c \lambda^t$ and write:

$$c \lambda^t = a_1 c \lambda^{t-1} + a_2 c \lambda^{t-2} + ... + a_p c \lambda^{t-p} \tag{3.12}$$

Since we already assumed that $c \neq 0$ we can divide the above equation by c and then by λ^t. Denoting $y = 1/\lambda$, we get:

$$1 - a_1 y + a_2 y^2 + ... + a_p y^p = 0 \tag{3.13}$$

This equation is known as characteristic equation of the homogeneous equation. Following the Fundamental Theorem of Algebra, this equation has p roots, denoted by $y_1, ..., y_p$, to each y corresponding a λ denoted by $\lambda_1, ..., \lambda_p$.

There are two cases that allow for a further discussion of the solution: distinct roots and multiple roots. In the former case, the set $\lambda_1^t, ..., \lambda_p^t$ is a fundamental set of solutions. In other words, the solution to the homogeneous equation can be written as:

$$x_t = c_1 \lambda_1^t + c_2 \lambda_2^t + ... + c_p \lambda_p^t \tag{3.14}$$

When there are multiple roots, for this particular case, we can assume that the distinct roots are denoted by the set $y_1, ..., y_r$, where $r < p$. Denoting their multiplicities by $m_1, ..., m_r$, following [5], we can rewrite the initial equation using the lag operators as follows:

$$(1 - a_1 L + a_2 L^2 + ... + a_p L^p) x_t = (1 - \lambda_1 L)^{m_1} (1 - \lambda_2 L)^{m_2} ... (1 - \lambda_r L)^{m_r} X_t = 0 \tag{3.15}$$

As stated before, λ_i with $1 \leq i \leq r$ verify the relationship $\lambda_i = 1/y_i$.

If ψ_t is a solution to the equation:

$$(1 - \lambda_i L)^{m_i} \psi_t = 0 \tag{3.16}$$

Then it is a solution to the original equation (3.15). Furthermore, it can be shown that the sets G_i given by $G_i = \{\lambda_i^t, t\lambda_i^t, ..., t^{m_i-1}\lambda_i^t\}$ are also a solution to Eq. (3.16). Furthermore, the union of these sets, i.e. $G = \bigcup_{i=1}^{r} G_i$ is actually a fundamental set of solutions to the homogeneous difference equation in (3.16). In the end, the solution to the homogeneous difference equation when multiple roots are present can be written as:

$$x_t = \sum_{i=1}^{r} (c_{i,0} + c_{i,1} t + c_{i,2} t^2 + ... + c_{i,m_i-1} t^{m_i-1}) \lambda_i^t \tag{3.17}$$

Non-Homogeneous Difference Equation of Order p

For this case of non-homogeneous equations, we can write the solution as the sum of the general solution of the homogeneous difference equation of order p and a particular solution to the homogeneous solution, in other words, we can write:

$$x_t = x_t^g + x_t^p \tag{3.18}$$

The general solution to the non-homogeneous difference equation can be found by solving for the homogeneous difference equation of order p, as seen above. To find a particular solution to the non-homogeneous we may follow the approaches already discussed for the one-dimensional difference equations. We can use the steady state solution, provided that the difference equation is autonomous. If it is not autonomous, i.e. the sequence z_t is time-varying, we may still find a particular solution either by backward iteration or by forward iteration.

Characterizing the Solutions to Higher Order Difference Equations

To better understand the behavior of the solutions for difference equations of order p, I focus on the second order difference equations. This is the simplest higher order difference equation and, additionally, it can be found in many simple macroeconomic models (e.g., the accelerator model).

The baseline non-autonomous second order difference equation can be written as:

$$x_{t+2} = ax_{t+1} + bx_t + cz_t \tag{3.19}$$

Again, z_t is an exogenous sequence of real values that is bounded.

Applying the operator lag, we may rewrite the equation as

$$(L^{-2} - aL^{-1} - b)x_t = cz_t \tag{3.20}$$

This equation has the following characteristic equation:

$$\lambda^2 - a\lambda - b = 0 \tag{3.21}$$

Given the non-homogeneous nature of this difference equation, we rely on writing the solution as the sum of a general solution and a particular solution:

$$x_t = x_t^g + x_t^p \tag{3.22}$$

Here, the particular solution can be derived based on the method of factorization, as outlined by [2]. Namely, Eq. (3.20) can be rewriting by factoring the expression on the left hand side. We get:

$$(L^{-1} - \lambda_1)(L^{-1} - \lambda_2)x_t = cz_t \tag{3.23}$$

Here, λ_1 and λ_2 are the solution to the characteristic equation in (3.21). They may be real or complex and they must satisfy the conditions $\lambda_1 + \lambda_2 = a$ and $\lambda_1\lambda_2 = -b$.

Based on the factorization above, a particular solution can be derived:

$$x_t^p = \frac{cz_t}{(L^{-1} - \lambda_1)(L^{-1} - \lambda_2)} \tag{3.24}$$

To fully characterize the solution, we need to derive the general solution. This can be done by relying on the homogeneous case of the original equation in (3.19). We may rewrite it as:

$$x_{t+2} = ax_{t+1} + bx_t \tag{3.25}$$

We can distinguish between three potential cases.

Real and Distinct Roots: $\lambda_1 \neq \lambda_2$ and $\lambda_1, \lambda_2 \in \mathbb{R}$

In this particular case, the solution to the difference equation is given by:

$$x_t^g = c_1\lambda_1^t + c_2\lambda_2^t \tag{3.26}$$

The coefficients c_1, c_2 are found by using the information provided by the initial value condition and the boundary condition. The values of the roots λ_1, λ_2 will lead to a different qualitative behavior, as follows.

- When both $|\lambda_1| > 1$ and $|\lambda_2| > 1$, the resulting solution is known as **a source**. In this particular case, the solution becomes explosive in time.
- When both $|\lambda_1| < 1$ and $|\lambda_2| < 1$, as seen from the one-dimensional recurrence equation, the solution converges to the stationary point. This particular solution is known in the literature as **a sink**. However the coefficients c_1 and c_2 cannot be uniquely determined except when a boundary condition is provided. If the latter is missing, the solution is said to be indeterminate.
- When $|\lambda_1| < 1$ but $|\lambda_2| > 1$, the solution is a saddle point.

Real but Identical Roots: $\lambda_1 = \lambda_2$ and $\lambda_1, \lambda_2 \in \mathbb{R}$

The solution to the homogeneous difference equation can be written as:

$$x_t^g = (c_1 + tc_2)\lambda_1^t \tag{3.27}$$

The coefficients c_1 and c_2 can be determined by the boundary condition. If the latter condition is not present, the solution is again indeterminate. The solution will be stable when $|\lambda_1| < 1$ (since the two roots are identical).

Complex and Distinct Roots: $\lambda_1 = \lambda_2$ and $\lambda_1, \lambda_2 \in \mathbb{C}$

Since the two roots are complex but distinct, we can write them as: $\lambda_1 = re^{i\theta}$ and $\lambda_2 = re^{-i\theta}$. Thus, the general solution becomes in this case:

$$x_t^g = c_1\lambda_1^t + c_2\lambda_2^t = r^t(c_1 re^{i\theta} + c_2 re^{-i\theta}) \tag{3.28}$$

Again, the coefficients c_1 and c_2 may be determined with the help of the boundary condition. Furthermore, since we are interested in a general solution that is real, we must additionally impose that the numbers $(c_1 + c_2)$ and $(c_1 - c_2)i$ are both real. To see why, we first can observed that the above solution may be further written as:

$$x_t^g = r^t(c_1 e^{i\theta} + c_2 e^{-i\theta}) \tag{3.29}$$
$$= r^t c_1[\cos(\theta t) + i\sin(\theta t)] + r^t c_2[\cos(\theta t) - i\sin(\theta t)] \tag{3.30}$$
$$= r^t(c_1 + c_2)\cos(\theta t) + r^t(c_1 - c_2)i\sin(\theta t) \tag{3.31}$$

If these two conditions are respected, then the general solution may be finally written as:

$$x_t^g = r^t(A\cos(\theta t) + B\cos(\sin t)) \tag{3.32}$$

Here, A and B are two coefficients that are real and are determined using the boundary conditions.

We may further analyze the qualitative behavior of the solution on the basis of the value of the coefficient r. There are three possible cases that are discussed below:

- When $r > 1$, both roots are outside the unit circle. The solution will oscillate, but the oscillations explode in amplitude.
- If $r = 1$, the two roots lie on the unit circle. The solution oscillates, but the amplitude is constant.
- For $r < 1$, both roots lie within the unit circle. The solution is oscillatory in nature, however the amplitude dampens in time.

An Example

As already underlined, deterministic difference equations are usually met within the context of standard Keynesian models. A classical reference is the multiplier-accelerator model due to Samuelson. The model is both illustrative for older style macroeconomics and as an application of higher order difference equations (in this case, a second order difference equation). The presentation follows [5].

We assume a closed economy such that the following income identity applies:

$$Y_t = C_t + I_t + G_t \tag{3.33}$$

The consumption is modeled as depending on the current income:

$$C_t = \alpha + \beta * Y_{t-1} \tag{3.34}$$

Here, it is further assumed that the coefficients α and β respect the following conditions: $0 < \beta < 1$ and $\alpha > 0$. The coefficient β is known in the literature as the marginal propensity towards consumption.

Finally, the investment depend on the change in income as follows:

$$I_t = \gamma * (Y_{t-1} - Y_{t-2}) \tag{3.35}$$

The coefficient γ is assumed to be positive, $\gamma > 0$.

To get a second order difference equation that can be characterized using the techniques developed above, we can the insert the behavioral equations for consumption C_t and investments I_t into the income identity equation. We get:

$$Y_t = (\beta + \gamma)Y_{t-1} - \gamma Y_{t-2} + (\alpha + G_t) \tag{3.36}$$

This is a second order non-autonomous difference equation. To further simplify, we assume constant government expenditures, namely that $G_t = \bar{G}$. This allows us to solve for the steady state:

$$Y^* = (\beta + \gamma)Y^* - \gamma Y^* + \alpha + \bar{G} \tag{3.37}$$

$$\implies Y^* = \frac{\alpha + \bar{G}}{1 - \beta} \tag{3.38}$$

Following the above results about the stability of the stationary point, we should verify:

1. $1 - (\beta + \gamma) + \gamma = 1 - \beta > 0$,
2. $1 + (\beta + \gamma) + \gamma = 1 + \beta + 2\gamma > 0$,
3. $1 - \gamma > 0$.

Since it can be easily checked that the first two conditions are fulfilled, the only condition that needs to be respected too is the third one, namely that the coefficient corresponding to the accelerator, γ, has not a too high value, i.e. $\gamma < 1$.

The inverse of the characteristic roots can be found from:

$$\lambda_{1,2} = \frac{(\beta + \gamma) \pm \sqrt{(\beta + \gamma)^2 - 4\gamma}}{2} \tag{3.39}$$

When the roots are complex, i.e. $(\beta + \gamma)^2 - 4\gamma < 0$, then Y_t will oscillate around its steady state. For real (and distinct) roots, the output initially increases, and afterwards, the initial positive impact fades away gradually.

3.2.4 Deterministic Linear Systems

This section extends the previous discussion about deterministic difference equations to deterministic dynamic systems.

$$Ax_{t+1} = Bx_t + Cz_t \tag{3.40}$$

Here x_t is a vector of real valued endogenous variables, i.e. $x_t \in R$, while z_t is a real valued vector of exogenous variables. A, B and C are matrices.

In the remaining of this section, I detail the solution proposed by Blanchard and Kahn, see [6]. The approach will be further detailed for stochastic dynamic systems in the next section, when alternative methods will be presented too.

It is assumed that the sequence z_t is stable. The stability is understood in the following sense:

Definition 3.1: A sequence z_t is stable if there exists $M > 0$ such that $||z_t||_{max} < M$ for all t, where $||z_t||_{max} = \max_j |x_j|$ for any $z \in \mathbb{R}^n$.

The role of this assumption is to ensure that the solution is nonexplosive. A further imposed solution is that of regularity. We impose that $det(A\alpha - B) \neq 0$ for a certain α. The role of this condition is to make Eq. (3.40) solvable.

There are two cases, which differ in whether the matrix A is singular or not.

A Is not Singular

When the matrix A is not singular, then, following Blanchard and Kahn, we can first rewrite the system as:

$$x_{t+1} = A^{(-1)}Bx_t + A^{(-1)}Cz_t \tag{3.41}$$

It can be shown that the assumption of regularity is always respected, see [3]. We can further define the matrix W as $W = A^{(-1)}B$. If we denote the eigenvalues of W by $\lambda_1, \lambda_2, ..., \lambda_l$, then, according to the Jordan decomposition, there is a matrix P such that we can perform the following decomposition:

$$W = P^{(-1)}JP \tag{3.42}$$

Here, the matrix P is nonsingular while J is a Jordan matrix. We write:

$$J = \begin{bmatrix} J_1 & & & \\ & J_2 & & \\ & & \cdots & \\ & & & J_l \end{bmatrix}, J_i = \begin{bmatrix} \lambda_i & 1 & & \\ & \lambda_i & 1 & \\ & & \cdots & 1 \\ & & & \lambda_i \end{bmatrix}_{m_i \times m_i}$$

Here, the matrices J_i are of dimensions $m_i \times m_i$.

By definition, it is said that an eigenvalue of a matrix is stable when its modulus is less than 1. We say that an eigenvalue is unstable when the modulus has a value larger than 1. In general, the given matrix is said to be stable when all its eigenvalues are stable.

To solve the system, we can further define:

$$x_t^* = P x_t \tag{3.43}$$

$$C^* = P A^{(-1)} C \tag{3.44}$$

Using this new notation, Eq. (3.40) may be rewritten as:

$$x_{t+1}^* = J x_t^* + C^* z_t \tag{3.45}$$

This equation can be solved backwards to yield:

$$x_t^* = J^t x_0^* + \sum_{j=0}^{t-1} J^j C^* z_{t-1-j} \tag{3.46}$$

Here, the matrices J^t and J_i^t are given by:

$$J^t = \begin{bmatrix} J_1^t & & & \\ & J_2^t & & \\ & & \cdots & \\ & & & J_l^t \end{bmatrix}, J_i^t = \begin{bmatrix} \lambda_i^t & t\lambda_i^{t-1} & \frac{t(t-1)}{2}\lambda_i^{t-2} & \cdots \\ & \lambda_i^t & t\lambda_i^{t-1} & \cdots \\ & & \cdots & \\ & & & \lambda_i^t \end{bmatrix}$$

Depending on whether we know the initial value of a variable, we may classify the variables as either predetermined or not-predetermined. The latter type is also known as a jump variable. The classification is widely used and it helps understanding the following key results.

When there are jumps variables, we cannot solve the system backwardly as above, and we need to rely on a different approach. To apply it, we can split the vector x_t of variables into the vector of predetermined variables k_t and the vector of jump variables y_t. Now, the original vector x_t can be rewritten as: $x_t = [k_t', y_t']$. We assume that there is a number of n_y variables in y_t and a number of n_k variables in k_t. Let us further suppose that the number of unstable eigenvalues in W is n_u while the number of stable values is simply n_s. Using this classification, the Jordan matrix can be partitioned as follows:

$$J^t = \begin{bmatrix} J_s & \\ & J_u \end{bmatrix}$$

Here, it is assumed that the eigenvalues of matrix J_s are stable, while the eigenvalues of the J_u matrix are unstable. We can also partition the vector x_t^* and the matrix C^* accordingly as follows:

$$x_t^* = \begin{bmatrix} s_t \\ u_t \end{bmatrix}, C^* = \begin{bmatrix} C_s^* \\ C_u^* \end{bmatrix}$$

Using this newly defined variables, we can rewrite Eq. (3.45) as follows:

$$\begin{bmatrix} s_{t+1} \\ u_{t+1} \end{bmatrix} = \begin{bmatrix} J_s & \\ & J_u \end{bmatrix} \begin{bmatrix} s_t \\ u_t \end{bmatrix} + \begin{bmatrix} C_s^* \\ C_u^* \end{bmatrix} z_t$$

Based on (3.43), we can further write:

$$\begin{bmatrix} s_t \\ u_t \end{bmatrix} = P \begin{bmatrix} k_t \\ y_t \end{bmatrix} = \begin{bmatrix} P_{sk} & P_{sy} \\ P_{uk} & P_{uy} \end{bmatrix} \begin{bmatrix} k_t \\ y_t \end{bmatrix}$$

Defining further $R = P^{-1}$, we rewrite:

$$\begin{bmatrix} k_t \\ y_t \end{bmatrix} = R \begin{bmatrix} s_t \\ u_t \end{bmatrix} = \begin{bmatrix} R_{ks} & R_{ku} \\ R_{ys} & R_{yu} \end{bmatrix} \begin{bmatrix} s_t \\ u_t \end{bmatrix}$$

These equations help us stating the key results in Blanchard-Kahn approach. I provide the theorem without proofs which can be found in the original paper or in [3].

Theorem 3.1: Assuming that the dynamic system fulfills the conditions below:

1. The number of unstable eigenvalues of $W = A^{-1}B$ equals the number of jump variables;
2. The matrix P_{uy} is not singular;
3. The matrix W does not have eigenvalus on the unit circles.

It follows that the dynamic system in (3.40) has a solution that is both stable and unique given the initial values of the predetermined values k_t, i.e. k_0 and any sequence z_t that is stable.

The first two conditions are more known in the literature as the Blanchard Kahn conditions. They are usually presented as (provided that the third condition is already met):

1. The order condition: $n_s = n_k$;
2. The rank condition: the matrix R_{ks} or the matrix P_{uy} is invertible.

A Is Singular

There are quite a few methods to deal with the matrix A being singular: see [7], [8], [9]. I follow here [3] and focus on presenting the key results base on the method proposed by [8]. However, I present both the method by Klein and the method by Sims for stochastic dynamic systems.

Before introducing the key result in Klein's approach, a few definitions are necessary.

Definition 3.2: We say that a scalar $\lambda \in \mathbb{C}$ is a generalized eigenvalue of the matrices (A,B) if there exists a vector $x \in \mathbb{C}^n$ with the property that: $Bx = \lambda Ax$. Conventionally, x is known as the right generalized eigenvector.

We further define $\lambda(A, B)$ to be the set of all the generalized eigenvalues of (A, B). Then, we can introduce the QZ decomposition, also known as the (complex) generalized Schur form.

Theorem 3.2: We assume that the matrices A and B, each of dimension $n \times n$ are regular (see above). Then, it can be proven that there are $n \times n$ unitary matrices of complex numbers Q and Z such that the following conditions are fulfilled:

1. $QAZ = S$ is upper triangular.
2. $QBZ = T$ is upper triangular.
3. s_{ii} and t_{ii} are not at the same time equal to zero, for any i.
4. $\lambda(A, B) = \{t_{ii}/s_{ii} : s_{ii} \neq 0\}$.
5. (s_{ii}, t_{ii}) can be arranged in any order for any $i = 1, .., n$.

We now give the key result in [8]. Assume that S and T and rearranged with the stable eigenvalues n_s first. Further define: $x_t^* = Z^H x_t$ and $Z^H = Z^{-1}$ the conjugate transpose of Z. We partition the model similarly to the method by Blanchard and Kahn:

$$x_t = \begin{bmatrix} k_t \\ y_t \end{bmatrix}, x_t^* = \begin{bmatrix} s_t \\ u_t \end{bmatrix}$$

The matrix Z is partitioned too:

$$Z = \begin{bmatrix} Z_{11} & Z_{12} \\ Z_{21} & Z_{22} \end{bmatrix}$$

The following theorem established under what conditions the solution provided using the Klein's method is both unique and stable.

Theorem 3.3: The following assumptions are made: 1) $n_s = n_k$; 2) Z_{11} is invertible; 3) (A,B) has no generalized eigenvalues that lie on the unit circle. Then, the system in Eq. (3.40) has a solution that is unique and stable, provided an initial condition for the predetermined variables, k_0 and a sequence z_t that is stable.

3.3 STOCHASTIC DIFFERENCE EQUATIONS

In this section, I discuss how to solve for stochastic difference equations. The emphasis is on a step by step approach from simple univariate stochastic difference equations, to stochastic dynamic systems. I introduce the use of expectations operator, and standard solutions for stochastic difference equations models. I also present several key approaches to solve rational expectations models. The section concludes by presenting applications in Julia that solve and simulate basic DSGE models.

3.3.1 Modeling the Rational Expectations

Rational expectations (RE, hereafter) lie at the core of modern macroeconomics. The mainstream DSGE models are basically RE multivariate models. Even if there are other ways to model expectations (i.e. adaptive expectations), RE remains the standard way to treat expectations in quantitative macroeconomic models. The DSGE models in this book are based on the idea of RE and this is why this section introduces to the reader how to model rational expectations.

Although Lucas, see [11], is credited with introducing rational expectations into macroeconomics, the idea can be traced back to an earlier contribution by Muth, see [10]. According to him, rational expectations are equivalent to stating that individuals do not make systematic errors in forming their expectations.

There are various ways to define rational expectations in the modern sense, but in the following parts of this chapter (and book) we will stick to following definition:

Definition 3.3: The expectations of the agents are formed such that, in equilibrium, the objective distribution of the variables coincides with the subjective distribution of the variables, with the later conditioned on the information available to the agents.

Formally, this definition amounts to:

$$x_t^e = E(x_t | \Omega) \tag{3.47}$$

Here, Ω is the available information set. The models in this chapter and book are based on the Markovian property. This implies that the current information set Ω consists in the realization of the stochastic variable in the model in the past from the moment $t = 0$. Formally, we might write that, for any i:

$$E_{t-i}(x_t) = E(x_t | \Omega_{t-i}) \tag{3.48}$$

Here, the information set at $t - i$ gives the past realization of the stochastic variable x_k from 0 to $t - i$, namely:

$$\Omega_{t-i} = \{x_k; k = 0, ..., t - i\} \tag{3.49}$$

An important property of expectations that is very useful in working with stochastic difference equations is the law of iterated expectations:

Proposition 3.1. Law of Iterated Expectations: Assume two information sets, Ω_t and Ω_{t-1} for which $\Omega_{t-1} \subset \Omega_t$. Then, the following relationship holds:

$$E(x_t | \Omega_{t-1}) = E(E(x_t | \Omega_t) | \Omega_{t-1}) \tag{3.50}$$

3.3.2 First-Order Stochastic Linear Equations

Here, I discuss the basic stochastic linear equation, modeled as:

$$E_t(x_{t+1}) = ax_t + bz_t \tag{3.51}$$

It is assumed that a, b are coefficients, while z_t is a bounded process see the definition above.

Depending on whether $|a| > 1$ or not, the solution might be derived using a forward-looking approach or a backward looking approach.

Backward Looking Solutions

This approach applies whenever $|a| < 1$. In this particular case, the original equation in (3.51) might be rewritten as:

$$x_{t+1} = (E_t(x_{t+1})) + (x_{t+1} - E_t(x_{t+1})) = ax_t + bz_t + \eta_{t+1} \tag{3.52}$$

Here η stands for the expectational error and it is given by: $\eta_{t+1} = x_{t+1} - E_t x_{t+1}$, which is a martingale.

The above equation can be iterated backwards to obtain:

$$x_t = a^t x_0 + \sum_{j=0}^{t-1} a^j (bz_{t-j} + \eta_{t-j}) \tag{3.53}$$

Because $|a| < 1$, the solution is stable. In this particular case, since any initial value x_0 is admissible, leading back x_t to its long run solution, the solution is indeterminate. Furthermore, $|\eta_{t-j}|$ is not necessarily correlated with innovations in x_t such that they behave like sunspots, irrespective to fundamental shocks.

Forward Looking Solutions

When $|a| > 1$ the solution is forward in nature. There are different ways to solve for the solution of x_t and we present below the most known ones.

Forward Substitution: This simply consists in iterating the difference equation in (3.51) forward and apply the law of iterated expectations k times to get:

$$x_t = a^{(-1)} E_t x_{t+1} - a^{(-1)} bz_t \tag{3.54}$$

$$= a^{(-1)} E_t(a^{(-1)} E_t x_{t+2} - a^{(-1)} bz_{t+1}) - a^{(-1)} bz_t \tag{3.55}$$

$$= a^{(-2)} E_t x_{t+2} - a^{(-1)} bz_t - a^{(-2)} bE_t z_{t+1} \tag{3.56}$$

$$= \dots \tag{3.57}$$

$$= a^{(-k-1)} E_t x_{t+k+1} - a^{(-1)} \sum_{j=0}^{k} a^{(-j)} bE_t z_{t+j} \tag{3.58}$$

Taking the limit $\lim_{k\to\infty}$, the solution can be written as follows:

$$x_t = \lim_{k\to\infty} a^{(-k-1)} E_t x_{t+k+1} - \lim_{k\to\infty} a^{(-1)} \sum_{j=0}^{k} a^{(-j)} bE_t z_{t+j} \tag{3.59}$$

In this case, since $|a| > 1$, the solution is again stable. Imposing $\lim_{k\to\infty} a^{(-k-1)} E_t x_{t+k+1} = 0$, the solution becomes:

$$x_t = -a^{(-1)} \sum_{j=0}^{\infty} a^{(-j)} bE_t z_{t+j} \tag{3.60}$$

This implies that x_t is the sum of the discounted sum of the future expected value of z_t.

Factorization: This approach exploits the lag operator which was already introduced in the deterministic difference equation section. In the case of stochastic equations, we may write:

$$L^j x_t = x_{t-j} \tag{3.61}$$

$$L^j E_t x_{t+i} = E_t x_{t+i-j} \qquad (3.62)$$

$$L^{(-j)} x_t = E_t x_{t+j} \qquad (3.63)$$

The above properties imply that the lag operator shifts the variable x_t but not the expectation operator E_t. Using these properties, we can rewrite the original stochastic difference equation:

$$E_t(x_{t+1}) = ax_t + bz_t \qquad (3.64)$$

as:

$$(L^{(-1)} - a)x_t = bz_t \qquad (3.65)$$

This is solvable using the forward substitution as:

$$x = \frac{bz_t}{(L^{(-1)} - a)} = \frac{-bz_t}{a(1 - a^{(-1)}L^{(-1)})} \qquad (3.66)$$

$$= -b \sum_{j=0}^{\infty} a^{(-j-1)} L^{(-j)} z_t \qquad (3.67)$$

$$= -b \sum_{j=0}^{\infty} a^{(-j-1)} E_t z_{t+j} \qquad (3.68)$$

Given that the sequence z_t is bounded, while $|a| > 1$, the solution is stationary.

The Method of Undetermined Coefficients: This method is widely used in economics in solving both scalar stochastic difference equations and stochastic dynamic systems. The method implies making an (educated) guess about the form of the solution and solve for the undetermined coefficients using the resulting equations.

In the particular case of the stochastic difference equation presented before, we may guess the following solution:

$$x_t = \sum_{j=0}^{\infty} c_j E_t z_{t+j} \qquad (3.69)$$

and use it in the initial stochastic difference equation. We get:

$$E_t(\sum_{j=0}^{\infty} c_j E_t z_{t+j+1}) = a \sum_{j=0}^{\infty} c_j E_t z_{t+j} + bz_t \qquad (3.70)$$

We may solve now for the undetermined coefficients by solving for the coefficients a_i such that they solve for the above equation:

$$j = 0 : c_0 = -b * a^{(-1)} \qquad (3.71)$$

$$j = 1 : c_1 = a^{(-1)} c_0 \qquad (3.72)$$

$$j = 2 : c_2 = a^{(-1)} c_1 \qquad (3.73)$$

Thus, the solution implied by the method of undetermined coefficients becomes identical to the previous forward looking solutions:

$$x_t = -b \sum_{j=0}^{\infty} a^{(-j-1)} E_t z_{t+j} \qquad (3.74)$$

That is, the current value of x_t equals the sum of the expected value of the discounted future shocks in the exogenous series z_t.

3.3.3 Multivariate Linear Rational Expectations Models

The main of this chapter is to introduce methods to solve and simulate Linear Rational Expectations (RE) models. Most of the mainstream DSGE models fall into this category and this section will outline some of the most used ways to solve such models. The previous sections on deterministic difference equations and uni-dimensional stochastic equations serve only as an introduction to what is actually the main topic of this chapter. This section draws mostly from [2], [3] and [4].

Since this chapter deals with stochastic processes, a few definitions are necessary. We work in a probability space $(\Omega, \mathcal{F}, \mathcal{P})$. Here, Ω is the sample space, $\mathcal{P}$ is a probability measure and $\mathcal{F}$ is a filtration. The latter is defined formally as modeling $\{F\}_{t \geq 0}$ as an increasing sequence of σ-algebras (see the section on measure theory in Chapter 4). We write: $\mathcal{F}_0 \subset \mathcal{F}_1 \subset \ldots \mathcal{F}$. We define a stochastic process $\{X_t\}_{t \geq 0}$ with a given state space X as a sequence of random variables on the state space X. $\{X_t\}$ is said to be adapted to the filtration $\{\mathcal{F}_t\}$ if X is measurable with respect to $\{\mathcal{F}_t\}$ for $t = 0, 1, \ldots$ (see again Chapter 4 on measure theory). A filtration $\{\mathcal{F}_t\}$ is interpreted from an economic point of view as the information set available at time t.

Similarly to the first order stochastic difference equation, a multivariate RE can be written as:

$$A E_t(x_{t+1}) = B x_t + C z_t \tag{3.75}$$

Here, x_t has become a $n \times 1$ random vector. Since this is a multivariate model, A and B are matrices of coefficients of dimension $n \times n$, while C is a matrix of dimension $n \times n_z$. Furthermore z_t is a stochastic process of dimension $n_z \times 1$. We assume that the stochastic process can be written as an AR(1) process. This is actually in line with the usual way the exogenous processes are modeled in empirical DSGE modeling. Formally, we can write:

$$(z_{t+1}) = \Phi z_t + \Sigma \epsilon_{t+1} \tag{3.76}$$

It is assumed that the initial value of the stochastic process, i.e. z_0 is known, while Φ is a matrix of dimension $n_z \times n_z$, while Σ is a matrix of dimensions $n_z \times n_\epsilon$. Finally, ϵ_t is a stochastic process that verifies:

$$E_t \epsilon_{t+1} = 0 \text{ and } E_t \epsilon_{t+1} \epsilon'_{t+1} = 0.$$

Using the standard notation, I is the identity matrix. It is further assumed, similarly to the unidimensional case, that the z_t process is stable. In the multivariate case, this is can be formulated as follows:

Definition 3.3: We say that a stochastic process z_t is stable whenever there is a $M > 0$ such that $||z_t||_{max} < M$ for all t, where $||x||_{max} = \max_j E|x_j|$ for any random variable $z_t \in \mathbb{R}^n$.

We focus on presenting three of the most widely used methods to solve RE models as proposed by: Blanchard and Kahn, see [6], Klein, see [8] and Sims, see [7]. While they all propose solutions to the RE model in (3.75), they differ in the way they address two essential issues: whether the matrix A is singular and how the predetermined variables are treated.

3.3.4 The Blanchard-Kahn Approach

There are two key characteristics of this approach: the matrix A is assumed to be nonsingular. Furthermore, according to the method they proposed a variable is classified as predetermined when it satisfies the following definition.

Definition 3.4: We say that a stochastic process $\{x_t\}_{t \geq 0}$ is predetermined if two conditions are met: x_0 is given and x_{t+1} is measurable with respect to $\mathcal{F}_t$, where $\mathcal{F}_t$ is defined as a filtration. The second condition can be formally written as: $E[x_{t+1}|\mathcal{F}_t] = x_{t+1}$.

Following the results for the deterministic case, we can split again the vector x_t into a sub-vector y_t of non-predetermined variables of dimension n_y and a sub-vector k_t of predetermined variables of dimension $n - n_y$. Thus we would write: $x_t = [k'_t, y'_t]$.

Assuming that there are a number of n_u unstable eigenvalues and a number of $n_s = n - n_u$ stable eigenvalues, following the results for the deterministic case, we may formally write a forward looking solution as follows:

$$u_t = -J_u^{(-1)}(I - L^{(-1)} J^{(-1)})^{(-1)} C_u^* z_t = \tag{3.77}$$

$$-\sum_{j=0}^{\infty} J_u^{(-j-1)} C_u^* E_t z_{t+j} \tag{3.78}$$

3.3.5 The Klein Approach

We have already seen the basics of the approach proposed by Klein for the case of deterministic dynamic systems. In contrast to the method by Blanchard and Kahn, Klein's method applies to the case when the matrix A is singular. The second difference relative to the approach by Blanchard and Kahn is in the way the predetermined variables are treated. However, a few additional definitions are necessary before doing this.

Definition 3.5: Let us consider a stochastic process x_t. If the condition: $E_t x_{t+1} = x_t$ for all $t \geq 0$ holds then this process is said to be a martingale. If the condition: $E_t x_{t+1} = 0$ holds, then the process is martingale difference.

Definition 3.6: We say that a stochastic process x_t is white noise if the following conditions are met:

1. $E_t[x_t] = 0$
2. $E_t[x_t x_s'] = \begin{cases} 0 & s \neq t \\ \Sigma & s = t \end{cases}$

The following definition elucidates why the use of predetermined variables in Klein's method is more general the one in the approach by Blanchard and Klein.

Definition 3.7: Given a stochastic process x_t, we say that it is predetermined (or backward-looking) if the following conditions are met:

1. The prediction error $\xi_t = x_{t+1} - E_t x_{t+1}$ is a martingale difference which is exogenously given;
2. The initial value x_0 is measurable with respect to the filtration $\mathcal{F}_0$ and it is exogenously given too.

When $\xi_{t+1} = 0$, the definition coincides with the definition used by Blanchard and Kahn. Assuming that the set of variables k_t is predetermined following the above definition, and that the prediction error ξ_t is exogenously given, it can be shown that the solution to the model can be written as:

$$y_t = A_{yk} k_t + A_{yz} z_t \tag{3.79}$$

$$k_{t+1} = A_{kk} k_t + A_{kz} z_t + \xi_{t+1} \tag{3.80}$$

Here, it is assumed that k_0, z_0 are given. More details can be found in [8] or [3].

3.3.6 The Sims Approach

In contrast to the other two approaches, Sims uses the following representation of the RE model:

$$\Gamma_0 y_t = \Gamma_1 y_{t-1} + C + \Psi z_t + \Pi \eta_t \tag{3.81}$$

Here, y_t is a random vector of dimension $n \times 1$, z_t is a random vector of dimension $n_z \times 1$ and it is also exogenously given, while η_t is a vector of dimension $m \times 1$ consisting in endogenously determined prediction errors. The latter ones are assumed to satisfy the equation: $E_t \eta_{t+1} = 0$. Γ_0, Γ_1 are matrices of coefficients of dimensions $n \times n$, C is a constant vector with dimensions $n \times 1$, Ψ is a $n \times n_z$ matrix and Π a matrix of dimensions $n \times m$.

The representation above can be simplified conveniently by assuming that the matrix $C = 0$, if we use change of variables, and that z_t is serially correlated such that z_t is appended to y_t and replaced by a process ϵ_t. With these assumptions, the system becomes:

$$\Gamma_0 y_t = \Gamma_1 y_{t-1} + \Psi \epsilon_t + \Pi \eta_t \tag{3.82}$$

Here, $E_t \epsilon_{t+1} = 0$.

As in the method proposed by Klein, Sims' approach allows for a singular matrix A which, in his notation, is given by Γ_0. However, what really differentiates this approach is that the method does not distinct between predetermined and jump variables. Instead Sims imposes that the model determines endogenously a linear combination of variables that are predetermined. He also assumes that all variables at moment t are also observable at time t.

The method proposed by Sims is also based on the generalized Schur decomposition. Here, we apply it matrices (Γ_0, Γ_1) which are assumed to be regular. According to the generalized Schur Decomposition, there are unitary complex matrices Q, Z as well as upper triangular matrices S, T such that the following relationships hold: $Q\Gamma_0 Z = S$ and $Q\Gamma_1 Z = T$.

We can order again the matrices S, T with the n_s stable eigenvalues first, and the n_u unstable eigenvalues last. We further define $y^* = Z^H y_t$ and use the following partition for it:

$$y_t^* = \begin{bmatrix} s_t \\ u_t \end{bmatrix}$$

If we make use of the transformation of y_t as well as the Schur decomposition, we multiply by the matrix Q and get:

$$S y_t^* = T y_{t-1}^* + Q(\Psi \epsilon_t + \Pi \eta_t) \tag{3.83}$$

Since the matrices S, T are upper triangular, we can partition them conveniently as follows:

$$\begin{bmatrix} S_{11} & S_{12} \\ 0 & S_{22} \end{bmatrix} \begin{bmatrix} s_t \\ u_t \end{bmatrix} = \begin{bmatrix} T_{11} & T_{12} \\ 0 & T_{22} \end{bmatrix} \begin{bmatrix} s_{t-1} \\ u_{t-1} \end{bmatrix} + \begin{bmatrix} Q_{1.} \\ Q_{2.} \end{bmatrix} (\Psi \epsilon_t + \Pi_t \eta_t) \tag{3.84}$$

Here, Q is partitioned using the same convention as for the matrices S, T: $Q_{1.}$ contains the first n_s rows from Q, while $Q_{2.}$ the last n_u rows. Given the unstable nature of u_t, we can solve for it by a forward-looking solution to get:

$$u_t = -T_{22}^{-1} \sum_{j=1}^{\infty} [T_{22}^{-1} S_{22}]^j Q_{2.} (\Psi \epsilon_{t+j} + \Pi \eta_{t+j}) \tag{3.85}$$

When we apply the expectations operator to the process u_t we get that: $E_t u_t = u_t = 0$. This can be further exploited when we extend the partition of y_t^* to:

$$y_t^* = \begin{bmatrix} s_t \\ u_t \end{bmatrix} = \begin{bmatrix} Z_1^H \\ Z_2^H \end{bmatrix} y_t$$

Given the expected value of u_t, this also implies $Z_2^H y_t = 0$, thus providing an initial value for y_t. Additionally, we also get:

$$Q_{2.}(\Psi \epsilon_{t+j} + \Pi \eta_{t+j}) = 0 \tag{3.86}$$

To advance with the solution, we also need to solve for the process η_t in terms of the exogenous shocks ϵ_t. We can use the following proposition:

Proposition 3.1: Given a series of exogenous shocks ϵ_t, there is always a process η_t, with $\eta_t \in \mathbb{R}$, that satisfies the equation above if and only if there is a matrix Λ of dimensions $m \times n_z$ such that the following relationship is verified: $Q_{2.} \Psi = Q_{2.} \Pi \Lambda$.

This proposition implies that, in order to solve for the relationship (3.86), we must make the following assumption:

Assumption 3.1: There is a matrix Λ of dimensions $m \times n_z$, such that $Q_{2.} \Psi = Q_{2.} \Pi \Lambda$. In other words, it must hold that the column space of $Q2.\Psi$ is contained in that of $Q_{2.} \Pi$.

While this assumption ensures that we can find a solution, we also need to impose an additional assumption in order to have a unique solution.

Assumption 3.2: There is a matrix Ξ of dimensions $n_s \times n_u$ so that the following relationship is verified: $Q_{1.} \Pi = \Xi Q_{2.} \Pi$.

We can premultiply Eq. (3.84) with $[I - \Xi]$ and get:

$$\begin{bmatrix} S_{11} & S_{12} - \Xi S_{22} \\ 0 & I \end{bmatrix} \begin{bmatrix} s_t \\ u_t \end{bmatrix} = \begin{bmatrix} T_{11} & T_{12} - \Xi T_{22} \\ 0 & 0 \end{bmatrix} \begin{bmatrix} s_{t-1} \\ u_{t-1} \end{bmatrix} + \begin{bmatrix} Q_{1.} - \Xi Q_{2.} \\ 0 \end{bmatrix} (\Psi \epsilon_t + \Pi_t \eta_t) \tag{3.87}$$

Premultiplying matrices of dimensions 2×2 with a vector of matrix of dimensions 2×1 would result in matrices of dimensions 2×1. However, the lower block is also appended such that we include in the above equation $u_t = 0$. The last term of the above equation can be simplified further by taking into account the second assumption. The equation becomes:

$$\begin{bmatrix} S_{11} & S_{12} - \Xi S_{22} \\ 0 & I \end{bmatrix} \begin{bmatrix} s_t \\ u_t \end{bmatrix} = \begin{bmatrix} T_{11} & T_{12} - \Xi T_{22} \\ 0 & 0 \end{bmatrix} \begin{bmatrix} s_{t-1} \\ u_{t-1} \end{bmatrix} + \begin{bmatrix} Q_{1.} - \Xi Q_{2.} \\ 0 \end{bmatrix} (\Psi \epsilon_t) \tag{3.88}$$

To derive a solution for this equation, we use the fact that $y_t = Zy_t^*$ and solve to get a solution that is also a solution to the original representation in (3.82):

$$y_t = \Theta_1 y_{t-1} + \Theta_2 \epsilon_t \tag{3.89}$$

Here, the matrices Θ_1, Θ_2 are written as follows:

$$\Theta_1 = Z \begin{bmatrix} S_{11} & S_{12} - \Xi S_{22} \\ 0 & I \end{bmatrix}^{-1} \begin{bmatrix} T_{11} & T_{12} - \Xi T_{22} \\ 0 & 0 \end{bmatrix} Z^H, \tag{3.90}$$

$$\Theta_2 = Z \begin{bmatrix} S_{11} & S_{12} - \Xi S_{22} \\ 0 & I \end{bmatrix} \begin{bmatrix} Q_{1.} & -\Xi Q_{2.} \\ 0 & 0 \end{bmatrix}^{-1} \Psi \tag{3.91}$$

We can extract the main results of the Sims' approach using the following theorem:

Theorem 3.4: If Assumptions 3.1 and 3.2 hold, then this is a necessary and sufficient condition that the solution to Eq. (3.82) exists and is unique.

3.4 APPLICATIONS IN JULIA

This section introduces two of the reference DSGE models: the real business cycle model and the New Keynesian model. I present the two models, and then implement them in Julia. I also discuss Julia libraries that specifically deal with solving and simulating DSGE models, even estimating them.

3.4.1 A Real Business Cycle Model

I start by presenting a canonical real business cycles (RBC, hereafter) model following [4]. The aims of this part is to present one of the reference DSGE models, to introduce linearization techniques and to solve and simulate the model in Julia.

The RBC model is a closed economy model where there a large number of infinitely living identical households and firms. Households maximize their lifetime utility given by:

$$E_t \sum_{t=0}^{\infty} \beta^t log(c_t) - \gamma \frac{h_t^{1+\psi}}{1+\psi} \tag{3.92}$$

The household chooses optimally the consumption c_t and the hours worked h_t. Here, the parameter β stands for the discount parameter.

The household faces the following budget constraint:

$$y_t = c_t + i_t \tag{3.93}$$

The representative firm produces a homogeneous final good that is consumed or invested. The firms own the capital stock and they hire labor services from household. The technology of the representative firm is characterized by the following Cobb-Douglas production function:

$$y_t = a_t k_t^{\alpha} h_t^{1-\alpha} \tag{3.94}$$

Here α is the capital share while a_t is the total factor productivity. It is further assumed that the total factor productivity evolves according to an AR(1) process:

$$log(a_t) = (1 - \rho)log(\bar{a}) + \rho log(a_{t-1}) + \epsilon_t \tag{3.95}$$

Here, ϵ_t is assumed to be normally distributed with mean zero and standard deviation σ.

Finally, the capital stock follows:

$$k_{t+1} = (1 - \delta)k_t + i_t \tag{3.96}$$

Here, the parameter δ stands for the depreciation rate.

Solution

Solving from the perspective of a central planner, we get the following first order conditions (after combining the capital stock dynamics with the resource constraint):

$$\gamma h_t^{\psi} c_t = (1 - \alpha)\frac{y_t}{h_t} \tag{3.97}$$

$$y_t = a_t k_t^{\alpha} h_t^{1-\alpha} \tag{3.98}$$

$$y_t = c_t + i_t \tag{3.99}$$

$$k_{t+1} = i_t + (1 - \delta)k_t \tag{3.100}$$

$$1 = \beta E_t(\frac{c_t}{c_{t+1}}(\alpha\frac{y_{t+1}}{k_{t+1}} + 1 - \delta)) \tag{3.101}$$

There are solution methods that specifically deal with nonlinear models like this one, however, the focus of this chapter lies on linear systems. Before linearizing the model, we must however determine the steady state of the model.

Deterministic Steady State

We compute here the deterministic steady state of the model. The steady state $\bar{x}$ of a variable x_t is such that $x_t = \bar{x}$ for all the values of t. We can write the steady state of the RBC model as:

$$\gamma \bar{h}^{\psi} \bar{c} = (1 - \alpha)\frac{\bar{y}}{\bar{h}} \tag{3.102}$$

$$\bar{y} = \bar{a}\bar{k}^{\alpha}\bar{h}^{1-\alpha} \tag{3.103}$$

$$\bar{y} = \bar{c} + \bar{i} \tag{3.104}$$

$$\bar{k} = \bar{i} + (1 - \delta)\bar{k} \tag{3.105}$$

$$1 = \beta((\alpha\frac{\bar{y}}{\bar{k}} + 1 - \delta)) \tag{3.106}$$

We use the above equations to determine the steady state values for the individual variables. Using the steady state formula for the capital stock process we get:

$$\bar{i} = \delta\bar{k} \tag{3.107}$$

$$\frac{\bar{i}}{\bar{y}} = \delta\frac{\bar{k}}{\bar{y}} \tag{3.108}$$

Using this relationship, we can rewrite Eq. (3.106) as:

$$\frac{\bar{y}}{\bar{k}} = \frac{1 - \beta(1 - \delta)}{\alpha\beta} \tag{3.109}$$

Combining the last two equations, we get:

$$\frac{\bar{i}}{\bar{y}} = \frac{\alpha\beta\delta}{1 - \beta(1 - \delta)} \tag{3.110}$$

Using the resource constraint, we may also write:

$$\frac{\bar{c}}{\bar{y}} = 1 - \frac{\bar{i}}{\bar{y}} \tag{3.111}$$

Using this, we can derive the steady state value for hours worked:

$$\bar{h} = (\frac{1 - \alpha}{\gamma(1 - \bar{i}/\bar{y})})^{\frac{1}{1+\psi}} \tag{3.112}$$

Using the state output to capital stock share and the steady state value of hours worked, we can compute now the steady state value of output as:

$$\bar{y} = \bar{a}\left(\frac{\alpha\beta}{1 - \beta(1 - \delta)}\right)^{\frac{\alpha}{1-\alpha}} \tag{3.113}$$

Using the shares $\bar{y}/\bar{k}$, $\bar{i}/\bar{y}$ and $\bar{c}/\bar{y}$, we can determine how the steady state value of the other variables too.

Linearization

In Section 2.4.2 of the 2nd chapter, I introduced the idea of local approximation in the context of doing function approximation. However, I delayed a more extensive discussion until here, in order to introduce it in a more convenient framework, that of linearizing macroeconomic models. Linearizing a macroeconomic model leads to a reasonable approximation provided that the model is not too far away from the steady state.

There are basically two ways to deal with linearizing a nonlinear macroeconomic model: one based on the Taylor expansion, and a second one due to Uhlig, see [13]. A good source presenting comparatively both methods is [12]. I follow mostly the latter in presenting the two approaches.

A Taylor Expansion Approach: Assume that an equation of a given model can be written as follows:

$$f(x_t) = \frac{g(x_t)}{h(x_t)} \tag{3.114}$$

We can first apply the natural logarithm and get:

$$ln(f(x_t)) = ln(g(x_t)) - ln(h(x_t)) \tag{3.115}$$

We can apply to this last expression a first order Taylor expansion and get:

$$ln(f(\bar{x})) + \frac{f'(\bar{x})}{f(\bar{x}}(x_t - \bar{x}) \approx ln(g(\bar{x})) + \frac{g'(\bar{x})}{g(\bar{x})}(x_t - \bar{x}) - ln(h(\bar{x})) - \frac{h'(\bar{x})}{h(\bar{x}}(x_t - \bar{x}) \tag{3.116}$$

What we obtained is a linear approximation of the initial equation (3.114). It must be noted that the fractions $\frac{f'(\bar{x})}{f(\bar{x})}$ and so on are linear since they involve only constants. We also know that, in steady state, it holds that:

$$ln(f(\bar{x})) = ln(g(\bar{x})) - ln(h(\bar{x})) \tag{3.117}$$

Then, we get the final linearized version of the initial equation.

$$\frac{f'(\bar{x})}{f(\bar{x}}(x_t - \bar{x}) \approx \frac{g'(\bar{x})}{g(\bar{x})}(x_t - \bar{x}) - \frac{h'(\bar{x})}{h(\bar{x}}(x_t - \bar{x}) \tag{3.118}$$

Uhlig's Approach: In contrast to the above approach based on Taylor's rule and differentiation, Uhlig's method is much simpler, involving a set of simple rules. We define first the log-difference of a variable from its equilibrium value as:

$$\tilde{x}_t = ln(x_t) - ln(\bar{x}) \tag{3.119}$$

Uhlig showed that a variable x_t can be written as $x_t = \bar{x}e^{\tilde{x}_t}$. Below, I present the demonstration:

$$x_t = \bar{x}\frac{x_t}{\bar{x}} = \bar{x}e^{ln\frac{x_t}{\bar{x}}} = \bar{x}e^{lnx_t - ln\bar{x}} = \bar{x}e^{\tilde{x}_t} \tag{3.120}$$

Uhlig's method basically consists in writing each variable x_t in its equivalent form $x_t = \bar{x}e^{\tilde{x}_t}$ and then applying a few basic rules, namely:

$$e^{\tilde{x}_t + a\tilde{y}} \approx 1 + \tilde{x}_t + a\tilde{y}_t \tag{3.121}$$

$$\tilde{x}_t \tilde{y}_t \approx 0 \tag{3.122}$$

$$E_t[ae^{\tilde{x}_{t+1}}] \approx a + aE_t[\tilde{x}_{t+1}] \tag{3.123}$$

An Application: I present below the log-linearization of one of the equations in the RBC model above, the production function, see Eq. (3.98). I write the equation again below:

$$y_t = a_t k_t^{\alpha} h_t^{1-\alpha} \tag{3.124}$$

We apply the natural logarithm function to get:

$$ln(y_t) = ln(a_t) + \alpha ln(k_t) + (1-\alpha)ln(h_t) \tag{3.125}$$

We can use now a first order Taylor expansions and obtain:

$$ln(\bar{y}) + \frac{1}{\bar{y}}(y_t - \bar{y}) \approx ln(\bar{a}) + \frac{1}{\bar{a}}(a_t - \bar{a}) +$$
$$\alpha ln(\bar{k}) + \alpha \frac{1}{\bar{k}}(k_t - \bar{k}) + (1-\alpha)ln(\bar{h}) + (1-\alpha)\frac{1}{\bar{h}}(h_t - \bar{h}) \tag{3.126}$$

Again, as in the theoretical exposition, the variables in steady state cancel each other since it holds that:

$$ln(\bar{y}) = ln(\bar{a}) + \alpha ln(\bar{k}) + (1-\alpha)ln(\bar{h}) \tag{3.127}$$

We finally get:

$$\frac{1}{\bar{y}}(y_t - \bar{y}) \approx \frac{1}{\bar{a}}(a_t - \bar{a}) + \alpha\frac{1}{\bar{k}}(k_t - \bar{k}) + (1-\alpha)\frac{1}{\bar{h}}(h_t - \bar{h}) \tag{3.128}$$

Which can be further simplified to:

$$\frac{1}{\bar{y}} + 1 \approx \frac{a_t}{\bar{a}} + \alpha\frac{k_t}{\bar{k}} + (1-\alpha)\frac{h_t}{\bar{h}} \tag{3.129}$$

We can also apply the Uhlig's approach to log-linearize the model. We start again from the same specification of the production function. For each variable x_t, we replace it with $x_t = \bar{x}e^{\tilde{x}_t}$. The equation becomes now:

$$\bar{y}e^{\tilde{y}_t} = \bar{a}\bar{k}^{\alpha}\bar{h}^{1-\alpha}e^{\tilde{a}+\alpha\tilde{k}+(1-\alpha)\tilde{h}} \tag{3.130}$$

This can be further approximated using Uhlig's rules to:

$$\bar{y}(1 + \tilde{y}_t) = \bar{a}\bar{k}^{\alpha}\bar{h}^{1-\alpha}(1 + \tilde{a}_t + \alpha\tilde{k}_t + (1-\alpha)\tilde{h}_t) \tag{3.131}$$

We can now use the equation in steady state: $\bar{y} = \bar{a}\bar{k}^{\alpha}\bar{h}^{1-\alpha}$. We finally get:

$$\tilde{y}_t = \tilde{a}_t + \alpha\tilde{k}_t + (1-\alpha)\tilde{h}_t \tag{3.132}$$

This is equivalent to the first log-linearization, provided that one makes the transformation: $x_t \approx \bar{x}(1 + \tilde{x})$.

The Log-Linearized Model

I present below the fully log-linearized model:

$$(1 + \psi)\tilde{h}_t + \tilde{c}_t - \tilde{y}_t = 0 \tag{3.133}$$

$$\tilde{y}_t - (1-\alpha)\tilde{h}_t - \alpha\tilde{k}_t - \tilde{a}_t = 0 \tag{3.134}$$

$$\tilde{y}_t = \frac{\bar{c}}{\bar{y}}\tilde{c}_t + \frac{\bar{i}}{\bar{y}}\tilde{i}_t \tag{3.135}$$

$$\tilde{k}_{t+1} = \delta\tilde{i}_t + (1-\delta)\tilde{k}_t \tag{3.136}$$

$$E_t\tilde{c}_{t+1} = \tilde{c}_t + (1 - \beta(1-\delta))(E_t\tilde{y}_{t+1} - E_t\tilde{k}_{t+1}) \tag{3.137}$$

$$\tilde{a}_t = \rho\tilde{a}_{t-1} + \tilde{\epsilon}_t \tag{3.138}$$

Julia Code

Below, I present the code for solving and simulating the RBC model in Julia. The code is uses Sim's approach for solving it. I follow the implementation in [4]. I group first the variables into two sets, $y_t = \{\tilde{k}_{t+1}, \tilde{a}_t, E_t \tilde{c}_{t+1}\}$ and $x_t = \{\tilde{y}, \tilde{c}_t, \tilde{i}_t, \tilde{h}_t\}$. Using these definitions, we can write the system as a set of two equations, with the first one grouping the static equations and the second one collecting the dynamics ones, as seen below:

$$\Gamma_x x_t = \Gamma_y y_{t-1} + \Gamma_\epsilon \epsilon_t + \Gamma_\eta \eta_t$$
$$\Gamma_y^0 y_t + \Gamma_x^0 E_t x_{t+1} = \Gamma_y^1 y_{t-1} + \Gamma_x^1 x_t + \Gamma_\epsilon \epsilon_t + \Gamma_\eta \eta_t \tag{3.139}$$

Using the first equation, we can solve for x_t and get:

$$x_t = \Pi_y y_{t-1} + \Pi_\epsilon \epsilon_t + \Pi_\eta \eta_t \tag{3.140}$$

Here, I denote through $\Pi_j = (\Gamma_x)^{-1} \Gamma_j$, with $j = \{y, \epsilon, \eta\}$. We also know that the expected value of the errors is zero, that is $E_t \epsilon_{t+1} = E_t \eta_{t+1}$ which implies that the above equation can be written as $E_t x_{t+1} = \Pi_y y_t$. We can thus rewrite the second equation now as:

$$A_0 y_t = A_1 y_{t+1} + B \epsilon_t + C \eta_t \tag{3.141}$$

Here, the coefficient matrices are defined as follows: $A_0 = \Gamma_y^0 + \Gamma_x^0 \Pi_y$, $A_1 = \Gamma_y^1 + \Gamma_x^1 \Pi_y$, $B = \Gamma_\epsilon + \Gamma_x^1 \Pi_\epsilon$ and $C = \Gamma_\eta + \Gamma_x^1 \Pi_\eta$. We can also write the expectations errors η_t using the fundamental shocks ϵ_t, see [4] for details, namely:

$$\eta_t = -V_1 D_{11}^{-1} U_1' Q_2 B \epsilon_t \tag{3.142}$$

I first show the code to solve for the RBC using Sims' approach:

```julia
alpha = 0.4;
delta = 0.025;
rho  = 0.95;
beta= 0.988;
hs   = 0.31;
sz   = 0.00217;

# Deterministic Steady state
ysk = (1-beta*(1-delta))/(alpha*beta);
ksy = 1/ysk;
si  = delta/ysk;
sc  = 1-si;

#Define:
#Y=[k(t+1) a(t+1) E_tc(t+1)]
#X=[y,c,i,h]

ny  = 3;  # of variables in vector Y
nx  = 4;  # of variables in vector X
ne  = 1;  # of fundamental shocks
nn  = 1;  # of expectation errors

# Initialize the Upsilon matrices
UX=zeros(nx,nx);
UY=zeros(nx,ny);
UE=zeros(nx,ne);
UN=zeros(nx,nn);

G0Y=zeros(ny,ny);
G1Y=zeros(ny,ny);
G0X=zeros(ny,nx);
```

```
G1X=zeros(ny,nx);
GE=zeros(ny,ne);
GN=zeros(ny,nn);

# Production function
UX[1,1]=1;
UX[1,4]=alpha-1;
UY[1,1]=alpha;
UY[1,2]=rho;
UE[1]=1;

#Consumption c(t)=E(c(t)|t-1)+eta(t)
UX[2,2]=1;
UY[2,3]=1;
UN[2]=1;

# Resource constraint
UX[3,1]=1;
UX[3,2]=-sc;
UX[3,3]=-si;

# Consumption-leisure arbitrage
UX[4,1]=-1;
UX[4,2]=1;
UX[4,4]=1;

# Accumulation of capital
G0Y[1,1]=1;
G1Y[1,1]=1-delta;
G1X[1,3]=delta;

# Productivity shock
G0Y[2,2]=1;
G1Y[2,2]=rho;
GE[2]=1;

# Euler equation
G0Y[3,1]=1-beta*(1-delta);
G0Y[3,3]=1;
G0X[3,1]=-(1-beta*(1-delta));
G1X[3,2]=1;

# Solution
# Step 1: solve the first set of equations
PIY = inv(UX)*UY;
PIE = inv(UX)*UE;
PIN = inv(UX)*UN;

# Step 2: build the standard System
A0  = G0Y+G0X*PIY;
A1  = G1Y+G1X*PIY;
B   = GE+G1X*PIE;
C   = GN+G1X*PIN;

#First we compute the Schur decomposition A0=Q'*T*Z' and A1=Q'*S*Z'
r = schurfact(complex(A1),complex(A0))
tol_=1e-8;
cutoff=1
sel = (abs.(diag(r[:S])./diag(r[:T]))).<cutoff)
```

```
ordschur!(r,sel)
S = r[:S]
T = r[:T]
Q = r[:Q]'   # So now q*a*z = s and q*b*z = t
Z = r[:Z]

n          = size(A0,1);   # number of variables
nf         = size(B,2);    # number of fundamental shocks
ne         = size(C,2);    # number of expectation errors

# Calculate the number of unstable eigenvalues
m = n-sum(sel);

Q1         = Q[1:n-m,:];
Q2         = Q[n-m+1:n,:];
Z1         = Z[:,1:n-m]';
Z2         = Z[:,n-m+1:n]';

r_svd      = svdfact(Q2*C);
U1      = r_svd[:U]
D1      = r_svd[:S]
V1      = r_svd[:V]
r       = rank(Q2*C);                # number of linearly independent forecast errors


T11        = T[1:n-m,1:n-m];
T12        = T[1:n-m,n-m+1:n];
T22        = T[n-m+1:n,n-m+1:n];

T1i        = inv(T11);
S11        = S[1:n-m,1:n-m];
S12        = T[1:n-m,n-m+1:n];
S22        = T[n-m+1:n,n-m+1:n];

r_svd      = svdfact(Q1*C);
U1      = r_svd[:U]
D1      = r_svd[:S]
V1      = r_svd[:V]

r1          = rank(Q1*C);

r_svd      = svdfact(Q2*C);
U2      = r_svd[:U]
D2      = r_svd[:S]
V2      = r_svd[:V]
r2          = rank(Q2*C);

Phi        = ((U2[:,1:r2]*(D2[1:r2,1:r2]\V2[:,1:r2]'))*(V1[:,1:r1]*D1[1:r1,1:r1]*U1[:,1:r1]'))';


Transfo    = [eye(n-m) -Phi];
MY0        = inv([Transfo*T;zeros(m,n-m) eye(m)]);
MY1        = ([Transfo*S;zeros(m,n)]);
MY         = Z*(MY0*MY1)*Z';

if ne>r2;
println("Indeterminacy: adding beliefs")
ME          = MY0*[Transfo*Q*[B C];zeros(m,size([B C],2))];
ME          = Z*ME;
```

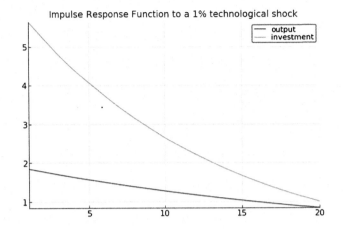

FIGURE 3.1 RBC IRF.

```
ETA          = (U2[:,1:r2]*(D2[1:r2,1:r2]\V2[:,1:r2]'))'*Q2*[B C];
else
ME           = MY0*[Transfo*Q*B;zeros(m,size(B,2))];
ME           = Z*ME;
ETA          = (U2[:,1:r2]*(D2[1:r2,1:r2]\V2[:,1:r2]'))'*Q2*B;
end

#solutions
MY  = real(MY);
ME  = real(ME);
ETA = real(ETA);
```

To draw the impulse response functions (IRFs, hereafter) I use this simple code:

```
#simulate
# Step 4: Recover the impact function

PIE=PIE-PIN*ETA;

#horizon of responses
nrep     = 20;
YS       = zeros(3,nrep);
XS       = zeros(4,nrep);
Shock    = 1;
YS[:,1] = ME*Shock;
XS[:,1] = PIE;
for t=2:nrep;
YS[:,t] = MY*YS[:,t-1];
XS[:,t] = PIY*YS[:,t-1];
end

using Plots
pyplot()
plot(XS[1,:],linewidth=1,label="output",title="Impulse Response Function for RBC model")
plot!(XS[3,:],linewidth=1,label="investment")
```

The result is presented in Fig. 3.1.

3.4.2 A Basic New Keynesian Model

I introduce here a basic New Keynesian model which I solve and simulate and Julia. The model is quite basic and I implement an alternative solution method using Blanchard and Kahn's method. There are many good materials covering in an extensive manner the New Keynesian model. The reader might want to consult [14] or [15]. In this section, I rather choose a simplified version, following [16]. I rather prefer following this approach to keep things simple and allow the reader to compare the implementation in Julia here with the original implementation in Matlab that accompanies [16].

The model is a simpler version of the baseline New Keynesian model as outlined in [15]. Since the model is standard, I choose only to sketch the model, while the interested reader might want to consult the suggested materials. This is a typical New Keynesian model which consists in three block: households, firms and government (the monetary authority). Households maximize their utility function. The following utility function $U(\cdot)$ is assumed to follow a CRRA specification:

$$U(c_t) = \frac{C^{1-\sigma}}{1-\sigma} \tag{3.143}$$

Where c_t is the consumption, while σ is the coefficient of relative risk aversion. Households maximize their expected lifetime utility function, under the given budget constraint.

A further simplifying assumption is that there is not capital, such that output is equal to consumption, that is: $y_t = c_t$. Firms are profit maximizing profits facing three types of constraints: the technology or production function, the demand curve faced by them as well as the fact that not all the firms change their price in each period.

Finally, the monetary authority set the current nominal interest rate i_t following a simplified Taylor rule such that the central bank reacts only to changes in current inflation π_t. The final log-linearized version of the model, consisting in an IS curve, a New Keynesian Phillips curve, a Taylor rule for monetary policy as well as a AR process for technological shocks, is outlined below:

$$\tilde{x}_t = E_t \tilde{x}_{t+1} - \sigma^{-1}(\tilde{i}_t - E_t \tilde{\pi}_{t+1}) \tag{3.144}$$

$$\tilde{\pi}_t = E_t \tilde{\pi}_{t+1} + \kappa \tilde{x}_t \tag{3.145}$$

$$\tilde{i}_t = \delta \tilde{\pi}_t + v_t \tag{3.146}$$

$$v_{t+1} = \rho v_t + \epsilon_{t+1} \tag{3.147}$$

Here, the parameter κ is given by $\frac{(1-\omega)(1-\beta\omega)}{\alpha\omega}$. Eqs. (3.144) and (3.146) and can grouped together and the model rewritten in a more convenient manner as follows:

$$E_t \tilde{x}_{t+1} + \sigma^{-1} E_t \tilde{\pi}_{t+1} = \tilde{x}_t + \sigma^{-1}\delta \tilde{\pi}_t + \sigma^{-1} v_t \tag{3.148}$$

$$E_t \tilde{\pi}_{t+1} = \tilde{\pi}_t - \kappa \tilde{x}_t \tag{3.149}$$

$$v_{t+1} = \rho v_t + \epsilon_{t+1} \tag{3.150}$$

This can be represented using the already familiar representation of DSGE models from (3.75):

$$A_0 E_t X_{t+1} = A_1 X_t + B_0 v_{t+1} \tag{3.151}$$

This can be implemented in Julia using the algorithm already outlined above. I present the code below to solve the model:

```
#Calibrated parameter values
beta=0.99;
sigma=1.0;
chi=1.55;
eta=0;
theta=2.064;
omega=0.5;
alpha=3;
delta=1.5;
rho=0.5;
kappa=(1-omega)*(1-beta*omega)/(alpha*omega);

#Number of predetermined and jump variables
n=1;#predetermined variables
m=2;#jump variables
```

```julia
nu=1;
cutoff=1.0;

#Define state space matrices
A0=zeros(3,3);
A0[1,1]=1;
A0[2,2]=1;
A0[2,3]=sigma^-1;
A0[3,3]=beta;

A1=zeros(3,3);
A1[1,1]=rho;
A1[2,1]=sigma^-1;
A1[2,2]=1;
A1[2,3]=sigma^-1*delta;
A1[3,2]=-kappa;
A1[3,3]=1;

B0=zeros(3,1);
B0[1,1]=1;

#Calculate alternative state space matrices
A=inv(A0)*A1;
B=inv(A0)*B0;
lambda=eigvals(A);

println("lambda=");
println(transpose(real(lambda)));

#Blanchard-Kahn Conditions

bk_n = 0;
for i = 1:length(lambda)
if    abs.(lambda[i]) > 1.0
bk_n = bk_n+1;
end
end;

println("BK condition");
println("Number of jump variables:",m);
println("Number of unstable roots:",bk_n);

if bk_n==m;
println("BK satisfied")
elseif bk_n>n
println("Too many unstable roots")
else
println("Too few unstable roots")
end;
#Sort eigenvectors and eigenvalues
v,w = eig(A)
r=[abs.(v) w']

for i = 1:(m+n)
for j = i+1:(m+n)
if  real(r[i,1])> real(r[j,1])
tmp = r[i,:];
r[i,:]=r[j,:];
r[j,:]=tmp;
```

```
elseif real(r[i,1])== real(r[j,1])
if imag(r[i,1])> imag(r[j,1])
tmp = r[i,:];
r[i,:]=r[j,:];
r[j,:]=tmp;
end;
end;
end;
end;

lam= r[:,1];
M=r[:,2:4]';

P=inv(M);
lam=diagm(lam);

#solutions
LAMBDA1=lam[1:n,1:n];
LAMBDA2=lam[(n+1):n+m,(n+1):n+m];

P11 = P[1:n,1:n];
P12 = P[1:n,(n+1):n+m];
P21 = P[(n+1):n+m,1:n];
P22 = P[(n+1):n+m,(n+1):n+m];
R=P*B;

#decision rules
C11=real(inv(P11-P12*inv(P22)*P21)*LAMBDA1*(P11-P12*inv(P22)*P21));
C12=real(inv(P11-P12*inv(P22)*P21)*R[1]);
C21=real(-inv(P22)*P21);
```

I can simulate the impulse response functions as in the case of the RBC model, as shown below:

```
horiz=24;
e=zeros(horiz,1);
x=zeros(horiz,2);
eps=zeros(horiz,1);
eps[1,1]=1;

for i = 1:horiz-1
e[i+1,:]=C11*e[i,1]+C12*eps[i,1]
x[i+1,:]=C21*e[i,1]
end

using Plots
pyplot()
plot(x[:,2],linewidth=1,label="Inflation",title="Impulse Response Function to a monetary policy shock")
plot!(x[:,1],linewidth=1,label="Output Gap")
```

The IRF's for both output gap and inflation are shown in Fig. 3.2. Finally, I can also simulate the model and determine the theoretical moments of the output gap and inflation.

```
#Simulation and moments
#variable names
name=['x','pi'];
periods=500;
drop=250;
rep=100;
nlag=4;
nvars=size(name,1);
```

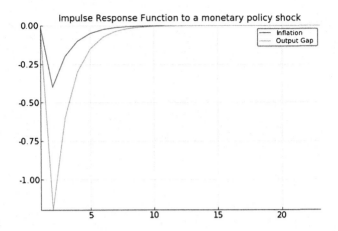

FIGURE 3.2 NK IRF.

```
#matrices store results
stdst=zeros(rep,nvars);
corst=zeros(rep,nvars*nvars);
auto=zeros(rep,nvars*nlag);

for i = 1:rep
eps=sqrt(0.01)*rand(1,periods);
x=zeros(periods,2);
e=zeros(periods,1);

#compute variables
e[1,1]=0;
x[1,:]=0;
for j = 1:periods-1
e[j+1,:]=C11*e[j]+C12*eps[j]
x[j+1,:]=C21*e[j,1]

end
#drop burnins
stdst[i,1]=std(x[:,1])
stdst[i,2]=std(x[:,2])
end

#Display results
println("Simulation results");
println("Average standard deviation of output gap:",mean(stdst[:,1]));
println("Average standard deviation of inflation:",mean(stdst[:,2]));

Simulation results
Average standard deviation of output gap:0.04056
Average standard deviation of inflation: 0.01352
```

3.4.3 DSGE Models in Julia

Maybe a bit surprising, given how young is this language, there is a library dealing with solving and simulating DSGE models in Julia, SolveDSGE, due to Richard Dennis from the University of Glasgow. The package contains solution methods for the most used methods to solve for DSGE models, including the ones discussed in this chapter, namely Blanchard and Kahn method, Klein's method or Sim's method. The package also allows for both first and second order accurate solutions. Additionally, the package includes functions that solve for Linear Quadratic optimal policy models under discretion, commitment or timeless-perspective.

Another contribution worth-mentioning is the package Dolo by Pablo Winant that implements many state-of-art algorithms, like perturbation, parametrized expectations or time iteration. This book also covers the first two of these approaches in Chapter 5.

Not at last, there is also the package DSGE that not only implements the DSGE model of the Federal Reserve Bank in New York, but it also allows the estimation of user-defined DSGE models.

REFERENCES

[1] L. Ljungqvist, Th. Sargent, Recursive Macroeconomic Theory, 3rd edition, MIT Press, 2012.

[2] Th. Sargent, Macroeconomic Theory, 2nd edition, Emerald Group Publishing Limited, 1987.

[3] J. Miao, Economic Dynamics in Discrete Time, MIT Press, 2014.

[4] F. Collard, Notes on numerical methods, Mimeo, 2015.

[5] K. Neusser, Difference equations for economists, Mimeo, 2016.

[6] O. Blanchard, Ch. Kahn, The solution of linear difference models under rational expectations, Econometrica 48 (5) (1980) 1305–1312.

[7] Ch. Sims, Solving linear rational expectations models, Computational Economics 20 (2001) 1–20.

[8] P. Klein, Using the generalized Schur form to solve a multivariate linear rational expectations model, Journal of Economic Dynamics & Control 24 (5) (2000) 1405–1423.

[9] R. King, M. Watson, The solution of singular linear difference systems under rational expectations, International Economic Review 39 (4) (1998) 1015–1026.

[10] J.F. Muth, Rational expectations and the theory of price movements, Econometrica 29 (1961) 315–335.

[11] R. Lucas, Expectations and the neutrality of money, Journal of Economic Theory 4 (1972) 103–124.

[12] G. McCandless, The ABCs of RBCs: An Introduction to Dynamic Macroeconomic Models, Harvard University Press, 2008.

[13] H. Uhlig, A toolkit for analysing nonlinear dynamic stochastic models easily, in: R. Marimon, A. Scott (Eds.), Computational Methods for the Study of Dynamic Economies, 2001, pp. 30–61.

[14] J. Gali, Monetary Policy, Inflation, and the Business Cycle: An Introduction to the New Keynesian Framework and Its Applications, 2nd edition, Princeton University Press, 2015.

[15] C. Walsh, Monetary Theory and Policy, 3rd edition, MIT Press, 2010.

[16] M. Ellison, Practical DSGE modelling, Mimeo, Bank of England, 2005.

Chapter 4

Dynamic Programming

Contents

4.1 INTRODUCTION

Modern macroeconomics relies heavily on dynamic programming. This chapter introduces the topic and keeps a balanced approach between theory, numerical algorithms and practical implementations in Julia. While it is not the aim of this chapter to thoroughly present the theory behind dynamic programming, nevertheless it is necessary to discuss the theoretical foundations such that the numerical algorithms are well understood.

4.2 DETERMINISTIC DYNAMIC PROGRAMMING

I start by presenting first deterministic dynamic programming. Deterministic dynamic programming is easier to be understood for many reasons, including pedagogical ones. On this ground, it is usually presented before stochastic dynamic programming. I start from presenting the theoretical background before moving to numerical methods and implementing a baseline model in Julia.

4.2.1 Theory

There are many good books that present in detail the deterministic dynamic programming. I follow here mainly [3] and [4] for the theory, and [1] and [5] for the numerical implementations. The emphasis is here on ensuring a balance between theory and the actual application, although the reader is redirected for the proofs to key books on this topic (given the limited space and the general emphasis of the book on applications).

Representations

There are two alternative representations of the dynamic programming approach: a sequential one and a functional one. They are equivalent as it will be shown. The Sequential Representation (SR, hereafter), may be written as follows:

Sequential Representation:

$$V^*(x_0) = \sup_{\{x_{t+1}\}_{t=0}^{\infty}} \sum_{t=0}^{\infty} \beta^t U(t, x_t, x_{t+1}) \tag{4.1}$$

This is subject to the following constraint:

$$x_{t+1} \in G(x_t), \tag{4.2}$$

with $x_0 \in X$ given. Here $G(x)$ is a correspondence, mapping a value into a set. The function $U(x)$ is the instantaneous utility, while β is the discount factor.

Introduction to Quantitative Macroeconomics Using Julia. https://doi.org/10.1016/B978-0-12-812219-8.00011-2

We distinguish between x_t, a state variable at moment t, since its value is known before t given $G(x_{t-1})$, and x_{t+1}, a control variable at t.

Two more remarks should be further made. The operator sup is used here, which is needed on the basis that it is not sure whether the maximal value is obtainable for a feasible plan. Furthermore, $V^*(x_0)$ denotes the value function, or the value of following the optimal plan starting with x_0.

The alternative representation, which is actually preferable when solving a dynamic programming problem, is that of a functional equation (FE, hereafter).

Functional Equation:

$$V(x) = \sup_{y \in G(x)} [U(x, y) + \beta V(y)] \tag{4.3}$$

Here, $V(x)$ is the value function. In this formulation, we do not focus on choosing the sequence $\{x_t\}_{t=0}^{\infty}$, but on choosing a policy function through which we can determine x_{t+1} given x_t.

In contrast to previous representation, the time subscripts are not used since the instantaneous utility $U()$ does not depend on time and neither does the policy function.

Since this representation contains $V()$ on the right hand side, it is also called the recursive representation. The main appeal (besides being computationally easier to deal with) from an economic point of view is that it relates the return today, $U(x, y)$ and the return tomorrow, $\beta V(y)$, or the continuation return (starting from next day).

Equivalence of Representations:
It is easy to be shown that the FE and the SR are equivalent. Assume that the SR has a maximum starting at x_0 which is attained by the sequence $\{x_t^*\}_{t=0}^{\infty}$ for which $x_0^* = x_0$. Following [3], we can write:

$$V^*(x_0) = \sum_{t=0}^{\infty} \beta^t U(x_t^*, x_{t+1}^*) \tag{4.4}$$

$$= U(x_0, x_1^*) + \beta \sum_{s=0}^{\infty} \beta^s U(x_{s+1}^*, x_{s+2}^*) \tag{4.5}$$

$$= U(x_0, x_1^*) + \beta V^*(x_1^*) \tag{4.6}$$

Assumptions

To solve the SR problem, we need a number of assumptions which ensure that they are a solution to both SR problem and the FE problem. We start assuming a sequence $\{x_t^*\}_{t=0}^{\infty}$ which ensures that the supremum of SR is reached. We want to make sure that this series satisfies FE:

$$V(x_t^*) = U(x_t^*, x_{t+1}^*) + \beta V(x_{t+1}^*) \tag{4.7}$$

For any $t = 0, 1, 2...$.

As we can see from the formulation above, the problem assumes that we are given $X, G(x), U(x), \beta$. Here, X is the set of possible values for the state variable x.

A key concept in dynamic programming is the concept of feasible plan (or feasible sequence). Assuming a starting point in x_t, we call $\Phi(x_t)$ a feasible plan if it consists in the feasible choices of vectors starting from x_t. We denote by $\bar{x} = (x_0, x_1, ...)$ a typical element in the set $\Phi(x_0)$. Thus, formally we have that $\Phi(x_0) = \{\{x_t\}_{t=0}^{\infty} : x_{t+1} \in \Gamma(x_t)\}$.

We also introduce the concept of policy correspondence. Given a solution V, the policy correspondence $g(x)$ can be defined as:

$$g(x) = \{y \in G(x) : V(x) = U(x) + \beta V(y)\} \tag{4.8}$$

If g is single-valued, then we call it as a policy function. When a sequence $\bar{x} = \{x_0, x_1, ...\}$ has the property that $x_{t+1} \in G(x_t)$, $\bar{x}$ is said to be generated from x_0 by G. The optimal policy correspondence is defined as:

$$g^* = \{y \in G(x) : V^*(x) = U(x, y) + \beta V^*(y)\} \tag{4.9}$$

Here, V^* is the supremum function in SR. We will denote the graph of G by $A = \{(x, y) \in X \times X : y \in G(x)\}$ while $U : A \to \mathbb{R}$.

Assumption 4.1: It is assumed that the correspondence $G(x)$ is nonempty for all $x \in X$.

It is also imposed that we can actually evaluate all the feasible plans using $U()$ and the discount rate β.

Assumption 4.2: For all $x_0 \in X$ and $\bar{x} \in \Phi(x_0)$ the following limit exists and is finite:

$$\lim_{n \to \infty} \sum_{t=0}^{n} \beta^t U(x_t, x_{t+1}) \tag{4.10}$$

The assumption of the existence of the limit is a key one for the following results. The assumption of a finite limit however, though not necessary, it does ensure that the maximized values achieved by the agents are not infinite, which does make sense from an economic point of view.

Assumption 4.3: The set X is a convex subset of $\mathbb{R}^K$, while G is assumed to be nonempty, compact valued and continuous.

Assumption 4.4: The function U is bounded and continuous, while the discount factor β has the property that $0 < \beta < 1$.

The assumption of the continuity of the utility function is rather natural for the usual forms of utility functions assumed in macroeconomics.

Another key assumption is that of an increasing objective function in the state variable. This can be stated as:

Assumption 4.5: For each $y \in X$, the function $U(\cdot, y)$ is strictly increasing in each of its first K arguments.

Assumption 4.6: G is assumed to be monotone, i.e. $x_1 \leq x_2$ implies that $G(x_1) \subseteq G(x_2)$.

Assumption 4.7: The function U is strictly concave. Formally, given a $\alpha \in (0, 1)$, for any $(x_1, y_1), (x_2, y_2) \in A$ it holds that:

$$U[\alpha(x_1, y_1) + (1 - \alpha)(x_2, y_2)] \geq \alpha U(x_1, y_1) + (1 - \alpha)U(x_2, y_2) \tag{4.11}$$

Assumption 4.8: The correspondence G is convex. For $\alpha \in (0, 1)$, $y_1 \in G(x_1)$, $y_2 \in G(x_2)$, the convexity of G can be formally written as:

$$\alpha y_1 + (1 - \alpha)y_2 \in G[\alpha x_1 + (1 - \alpha)x_2] \tag{4.12}$$

Assuming G is convex is also self-understood given the assumptions needed to carry an optimization. To perform an optimization, one needs to assume a convex constraint set and a concave utility function.

Finally, since we are interested in dealing with first order condition, a final condition imposed is that of differentiability.

Assumption 4.9: U is continuously differentiable at each point in the interior of its domain A.

Theorems

Based on these assumptions, we can derive a number of key results that can help us finding a solution to the dynamic programming problems represented as SR and as FE. Proofs can be found in [4] and [3].

The following theorem establishes that, if Assumptions 4.1 and 4.2 hold, then the SR approach and the FE approach yield the same result:

Theorem 4.1: If X, G, U, β verify Assumptions 4.1 and 4.2, then, for any $x \in X$, the function V^* solves the FE.

The converse to the above theorem (at least in partial sense) is shown below. It basically shows that V^* is also the only solution to the FE that also satisfies a limit condition.

Theorem 4.2: If X, G, U, β verify Assumptions 4.1 and 4.2, V is a solution to the functional equations FE, and it also satisfies: $\lim_{n \to \infty} \beta^n V(x_n) = 0$ for all $(x_0, x_1, ...) \in \Phi(x_0)$, all $x_0 \in X$, then it holds that:

$$V = V^* \tag{4.13}$$

A more important result is shown below and it focuses on optimal plans. A feasible plan $\bar{x} \in \Phi(x_0)$ is an optimal plan from x_0 provided it attains the supremum in the sequence problem (SP). This is equivalent to saying: $U(\bar{x}) = V^*(x_0)$. The following two theorems establish a relationship between optimal plans and those plans that satisfy the policy equation $V = V^*$ for (4.7).

Theorem 4.3: If X, G, U, β verify Assumptions 4.1 and 4.2, $\bar{x}^* \in \Phi(x_0)$ is a feasible plan reaching the supremum in the SR problem for an initial state x_0, then it holds that:

$$V^*(x_t^*) = U(x_t^*, x_{t+1}^*) + \beta V^*(x_{t+1}^*) \tag{4.14}$$

Here $t = 0, 1, 2...$ and $x_0^* = x_0$. The next theorem establishes a partial converse to the above result.

Theorem 4.4: Suppose X, G, U, β verify Assumption 4.1 and 4.2. Consider a feasible plan $\bar{x}^* \in \Phi(x_0)$ from initial state x_0 for which it also holds that:

$$V^*(x_t^*) = U(x_t^*, x_{t+1}^*) + \beta V^*(x_{t+1}^*) \tag{4.15}$$

and for which $\lim_{t \to \infty} \sup \beta^t v^*(x_t^*) \leq 0$. Then it holds that $\bar{x}^*$ attains the supremum in the sequential problem SR for an initial state x_0.

It is quite obvious that, if Assumptions 4.3 and 4.4 hold, so do Assumptions 4.1 and 4.2, implying that the SP problem that corresponds to (4.7) is well defined. We also restrict the discussion to the case of FE representation in Eq. (4.7) for which the function $U()$ is bounded while $\beta < 1$.

Consider a bound B for $|U(x, y)|$. It can be easily shown that the supremum function V^* satisfies the equation:

$$|V^*(x)| \leq B/(1 - \beta) \tag{4.16}$$

for all $x \in X$. Consequently, we look for solutions in the space $C(X)$ of bounded continuous functions $U : X \to \mathbb{R}$ having the norm $||U|| = \sup_{x \in X} |U(x)|$.

Let us define first the operator T on $C(X)$ for which:

$$(TV)(x) = \max_{y \in G(x)} [U(x) + \beta V(y)] \tag{4.17}$$

such that Eq. (4.7) can now be written as: $V = TV$. We establish first that, under Assumptions 4.3 and 4.4, T has a unique fixed point on $C(X)$ and that the policy correspondence $g(x)$ is both nonempty and upper hemicontinuous (see below).

However, before getting here, a few more results are necessary. To introduce them, a few definitions and results from real analysis must be introduced. The next paragraphs introduce the Contraction Mapping Theorem, a key result in the dynamic programming approach, as well as the Theory of the Maximum. It is assumed that the reader has a basic exposure to real analysis. One may also consult [3], [4] for a presentation in the context of economics, or [11] for a pure mathematical text. I first introduce the concept of metric spaces and contraction functions. A few definitions are necessary.

Definition 4.1: Let S be a set endowed with a function $\rho : S \times S \to \mathbb{R}$ such that, for all $x, y, z \in S$ it holds that:

1. $\rho(x, y) \geq 0$ while $\rho(x, y) = 0$ iff $x = y$
2. $\rho(x, y) = \rho(y, x)$
3. $\rho(x, y) \leq \rho(y, x) + \rho(y, z)$

Then S is a metric space.

Definition 4.2: Assume (S, ρ) is a metric space. The series $\{x_n\}_{n=0}^{\infty}$ in S converges to $x \in S$ if, for each $\epsilon > 0$, there exists $n_\epsilon \in \mathbb{N}$ such that: $\rho(x_n, x) < \epsilon$ for all $n \geq n_\epsilon$.

Definition 4.3: Let (S, ρ) be a metric space. A sequence in S $\{x_n\}_{n=0}^{\infty}$ is said to be a Cauchy sequence if, for each $\epsilon > 0$, there exists $n_\epsilon \in \mathbb{N}$ such that: $\rho(x_n, x_m) < \epsilon$ for all $m, n \geq n_\epsilon$.

Definition 4.4: Let (S, ρ) be a metric space. We say that S is complete if every Cauchy sequence which is in S converges to a point which is also in S.

Definition 4.5: Let (S, ρ) be a metric space. Let $T : S \to S$ be a function that maps S into itself. If the function T has the following property: $\rho(Tx, Tx) \leq \beta\rho(x, y)$ for any $x, y \in S$ and $\beta \in (0, 1)$, then we say that the function T is a contraction (of modulus β).

Equipped with these definitions, we may state now a first key result, the Contraction Mapping Theorem.

Theorem 4.5: Let (S, ρ) be a complete metric space and $T : S \to S$ a contraction mapping. Then it holds that:

1. T has exactly one fixed point $V \in S$ for which $V = TV$.
2. for any $V_0 \in S$, it holds that $\rho(T^n V_0, V) < \beta^n \rho(V_0, V)$ with $n = 0, 1, 2, \dots$.

The proof might be found in [4] or [3]. The main implication of this theorem is that we can design an algorithm that, whatever the initial point, will converge to the optimal solution provided the value function satisfies the contraction property. The next step is to find a way which ensures that the value function has this property and this is done through the Blackwell's Sufficiency Theorem:

Theorem 4.6: Let $X \subseteq R^k$ and $B(X)$ be the space of bounded functions $V : X \to \mathbb{R}$ endowed with the uniform metric. Consider also an operator $T : B(X) \to B(X)$ which has the following two properties

1. For $V, W \in B(X)$, if $V(x) \leq W(x)$ for any $x \in X$, $TV(x) \leq TW(x)$ (the monotonicity property);
2. There is a parameter $\beta \in (0, 1)$ such that for all $V \in B(X)$ and $a \geq 0$, it holds that: $[T(V + a)](x) \leq TV(x) + \beta * a$ (discounting property).

Then it follows that T is a contraction with modulus β.

What we are interested in is to apply the Contraction Mapping Theorem in the context of generally specified dynamic programming problems as specified in Eq. (4.7). We would like to impose appropriate restrictions on the correspondence $g(x)$ and on the return function $U(x)$ such that if $V \in C(X)$ and $TV(x) = \sup_{y \in G(x)}[U(x, y) + \beta V(y)]$ then the operator T maps the space $C(X)$ into itself. We also need to have a result through which we can determine the properties of $g(x)$ correspondence that contain the maximizing values of y for each x. These results are established through the following result, known as the Theorem of the Maximum. First, let's rewrite the problem as:

$$h(x) = \max_{y \in G(x)} u(x, y) \tag{4.18}$$

$$g(x) = \{y \in G(x) : u(x, y = h(x))\} \tag{4.19}$$

I define first the concept of continuity for correspondences.

Definition 4.6: A correspondence $G : X \to Y$ is upper hemicontinuous (or u.h.c.) at x if $G(x)$ is nonempty and if, for every $x_n \to x$ and every $\{y_n\}$ with the property $y_n \in G(x_n)$ for all n, there is a convergent subsequence of $\{y_n\}$ with the limit in $y \in G(x)$.

Definition 4.7: A correspondence $G : X \to Y$ is lower hemicontinuous (or l.h.c.) at x if $G(x)$ is nonempty and if, for every $y \in G(x)$ and every sequence $x_n \to x$, there is an integer $N \geq 1$ as well as a sequence $\{y_n\}$ for which $y_n \to y$ and $y_n \in G(x_n)$ for all $n \geq N$.

Definition 4.8: A correspondence $G : X \to Y$ is continuous at x if it is both u.h.c. and l.h.c.

Theorem 4.7: (Theorem of the Maximum). Fix $X \subset \mathbb{R}^k$ and $Y \subset \mathbb{R}^m$. Consider a continuous function $u : X \times Y \to \mathbb{R}$ and a continuous and compact-valued correspondence $G : X \to Y$. Then the function $h : X \to \mathbb{R}$, as defined above, is continuous while the correspondence $g : X \to Y$ is nonempty, compact valued and upper hemi-continuous.

We can now use Assumptions 4.3 and 4.4 with the above results to establish that T maps $C(x)$ into itself, that T does have only one fixed point and that $g(x)$ is both nonempty and u.h.c.

Theorem 4.8: Suppose X, G, U, β satisfy Assumption 4.3 and 4.4. Consider $C(X)$ the space of bounded continuous functions $U : X \to \mathbb{R}$ with the sup norm. It can be shown that the operator T maps $C(X)$ into itself, i.e. $T : C(X) \to C(X)$, that T has a unique fixed point $V \in C(X)$ and that for all $v_0 \in C(X)$, it holds that:

$$||T^n V_0 - V|| \leq \beta^n ||V_0 - V|| \tag{4.20}$$

Where $n = 0, 1, 2, \dots$. It also implies that, for a given V, the optimal policy correspondence $g : X \to X$ as defined above in (4.8) is both compact-valued and upper hemi-continuous.

We can also combine Theorem 4.2 and Theorem 4.8 and establish that an optimal policy function that attains the supremum V^* exists and, that, furthermore, V^* is both continuous and bounded.

Theorem 4.9: Suppose X, G, U, β satisfy Assumptions 4.3–4.6. Then the unique value function $V : X \to \mathbb{R}$ satisfying FE is strictly increasing in all its arguments.

Theorem 4.10: Suppose X, G, U, β satisfy Assumptions 4.3–4.4 and 4.7–4.8, then the unique value function $V : X \to \mathbb{R}$ satisfying FE is strictly concave, while g is a continuous and single-valued function.

By now, it was established that there exists a unique solution $V \in C(X)$ to the original problem in Eq. (4.7). To characterize more sharply the policy functions, we would need additional assumptions and results. First, we state the result by Benveniste and Scheinkman, see [10] which shows that, provided certain general conditions are met, the value function V is once differentiable. Unfortunately, the conditions needed to ensure that V is twice differentiable and thus G is once differentiable are very strong. Though, when g is monotone, we can establish this using a direct approach based on a first order condition.

Theorem 4.11: (Benveniste and Scheinkman). Consider a convex set $X \subset \mathbb{R}^k$. Consider also a concave function $V : X \to \mathbb{R}$. Set $x_0 \in int\, X$ with D a neighborhood of x_0. If it exists a function $W : D \to \mathbb{R}$ that is both concave and differentiable for which $W(x_0) = V(x_0)$ and $W(x) \leq V(x)$ for all $x \in D$, then it holds that V is differentiable at x_0 and that: $V_i(x_0) = W_i(x_0)$ for $i = 1, 2, \dots, k$.

Theorem 4.12: Let Assumptions 4.3–4.4 and 4.7–4.9 hold, V satisfy Eq. (4.7) and g satisfy Eq. (4.8). Assuming that $x_0 \in Int\, X$ and that $g(x_0) \in Int\, G(x_0)$, then the value function V is continuously differentiable at x_0 and its derivatives are:

$$V_i(x_0) = U_i(x_0, g(x_0)) \tag{4.21}$$

Where $i = 1, 2, \dots, k$.

4.2.2 Numerical Algorithms and Applications

4.2.2.1 The Optimal Growth Model

Before moving to actual applications, I succinctly present the optimal growth model which will be used as an illustrative example for solving dynamic programming problems with numerical techniques.

Assume a one-sector economy in which there is a representative household. The instantaneous utility function is $u()$ while the discount factor $\beta \in (0, 1)$. The representative household maximizes the discounted lifetime utility:

$$\max_{\{c_t\}_{t=0}^{\infty}} \sum_{t=0}^{\infty} \beta^t u(c_t) \tag{4.22}$$

Each period, the household face the following constraint (combining the household budget constraint with the capital stock dynamics):

$$k_{t+1} = f(k_t) + (1 - \delta)k_t - c_t \tag{4.23}$$

It is further assumed that the initial capital stock k_0 is given while $k_t \geq 0$.

For this specific model, we can write the Bellman equation as:

$$V(k_t) = \max_{c_t}(u(c_t) + \beta V(k_{t+1})) \tag{4.24}$$

Since in the FE representation we can drop the time subscript, we can rewrite this by denoting next period capital stock by k'. After replacing the consumption using (4.23), we obtain:

$$V(k) = \max_{k'}(u(f(k) + (1 - \delta)k - k') + \beta V(k') \tag{4.25}$$

Let us construct the following operator:

$$(TV)(k) = \max_{k'}(u(f(k) + (1 - \delta)k - k') + \beta V(k')) \tag{4.26}$$

If certain properties conditions are met, it can be shown that this operator T verifies the properties of monotonicity and discounting and therefore it is a contraction with modulus β. This implies that the value function not only exists but it is also unique. Using Eq. (4.26) we can design algorithms to solve for the value function.

4.2.2.2 Value Function Iteration

This is the simplest algorithm one can use to solve the dynamic programming. It exploits the recursive nature of the operator T such that, by iterating on Eq. (4.26), it can find a solution for the value function. I sketch a basic value function iteration algorithm below which is further implemented in Julia in this section.

1. Construct a grid of admissible values for the state variable k of the form: $\mathcal{K} = \{k_1, ..., k_n\}$
2. Propose a starting point for the value function $V_0(x)$ and set an approximation criterion ϵ
3. Iterate on the grid such that for each $k_i \in \mathcal{K}$ with $(i = 1, .., n)$, we solve for: $V_{j+1}(k_i) = \max_{k'}(u(f(k_i, k'), k_i) + \beta V_j(k'))$
4. Stop if the error is smaller than the criterion ϵ, i.e.: $||V_{j+1}(k) - V_j(k)|| < \epsilon$
5. Determine the solution: $f^*(k) = f(k, k')$ and $V^*(k) = \frac{u(f^*(k), k)}{1 - \beta}$

I implement this algorithm in Julia, basically following [5]. I focus on the optimal growth model and use the following specification for the utility function:

$$u(c) = \frac{c^{1-\sigma} - 1}{1 - \sigma} \tag{4.27}$$

While the next period k' capital stock can be written as:

$$k' = k^\alpha - c + (1 - \delta)k \tag{4.28}$$

This implies that the Bellman equation becomes now:

$$V(k) = \max_c \frac{c^{1-\sigma} - 1}{1 - \sigma} + \beta V(k') \tag{4.29}$$

But consumption can be replaced using: $c = k^\alpha + (1 - \delta)k - k'$. We rewrite the Bellman equation as:

$$V(k) = \max_{k'} \frac{(k^\alpha + (1 - \delta)k - k')^{1-\sigma} - 1}{1 - \sigma} + \beta V(k') \tag{4.30}$$

For each i point on the grid, we evaluate the value function:

$$V_{i,h} = \frac{(k_i^\alpha + (1 - \delta)k_i - k_h')^{1-\sigma} - 1}{1 - \sigma} + \beta V(k_h) \tag{4.31}$$

Here h refers to feasible values. This is one of the key points of the algorithm: the grid of length N of values for k_i must consist in feasible values. By feasible values it means that the consumption must be both positive and less than output, i.e. $c < y$. The next period capital stock must satisfy:

$$0 \leq k' \leq k^\alpha + (1 - \delta)k \tag{4.32}$$

Since the algorithm relies on a uniform scale, the next period in the grid can be computed using $k_h = \underline{k} + (h - 1)d_k$. Then we may compute the upper bound combining the last two equations, resulting in:

$$\bar{h} = E(\frac{k_j^\alpha + (1 - \delta)k_j - \bar{k}}{d_k}) + 1 \tag{4.33}$$

In each period, we try to find:

$$\mathcal{V}_{i,h}^* = \max_{h=1,\dots,\bar{h}} \mathcal{V}_{i,h} \qquad (4.34)$$

We update the value function using: $V_{j+1}(k_i) = \mathcal{V}_{i,h}^*$ and update next value capital using the index h^* such that: $k'(k_i) = k_{h^*}$.

The Julia code is shown below:

```julia
sigma  = 1.5;
delta  = 0.1;
beta   = 0.95;
alpha  = 0.30;
ks     = ((1-beta*(1-delta))/(alpha*beta))^(1/(alpha-1));
csy    = 1-alpha*beta*delta/(1-beta*(1-delta));
dev    = 0.9;
kmin   = (1-dev)*ks;
kmax   = (1+dev)*ks;
nbk    = 1000;
devk   = (kmax-kmin)/(nbk-1);
k      = collect(linspace(kmin,kmax,nbk));
v0     = zeros(nbk,1);
v0     = ((csy*k.^alpha).^(1-sigma)-1)./((1-sigma)*(1-beta));
v      = zeros(nbk,1);
ik1    = zeros(nbk,1);
iter   = 1;
crit   = 1;
tol    = 1e-6;
u      = 0;

while crit>tol;
for i=1:nbk
imin =  max(ceil((((1-delta)*k[i]-kmin)/devk)+1.0,1);
imax =  min(floor((k[i]^alpha+(1-delta)*k[i]-kmin)/devk)+1.0,nbk);

imin=trunc(Int, imin);
imax=trunc(Int, imax);
c = k[i]^alpha+(1-delta)*k[i]-k[imin:imax];
u = (c.^(1-sigma)-1)/(1-sigma);
(v[i],itmp)= findmax(u+beta*v0[imin:imax]);
ik1[i] = imin-1+itmp;
end;
error=abs.(v-v0);
crit= maximum(error);
copy!(v0, v)
iter= iter+1;
end

#solution
k1     = zeros(nbk,1);

for i=1:nbk
index=trunc(Int, ik1[i]);

k1[i]= k[index];

end;

c = k.^alpha+(1-delta)*k-k1;
```

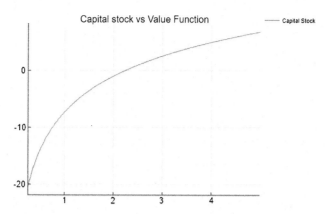

FIGURE 4.1 Capital stock vs value function.

```
u = (c.^(1-sigma)-1)/(1-sigma);
v =u/(1-beta);
```

I plot in Fig. 4.1 the capital stock versus the value function (or course, various other variables of interest can be easily be plotted). I use the following code:

```
using Plots
plotly()
plot(k,v,linewidth=1,label="Capital Stock",title="Capital stock vs Value Function")
```

4.2.2.3 Policy Iteration – The Howard Improvement

The main advantage of the value function iteration is that it is easy to design and program. Unfortunately, the algorithm implies a convergence rate equal to the value of β parameter. Since this parameter is close to 1, the algorithm will converge slowly.

An algorithm that addresses this shortcoming is the Howard improvement algorithm. The basic idea is very simple: instead of iterating on the value function, the algorithm iterates on the policy function. I describe the algorithm below following [5]:

1. Start from an initial guess of the control variable $c = f_0(k)$ and compute the implied value function for this initial guess using: $V(k_t) = \sum_{s=0}^{\infty} \beta^s u(f_i(k_{t+s}), k_{t+s})$. Here, we use $k_{t+1} = h(k_t, c_t) = h(k_t, f_i(k_t))$.
2. We compute a new policy rule $c = f_{i+1}(k)$ that verifies: $f_{i+1}(k) \in \arg\max_c u(c,k) + \beta V(k')$. Here, we use $k' = h(k, f_i(k))$.
3. Using a parameter ϵ as the stopping criteria, we check whether: $\|f_{i+1}(k) - f_i(k)\| < \epsilon$. If the condition is not fulfilled, the algorithm goes back to the second step.

I present the implementation in Julia below:

```
#  Policy Function iteration
sigma    = 1.50;                    # utility parameter
delta    = 0.10;                    # depreciation rate
beta     = 0.95;                    # discount factor
alpha    = 0.30;                    # capital elasticity of output
nbk      = 1000;                    # number of data points in the grid
crit     = 1;                       # convergence criterion
iter     = 1;                       # iteration
tol      = 1e-6;                    # convergence parameter
#steady state capital stock
ks       = ((1-beta*(1-delta))/(alpha*beta))^(1/(alpha-1));
dev      = 0.9;                     # maximal deviation from steady state
kmin     = (1-dev)*ks;             # lower bound on the grid
kmax     = (1+dev)*ks;             # upper bound on the grid
```

```
devk    = (kmax-kmin)/(nbk-1);      # implied increment
kgrid   = collect(linspace(kmin,kmax,nbk)); # builds the grid
#kgrid   = kgrid';
v       = zeros(nbk,1);             # value function
#c       = zeros(nbk,1);             # consumption
kp0     = kgrid;                    # initial guess on k(t+1)
dr      = zeros(nbk,1);             # decision rule (will contain indices)
kp      = zeros(nbk,1);

while crit>tol

for i=1:nbk

imin    = max(ceil((((1-delta)*kgrid[i]-kmin)/devk)+1,1);
imax    = min(floor((kgrid[i]^alpha+(1-delta)*kgrid[i]-kmin)/devk)+1,nbk);
imin=trunc(Int, imin);
imax=trunc(Int, imax);

c_temp      = kgrid[i]^alpha+(1-delta)*kgrid[i]-kgrid[imin:imax];
util_temp   = (c_temp.^(1-sigma)-1)/(1-sigma);
(v1,idr)= findmax(util_temp+beta*v[imin:imax]);
dr[i]   = imin-1+idr;
dr[i]   = trunc(Int, dr[i]);
end;

# decision rules
kp  = zeros(nbk,1);
for i=1:nbk
index=trunc(Int, dr[i]);

kp[i]= kgrid[index];

end;

c   = kgrid.^alpha+(1-delta)*kgrid-kp;
util= (c.^(1-sigma)-1)/(1-sigma);
Q   = zeros(nbk,nbk);

for i=1:nbk;
index=trunc(Int, dr[i]);
Q[i,index] = 1;
end

A=(eye(nbk)-beta*Q);
B=util;
Tv  = \(A, B);
crit= maximum(abs.(kp-kp0));
v   = copy(Tv);
kp0 = copy(kp);
iter= iter+1;
end;

using Plots
plotly() # Choose the Plotly.jl backend for web interactivity
plot(kp,c,linewidth=1,label="Consumption",title="Consumption vs Capital stock")
```

The last lines plot consumption versus capital stock. I include Fig. 4.2.

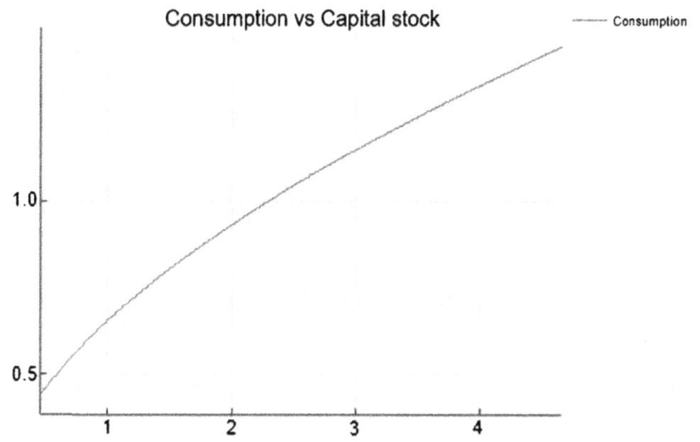

FIGURE 4.2 Consumption.

4.3 STOCHASTIC DYNAMIC PROGRAMMING

This section focuses on the stochastic case of dynamic programming. Most of the macroeconomic applications involve the presence of uncertainty and therefore the stochastic dynamic programming approach is more relevant to macroeconomic applications as compared to the deterministic dynamic programming.

4.3.1 Theory

The presentation draws mostly on [3] and [4]. In the former approach, Acemoglu, see [3], rather focuses on the simpler case of finite values stochastic variables. There are two reasons for doing this: one is making the transition from deterministic dynamic programming smoother, and, second, is avoiding the use of measure theory. However, I mostly follow [4] since the measure based approach is more general. I also believe that the reader might benefit more from this exposure, given the increased use of measure theory in macroeconomics.

4.3.1.1 Representations

Similarly to the deterministic dynamic programming, there are two alternative representations of the stochastic dynamic programming approach: a sequential one and a functional one. I follow first [3] and develop the two alternative representations before moving to the measured based recursive approach.

First, let us consider the introduction of a random (stochastic) variable $z_t \in Z$, where $Z = \{z_1, z_2, ..., z_n\}$. It is assumed that the set Z is finite (this implies compactness too). The utility function becomes now:

$$U(x_t, x_{t+1}, z_t) \tag{4.35}$$

Here, the utility function is extended to take into account the fact that the payoff now depends on the random variable z_t. Again, there is a discount factor $\beta \in (0, 1)$, x_t stands for the state variable, while x_{t+1} stands for the control variable, both relative to time t. It is assumed that the initial values of the state vector, i.e. x_0, and of the stochastic variable, z_0 are given at the beginning.

Furthermore, each period constraint is conditioned now to be: $x_{t+1} \in G(x_t, z_t)$, with $G(x, z)$ a correspondence that depends in this case on the stochastic variable too and which is written as $G : X \times Z \to X$.

Finally, the random variable z_t is assumed to follow a Markov chain, implying that the current value z_t depends only on the value in the last period z_{t-1}. In other words, the probability of the current value being $z_t = z_j$ depends only on the value in the past period z_{t-1}. We could write this formally as:

$$P[z_t = z_j | z_0, ..., z_{t-1}] = P[z_t = z_j | z_{t-1}] \tag{4.36}$$

The stochastic optimal problem can be easily written in both the sequential representation and the functional representation. I start again from the sequential representation, which, following Acemoglu, see [3], can be easily written as follows:

Sequential Representation:

$$V^*(x_0, z_0) = \sup_{\{\tilde{x}[z^t]\}_{t=0}^{\infty}} \mathbb{E}_0 \sum_{t=0}^{\infty} \beta^t U(\tilde{x}[z^{t-1}], \tilde{x}[z^t], z_t) \tag{4.37}$$

Here $z^t = \{z_1, ..., z_t\}$ is the history of z_t up to date t, with z_0 considered as given.

This is subject to the following constraint:

$$\tilde{x}[z^t] \in G(\tilde{x}[z^{t-1}], z_t) \tag{4.38}$$

with x_0, z_0 given and $\tilde{x}[z^{-1}] = x_0$ as well as $z^0 = z_0$. Here $G(x, z)$ is the correspondence which depends on the stochastic term too. The function $U()$ is the instantaneous utility, while β is the discount factor. $\mathbb{E}_0$ stands for the expectation operator at time $t = 0$ and it is conditioned on z_0.

The alternative representation, which is actually preferable when solving a dynamic programming problem, is that of a functional equation. However there are two ways to achieve this. In the simplest form, we could use the expectation operator and write:

Functional Equation:

$$V(x, z) = \sup_{y \in G(x)} [U(x, y, z) + \beta \mathbb{E}[V(y, z')|z]] \tag{4.39}$$

Here, $V(x)$ is a real-valued function, with $V : X \times Z \to \mathbb{R}$. Again, as in the deterministic approach, we do not focus on choosing the sequence $\{x_t\}_{t=0}^{\infty}$, but on choosing a policy function through which we can determine x_{t+1} given x_t and z_t. We can drop here the time subscripts too since neither the instantaneous utility $U()$ nor the policy function depend on it. The key difference from the deterministic (FE) is that we use now an expectation operator. To understand its function, we remember that $z \in Z$ and thus is takes values in a finite set. Assume now that the probabilities associated to these events, i.e. $\{z_1, z_2, ..., z_i, ...\}$ are denoted by $\{\pi_1, \pi_2, ..., \pi_i, ...\}$. This also implies that the values are positive and that they sum up to 1, i.e. $\pi_i \geq 0$ and $\sum_{i=1}^{\infty} \pi_1 = 1$ with $i = 1, 2, ...$ Then, we could simply replace the expectation operator $\mathbb{E}$ and rewrite the (FE):

$$V(x, z) = \sup_{y \in G(x)} [U(x, y, z) + \beta \sum_{i=1}^{\infty} V(y, z_i)\pi_i] \tag{4.40}$$

The FE representation can also be written by drawing on the language of measure theory. We would write:

Functional Equation Based on Lebesgue Integral:

$$V(x, z) = \sup_{y \in G(x)} [U(x, y, z) + \beta \int V(y, z')Q(z, dz')] \tag{4.41}$$

Here $Q(z,)$ is a transition function which gives the value of next period random variable z' given its value in the current period z, while $\int V(y, z')Q(z, dz')$ is the Lebesgue integral of the function f with respect to the Markov process for the random variable z.

4.3.1.2   Measure Theory and Integration

This section generally follows the general presentation from [4]. However, where the exposition by the latter does not build up the intuition enough, which fortunately does not happen too often, the presentation here also relies on reference texts in mathematics, see [11], [12] or [13]. The main role of the section is to introduce a way to deal with the Lebesgue integral with respect to the Markov process for z. This is done through measurable function which allow the use of a more generalized way to integrate that includes the expectations operator used before as a particular case. But before this, the reader is introduced to the concept of measure.

Intuitively, a measure is a way to assign a number or quantity to a set. For the case of the real line, this would be equivalent to the length of that line, i.e. for $[a, b]$ the measure of this line is $b - a$. For areas, the measure of an area is equal to the surface the area. However, we would like to be able to work with measures on abstract sets, and therefore we proceed from the basics.

In order to define measures, one starts by establishing what kind of sets or subsets can the measures be defined. Considering that we are equipped with a set S, we may start by defining a sigma-algebra or σ-*algebra* using the following definition:

Definition 4.7: σ-Algebras: If S is a set, and $\mathcal{S}$ is a family of subsets of S, $\mathcal{S}$ is a σ-algebra if the following three conditions are met:

1. $\varnothing, S \in \mathcal{S}$
2. $A \in \mathcal{S}$ implies that $A^c = S \setminus A \in \mathcal{S}$
3. $A_n \in \mathcal{S}$ for $n = 1, 2, \ldots$ implies that $\bigcup_{n=1}^{\infty} A_n \in \mathcal{S}$

The definition implies that a σ-*algebra* is closed under complementation and countable union. If we consider the pair $(S, \mathcal{S})$, with $\mathcal{S}$ a σ-*algebra*, then this is a measurable space and any subset $A \in \mathcal{S}$ is called a $\mathcal{S}$-measurable space.

To further advance the discussion, we are interested to construct measures, that is functions that assign numbers in the sense of probability to the $\mathcal{S}$-measurable spaces.

Definition 4.8: Measures: Let us consider the measurable space the pair $(S, \mathcal{S})$. We define a measure as an extended real function $\mu : \mathcal{S} \to [0, \infty]$ which satisfies the following three conditions:

1. $\mu(\varnothing) = 0$
2. $\mu(A) \geq 0$ for all $A \in \mathcal{S}$
3. If $A_n \in \mathcal{S}$ is a sequence of disjoint subsets in $\mathcal{S}$ which is also countable, then it holds that $\mu(\bigcup_{n=1}^{\infty} A_n) = \sum_{n=1}^{\infty} \mu(A_n)$

Definition 4.9: Measure Spaces: Let S be a set, $\mathcal{S}$ a σ-*algebra* and μ a measure defined as above on $\mathcal{S}$. A measure space is given by a triple $(S, \mathcal{S}, \mu)$.

For a certain measure space $(S, \mathcal{S}, \mu)$, a proposition is said to hold μ – almost everywhere (μ-a.e.) if there is a set $A \in \mathcal{S}$ with $\mu(A) = 0$ such that the proposition holds on the complement of A. A basic example would be illustrative: we say that on a measure space $(S, \mathcal{S}, \mu)$, two functions f, g are equal almost everywhere, $f = g$ a.e., if $f(s) = g(s)$ for all $s \in A^c$ for $A \in \mathcal{S}$ and $\mu(A) = 0$.

The definitions up to now allow us to introduce the concept of probability measure. If the measure μ has the property that $\mu(S) = 1$ then μ is called a probability measure and $(S, \mathcal{S}, \mu)$ is a probability space.

The results until now allow us to define measures on subintervals of a given interval $[a, b]$. However, we would also be interested to extend the measures defined on subintervals of $[a, b]$ to all the Borel subsets of $[a, b]$. The Borel algebra for $\mathbb{R}^1$ is the smallest σ-algebra containing all the open sets.

We can start first from defining a smaller class of sets relative to σ-algebras, that of algebras:

Definition 4.10: Algebras: If S is a set, and $\mathcal{A}$ is a family of subsets of S, then $\mathcal{A}$ is an algebra if the following three conditions are met:

1. $\varnothing, S \in \mathcal{A}$
2. $A \in \mathcal{A}$ implies that $A^c = S \setminus A \in \mathcal{A}$
3. $A_n \in \mathcal{A}$ for $n = 1, 2, \ldots, m$ implies that $\bigcup_{n=1}^{m} A_n \in \mathcal{A}$

By definition, an algebra is closed under two operations: complementation and finite union. Since a σ-algebra is closed under a countable union, clearly an algebra is "smaller" than a σ-algebra. Nevertheless, when we try to define a measure on an algebra, a small but significant difference will appear, as seen from below.

Definition 4.11: Measures on Algebras: Let us consider the measurable space the pair $(S, \mathcal{S})$. We define a measure as an extended real function $\mu : \mathcal{S} \to [0, \infty]$ which satisfies the following three conditions:

1. $\mu(\varnothing) = 0$
2. $\mu(A) \geq 0$ for all $A \in \mathcal{A}$
3. If $\{A_n\}_{n=1}^{\infty}$ is a disjoint sequence of sets in $\mathcal{A}$ for which $\bigcup_{n=1}^{\infty} A_n \in S$, then it holds that $\mu(\bigcup_{n=1}^{\infty} A_n) = \sum_{n=1}^{\infty} \mu(A_n)$

The significant difference between measures defined on algebras and measures defined on σ-algebras is that, for the specific case of countable unions, a measure for an algebra is defined if and only if the countable union is defined on it. Although it may seem that it is easier to work on algebras, we would also like to retain the properties of measures defined on σ-algebras. Achieving this can be done with the help of the extensions theorems due to Caratheodory and Hahn. But first, we need to introduce the concept of exterior measure.

Definition 4.12: Exterior Measure: We fix a set S and $\mathcal{A}$ an algebra of subsets in S. We consider B a given subset of S. We define μ^* as the exterior measure generated by μ as $\mu^*(B) = \inf \sum_{j=1}^{\infty} \mu(E_j)$ where the infimum is extended over all sequences (E_j) of sets in A with $B \subseteq \bigcup_{j=1}^{\infty} E_j$.

Although the outer measure is not always a proper measure, it can be shown that it is "close" to a true measure.

Lemma 4.13: Properties of Exterior Measure: The exterior measure μ^* defined in 4.12 has the following properties:

1. $\mu^*(\emptyset) = 0$;
2. $\mu^*(B) \geq 0$ for $B \subseteq S$;
3. If $A \subseteq B$, then it holds that: $\mu^*(A) \leq \mu^*(B)$;
4. If $B \in \mathcal{A}$, then $\mu^*(B) = \mu(B)$;
5. For a sequence of subsets of S denoted by (B_n), the countable sub-additivity property holds: $\mu^*(\bigcup_{n=1}^{\infty} B_n) \leq \sum_{n=1}^{\infty} \mu^*(B_n)$.

We can define μ^*-measurable sets as follows:

Definition 4.13: Outer Measurable Sets: A subset $E \subset S$ is μ^*-measurable if: $\mu^*(A) = \mu^*(A \cup E) + \mu^*(A \setminus E)$.

We can introduce now the Caratheodory Extension Theorem that essentially shows that a measure μ on an algebra $\mathcal{A}$ can always be extended to a measure μ^* on a σ-algebra S^* containing $\mathcal{A}$.

Theorem 4.14: Caratheodory Extension Theorem: The collection S of all μ^* measurable sets is a σ-algebra containing $\mathcal{A}$. Furthermore, for (E_n) a sequence in S of disjoint sets, it also holds that $\mu^*(\bigcup_{n=1}^{\infty} E_n) = \sum_{n=1}^{\infty} \mu^*(E_n)$.

While this theorem ensures that there is at least such an extension of the measure μ, it definitely does not preclude the existence of other extensions. To ensure the uniqueness of this extension, we need the following theorem. We define first σ-finite measures.

Definition 4.14: We fix a set S and an algebra of subsets of S on it denoted by $\mathcal{A}$. We consider a measure μ on $\mathcal{A}$. If there exists a countable sequence of sets $\{A_i\}_{i=1}^{\infty}$ in $\mathcal{A}$ such that $\mu(A_i) < \infty$ and $S = \bigcup_{i=1}^{\infty} A_i$ then we say that the measure μ is σ-finite.

Theorem 4.15: Hahn Extension Theorem: Consider as in the previous theorem a set S and $\mathcal{A}$ an algebra of the subsets in S. Let us also consider a measure μ defined on $\mathcal{A}$. We denote by S the smallest σ-algebra that contains $\mathcal{A}$. Further assuming that the measure μ is σ-finite, then it can be proved that the extension μ^* to S is unique.

The main motivation behind introducing the concepts of measurable set and measures, as seen from the introduction to this section, was to propose a way to deal with the expectations operator. In more general terms, we would like to deal the expected value of real valued functions, with the general form: $E(f)$.

There are various ways to define a measurable function. In the more general sense, we could use the following definition, see [11]:

Definition 4.15: Measurable Functions: We consider the measurable space (S, S) and (T, T). A function f defined as $f : S \to T$ is said to be (S, T) measurable if $A \in T$ implies that $f^{-1}(A) \in S$.

This definition is too general for what we usually need in dynamic programming. The following definition will be actually used throughout the remaining part of this section. Here, we take (T, T) to be $(\mathcal{R}, \mathcal{B}(\mathcal{R}))$.

Definition 4.16: Measurable Functions: We consider the measurable space (S, S). A function f : $S \to \mathbb{R}$ is said to be measurable with respect to S (or S-measurable) if $\{s \in S : f(s) \leq a\} \in S$ for all $a \in \mathbb{R}$.

The above definition is saying that it is actually enough that the set $\{s \in S : f(s) \leq a\}$ is an element of S for each $a \in \mathbb{R}$. It can be proven that we can equivalently use as measurability criteria:

1. $\{s \in S : f(s) \leq a\} \in S$ for all $a \in \mathbb{R}$;
2. $\{s \in S : f(s) \geq a\} \in S$ for all $a \in \mathbb{R}$;
3. $\{s \in S : f(s) > a\} \in S$ for all $a \in \mathbb{R}$;
4. $\{s \in S : f(s) < a\} \in S$ for all $a \in \mathbb{R}$

The next theorems make use of the concept of simple function that are shown that can be used to approximate measurable functions. I introduce first this concept.

We fix a measurable space $(S, \mathcal{S})$ and define on it the indicator function $\chi_A : S \to \mathbb{R}$ as:

$$
\chi_A = \begin{cases} 1, & \text{if } s \in A \\ 0, & \text{if } s \notin A \end{cases}
$$

An indicator function defined like this is $\mathcal{S}$-measurable provided that $A \in \mathcal{S}$. We can construct now simple functions that are weighted sum of the indicator function and thus they are measurable too.

$$
\phi(s) = \sum_{i=1}^{n} a_i \chi_{A_i}(s) \tag{4.42}
$$

Here, $\{A_i\}_{i=1}^{n}$ is defined as a sequence of subsets of S, while $\{a_i\}_{i=1}^{n}$ is a sequence of real numbers. Such functions as the function ϕ above are known as simple functions and they can only take a finite number of values.

Two important results that are very useful are presented below. The first basically says that the set of all functions that are measurable corresponds to set of functions that are pointwise limits of measurable simple functions. The second says that any measurable function f can be written as a pointwise limit of a sequence of measurable simple functions.

Theorem 4.16: On a measurable space $(S, \mathcal{S})$ we consider a sequence of $\mathcal{S}$-measurable functions $\{f_n\}$. If this sequence converges pointwise to f, i.e. $\lim_{n \to \infty} f_n(s) = f(s)$, for all $s \in S$, then f is $\mathcal{S}$-measurable too.

Theorem 4.17: Approximation of Measurable Functions by Simple Functions: We fix a measurable space $(S, \mathcal{S})$. For a $\mathcal{S}$-measurable function $f : S \to \mathbb{R}$, there is a sequence of measurable simple functions $\{\phi_n\}$ for which $\phi_n \to f$ in a pointwise manner.

Before moving to integration, it is useful to note that measurability is preserved under most basic algebraic operations.

Lemma 4.18: We fix a measurable space $(S, \mathcal{S})$. For $\mathcal{S}$-measurable functions f and g on S, and for a constant $c \in \mathbb{R}$, the functions cf, f^2, $f + g$, fg, $|f|$ are measurable too.

It can be further shown that measurability is also preserved when taking limits:

Lemma 4.19: We fix a measurable space $(S, \mathcal{S})$. For a sequence of $\mathcal{S}$-measurable functions $\{f_n\}$ on S, the functions $(sup_n f_n)(x) = sup_n(f_n(x))$, $(inf_n f_n)(x) = inf_n(f_n(x))$, $(lim_{n \to \infty} sup f_n)(x) = lim_{n \to \infty} sup_n(f_n(x))$ and $(lim_{n \to \infty} inf f_n)(x) = lim_{n \to \infty} inf_n(f_n(x))$ are measurable too.

Equipped with the definition of measurable functions we can proceed now to the main object of interest in this section: dealing with the expectations functional $E(f)$. To achieve this, we use the developed concepts of measurable space and measurable functions and introduce the Lebesgue integration. Although I don't follow here step by step this approach, the integration theory is best understood as developed in a sequence of steps as outlined below:

1. simple functions;
2. bounded functions having as a support a set of finite measure;
3. nonnegative functions;
4. general case of integrable functions.

The Lebesgue integration is a generalization of the more familiarly Riemann integration. A simple example following [11] illustrates the differences between the two very well. We start from a closed interval $[a, b]$ on which a function f is defined. The integral in Riemann sense is defined as:

$$
\sum_{k} f(\xi_k) \delta_k \tag{4.43}
$$

Where ξ_k are points chosen on the smaller intervals of the form $[x_k, x_{k+1}]$ such that the value of $f(x)$ at each point within this interval is replaced by the value of f in the arbitrary chosen point ξ_k.

The major problem with this approach is that the points that are close must also lead to close values of the function, in other words, the function must be continuous or, at least, do not present large jumps or discontinuities.

The alternative Lebesgue integral does not rely on grouping the points x on the criterion of being close on the x-axis, but on the criterion that the values of $f(x)$ are close, thus the points x are grouped according to whether the values are close on y-axis. The Lebesgue integral can be written as:

$$\sum_{k=1}^{\infty} y_k \lambda(A_k)$$ (4.44)

Here, as already stated, the integral relies on grouping the points according to close values of the function, i.e. y_k, and A_k is defined as $A_k = \{x : y_k \leq f(x) \leq y_{k+1}\}$ and $\lambda(A_k)$ is the measure of set A_k. The values of y_k are also ordered as: $0 = y_1 \leq ... \leq y_n$.

This approach makes it possible to deal with the inefficiencies of the Riemann integral and integrate functions that are not continuous or present significant discontinuities. In addition, we can use the Lebesgue integral with more general measure spaces. On a measure space (S, S) on which μ is a probability measure, we can compute the expected value of the random variable with respect to distribution μ as $\int_S f(s)\mu(ds)$.

The two integrals however are identical, provided the Riemann integral does exist. We can define now the Lebesgue integral for the case of a simple nonnegative measurable function.

In the following definitions we use the measure space (S, S, μ) and consider $M(S, S)$ as the space of measurable, extended real valued functions on S, while $M^+(S, S)$ is the subset containing only nonnegative functions. By default, a measurable function is understood as S-measurable.

Definition 4.17: Lebesgue Integral for Simple Functions: Consider the function $\phi \in M^+(S, S)$ a measurable simple function. It is further assumed that ϕ has the standard representation $\phi(s) = \sum_{i=1}^{n} a_i \chi_{A_i}(s)$. We define the integral of the function ϕ with respect to the measure μ as:

$$\int_S \phi(s)\mu(ds) = \sum_{i=1}^{n} a_i \mu(A_i)$$ (4.45)

The above definition which is limited to simple functions can be extended for all nonnegative functions on $M^+(S, S)$ with the following definition.

Definition 4.18: Lebesgue Integral for Nonnegative Functions: Consider the function $f \in M^+(S, S)$. We define the integral of the function f with respect to the measure μ as:

$$\int_S f(s)\mu(ds) = sup \int_S \phi(s)\mu(ds)$$ (4.46)

Here, the supremum operator is applied over all the simple functions $\phi \in M^+(S, S)$ for which $0 \leq \phi \leq f$.

When the set $A \in S$, we can define the integral of the function f over the set A with respect to μ as:

$$\int_A f(s)\mu(ds) = \int_S f(s)\chi_A(s)\mu(ds)$$ (4.47)

The notation above can be simplified, where possible to: $\int f d\mu$ and $\int_A d\mu$ respectively.

One of the main advantages of simple functions is that we can express any function in $M^+(S, S)$ as the limit of an increasing sequence $\{\phi_n\}$ of simple functions. This would suggest defining the integral $\int f d\mu$ as the limit of the sequence $\{\int \phi_n d\mu\}$. However, this might imply that the limit depends on the sequence $\{\phi_n\}$ that was chosen. We can first establish that we can use a simple function on a measure space to define a new measure on the same measure space.

Lemma 4.20: Consider a function $\phi \in M^+(S, S)$ and define a function $\lambda : S \to \mathbb{R}$ such that $\lambda(A) = \int_A \phi d\mu$ for all $A \in S$. Then it can be proven that λ is a measure on S too.

With the help of this lemma, we can establish a key result for the material to follow and which implies that the obtained limit is actually unique.

Theorem 4.21: Monotone Convergence Theorem: Consider $\{f_n\}$ a monotone increasing sequence of functions defined in $M^+(S, S)$, such that $f_n \leq f_{n+1}(x)$, $x \in S$, that is assumed to converge to $f \in M^+(S, S)$. Then, it holds that:

$$\int f d\mu = \lim_{n \to \infty} \int f_n d\mu \tag{4.48}$$

We have shown until now how to integrate simple functions and nonnegative functions. We would like now to integrate both positive and negative functions. To achieve this, we impose the condition that the integrals and the functions take finite values. We introduce first the positive and negative parts of a function f, denoted by f^+ and f^-. We define them as follows:

$$f^+ = \begin{cases} f(s), & \text{if } f(s) \geq 0 \\ 0, & \text{if } f(s) < 0 \end{cases}$$

$$f^- = \begin{cases} -f(s), & \text{if } f(s) \leq 0 \\ 0, & \text{if } f(s) > 0 \end{cases}$$

If the function f is measurable, then f^-, f^+ are in $M^+(S, S)$ and $f = f^+ - f^-$.

Definition 4.19: We consider the measure space (S, S, μ) and f a measurable function on S. If f^-, f^+ have finite integrals with respect to μ, then the function f is integrable with respect to the measure μ and:

$$\int f d\mu = \int f^+ d\mu - \int f^- d\mu \tag{4.49}$$

A very useful result can be derived with respect limits of integrals.

Theorem 4.22: Lebesgue Dominated Convergence Theorem: We consider the measure space (S, S, μ) and $\{f_n\}$ a sequence of integrable functions that converge a.e. to a measurable function f. If it exists a function g that is integrable such that $|f_n| \leq g$ for all n, then, it holds that f is integrable and:

$$\int f d\mu = \lim \int f_n d\mu \tag{4.50}$$

A measure λ on a space (S, S) can be obtained by also integrating a nonnegative function $f \in M^+(S, S)$ with respect to a measure μ, $\lambda(A) = \int_A f d\mu$, $A \in S$. The next theorem provides a converse of this result. We introduce first the notion of absolute continuous measure.

Definition 4.20: Absolute Continuous Measures: We fix a measurable space (S, S) and consider two measure on it, μ, ν. One says that λ is absolutely continuous with respect to μ and write $\lambda \ll \mu$ if, for every $S \in S$, $\mu(A) = 0$ implies that $\lambda(A) = 0$.

Theorem 4.23: Radon-Nikodym Theorem: Consider two σ-finite and positive measures on (S, S), λ and μ, such that $\lambda \ll \mu$. Then, there exists a function h that is integrable such that

$$\lambda(A) = \int_A h\mu, A \in S \tag{4.51}$$

This function is unique: if there is another function h' with the same property, then we have that $h' = h$ μ-a.e.

Measures can also be defined in a quite straight manner for product spaces. Let us consider (X, X, μ) and $(Y, \mathcal{Y}, \nu)$ as σ-finite measurable spaces and Z the Cartesian product between X and Y, i.e.:

$$Z = X \times Y = \{z = (x, y) : x \in X, y \in Y\} \tag{4.52}$$

Definition 4.21: Measurable Rectangle: If we define a set C as being given by $C = A \times B \subseteq Z$, then C is a measurable rectangle if $A \in X$ and $B \in \mathcal{Y}$.

We denote by C' the set of all measurable rectangles and by $Z = X \times \mathcal{Y}$ the σ-algebra generated by C'. The next theorem shows the main result with respect to product measure.

Theorem 4.24: Measures on Product Spaces: We fix the σ-finite measure spaces as above, i.e. (X, X, μ), $(Y, \mathcal{Y}, \nu)$ along with (C', Z). We define a measure on $Z = X \times \mathcal{Y}$ such that:

$$\pi(A \times B) = \mu(A)\nu(B) \tag{4.53}$$

For any $A \times B \in C'$. Then, it can be shown that this measure, also known as the product measure of μ and ν, exists, it is unique and σ-finite. We introduce now the notion of section and produce later a formula for the product measure.

Definition 4.22: Sections of a Set: We consider a subset E of $Z = X \times Y$ and take $x \in X$. The x-section of E is defined as:

$$E_x = \{y \in Y : (x, y) \in E\} \tag{4.54}$$

The y-section of E, for $y \in Y$ is defined as:

$$E^y = \{x \in X : (x, y) \in E\} \tag{4.55}$$

Definition 4.23: Sections of a Function: We consider a function $f : Z \to \bar{R}$ and take $x \in X$. The x-section of f is defined as:

$$f_x = f(x, y), \text{ for } y \in Y \tag{4.56}$$

The y-section of f, for $y \in Y$ is defined as:

$$f^y = f(x, y), \text{ for } x \in X \tag{4.57}$$

The following lemma can be established with respect to sections of sets and sections of functions.

Lemma 4.25: a) If E is a measurable subset of Z, then it holds that every section of E is measurable too. b) If $f : Z \to \bar{R}$ is a measurable function, then every section of f is measurable too.

Lemma 4.26: We fix the σ-finite measure spaces (X, X, μ) $(Y, \mathcal{Y}, \nu)$. We consider $E \in Z = X \times Y$. It holds then that the function defined as: $f(x) = \nu(E_x)$, $g(y) = \mu(E^y)$ are measurable and that:

$$\int_x f d\mu = \pi(E) = \int_y g d\nu \tag{4.58}$$

We introduce here first the Tonelli's theorem that applies to nonnegative functions:

Theorem 4.27: We fix the σ-finite measure spaces (X, X, μ) $(Y, \mathcal{Y}, \nu)$. We consider a nonnegative measurable function F on $Z = X \times Y$ to $\bar{R}$. It holds then that the functions defined on X and Y as: $f(x) = \int_Y F_x d\nu$, $g(y) = \int_X F^y d\mu$ are measurable and that:

$$\int_X f d\mu = \int_Z F d\pi = \int_Y g d\nu \tag{4.59}$$

Fubini's theorem refers to the more general case when the function can take both positive and negative values while being assumed as integrable. Consider a measurable space (X, X, μ). We say that a function $f : A \to \mathbb{R}$ is integrable with $\mu(X \setminus A) = 0$ if there is an integrable function $\tilde{f} : X \to \mathbb{R}$ such that $\tilde{f} = f$ on $A \subset X$, and, in this case, we say $\int f := \int \tilde{f}$.

Theorem 4.28: We consider σ-finite measure spaces (X, X, μ) $(Y, \mathcal{Y}, \nu)$. We also take the measure π on $Z = X \times Y$ to $\bar{R}$ to be the product-measure of μ and ν. If the function F defined on $Z = X \times Y$ to $\bar{R}$ is integrable with respect to the measure π then it holds that the real-extended functions which are defined a.e. as: $f(x) = \int_Y F_x d\nu$ and $g(y) = \int_X F^y d\mu$ have finite integrals and that also the following relationship holds:

$$\int_X f d\mu = \int_Z F d\pi = \int_Y g d\nu \tag{4.60}$$

Before moving to Markov Chains, I also introduce the conditional probability and conditional expectations. Let us start from a given probability space $(\Omega, \mathcal{F}, \mu)$. We consider a family of subsets $\{A_\eta\}_{\eta \in H}$. This family of subsets is a measurable partition of Ω provided that the following conditions are satisfied:

1. $A_\eta \in \mathcal{F}$ for all $\eta \in H$, where H is an index set
2. $\bigcup_{\eta \in H} A_\eta = \Omega$
3. $A_\eta \cap A_{\eta'} = \varnothing$ for all $\eta \neq \eta'$

If the index set H is countable, then the measurable partition is countable too.

Let us consider now $\{A_i\}_{i=1}^\infty$ any measurable partition of Ω that is countable and that, for all i, $\mu(A_i) > 0$. The conditional probability of an event can be defined in a standard manner as:

$$Pr(B|A_i) = \mu_{A_i}(B) = \mu(B \cap A_i)/\mu(A_i) \tag{4.61}$$

Here, the measurable set $B \in \mathcal{F}$. We can define in a similar manner the conditional expectation for a given integrable function f as follows:

$$E(f|A_i) = \int f d\mu_{A_i} \tag{4.62}$$

For all $f \in L(\Omega, \mathcal{F}, \mu)$, with L the space of integrable functions on $\mathcal{F}$.

We may be interested however to define conditional expectations on more general σ-algebras (not necessarily generated by a countable partition) and for integrable function.

Definition 4.24: Conditional Expectation: Let us consider the probability space $(\Omega, \mathcal{F}, \mu)$, $\mathcal{A} \subset \mathcal{F}$ a σ-algebra and $f : \Omega \to \mathbb{R}$ an integrable function. The conditional expectation of f relative to $\mathcal{A}$ is a $\mathcal{A}$-measurable function $E(f|\mathcal{A}) : \Omega \to R$ for which:

$$\int_C E(f|\mathcal{A})(\omega)\mu(d\omega) = \int_C f(\omega)\mu(d\omega) \tag{4.63}$$

for all $C \in \mathcal{A}$.

A key result regarding the conditional expectation defined above is that it can be proved that a $\mathcal{A}$-measurable function $E(f|\mathcal{A})$ always exists and it is unique.

4.3.1.3   Markov Chains

The purpose of this subsection is to build the mathematical apparatus necessary to deal with incorporating shocks in the representation of the dynamic programming models. The chapter deals with Markov processes for the reason that we must impose that the exogenous shocks are recursive and Markov processes fulfill this condition.

We fix a $(Z, \mathcal{Z})$ measurable space, λ a probability measure on $(Z, \mathcal{Z})$. The recursive representation can be rewritten such that to take into account the recursive nature of the shocks:

$$V(x, z) = \sup_{y \in G(x,z)} [U(x, y, z) + \beta * \int V(y, z')Q(z, dz')] \tag{4.64}$$

Here, x stands for the endogenous state variable in the current period, z is the exogenous shock in the current period, y is the endogenous state variable in the next period while z' stands for the next period exogenous shock. Furthermore, $Q(z,)$ is a probability measure. It is on the structure of Q functions that we first focus on.

Definition 4.25: Transition Functions: Let us fix the measurable space $(Z, \mathcal{Z})$. The function $Q : Z \times \mathcal{Z} \to [0, 1]$ is a transition function if it satisfies:

1. For each $z \in Z$, $Q(z, \cdot)$ is a probability measure on the measure space $(Z, \mathcal{Z})$
2. For each $A \in \mathcal{Z}$, $Q(\cdot, A)$ is a $\mathcal{Z}$-measurable function.

We assume that the function $Q(z, \cdot)$ is a transition function. Intuitively, $Q(a, A)$ can be interpreted as the probability that the next period exogenous shock z' lies in the set A given the current value of the exogenous shock $z = a$, i.e. $Q(a, A) = Pr\{z_{t+1} \in A | z_t = a\}$.

We can further define two essential operators which are very useful later. We can define an operator Tf for the $\mathcal{Z}$-measurable function f as:

$$(Tf)(z) = \int f(z')Q(z, dz') \tag{4.65}$$

For all $z \in Z$. Intuitively, $Tf(z)$ tells us what is the expected value of the function in the next period, conditional on the current value being z.

A second operator we can define is on the probability measure $(Z, \mathcal{Z})$. Given a probability measure λ on $(Z, \mathcal{Z})$, we can define the operator $T^*\lambda$ as:

$$(T^*\lambda)(A) = \int Q(z, A)\lambda(dz) \tag{4.66}$$

For all $A \in \mathcal{Z}$. If the current state is drawn following λ, then $T^*\lambda(A)$ is the probability that the next period lies in set A.

The next two theorems show key properties of the above defined operators, T and T^*. Here, we make use of the previously defined set $M^+(Z, \mathcal{Z})$, as the space of nonnegative, $\mathcal{Z}$-measurable real-valued functions.

Theorem 4.29: The operator T defined above maps the space $M^+(Z, \mathcal{Z})$ into itself, that is: $T : M^+(Z, \mathcal{Z}) \to M^+(Z, \mathcal{Z})$.

In a similar manner, for the operator T^*, given the space of probability measures $\Lambda(Z, \mathcal{Z})$, we can state the following theorem:

Theorem 4.30: The operator T^* defined above maps the space of probability measures $\Lambda(Z, \mathcal{Z})$ into itself, that is: $T^* : \Lambda(Z, \mathcal{Z}) \to \Lambda(Z, \mathcal{Z})$.

If we define $B(Z, \mathcal{Z})$ as the space of bounded, $\mathcal{Z}$-real valued functions, it can be also shown that the operator T maps this space into itself:

Theorem 4.31: The operator T defined above maps the space $B(Z, \mathcal{Z})$ into itself, that is: $T : B(Z, \mathcal{Z}) \to B(Z, \mathcal{Z})$.

The space $C(Z)$ of functions that are bounded and continuous is a subset of $B(Z, \mathcal{Z})$. In working with stochastic dynamic programming, we would like to ensure that the operator T maps the space $C(Z)$ into itself. The following definition introduces this specific property which will be very useful later.

Definition 4.26: Feller Property: We say that a transitions function Q defined on $(Z, \mathcal{Z})$ has the Feller property if the operator T associated to it maps the space $C(Z)$ into itself, namely: $T : C(Z) \to C(Z)$.

Using the above definitions and results, we can move now to define Markov processes. We start by defining a measurable space $(Z, \mathcal{Z})$ and define a produce space on it as:

$$(Z^t, \mathcal{Z}^t) = (Z \times ... \times Z, \mathcal{Z} \times ... \times \mathcal{Z}) \tag{4.67}$$

On the measurable space $(Z, \mathcal{Z})$, we define the transition function Q and consider a $z_0 \in Z$ as given. We can define now probability measures $\mu^t(z_0,) : \mathcal{Z}^t \to [0, 1]$ on such spaces. For any rectangle $B = A_1 \times ... \times A_t \in \mathcal{Z}^t$, we define:

$$\mu^t(z_0, B) = \int_{A_1} ... \int_{A_{t-1}} \int_{A_t} Q(z_{t-1}, dz_t)...Q(z_0, dz_1) \tag{4.68}$$

We can verify that it fulfills the following three conditions:

1. $\mu^t(z_0, \varnothing) = 0$
2. if $\{B_i\} = \{(A_{1i} \times ... \times A_{ti})\}_{i=1}^{\infty}$ is a sequence of disjoint sets in $\mathcal{Z}^t$ and $\bigcup_{i=1}^{\infty} B_i$ in $\mathcal{Z}^t$ then $\mu^t(z_0, \bigcup_{i=1}^{\infty} B_i) = \sum_{i=1}^{\infty} \mu^t(z_0, B_i)$
3. $\mu^t(z_0, Z^t) = 1$

Thus $\mu^t(z_0,)$ is a probability measure. Following Caratheodory and Hahn extensions theorems, $\mu^t(z_0,)$ can be shown to have a unique extension to a probability measure on Z^t. We can define probabilities on infinite sequences in a similar manner.

We define now stochastic processes and Markov processes as follows. We fix first a probability space $(\Omega, \mathcal{F}, P)$.

Definition 4.27: Stochastic Processes: On the probability space $(\Omega, \mathcal{F}, P)$, we define a stochastic process as an increasing sequence of σ-algebras, i.e. $\mathcal{F}_1 \subseteq \mathcal{F}_2 \subseteq ... \subseteq \mathcal{F}$, a measurable space $(Z, \mathcal{Z})$ as well as a sequence of function $\sigma_t : \Omega \to Z$, with $t = 1, 2, ...$ such that each function σ_t is $\mathcal{F}_t$-measurable.

For the specific case when the function σ_t takes values into $Z = \mathbb{R}$, the function is just a random variable on the given probability space $(\Omega, \mathcal{F}, P)$.

Definition 4.28: First-Order Markov Processes: On the probability space $(\Omega, \mathcal{F}, P)$, a Markov process is a stochastic process that has the following property:

$$P_{t+1...t+n}(C|a_{t-s}, ..., a_{t-1}, a_t) = P_{t+1...t+n}(C|a_t) \tag{4.69}$$

Here $t = 2, ..., n$; $n = 1, 2, ...$; $s = 1, 2, ..., t-1$ and $C \in \mathcal{Z}^n$. In words, a Markov process is a stochastic process that has the specific property that future realizations depend only on the current realization $\sigma_t = a_t$. A Markov process has stationary transitions if the conditional probabilities $P_{t+1}(A|a)$ are independent of time t for all $a \in Z$ and $A \in \mathcal{Z}$.

Using the measures $\mu^t(z_0,)$, we can define expected values rather straightforward as follows. If $z^t = (z_1, ...,)$ is an element of Z^t, with t taking values from $t = 1, 2, ...$, the expected value of any function U that is integrable with respect to the measure $\mu^t(z_0,)$ can be written as:

$$E(U|z_0) = \int_{Z^t} U(z^t) \mu^t(z_0, dz^t) \tag{4.70}$$

[4] further show (but the results would take too much space if they were presented here) that the above integral can be expressed as an iterated integral. Take $t \in \{2, 3, ...\}$ and consider $U : Z^t \to \mathbb{R}$ a function that is $\mathcal{Z}^t$-measurable. Further assume that U is $\mu^t(z_0, \cdot)$-integrable. We denote the z^{t-1} section of U by $U(z^{t-1}, \cdot) : Z \to \bar{\mathbb{R}}$. Then, it can be shown that:

$$\int_{Z^t} U(z^t) \mu^t(z_0, dz^t) = \int_{Z^{t-1}} [\int_Z U(z^{t-1}, z_t) Q(z_{t-1}, dz_t)] \mu^{t-1}(z_0, dz^{t-1}) \tag{4.71}$$

4.3.1.4 Assumptions

We assume that $(X, \mathcal{X})$, $(Y, \mathcal{Y})$ and $(Z, \mathcal{Z})$ are measurable spaces, while $(S, \mathcal{S}) = (X \times Z, \mathcal{X} \times \mathcal{Z})$ is a product space (S denotes the set of the state values). The endogenous state variables takes value in X, while Z is the set of values for the exogenous shock z. We use Y to define the set of possible actions which the decision maker could take. The stochastic shocks evolve according to the stationary transition function $Q(Z, \mathcal{Z})$.

As already mentioned above, the constraint correspondence $G(x, z)$ depends now on the stochastic shock too, with $G : X \times Z \to Y$. The graph of G is $A = \{(x, y, z) \in X \times Y \times Z : y \in G(x, z)\}$.

We extend first the concepts of plan and feasible plan for stochastic case. We define the product spaces $(Z^t, \mathcal{Z}^t)$, and denote by $z^t = (z_1, ..., z_t) \in Z^t$ a partial history of shocks from period 1 to period t.

The utility function $U(x, y, z)$ is defined on set A, i.e. $U : A \to \mathbb{R}$. To describe the dynamics of the variable x we define the set D as: $D = \{(x, y) \in X \times Y : y \in G(x, z)\}$ for a particular value of $z \in Z$. The law of motion for x is described by function $\phi : D \times Z \to X$, with $x' = \phi(x, y, z')$ or the next value of x, x', is determined by the current value, the action y taken and the next period realization z' of the stochastic process.

Definition 4.29: A plan is defined as sequence of measurable functions $\pi = \{\pi_t\}_{t=0}^\infty$ for which $\pi_t : Z^t \to X$ is $\mathcal{Z}^t$-measurable.

Definition 4.30: A plan π is said to be feasible starting with $s_0 \in S$, if:

1. $\pi_0 \in G(s_0)$
2. $\pi^t(z_t) \in G(x_t^\pi(z^t), z_t)$, for all $z^t \in Z^t$, and $t = 1, 2, ...$.

The functions $x_t^\pi : Z^t \to X$, with $t = 1, 2, ...$ are defined as:

$$x_1^\pi(z_1) = \phi(x_0, \pi_0, z_1), z_1 \in Z$$
$$x_t^\pi(z^t) = \phi(x_{t-1}^\pi(z^{t-1}), \pi_{t-1}(z^{t-1}), z_t), z_t \in Z^t, t = 2, ... \tag{4.72}$$

I present below the assumptions that will be made before moving to the key results regarding stochastic dynamic programming. The assumptions generally correspond to the deterministic case, except a few cases where supplementary assumptions are needed in order to deal with the stochastic nature of the problem. To mirror the presentation for the deterministic case, I denote the assumptions for stochastic case by adding the sign prime to the corresponding assumption's number for deterministic case. The givens for the stochastic dynamic programming problem are $(X, \mathcal{X}), (Y, \mathcal{Y}), (Z, \mathcal{Z}), (S, \mathcal{S}), Q, G, U, \beta, \phi$.

Assumption 4.1′: It is assumed that the correspondence $G(x)$ is nonempty. The graph of G is $(\mathcal{X} \times \mathcal{Y} \times \mathcal{Z})$-measurable. It is also assumed that G has a measurable selection; in other words, there is a measurable function $h : S \to X$ such that $h(s) \in G(s)$ for all $s \in S$. Furthermore, the function $\phi : D \times Z \to X$ is measurable.

We take a look now at the way the total discounted expected returns are calculated in the case of a given feasible plan. We fix the probability measures $\mu^t(z_0, \cdot)$ and define the set $\mathcal{A}$ as $\mathcal{A} = \{C \in \mathcal{X} \times \mathcal{Y} \times \mathcal{Z} : C \subset A\}$.

Assumption 4.2′: The function $U : A \to \mathbb{R}$ is $\mathcal{A}$-measurable and one of the following two conditions holds:

1. $U \geq 0$ or $U \leq 0$
2. For each $(x_0, z_0) = s_0 \in S$, and each plan $\pi \in \Pi(s_0)$, then:

$U[x_t^\pi(z^t), \pi_t(z^t), z_t]$ is $\mu^t(z_0,)$-integrable, and the following limit exists:
$U(x_0, \pi_0, z_0) + \lim_{n \to \infty} \sum_{t=1}^{n} \int_{Z^t} \beta^t U[x_t^\pi(z^t), \pi_t(z^t), z_t] \mu^t(z_0, dz^t)$

Assumption 4.3′: Assume that the function U takes on both signs. Then, there exists a collection of nonnegative measurable functions $L_t : S \to \mathbb{R}_+$, with the property that, for all $\pi \in \Pi(s_0)$ and all $s_0 \in S$, we have:

1. $|U(x_0, \pi_0, z_0)| \leq L_0(s_0)$
2. $|U[x_t^\pi(z^t), \pi_t(z^t), z_t]| \leq L_t(s_0)$, for all $z^t \in Z^t$
3. $\sum_{t=0}^{\infty} \beta^t L_t(s_0) < \infty$

To carry on with the results similar to the ones for the deterministic case, I assume in the following that the return function U is bounded and continuous, the discount factor β is less than one while the transition function Q has the Feller property.

First, we impose a condition on X, mirroring the deterministic case, and then move to impose further conditions on Z, Q, which are specific to the stochastic case.

Assumption 4.4′: X is a Borel set in $\mathbb{R}^k$, which is also convex. Its Borel subsets are denoted by $\mathcal{X}$.

Assumption 4.5′: It is assumed that one of the following two statements holds:

1. Z is a countable set, while $\mathcal{Z}$ is a σ-algebra containing all the subsets of Z;
2. Z is a compact Borel set in $\mathcal{R}^k$, its Borel subsets are denoted by $\mathcal{Z}$, and the transition function Q defined on $(Z, \mathcal{Z})$ has the Feller property.

The following assumptions are the similar to the ones used in the deterministic case.

Assumption 4.6′: The correspondence $G : X \times Z \to X$ is nonempty, continuous and compact-valued.

Assumption 4.7′: The return function $U : A \to \mathbb{R}$ is bounded, continuous. The discount factor β takes values in $(0, 1)$.

The following two assumptions impose monotonicity on the return function U and the correspondence G:

Assumption 4.8′: For each $(y, z) \in X \times Z$, the return function $U(\cdot, y, z) : A_{yz} \to \mathbb{R}$ is strictly increasing.

Assumption 4.9′: The correspondence $G(\cdot, z) : X \to X$, is increasing, that is $x \leq x'$ implies $G(x, z) \subseteq G(x', z)$, for each $z \in Z$.

We can further impose concavity restrictions on U and G:

Assumption 4.10′: For each $z \in Z$, the return function $U(\cdot, \cdot, z) : A_z \to \mathbb{R}$ is concave, that is, for all $\theta \in (0, 1)$ and all $(x, y), (x', y') \in A_z$, the following holds:

$$U[\theta(x, y) + (1 - \theta)(x', y'), z] \geq \theta U(x, y, z) + (1 - \theta)U(x', y', z) \tag{4.73}$$

Assumption 4.11′: For each $z \in Z$, $x, x' \in X$, the correspondence G is convex, that is:

$$\theta y + (1 - \theta)y' \in G[\theta x + (1 - \theta)x', z] \tag{4.74}$$

For all $\theta \in [0, 1]$, and each $y \in G(x, z)$ and $y' \in G(x', z)$.

To also establish the differentiability of the value function, we need a further assumption on the differentiability of the return function F:

Assumption 4.12′: The return function $U(\cdot, \cdot, z) : A_z \to \mathbb{R}$, for each fixed $z \in Z$, is continuously differentiable in (x, y) on the interior of A_z.

4.3.1.5 Theorems

Using the above assumptions, a number of results can be established. First, a direct result when Assumption 4.1' holds is the following.

Lemma 4.32: Let Assumption 4.1' hold, and fix $(X, \mathcal{X})$, $(Z, \mathcal{Z})$. Assume a given correspondence G, as described above. Then, $\Pi(s)$ is not empty for all $s \in S$.

If Assumption 4.2' holds too, then, for each $s_0 \in S$, it is possible to define the functions $u_n(, s_0) : \Pi \to \mathbb{R}$ and $u(, s_0) : \Pi \to \mathbb{R}$ as follows:

1. $u_0(\pi, s_0) = U[x_0, \pi_0, z_0]$
2. $u_n(\pi, s_0) = U[x_0, \pi_0, z_0] + \sum_{t=1}^{n} \int_{Z^t} \beta^t U[x_t^{\pi}(z^t), \pi_t(z^t), z_t]\mu^t(z_0, dz^t)$
3. $u(\pi, s_0) = \lim_{n \to \infty} u_n(\pi, s_0)$

Here, $u_n(\pi, s_0)$ is the sum of the expected discounted returns from period 0 to period n for the plan π assuming as given the initial state s_0. If Assumptions 4.1' and 4.2' hold, then the function $u(, s_0)$ is well defined on the set $\Pi(s_0)$ for any $s_0 \in S$. It is possible then to define the supremum function $V^* : S \to \mathbb{R}$ as given by:

$$V^*(s) = \sup_{\pi \in \Pi(s)} u(\pi, s) \tag{4.75}$$

The corresponding functional equation can be written as:

$$V(s) = \sup_{y \in G(s)} [U(x, y, z) + \beta \int V[\phi(x, y, z'), z']Q(z, dz')] \tag{4.76}$$

If a function v satisfies Eq. (4.76), then a policy correspondence g associated to it can be written as:

$$g(s) = \{y \in G(s) : V(s) = [U(x, y, z) + \beta \int V[\phi(x, y, z'), z']Q(z, dz')]\} \tag{4.77}$$

For a nonempty g, and in case there is a measurable selection from g, it is said that π is generated from s_0 by g in case it is constructed as follows. Define first a sequence of measurable selections from g as $g_0, g_1, ...$ for which:

1. $\pi_0 = g_0(x_0, z_0)$
2. $\pi_t(z^t) = g_t[x_t^{\pi}(z^t), z_t]$, for all $z^t \in Z^t$.

Since each g_t is measurable, and π satisfies the previously defined conditions, π is measurable too, and thus any plan that is generated by g from s_0 is a feasible plan from s_0.

If Assumptions 4.1' and 4.2' hold, and if V^* is well defined, then, the following result can be established.

Theorem 4.33: We fix $(X, \mathcal{X})$, $(Y, \mathcal{Y})$, $(Z, \mathcal{Z})$, Q, G, U, β and ϕ as until now. Suppose Assumptions 4.1' and 4.2' hold and consider a function V^* defined as in (4.75). Further assume a correspondence g defined as above, while also assume g is both nonempty and it allows measurable selections. Assume V is a measurable function given by (4.76) which satisfies:

$$\lim_{t \to \infty} \int_{Z^t} \beta^t V[x_t^{\pi}(z^t), z_t]u^t(z_0, dz^t) = 0 \tag{4.78}$$

for all $\pi \in \Pi(x_0, z_0)$ and all $(x_0, z_0) \in X \times Z$. Then, it can be proven that: $V = V^*$ as well as that any plan π^* generated by the correspondence g attains the supremum in (4.75).

Theorem 4.33 has also a partial converse, to be presented below in Theorem 4.35. The main result in Theorem 4.35 is that for a set of more strict hypotheses, a plan is optimal only when it is generated by g. To present it, first a new concept has to be introduced.

Given $s_0 \in S$, $\pi \in \Pi(s_0)$ and $z_1 \in Z$, the continuation of π following z_1 is denoted by $C(\pi, z_1)$ and it is defined as follows:

1. $C_0(\pi, z_1) = \pi_1(z_1)$
2. $C_t(z_2^{t+1}; \pi, z_1) = \pi_{t+1}(z^{t+1})$, for all $z_2^{t+1} \in Z^T$, $t = 1, 2, \dots$.

By definition, each function $C_t(\cdot; \pi, z_1) : Z^t \to X$ is the z_1-section of the function π_{t+1}. As shown previously, these functions are measurable too, and they also satisfy the feasibility constraints. Letting Assumptions 4.1' to 4.3' hold, the following result can now be established.

Lemma 4.34: Let Assumptions 4.1' to 4.3' hold, and fix $(X, \mathcal{X})$, $(Z, \mathcal{Z})$, Q, G, U, β and ϕ as before. Then, it can be shown that, for any $(x_0, z_0) = s_0 \in S$ and any $\pi \in \Pi(s_0)$ it holds that:

$$u(\pi, s_0) = U(x_0, \pi_0, z_0) + \beta \int_Z u[C(\pi, z_1), (\pi_1^\pi(z_1), z_1)] Q(z_0, dz_1) \tag{4.79}$$

with $C(\pi, z_1)$ being the continuation of π following z_1 for each $z_1 \in Z$.

Once this partial but key result in Lemma 4.34 has been established, we can proceed and further establish that any plan π^* which attains the supremum in Eq. (4.75) is generated almost everywhere by g.

Theorem 4.35: Fix, as before, $(X, \mathcal{X})$, $(Z, \mathcal{Z})$, Q, G, U and β. Consider that Assumptions 4.1' to 4.3' apply and further consider the function V^* as in (4.75), taken as measurable and satisfying Eq. (4.76). The correspondence g is defined by Eq. (4.77), with g assumed as both nonempty and allowing measurable selections. Also, we take $(x_0, z_0) = s_0 \in S$ and we let $\pi^* \in \Pi(s_0)$ a plan that attains the supremum defined by Eq. (4.75), assuming an initial condition s_0. It can be shown that, under these conditions, there is a plan generated by g from s_0 and denoted by π^g such that:

1. $\pi_0^g = \pi_0^*$
2. $\pi_t^g(z^t) = \pi_t^*(z^t)$

$\mu^t(z_0,)$-a.e. and $t = 1, 2, \dots$.

Assumptions 4.4' and 4.5' allow us to parallel the results for the deterministic case, since under these two assumptions, the application of the integration preserves the needed properties of the integrand in (4.75), that is the properties of boundedness, continuity, monotonicity and concavity. To further advance, the following result is necessary:

Lemma 4.36: Suppose $(X, \mathcal{X})$, $(Z, \mathcal{Z})$, and the transition function Q satisfy Assumptions 4.4' and 4.5'. Further assume a function $u : X \times Z \to \mathcal{R}$ that is both bounded and continuous. Let us define a function Mu by:

$$(Mu)(y, z) = \int u(y, z') Q(z, dz') \tag{4.80}$$

For all $(y, z) \in X \times Z$, such that $M : C(S) \to C(S)$. Then, if the function u is increasing in each of the first k arguments, then so is Mu, and if u is concave jointly in the first k arguments, so is Mu.

The main implication of this key result is that it becomes possible to extend the results from the deterministic to the stochastic case. First, we further let Assumptions 4.6' and 4.7' hold to establish the following result.

Theorem 4.37: We fix $(X, \mathcal{X})$, $(Z, \mathcal{Z})$, Q, G, U and β as previously and suppose that they satisfy Assumptions 4.4' to 4.7'. We further define the operator T on $C(S)$ as:

$$(TU)(x, z) = \sup_{y \in G(x, z)} \{U(x, y, z) + \beta \int U(y, z') Q(z, dz')\} \tag{4.81}$$

It can be shown that T maps $C(S)$ into itself, that is $T : C(S) \to C(S)$, that T has a unique fixed point $V \in C(S)$ and for a $V_0 \in C(S)$ it also holds that:

$$\|T^n V_0 - V\| \leq \beta^n \|V_0 - V\| \tag{4.82}$$

Additionally, it holds that the correspondence $g : S \to X$ as defined by equation $g(x, z) = \{y \in (G, z) : V(x, z) = U(x, y, z) + \beta \int V(y, z')Q(z, dz'))\}$ is nonempty, compact-valued and upper-hemicontinuous.

If we also assume monotonicity about the return function U and the correspondence G, then the following result characterizes more sharply the fixed point of operator T:

Theorem 4.38: Fix again $(X, \mathcal{X})$, $(Z, \mathcal{Z})$, Q, G, U and β as previously and suppose that they satisfy Assumptions 4.4' to 4.9'. Let V be the unique fixed point operator of T in Eq. (4.81). For any $z \in Z$, the function $V(\cdot, z) : X \to \mathbb{R}$ is strictly increasing.

Once the assumptions of concavity are imposed, the value function is shown to concave.

Theorem 4.39: Take again $(X, \mathcal{X})$, $(Z, \mathcal{Z})$, Q, G, U and β as previously and suppose that they satisfy Assumptions 4.4'–4.7', as well as 4.10'–4.11'. Let V be the unique fixed point operator of T in Eq. (4.81). Furthermore, let the correspondence g be defined as above. For any $z \in Z$, the value function $V(\cdot, z) : X \to \mathbb{R}$ is strictly concave while the correspondence $g(\cdot, z) : X \to X$ is a continuous function.

The assumption of concavity also implies that the sequence of approximate policy functions denoted by $\{g_n\}$ converges to the optimal policy function g. This result is presented below:

Theorem 4.40: Suppose $(X, \mathcal{X})$, $(Z, \mathcal{Z})$, Q, G, F and β satisfy Assumptions 4.4'–4.7', as well as 4.10'–4.11'. Let $C'(S) \subset C(S)$ be the set of bounded continuous functions on S that are weakly concave jointly in their first k arguments. Also, $V \in C'(S)$ is the unique fixed point of the operator in (4.81), while $g = G$ is the function defined by as above. If $V_0 \in C'(S)$ and we define $\{(V_n, g_n)\}$ by:

1. $V_n = T V_{n-1}$
2. $g_n(x, z) = \arg\max_{y \in G(x,z)} \{U(x, y, z) + \beta \int V_n(y, z')Q(z, dz')\}$

The, it can be shown then that $g_n \to g$ pointwise. Furthermore, if X, and Z are both compact sets, the convergence is uniform.

When we further assume that the return function U is differentiable, then the following result about the differentiability of the value function can be established:

Theorem 4.41: Suppose $(X, \mathcal{X})$, $(Z, \mathcal{Z})$, Q, G, U and β satisfy Assumptions 4.4'–4.7', as well as 4.10'–4.12'. Assume that $V \in C'(S)$ is the unique fixed point of the operator in (4.81), while $g = G$ is the function defined as above. If $x_0 \in int(X)$ and $g(x_0, z_0) \in int(G(x_0, z_0))$, then it can be shown that $V(\cdot, z_0)$ is continuously differentiable in x at x_0 with the derivatives written as:

$$V_i(x_0, z_0) = U_i[x_0, g(x_0, z_0), z_0] \tag{4.83}$$

For $i = 1, ..., k$.

4.3.2 Numerical Algorithms and Applications

4.3.2.1 The Stochastic Optimal Growth Model

Before moving to actual applications, I introduce the stochastic optimal growth model which will be used as an illustrative example for solving dynamic programming problems with numerical techniques. The presentation follows [4] and [5].

Assume a one-sector economy in which there is a representative household. The instantaneous utility function is $u()$ while the discount factor $\beta \in (0, 1)$. The representative household maximizes the lifetime utility:

$$\max_{\{c_t\}_{t=0}^\infty} \mathbb{E}_0 \sum_{t=0}^\infty \beta^t u(c_t) \tag{4.84}$$

The notation is similar to the deterministic optimal growth model: k_t, c_t are the capital stock and consumption. Each period, the household face the following constraint:

$$k_{t+1} = exp(a_t) f(k_t) + (1 - \delta)k_t - c_t \tag{4.85}$$

a_t is the productivity. It is further assumed that the initial capital stock k_0 is given while $k_t \geq 0$. We can remove the time subscripts as before, and assuming the production function is given by $f(k_t) = k^\alpha$, we can write it as:

$$k' = exp(a)k^\alpha + (1 - \delta)k - c \tag{4.86}$$

Here, the productivity evolves according to $a' = \rho a + \epsilon'$. Furthermore, we can assume the same specification of the utility function as for the

$$u(c) = \frac{c^{1-\sigma} - 1}{1 - \sigma} \tag{4.87}$$

Given these assumptions, we can write the Bellman equation as:

$$V(k, a) = \max_c \frac{c^{1-\sigma} - 1}{1 - \sigma} + \beta \int V(k', a')d\mu(a'|a) \tag{4.88}$$

Eq. (4.86) allows us to determine the consumption as follows:

$$c = exp(a)k^\alpha + (1 - \delta)k - k' \tag{4.89}$$

We can rewrite the Bellman equation as:

$$V(k, a) = \max_{k'} \frac{(exp(a)k^\alpha + (1 - \delta)k - k')^{1-\sigma} - 1}{1 - \sigma} + \beta \int V(k', a')d\mu(a'|a) \tag{4.90}$$

4.3.2.2 Discretization of the Shocks

A key issue in numerically solving a stochastic dynamic programming problem is dealing with space spanned by the shocks. In theory, the support for the stochastic shocks is continuous, however, to numerically solve such problems, we need to transform the shocks into discrete one, while keeping the properties for the continuous process.

Fortunately, there are a few sound solutions proposed in the literature that deal with the process of discretization the shocks. In this subsection, I cover the algorithm proposed by [8]. The focus is rather on the simpler case of AR(1) processes, though the initial contribution covers the more general case of VAR shocks.

The presentation follows Tauchen and Hussey, see [8], as well as Collard, see [5]. I focus on the following specification:

$$s_{t+1} = \rho s_t + (1 - \rho) * \bar{s} + \epsilon_{t+1} \tag{4.91}$$

Here, the shocks ϵ_{t+1} are assumed to follow a normal distribution $\mathcal{N}(0, \sigma^2)$.

Since s is a continuous random variable, we can write:

$$\frac{1}{\sigma\sqrt{2\pi}} \int_{-\infty}^{\infty} exp\{\frac{-1}{2}(\frac{s_{t+1} - \rho s_t - (1 - \rho)\bar{s}}{\sigma})^2\}ds_{t+1} = \int f(s_{t+1}|s_t)ds_{t+1} = 1 \tag{4.92}$$

In the algorithm by Tauchen and Hussey, the integral on the right is replaced by:

$$\int \Phi(s_{t+1}; s_t, \bar{s})f(s_{t+1}|\bar{s})ds_{t+1} = \int \frac{f(s_{t+1}|s_t)}{f(s_{t+1}|\bar{s})}f(s_{t+1}|\bar{s})ds_{t+1} = 1 \tag{4.93}$$

Here $f(s_{t+1}|s_t)$ is interpreted as standing for the density of s_{t+1} conditional on $s_t = \bar{s}$. Then, it holds that:

$$\Phi(s_{t+1}; s_t, \bar{s}) = \frac{f(s_{t+1}|s_t)}{f(s_{t+1}|\bar{s})} = exp\{\frac{-1}{2}[(\frac{s_{t+1} - \rho s_t - (1 - \rho)\bar{s}}{\sigma})^2 - (\frac{s_{t+1} - \bar{s}}{\sigma})^2]\} \tag{4.94}$$

When we use the standard linear transformation and write $z_t = (s_t - \bar{s})/\sigma\sqrt{2}$, then we obtain:

$$\frac{1}{\sqrt{\pi}} \int_{-\infty}^{\infty} exp\{-((z_{t+1} - \rho z_t)^2 - z_{t+1}^2 j)\}exp(-z_{t+1}^2)dz_{t+1} \tag{4.95}$$

For this specification, it is possible to use the Gauss-Hermite quadrature (see Chapter 2, the section on numerical integration). The following formula can be used:

$$\frac{1}{\sqrt{\pi}} \sum_{j=1}^{n} \omega_j \Phi(z_j; z_i; \bar{x}) \simeq 1 \tag{4.96}$$

Where it is assumed that the quadrature nodes z_i as well as the weights ω_i with $i = 1, ..., n$ are given.

The interpretation of the above formula is quite intuitive. The expression $\omega_i \Phi(z_j; z_i; \bar{x})$ can be understood as an estimator of the transition probability of the Markov chain from the state i to the state j, i.e. $\hat{\pi}_{ij} = Prob(s_{t+1} = s_j | s_t = s_i)$. Since this expression is just an approximation, generally, the condition $\sum_{j=1}^{n} \hat{\pi}_{ij} = 1$ will hold only approximately. To address this issue, Tauchen and Hussey proposed this formula:

$$\hat{\pi}_{ij} = \frac{\omega_j \Phi(z_j; z_i; \bar{s})}{\sqrt{\pi} \zeta_i} \tag{4.97}$$

Here, $\zeta_i = \frac{1}{\sqrt{\pi}} \sum_{j=1}^{n} \omega_j \Phi(z_j; z_i; \bar{x})$.

For the algorithms below, we can assume that the productivity shocks can be approximated with the help of a Markov chain with 2 states (that is, the productivity a can take two values a_1, a_2, with $a_1 < a_2$). It is further assumed that the transition matrix is symmetric, such that we can write it was: $\Pi = \begin{bmatrix} \pi & 1 - \pi \\ 1 - \pi & \pi \end{bmatrix}$.

It is also essential that the two state values a_1, a_2 are chosen in such a way that they reproduce the conditional first and second order moments of the $AR(1)$ process.

The conditional first order moments are: $\pi a_1 + (1 - \pi)a_2 = \rho a_1$, and $(1 - \pi)a_2 + \pi a_2 = \rho a_2$, while the second order moments can be written as: $\pi a_1^2 + (1 - \pi)a_2^2 - (\rho a_1)^2 = \sigma_\epsilon^2$, and: $(1 - \pi)a_2^2 + \pi a_2^2 - (\rho a_2)^2 = \sigma_\epsilon^2$. Using the first two equations, we can get the relationship between a_1 and a_2 as: $a_1 = -a_2$, while we also get that: $\pi = (1 + \rho)/2$. This allows us to solve for a_1 using the last equations such that we obtain: $a_1 = \sqrt{\sigma_\epsilon^2/(1 - \rho^2)}$.

Given this specification of the Markov chain, when coding the algorithm, we rely on the following specification of the value function:

$$V(k, a_k) = \max_c \frac{c^{1-\sigma} - 1}{1 - \sigma} + \beta \sum_{j=1}^{2} \pi_{kj} V_j(k', a_j')) \tag{4.98}$$

4.3.2.3 Value Function Iteration

Te algorithm for the value function iteration for the stochastic case is based on the same idea as the deterministic case. Again, the convergence is based on the contraction mapping theorem, though it is a bit more complicated since we are dealing with the convergence of a probability measure.

I present below the algorithm for value function iteration, before implementing it in Julia for the optimal growth model.

1. Construct a grid of admissible values for the state variable k of the form: $\mathcal{K} = \{k_1, ..., k_n\}$. In addition, consider also the shocks s in $\mathcal{S} = \{s_1, ..., s_M\}$, along the transition matrix $\Pi = (\pi_{ij})$.
2. Propose a starting point for the value function $V_0(x)$ and set an approximation criterion $\epsilon > 0$.
3. Iterating on the grid such that for each $k_l \in \mathcal{K}$ with $l = 1, ..., N$, as well for each $s_k \in \mathcal{S}$ with $k = 1, ..., M$, solve for: $V_{j+1}(k_l, s_k) = \max_{k'}(u(f(k_l, k', s_k), k_l, s_k) + \beta \sum_{i=1}^{M} \pi_{ki} V_j(k', s_i'))$.
4. Stop if the error is smaller than the criterion ϵ, i.e.: $||V_{j+1}(k, s) - V_j(k, s)|| < \epsilon$.
5. Determine the solution: $f^*(k, s) = f(k, k', s)$.

I show below the implementation in Julia.

```
sigma    = 1.5;
delta    = 0.1;
beta     = 0.95;
alpha    = 0.30;
p        = 0.9;
PI       = [p 1-p;1-p p];
se       = 0.2;
```

```julia
ab      = 0;
am      = exp(ab-se);
as      = exp(ab+se);
A       = [am as];
nba     = 2;

ks      = ((1-beta*(1-delta))/(alpha*beta))^(1/(alpha-1));
csy     = 1-alpha*beta*delta/(1-beta*(1-delta));
dev     = 0.9;
kmin    = (1-dev)*ks;
kmax    = (1+dev)*ks;
nbk     = 1000;
devk    = (kmax-kmin)/(nbk-1);
k       = collect(linspace(kmin,kmax,nbk));
kp      = zeros(nbk, nba);
c       = zeros(nbk,nba);
u       = zeros(nbk,nba);
v       = zeros(nbk,nba);
Tv      = zeros(nbk,nba);
iter    = 1;
crit    = 1;
tol     = 1e-6;

dr      = zeros(nbk,nba);              # decision rule (will contain indices)


while crit>tol
for i=1:nbk
for j=1:nba
c       = A[j]*k[i]^alpha+(1-delta)*k[i]-k;
neg     = find(x -> x <=0.0,c);
c[neg]  = NaN;
u[:,j]  = (c.^(1-sigma)-1)/(1-sigma);
u[neg,j] = -1e12;
end;
(Tv[i,:],dr[i,:]) = findmax(u+beta*(v*PI),1);
dr[i,2]=dr[i,2]-nbk;
end;
error = abs.(Tv-v);
crit  = maximum((error));
v       = copy(Tv);
iter    = iter+1;
end;

for i=1:nbk
for j=1:nba
index=trunc(Int, dr[i,j]);
kp[i,j]= k[index];
end;end;

c       = zeros(nbk,nba);

for j=1:nba;
c[:,j] = A[j]*k.^alpha+(1-delta)*k-kp[:,j];
end
u       = (c.^(1-sigma)-1)/(1-sigma);
v       = u/(1-beta);

using Plots
```

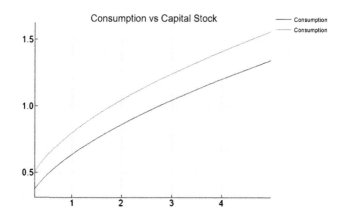

FIGURE 4.3 Consumption.

```
plotly() # Choose the Plotly.jl backend for web interactivity
plot(k,c, linewidth=1,title="Consumption vs Capital Stock", label="Consumption")
```

I also present a graphic of consumption versus capital stock in Fig. 4.3.

4.3.2.4   Policy Iteration – The Howard Improvement

Since the stochastic version of the value function iteration algorithm relies on the same contraction mapping theorem as its deterministic counterpart, the algorithm converges slowly. We may use again the policy iteration algorithm to speedup the computation.

1. Start from an initial feasible guess of the control variable $c = f_0(k, s_n)$, with $n = 1, ...M$, and compute the implied value function for this initial guess. Here, we use $k' = h(k, c, s) = h(k, f_j(k, s), s)$, for $j = 0$.

2. We compute a new policy rule $c = f_{j+1}(k, s_n)$ that verifies: $f_{j+1}(k, s_n) \in \arg\max_c u(c, k, s_n) + \beta \sum_{i=1}^{M} \pi_{ki} V(k', s_i')$. We use here the relation $k' = h(k, f_j(k, s_n), s_n)$.

3. Using a parameter ϵ as the stopping criterion, with $\epsilon > 0$, we check whether: $||f_{j+1}(k, s) - f_j(k, s)|| < \epsilon$. If the condition is not fulfilled, the algorithm goes back to the second step.

   To compute value function, we use: $V_{j+1}(k_l, s_n) = u(f_{j+1}(k_l, s_n), k_l, s_n) + \beta \Pi_k.QV_{j+1}(k_l, .)$.

   Here, the matrix $Q(N \times N)$ is given by:

$$
Q_{li} = \begin{cases} 1, & \text{if } k_i' = h(f_{j+1}(k_l), k_l) = k_l \\ 0, & \text{otherwise} \end{cases}
$$

The implementation in Julia is shown below.

```
sigma   = 1.50;                  # utility parameter
delta   = 0.10;                  # depreciation rate
beta    = 0.95;                  # discount factor
alpha   = 0.30;                  # capital elasticity of output
p       = 0.9;
PI      = [p 1-p;1-p p];
se      = 0.2;
ab      = 0;
am      = exp(ab-se);
as      = exp(ab+se);
A       = [am as];
nba     = 2;
nbk     = 1000;                  # number of data points in the grid
crit    = 1;                     # convergence criterion
iter    = 1;                     # iteration
tol     = 1e-6;                  # convergence parameter
ks      = ((1-beta*(1-delta))/(alpha*beta))^(1/(alpha-1));
```

```
kmin     = 0.2;                     # lower bound on the grid
kmax     = 6;                       # upper bound on the grid
devk     = (kmax-kmin)/(nbk-1);     # implied increment
kgrid    = collect(linspace(kmin,kmax,nbk)); # builds the grid
v        = zeros(nbk,nba);          #  value function
u        = zeros(nbk,nba);          # utility function
u_temp   = zeros(nbk,nba);
c_temp   = zeros(nbk,1);
c        = zeros(nbk,1);
Tv       = zeros(nbk,nba);
Ev       = zeros(nbk,nba);
kp0      = repmat(kgrid,1,nba);     # initial guess on k(t+1)
kp       = zeros(nbk,nba)
dr       = zeros(nbk,nba);          # decision rule (will contain indices)

#Main loop
while crit>tol
for i=1:nbk;
for j=1:nba;
c_temp   = A[j]*kgrid[i]^alpha+(1-delta)*kgrid[i]-kgrid;
neg      = find(x -> x <=0.0,c_temp);
c_temp[neg]  = NaN;
u_temp[:,j]  = (c_temp.^(1-sigma)-1)/(1-sigma);

u_temp[neg,j] = -1e30;
Ev[:,j]      = v*PI[j,:];

end
(Tv[i,:],dr[i,:]) = findmax(u_temp+beta* Ev,1);
dr[i,2]=dr[i,2]-nbk;
end;

#decision rules
for i=1:nbk
for j=1:nba

index=trunc(Int, dr[i,j]);
kp[i,j]= kgrid[index];

end;
end;

Q  = spzeros(nbk*nba,nbk*nba);
for j=1:nba;
c = A[j]*kgrid.^alpha+(1-delta)*kgrid-kp[:,j];
#update the value
u[:,j]= (c.^(1-sigma)-1)/(1-sigma);
Q0  = spzeros(nbk,nbk);

for i=1:nbk;
index=trunc(Int, dr[i,j]);
Q0[i,index] = 1;
end;
Q[(j-1)*nbk+1:j*nbk,:]= kron(PI[j,:]',Q0);
end;

AA   = (speye(nbk*nba)-beta*Q);
BB   = vec(u);
Tvv  = \(AA, BB);
```

```
crit = maximum(abs.(kp-kp0));
vv   = reshape(Tvv,nbk,nba);
v    = copy(vv);
kp0  = copy(kp);
iter = iter+1;
end;
```

4.4 LINEAR QUADRATIC DYNAMIC PROGRAMMING

The two previous sections have dealt with standard techniques to solve both deterministic and stochastic dynamic programming. The techniques were applied to the optimal growth model. Unfortunately, when the number of state variables increases, these techniques run into the so-called "dimensionality curse", i.e. the computational effort increases exponentially. Fortunately, a large class of dynamic programming models can be cast into a quite simple framework which can be iteratively solved with linear algebra techniques.

In this section I present a solution technique that is fast and easy to implement. This can be applied to a large class of economic models that satisfy two criteria: the payoff function is quadratic while the transition equation is linear. I present again both the deterministic and the stochastic case and introduce relevant examples in Julia. The theoretical exposition follows mainly [2], while the examples are drawn from [6] and [7].

4.4.1 The Deterministic Optimal Linear Regulator Problem

4.4.1.1 Theory

The Undiscounted Linear Regulator Problem

I present first the undiscounted version of the deterministic linear regulator problem. The problem consists in maximizing the following expression:

$$-\sum_{t=0}^{\infty}\{x_t' R_t x_t + u' Q u_t\} \tag{4.99}$$

Here, the control variable is $\{u_t\}_{t=0}^{\infty}$ of dimensions $(k \times 1)$, while x_t is the state variable of dimensions $(n \times 1)$. The transition equation for the state variable is linear, of dimensions $n \times 1$ and of the form $Ax_t + Bu_t$, with x_0 given. The matrix R is positive semidefinite symmetric, while Q is a positive definite symmetric matrix. Furthermore, the matrix A is of dimensions $(n \times n)$, while the matrix B is of dimensions $(n \times k)$.

We make the following guess about the form of the value function: $V(x) = -x'Px$, with the matrix P being a positive semidefinite symmetric. To differentiate quadratic and bilinear matrix forms, the following rules are to be used:

$$\frac{\partial x' A x}{\partial x} = (A + A')x$$

$$\frac{\partial y' B z}{\partial y} = Bz \tag{4.100}$$

$$\frac{\partial y' B z}{\partial z} = B'y$$

Using the assumed form of the value function, the Bellman equation can be written as:

$$-x'Px = \max_u\{-x'Rx - u'Qu - (Ax + Bu)'P(Ax + Bu)\} \tag{4.101}$$

Using the specific rules about differences matrix forms from above, it can be shown that the first-order condition can be written as:

$$(Q + B'PB)u = -B'PAx \tag{4.102}$$

We can use this to solve for the control variable u:

$$u = -(Q + B'PB)^{-1}B'PAx \tag{4.103}$$

We can further write $u = -Fx$, with $F = (Q + B'PB)^{-1}B'PA$. The optimal value of u from (4.103) can be plugged back in the Bellman equation and we get:

$$P = R + A'PA - A'PB(Q + B'PB)^{-1}B'PA \tag{4.104}$$

This is the so-called algebraic matrix Riccati equation. We can iterate on this equation since this can be rewritten as a matrix difference equation:

$$P_{j+1} = R + A'P_jA - A'P_jB(Q + B'P_jB)^{-1}B'P_jA \tag{4.105}$$

Assuming a starting point P_0, as $j \to \infty$, it can be shown that, under certain conditions, we get a unique positive semidefinite solution. We can also derive a policy function corresponding to iteration j:

$$F_{j+1} = (Q + B'P_jB)^{-1}B'P_jA \tag{4.106}$$

The Discounted Linear Regulator Problem

I move now to the discounted version of the deterministic linear regulator problem. This is also the far more common case in macroeconomic modeling. The problem consists in maximizing the following expression:

$$-\sum_{t=0}^{\infty} \beta^t \{x_t'R_tx_t + u'Qu_t\} \tag{4.107}$$

Here, the control variable is $\{u_t\}_{t=0}^{\infty}$ of dimension $(k \times 1)$, while $0 < \beta < 1$ is the usual discount factor. The transition equation for the state variable (x_{t+1}) is linear and of the form $Ax_t + Bu_t$, with x_0 given. The matrices A, B, P, Q are the same as for the undiscounted version of the problem.

In this particular case, the matrix Riccati difference equation becomes:

$$P_{j+1} = R + \beta A'P_jA - \beta^2 A'P_jB(Q + \beta B'P_jB)^{-1}B'P_jA \tag{4.108}$$

This also assumes a starting value P_0. If certain conditions are met, see again [2], then the matrix difference equation delivers a unique solution. The optimal policy is given by $u_t = -Fx_t$, with:

$$F = \beta(Q + \beta B'PB)^{-1}B'PA \tag{4.109}$$

The Approach by Kydland and Prescott

I detail here an alternative approach to solving linear quadratic dynamic programming models. The approach is due to Kydland and Prescott, see [9]. They use a second order Taylor series approximation for the discounted quadratic objective function in their model.

The problem can be stated as follows. I follow here the simplified presentation from [6] who focuses on the simpler Hansen model. The discounted quadratic objective function is given by:

$$\sum_{t=0}^{\infty} \beta^t F(x_t, y_t) \tag{4.110}$$

In this problem, the variable x_t is the state variable while the variable y_t is the control variable. The process for the dynamics of x_{t+1} is written as $x_{t+1} = Ax_t + By_t$. The main particularity of the approach proposed by Kydland and Prescott is the use of a second-order Taylor expansion of the function $F(x_t, y_t)$. We can write as follows:

$$F(x_t, y_t) \approx F(\bar{x}, \bar{y}) + [F_x(\bar{x}, \bar{y})' \, F_y(\bar{x}, \bar{y})'] \begin{bmatrix} x_t - \bar{x} \\ y_t - \bar{y} \end{bmatrix} + [(x_t - \bar{x})'(y_t - \bar{y})'] \begin{bmatrix} \frac{F_{xx}(\bar{x}, \bar{y})}{2} & \frac{F_{xy}(\bar{x}, \bar{y})}{2} \\ \frac{F_{yx}(\bar{x}, \bar{y})}{2} & \frac{F_{yy}(\bar{x}, \bar{y})}{2} \end{bmatrix} \begin{bmatrix} x_t - \bar{x} \\ y_t - \bar{y} \end{bmatrix} \tag{4.111}$$

The next step is to get above Taylor approximation into a quadratic form. To achieve this, we define first a new variable z_t as: $z_t = \begin{bmatrix} 1 \\ x_t \\ y_t \end{bmatrix}$. We denote the stationary value of z_t by: $\bar{z} = \begin{bmatrix} 1 \\ \bar{x} \\ \bar{y} \end{bmatrix}$.

The length of the new variable z_t is a function of the length of the state variable x_t and control variable y_t. Since x_t has a length k, y_t a length l then, the length of z_t will be $1 + k + l$. We define the matrix M of dimensions $(1 + k + l) \times (1 + k + l)$ given by:

$$M = \begin{bmatrix} m_{11} & m_{12} & m_{13} \\ m_{21} & m_{22} & m_{23} \\ m_{31} & m_{32} & m_{33} \end{bmatrix} \tag{4.112}$$

The components are designed in such a way that the product $z_t' M z_t$ gives the quadratic Taylor expansion from (4.111). The product $z_t' M z_t$ is written as:

$$z_t' M z_t = m_{11} + (m_{12} + m_{21}')x_t + (m_{13} + m_{31}')y_t + x_t'm_{22}x_t + \\ x_t'(m_{23} + m_{32}'y_t) + y_t'm_{33}y_t \tag{4.113}$$

The constant groups can be grouped together in the constant term of the above equation, i.e. in m_{11}. Then we write this term as:

$$m_{11} = F(\bar{x}, \bar{y}) - \bar{x}'F_x(\bar{x}, \bar{y}) - \bar{y}'F_y(\bar{x}, \bar{y}) + \frac{\bar{x}'F_{xx}(\bar{x}, \bar{y})\bar{y}}{2} + \\ \bar{x}'F_{xy}(\bar{x}, \bar{y})\bar{y} + \frac{\bar{y}'F_{yy}(\bar{x}, \bar{y})\bar{y}}{2} \tag{4.114}$$

We can further define the matrix M by grouping together the linear components and making the matrix symmetric, as follows:

$$m_{12} = m_{21} = \frac{F_x(\bar{x}, \bar{y})' - \bar{x}'F_{xx}(\bar{x}, \bar{y}) - \bar{y}'F_{yx}(\bar{x}, \bar{y})}{2} \tag{4.115}$$

$$m_{13} = m_{31} = \frac{F_y(\bar{x}, \bar{y})' - \bar{x}'F_{xy}(\bar{x}, \bar{y}) - \bar{y}'F_{yy}(\bar{x}, \bar{y})}{2} \tag{4.116}$$

Finally, we proceed similarly with the quadratic terms, as follows:

$$m_{22} = \frac{F_{xx}(\bar{x}, \bar{y})}{2} \tag{4.117}$$

$$m_{23} = m_{32} = \frac{F_{xy}(\bar{x}, \bar{y})}{2} \tag{4.118}$$

$$m_{33} = \frac{F_{yy}(\bar{x}, \bar{y})}{2} \tag{4.119}$$

Using the matrix M as defined above, the problem can be now recast as a linear quadratic problem defined by the following objective function:

$$\sum_{t=0}^{\infty} \beta^t z_t' M_t z_t \tag{4.120}$$

Where $z_t' = \begin{bmatrix} 1 & x_t & y_t \end{bmatrix}$ is subject to the following constraint:

$$\begin{bmatrix} 1 \\ x_{t+1} \end{bmatrix} = A \begin{bmatrix} 1 \\ x_t \end{bmatrix} + B y_t \tag{4.121}$$

4.4.1.2 An Example in Julia

In this section I introduce an example of model solved using the optimal LQ approach following the method by Kydland and Prescott in [9]. The model is the basic Hansen's real business cycle model, see [14], and the presentation follows [6]. The section concludes by showing how the model can be coded in Julia.

The representative household chooses the consumption and hours worked each period to maximize the lifetime utility function as given by:

$$\sum_{t=0}^{\infty} \beta u(c_t, h_t) \tag{4.122}$$

The household faces the following budget constraint:

$$c_t = f(k_t, h_t) + (1 - \delta)k_t - k_{t+1} \tag{4.123}$$

A standard utility function is assumed, with the specification:

$$u(c_t, h_t) = \ln c_t + A\ln(1 - h_t) \tag{4.124}$$

Which might be rewritten to include in it the budget constraint:

$$u(k_t, k_{t+1}, h_t) = \ln(f(k_t, h_t) + (1 - \delta)k_t - k_{t+1}) + A\ln(1 - h_t) \tag{4.125}$$

The production function is a Cobb-Douglas one and it is specified as follows:

$$f(k_t, h_t) = k_t^{\theta} h_t^{1-\theta} \tag{4.126}$$

The first step of applying the LQ approach consists in doing a second order Taylor expansion of the objective function.

$$u(k_t, k_{t+1}, h_t) \approx \ln(f(\bar{k}, \bar{h}) - \delta\bar{k}) + A\ln(1 - \bar{h}) + \frac{1}{\bar{c}}[\theta\frac{\bar{y}}{\bar{k}} + (1 - \delta)](k_t - \bar{k}) - \frac{1}{\bar{c}}(k_{t+1} - \bar{k})$$

$$+ [(1 - \theta)\frac{1}{\bar{c}}\frac{\bar{y}}{\bar{h}} - \frac{A}{1 - \bar{h}}](h_t - \bar{h}) + \begin{bmatrix} (k_t - \bar{k}) \\ (k_{t+1} - \bar{k}) \\ (h_t - \bar{h}) \end{bmatrix}' \begin{bmatrix} a_{11} & a_{12} & a_{13} \\ a_{21} & a_{22} & a_{23} \\ a_{31} & a_{32} & a_{33} \end{bmatrix} \begin{bmatrix} (k_t - \bar{k}) \\ (k_{t+1} - \bar{k}) \\ (h_t - \bar{h}) \end{bmatrix} \tag{4.127}$$

Here the constant elements of the matrix $(a_{ij}) \in \mathbb{R}^{3\times3}$ are defined as follows:

$$a_{11} = -\frac{1}{2\bar{c}^2}[\theta\frac{\bar{y}}{\bar{k}} + 1 - \delta]^2 - \frac{1}{2\bar{c}}\theta(1 - \theta)\frac{\bar{y}}{2\bar{k}^2} \tag{4.128}$$

$$a_{12} = a_{21} = \frac{1}{2\bar{c}^2}[\theta\frac{\bar{y}}{\bar{k}} + 1 - \delta] \tag{4.129}$$

$$a_{22} = -\frac{1}{2\bar{c}^2} \tag{4.130}$$

$$a_{13} = a_{31} = -\frac{1}{2\bar{c}^2}[\theta\frac{\bar{y}}{\bar{k}} + 1 - \delta](1 - \theta)\frac{\bar{y}}{\bar{h}} + \frac{1}{2\bar{c}}\theta(1 - \theta)\frac{\bar{y}}{\bar{k}\bar{h}} \tag{4.131}$$

$$a_{23} = a_{32} = \frac{1}{2\bar{c}^2}(1 - \theta)\frac{\bar{y}}{\bar{h}} \tag{4.132}$$

$$a_{33} = -\frac{1}{2\bar{c}^2}[(1 - \theta)\frac{\bar{y}}{\bar{h}}]^2 - \frac{1}{2\bar{c}}\theta(1 - \theta)\frac{\bar{y}}{\bar{h}^2} - \frac{A}{2(1 - \bar{h})^2} \tag{4.133}$$

To further proceed with the LQ approach as outlined in the previous section, we need to define the function M. The vector z_t is defined now as a four element vector with $z_t = \begin{bmatrix} 1 & k_t & k_{t+1} & h_t \end{bmatrix}'$. This leads to a matrix M of dimensions 4×4:

$$M = \begin{bmatrix} m_{11} & m_{12} & m_{13} & m_{14} \\ m_{21} & a_{11} & a_{23} & a_{13} \\ m_{31} & a_{21} & a_{33} & a_{23} \\ m_{41} & a_{31} & a_{32} & a_{33} \end{bmatrix} \tag{4.134}$$

Since the elements (a_{ij}) are already defined above, we need to define now the elements m_{ij}. We proceed as in the theoretical presentation and define (m_{ij}) according to the order of variables.

$$m_{11} = ln(f(\bar{k}, \bar{h}) - \delta\bar{k}) + Aln(1 - \bar{h}) - \frac{1}{\bar{c}}[\theta\frac{\bar{y}}{\bar{k}} + (1 - \delta) - 1]\bar{k} - $$

$$[(1-\theta)\frac{1}{\bar{c}}\frac{\bar{y}}{\bar{h}} - \frac{A}{1-\bar{h}}]\bar{h} + \begin{bmatrix} \bar{k} \\ \bar{k} \\ \bar{h} \end{bmatrix}' \begin{bmatrix} a_{11} & a_{12} & a_{13} \\ a_{21} & a_{22} & a_{23} \\ a_{31} & a_{32} & a_{33} \end{bmatrix} \begin{bmatrix} \bar{k} \\ \bar{k} \\ \bar{h} \end{bmatrix} \tag{4.135}$$

$$m_{12} = m_{21} = \frac{1}{\bar{c}}[\theta\frac{\bar{y}}{\bar{k}} + (1 - \delta)] - \begin{bmatrix} \bar{k} & \bar{k} & \bar{h} \end{bmatrix} \begin{bmatrix} a_{11} \\ a_{21} \\ a_{31} \end{bmatrix} \tag{4.136}$$

$$m_{13} = m_{31} = -\frac{1}{\bar{c}} - \begin{bmatrix} \bar{k} & \bar{k} & \bar{h} \end{bmatrix} \begin{bmatrix} a_{12} \\ a_{22} \\ a_{32} \end{bmatrix} \tag{4.137}$$

$$m_{14} = m_{41} = [(1-\theta)\frac{1}{\bar{c}}\frac{\bar{y}}{\bar{h}} - \frac{A}{1-\bar{h}}] - \begin{bmatrix} \bar{k} & \bar{k} & \bar{h} \end{bmatrix} \begin{bmatrix} a_{13} \\ a_{23} \\ a_{33} \end{bmatrix} \tag{4.138}$$

We can write now the problem as a Linear Quadratic dynamic programming one. The problem consists in maximizing the following quadratic form:

$$\sum_{t=0}^{\infty} \beta^t z_t' M_t z_t \tag{4.139}$$

This is a subject to a linear constraint written in matrix form as:

$$\begin{bmatrix} 1 \\ k_{t+1} \end{bmatrix} = A \begin{bmatrix} 1 \\ k_t \end{bmatrix} + B \begin{bmatrix} k_{t+1} \\ h_t \end{bmatrix} \tag{4.140}$$

Here, the matrices A, B are defined as $A = \begin{bmatrix} 1 & 0 \\ 0 & 0 \end{bmatrix}$ and $B = \begin{bmatrix} 0 & 0 \\ 1 & 0 \end{bmatrix}$.

The implementation in Julia is shown below:

```
#calibration
theta  =.36;
beta   =.99;
delta  =.025;
A      =1.72;

#steady state
kbar   =12.6695;
```

```
hbar    =.3335;
ybar    =kbar^theta*hbar^(1-theta);
cbar    =ybar-delta*kbar;
aa      =(theta*ybar/kbar+1-delta);

#setup matrices
a=zeros(3,3);
a[1,1]=-1/(2*cbar*cbar)*aa*aa-1/(2*cbar)*theta*(1-theta)*ybar/(kbar*kbar);
a[1,2]=1/(2*cbar*cbar)*aa;
a[2,1]=1/(2*cbar*cbar)*aa;
a[1,3]=-1/(2*cbar*cbar)*aa*(1-theta)*ybar/hbar;
a[1,3]=a[1,3]+1/(2*cbar)*theta*(1-theta)*ybar/(kbar*hbar);
a[3,1]=a[1,3];
a[2,2]=-1/(2*cbar*cbar);
a[2,3]=1/(2*cbar*cbar)*(1-theta)*ybar/hbar;
a[3,2]=a[2,3];
a[3,3]=-1/(2*cbar*cbar)*(1-theta)*ybar/hbar*(1-theta)*ybar/hbar;
a[3,3]=a[3,3]-1/(2*cbar)*theta*(1-theta)*ybar/(hbar*hbar);
a[3,3]=a[3,3]-A/(2*(1-hbar)*(1-hbar));


x=[kbar kbar hbar]';
m=zeros(4,4)
m[1,1]=log(kbar^theta*hbar^(1-theta)-delta*kbar)+A*log(1-hbar);
mm1=1/cbar*(theta*ybar/kbar+1-delta);
mm2=(1-theta)*ybar/(cbar*hbar)-A/(1-hbar);
m[1,1]=m[1,1]-mm1*kbar+kbar/cbar-mm2*hbar;
e=m[1,1]+(x')*a*x;
m[1,1]=e[1]
e=mm1/2-1*a[1:3,1]'*x;
m[1,2]=e[1];
m[2,1]=m[1,2];
e=-1/(2*cbar)-1*a[1:3,2]'*x;
m[1,3]=e[1]
m[3,1]=m[1,3];
e=mm2/2-1*a[1:3,3]'*x;
m[1,4]=e[1];
m[4,1]=m[1,4];
m[2:4,2:4]=a;

AA=[1 0; 0 0];
B=[0 0; 1 0];
R=m[1:2,1:2];
Q=m[3:4,3:4];
W=m[1:2,3:4]';
P=[1 0 ;0 1];

inv(Q+beta*B'*P*B);

#Iteration
zinv=zeros(2,2)
for i=1:1000
zinv=inv(Q+beta*B'*P*B);
z2=beta*AA'*P*B+W';
P=R+beta*AA'*P*AA-z2*zinv*z2'
end

# Display results
println("The matrix P is:", P)
```

```
F=-zinv*(W+beta*B'*P*AA)
println("The matrix F is:", F)
```

```
The matrix P is:[-96.3655 0.87792; 0.87792 -0.0258972]
The matrix F is:[0.586944 0.953674; 0.414565 -0.00639755]
```

4.4.2   The Stochastic Optimal Linear Regulator Problem

4.4.2.1   Theory

The stochastic case considered here features discounting. The problem is choosing the decision rule for u_t such that the following expression is maximized:

$$-E_0 \sum_{t=0}^{\infty} \beta^t \{x_t' R_t x_t + u' Q u_t\} \tag{4.141}$$

Here, the initial value of x, x_0 is given, while x is characterized by the following law of motion: $x_{t+1} = Ax_t + Bu_t + C\epsilon_{t+1}$. For ϵ_{t+1} it is further assumed that it is a $n \times 1$ vector of random i.i.d. variables, having a mean zero and a covariance matrix $E_t \epsilon_t \epsilon_t' = I$.

In this particular case, the value function will be written as:

$$v(x) = -x' P x - d \tag{4.142}$$

Here, the matrix P results from the same matrix Riccati equation as for the discounted linear regulator problem. The scalar d from the value function is written as follows:

$$d = \beta(1 - \beta)^{-1} trace(PCC)' \tag{4.143}$$

The optimal policy from $u_t = -Fx_t$ is given by:

$$F = \beta(Q + \beta B' P' B)^{-1} B' P A \tag{4.144}$$

The decision rule is identical to the one from the discounted optimal linear regulator. This result comes from the so-called Certainty Equivalence Principle which is stated below:

Certainty Equivalence Principle: Considering a given optimal regulator problem, then it holds that the decision rule for the stochastic optimal linear regulator version is identical to the decision rule for the corresponding nonstochastic optimal linear regulator version.

The proof can be found in [2].

4.4.2.2   An Example in Julia

In this section, I illustrate the stochastic LQ dynamic programming using a simple model. The model is taken from Ellison's lecture notes on optimal linear quadratic control, see [7], and, again, it is preferred for both simplicity and Maltab code availability.

We assume a central bank that controls the inflation π_t and the output y_t using the current interest rate as an instrument r_t. The following instantaneous payoff function for the central bank is assumed (which is quadratic in all three variables):

$$\mathcal{L}_t = \pi_t^2 + y_t^2 + 0.1 r_t^2 \tag{4.145}$$

This specification for the payoff function implies equal weights for the output and inflation, but much smaller values for the interest rate. The main objective of the central bank is to minimize the present discounted value of expected losses, assuming a discount rate β. We further assume that the endogenous variables π_t and y_t are characterized by the following processes:

$$\pi_{t+1} = 0.75\pi_t - 0.5r_t + \epsilon_t^{\pi} \tag{4.146}$$

$$y_{t+1} = 0.25y_t - 0.5r_t + \epsilon_t^{y} \tag{4.147}$$

Given these assumptions, the problem can now be casted as a LQ dynamic programming one as follows:

$$\min_{r_t} E \sum_{t=0}^{\infty} \beta^t [\pi_t^2 + y_t^2 + 0.1 r_t^2] \qquad (4.148)$$

With the linear constraints for inflation and output as given by Eqs. (4.146)–(4.147). We can write it further in a more general manner as:

$$\min_{u_t} E \sum_{t=0}^{\infty} \beta^t [x_t' R x_t + u_t' Q u_t] \qquad (4.149)$$

The associated constraint is: $x_{t+1} = A x_t + B u_t + \epsilon_t$. Here we define the state variable as $x_t = \begin{pmatrix} \pi_t & y_t \end{pmatrix}'$ and the control variable as $u_t = r_t$, while the disturbances are written as $\epsilon_t = \begin{pmatrix} \epsilon_t^\pi & \epsilon_t^y \end{pmatrix}'$.

The matrices R, Q, A, B are defined as follows: $R = \begin{bmatrix} 1 & 0 \\ 0 & 1 \end{bmatrix}$, $Q = 0.1$, $A = \begin{bmatrix} 0.75 & 0 \\ 0 & 0.75 \end{bmatrix}$, $B = \begin{bmatrix} -0.5 \\ 0.5 \end{bmatrix}$.

The code in Julia is shown below:

```
beta =0.99;
Q    =zeros(1,1);
R    =zeros(2,2);
A    =zeros(2,2);
B    =zeros(2,1);

Q[1,1]=0.1;
R[1,1]=1;
R[1,2]=0;
R[2,1]=0;
R[2,2]=1;
A[1,1]=0.75;
A[1,2]=0;
A[2,1]=0;
A[2,2]=0.25;
B[1,1]=-0.5;
B[2,1]=-0.5;

d=1;
D=0;
I=0;
i=0;

#Iterate on Ricatti equation
while d>0.0000000001
P1=R+beta*A'*P0*A-(beta*A'*P0*B)*(inv(Q+beta*B'*P0*B))*(beta*B'*P0*A);
Pd=P1-P0;
d=maximum(abs.(Pd));
d=maximum(d');
D=[D d];
P0=P1;
i=i+1;
I=[I i];
println("Iteration:",i,"d:",d)
end
P=P0;

# Display results
F=-inv(Q+beta*B'*P*B)*(beta*B'*P*A);
```

```
println("P matrix:")
println(P)
println("F matrix:")
println(F)

P matrix:
[1.43029 -0.106183; -0.106183 1.04419]
F matrix:
[0.744954 0.17591]
```

REFERENCES

[1] K. Judd, Numerical Methods in Economics, MIT Press, 1998.

[2] L. Ljungqvist, Th. Sargent, Recursive Macroeconomic Theory, 3rd edition, MIT Press, 2012.

[3] D. Acemoglu, Introduction to Modern Economic Growth, Princeton University Press, 2009.

[4] N. Stokey, R. Lucas, Recursive Methods in Economic Dynamics, Harvard University Press, 1989.

[5] F. Collard, Notes on numerical methods, Mimeo, 2015.

[6] G. McCandless, The ABCs of RBCs: An Introduction to Dynamic Macroeconomic Models, Harvard University Press, 2008.

[7] M. Ellison, Recursive methods for macroeconomics, Mimeo, University of Oxford.

[8] G. Tauchen, R. Hussey, Quadrature-based methods for obtaining approximate solutions to nonlinear asset pricing models, Econometrica 59 (1991) 371–396.

[9] F. Kydland, R. Prescott, Time to build and aggregate fluctuations, Econometrica 50 (1982) 1345–1371.

[10] L.M. Benveniste, J.A. Scheinkman, On the differentiability of the value function in dynamic models of economics, Econometrica 47 (1979) 727–732.

[11] A.M. Kolmogorov, S.V. Fomin, Elements of the Theory of Functions and Functional Analysis, Dover Books, 1999.

[12] E.M. Stein, R. Shakarchi, Real Analysis. Measure Theory, Integration & Hilbert Spaces, Princeton University Press, 2005.

[13] R.G. Bartle, The Elements of Integration, John Wiley & Sons, 1966.

[14] G. Hansen, Indivisible labour and the business cycle, Journal of Monetary Economics 16 (1985) 309–328.

Chapter 5

Advanced Numerical Techniques

Contents

5.1 INTRODUCTION

This chapter makes one step further in presenting the reader the modern tools used in quantitative macroeconomics. In this chapter I present three of the more advanced techniques to numerically solve for dynamic stochastic general equilibrium models: the perturbation methods, the parameterized expectations algorithm and the weighted residual or the projection method. The presentations will focus on a clear outline of the theory and implementations of baseline DSGE models in Julia. The state of art with respect to solving DSGE models can be found in the monograph by [10] published in the latest issue of Handbook of Macroeconomics. The monograph covers also the solution methods presented in this chapter.

5.2 PERTURBATION METHODS

I start by discussion the one of the widely used techniques, the perturbation method. Traditionally, the macroeconomics discipline has relied on particular cases of the more general perturbation theory, such as linearizing around the steady state. But, as [1] underscored, too often the approach was rather ad-hoc than rigorous.

For these reasons, I will start by presenting a general framework for the perturbation approach, before moving to the specific case of applying it to DSGE models.

5.2.1 The General Framework

In this section, I focus on presenting the general idea of the perturbation technique, as well as the basic techniques underlying it. I follow mainly [1].

The perturbation techniques (also known as the asymptotic techniques), are methods that are used to compute approximate solutions. Intuitively, they are quite simple. Suppose a general problem which has a particular case to which we can find a solution. Then, we can use the particular solution as a starting point in order to find an approximate solution to the general problem.

There are few mathematical results that are essential in applying this technique, especially the implicit function theorem and the Taylor series expansion. I present them below before sketching more formally the baseline perturbation approach.

Theorem 5.1. Implicit Function Theorem

Let us assume a function $H(x, y) : \mathbb{R}^n \times \mathbb{R}^m \to \mathbb{R}^m$ that is C^k. Assume further that $H(x_0, y_0) = 0$ and that $H_y(x_0, y_0)$ is not singular. Then, it can be proven that there exists a function $h : \mathbb{R}^n \to \mathbb{R}^m$ that is unique as well as C^0, for which $y_0 = h(x_0)$ and whenever x is close to x_0, it holds that $H(x, h(x)) = 0$. If the function H is C^k, then it further holds that h is C^k and we can determine the derivatives of the latter by using the implicit differentiation of $H(x, h(x)) = 0$.

The implicit function theorem, along the Taylor rule, are used to compute the derivatives of the function h with respect to x at x_0.

Introduction to Quantitative Macroeconomics Using Julia. https://doi.org/10.1016/B978-0-12-812219-8.00012-4

Approximation

It is essential to understand in which sense the perturbation technique uses the concept of approximation. In the most general sense, one could say that a function $f(x)$ is an approximation of the function $g(x)$ for x near x_0 if it holds that $f(x_0) = g(x_0)$. However, this is only a necessary condition. A sufficient condition for an approximation of a function using another function at a point x_0 is that:

$$f'(x_0) = g'(x_0) \tag{5.1}$$

holds (along the already mentioned necessary condition). When these two conditions holds, we say that "f is a first-order approximation of g at $x = x_0$".

This can be generalized to the case of an n-th order approximation of g using f when the following condition holds:

$$lim_{x \to x_0} \frac{||f(x) - g(x)||}{||x - x_0||^n} = 0 \tag{5.2}$$

Assuming the function f, g are C^n, then this latter condition is true if and only if the following relationship holds:

$$f^{(k)}(x_0) = g^{(k)}(x_0) \tag{5.3}$$

for $k = 0, ..., n$.

A Formal Exposition

Following [1], I present more formally the idea of perturbation. We assume that our problem of interest can be written as:

$$f(x, \epsilon) = 0 \tag{5.4}$$

Here x is a variable, while ϵ is a parameter. Assuming that for each value of the parameter ϵ there is a solution for the above equation that is also unique, then each such solution can be parameterized $x(\epsilon)$. We assume that such a function is smooth and that $f(x(\epsilon), \epsilon) = 0$.

Although the equation above might not be solvable for any ϵ, we can still find some values of ϵ for which the equation can be solved. Let us further assume that the function f is differentiable, x, ϵ are scalars, $x(\epsilon)$ is unique while $x(0)$ is known. Using the Implicit Function Theorem and applying it to equation above, we get:

$$f_x(x(\epsilon), \epsilon)x'(\epsilon) + f_\epsilon(x(\epsilon), \epsilon) = 0 \tag{5.5}$$

To advance with it, we may set $\epsilon = 0$ and, since $x(0)$ is known, we might evaluate $x'(0)$ by using:

$$x'(0) = -\frac{f_\epsilon(x(0), 0)}{f_x(x(0), 0)} \tag{5.6}$$

Then we can produce a linear approximation of $x(\epsilon)$ for ϵ by writing:

$$x(\epsilon) \equiv x(0) - \frac{f_\epsilon(x(0), 0)}{f_x(x(0), 0)}\epsilon \tag{5.7}$$

We can use a similar approach to compute finer approximation relying on higher-order derivatives of $x(\epsilon)$. When we differentiate once more Eq. (5.5), we get:

$$f_x x'' + f_{xx}(x')^2 + 2f_{x\epsilon}x' + f_{\epsilon\epsilon} = 0 \tag{5.8}$$

Setting again $\epsilon = 0$, we may derive a solution for $x''(0)$ as follows:

$$x''(0) = -\frac{f_{xx}(x(0), 0)(x'(0))^2 + 2f_{x\epsilon}(x(0), 0)x'(0) + f_{\epsilon\epsilon}(x(0), 0)}{f_x(x(0), 0)} \tag{5.9}$$

We can write now a 2nd order approximation as follows:

$$x(\epsilon) \equiv x(0) + \epsilon x'(0) + \frac{1}{2}\epsilon^2 x''(0) \tag{5.10}$$

The second step after getting an approximation for $x(\epsilon)$ in terms of ϵ is to check whether the derived approximation is good for any value of the parameter ϵ. In practice, to check for a certain value $\epsilon = a$, we may compute the residual of the approximation for this value of the parameter as $residual = f(x^k(a), a)$. A small residual implies that the approximation is reliable for $x(a)$.

5.2.2 Solving DSGE Models With the Perturbation Method

A General Representation of a DSGE Model

I focus in this section on presenting the solution of DSGE models using the perturbation approach. I follow mainly [4] and [3]. The equilibrium conditions of many DSGE models can be written using the following representation:

$$E_t f(y_{t+1}, y_t, x_{t+1}, x_t) = 0 \tag{5.11}$$

Here E_t is the expectations operator which is conditioned on the information that the agents have at their disposition at time t. x_t is the vector predetermined variables of dimension $n_x \times 1$, while y_t is the vector of non-predetermined variables having a dimension $n_y \times 1$. Furthermore, n is defined as $n = n_x + n_y$. Additionally, $f : \mathbb{R}^{n_y} \times \mathbb{R}^{n_y} \times \mathbb{R}^{n_x} \times \mathbb{R}^{n_x} \to \mathbb{R}^n$.

Since this is a stochastic model, the state variable vector can be further split into endogenous and exogenous predetermined variables. We write that $x_t = [x_t^1; x_t^2]$. The exogenous state variables follow an autoregressive law of motion:

$$x_{t+1}^2 = \Lambda x_t^2 + \tilde{\eta} \sigma \epsilon_{t+1} \tag{5.12}$$

The vectors x_t^2 and ϵ_t are of size $n_\epsilon \times 1$. It is assumed that the vector ϵ_t is independently identically distributed, having a zero mean and a covariance matrix I. Furthermore, the parameters $\sigma \gg 0$, as well as the matrix $\tilde{\eta}$ are known. The matrix $\tilde{\eta}$ is of dimensions $n_\epsilon \times n_\epsilon$.

The solution to the model in Eq. (5.11) can be written as:

$$y_t = g(x_t, \sigma) \tag{5.13}$$
$$x_{t+1} = h(x_t, \sigma) + \eta \sigma \epsilon_{t+1} \tag{5.14}$$

Here, the function g is mapping $\mathbb{R}^{n_x} \times \mathbb{R}^+$ into $\mathbb{R}^{n_y}$, while the function h is mapping $\mathbb{R}^{n_x} \times \mathbb{R}^+$ into $\mathbb{R}^{n_x}$. The matrix η can be written as:

$$\begin{bmatrix} \varnothing \\ \hat{\eta} \end{bmatrix} \tag{5.15}$$

We are interested in deriving first and second-order solutions around the non-stochastic steady state. This is defined by the vectors $(\bar{x}, \bar{y})$ such that the function f verifies the relationship:

$$f(\bar{y}, \bar{y}, \bar{x}, \bar{x}) = 0 \tag{5.16}$$

This implies that $\bar{y} = g(\bar{x}, 0)$ and $\bar{x} = h(\bar{x}, 0)$.

Approximate Solutions

The solution as given in Eqs. (5.13) and (5.14) can be substituted back in the original equation (5.11). Using the prime for $t + 1$ and dropping the time subscripts, we would get:

$$F(x, \sigma) = E_t f(g(h(x, \sigma) + \eta \sigma \epsilon', \sigma), g(x, \sigma), h(x, \sigma) + \eta \sigma \epsilon', x) = 0 \tag{5.17}$$

Since $F(x, \sigma)$ is equal to zero for any values of the variable x and parameter σ, it also follows that the derivatives of F (for any order) are zero too. We formally write:

$$F_{x^k, \sigma^j}(x, \sigma) = 0, \forall x, \sigma, j, k \tag{5.18}$$

The notation F_{x^k, σ^j} implies that we compute the k-th order derivative of F with respect to x, and the j-th order derivative with respect to σ.

First Order Approximation

A first order approximation implies finding approximate solutions to the functions h, g around the point $(x, \sigma) = (\bar{x}, 0)$ such that the following relationships hold:

$$g(x, \sigma) = g(\bar{x}, 0) + g_x(\bar{x}, 0)(x - \bar{x}) + g_\sigma(\bar{x}, 0)\sigma \tag{5.19}$$

$$h(x, \sigma) = h(\bar{x}, 0) + h_x(\bar{x}, 0)(x - \bar{x}) + h_\sigma(\bar{x}, 0)\sigma \tag{5.20}$$

The relationships can be simplified since we already know that: $g(\bar{x}, 0) = \bar{y}$ as well as that $h(\bar{x}, 0) = \bar{x}$. To further proceed with the approximation, we exploit the result in Eq. (5.17) which implies that: $F_x(\bar{x}, 0) = 0$ and $F_\sigma(\bar{x}, 0) = 0$.

We can use the first expression to compute g_x and h_x by solving the following system of equations:

$$[F_x(\bar{x}, 0)]^i_j = [f_{y'}]^i_\alpha [g_x]^\alpha_\beta [h_x]^\beta_j + [f_y]^i_\alpha [g_x]^\alpha_j + [f_{x'}]^i_\beta [h_x]^\beta_j + [f_x]^i_j = 0 \tag{5.21}$$

Here $i = 0, ..., n$, $\alpha = 1, ...n_y$ and $j, \beta = 1, .., n_x$. This equation is a system of $n \times n_x$ equations in $n \times n_x$ unknowns which are the elements of functions g_x and h_x. Following [5], an element $[f_{y'}]^i_\alpha$ is the i-th row and α-th column element of the matrix that results from differentiating the function f with respect to y'.

A similar strategy can be used to identify the remaining two coefficients of the approximations of f and g, that is g_σ and h_σ. We use:

$$[F_\sigma(\bar{x}, 0)]^i =$$
$$E_t\{[f_{y'}]^i_\alpha [g_x]^\alpha_\beta [h_\sigma]^\beta + [f_{y'}]^i_\alpha [g_x]^\alpha_\beta [\eta]^\beta_\phi [\epsilon']^\phi + [f_{y'}]^i_\alpha [g_\sigma]^\alpha$$
$$+ [f_y]^i_\alpha [g_\sigma]^\alpha + [f_{x'}]^i_\beta [h_\sigma]^\beta + [f_{x'}]^i_\alpha [\eta]^\beta_\phi [\epsilon']^\phi\} \tag{5.22}$$
$$= [f_{y'}]^i_\alpha [g_x]^\alpha_\beta [h_\sigma]^\beta + [f_{y'}]^i_\alpha [g_\sigma]^\alpha + [f_y]^i_\alpha [g_\sigma]^\alpha + [f_{x'}]^i_\beta [h_\sigma]^\beta$$
$$= 0$$

Here $i = 0, ..., n$, $\alpha = 1, ...n_y$, $\beta = 1, .., n_x$ and $\phi = 1, ..., n_\epsilon$. Since Eq. (5.22) is both linear and homogeneous in g_σ and h_σ, given a unique solution, it must hold that: $g_\sigma = h_\sigma = 0$.

Second Order Approximation

We perform a second-order approximation for the functions g, h by considering the same steady state value given by $(x, \sigma) = (\bar{x}, 0)$.

The second order approximations for g and h can be written as follows:

$$[g(x, \sigma)]^i = [g(\bar{x}, 0)]^i + [g_x(\bar{x}, 0)]^i_\alpha [(x - \bar{x})]_\alpha + [g_\sigma(\bar{x}, 0)]^i [\sigma]$$
$$+ \frac{1}{2}[g_{xx}(\bar{x}, 0)]^i_{ab} [(x - \bar{x})]_\alpha [(x - \bar{x})]_b$$
$$+ \frac{1}{2}[g_{x\sigma}(\bar{x}, 0)]^i_a [(x - \bar{x})]_\alpha [\sigma]$$
$$+ \frac{1}{2}[g_{\sigma x}(\bar{x}, 0)]^i_a [(x - \bar{x})]_\alpha [\sigma] \tag{5.23}$$
$$+ \frac{1}{2}[g_{\sigma\sigma}(\bar{x}, 0)]^i_a [\sigma][\sigma]$$

$$[h(x, \sigma)]^i = [h(\bar{x}, 0)]^j + [h_x(\bar{x}, 0)]^j_\alpha [(x - \bar{x})]_\alpha + [h_\sigma(\bar{x}, 0)]^j [\sigma]$$
$$+ \frac{1}{2}[h_{xx}(\bar{x}, 0)]^j_{ab} [(x - \bar{x})]_\alpha [(x - \bar{x})]_b$$
$$+ \frac{1}{2}[h_{x\sigma}(\bar{x}, 0)]^j_a [(x - \bar{x})]_\alpha [\sigma]$$
$$+ \frac{1}{2}[h_{\sigma x}(\bar{x}, 0)]^j_a [(x - \bar{x})]_\alpha [\sigma] \tag{5.24}$$
$$+ \frac{1}{2}[h_{\sigma\sigma}(\bar{x}, 0)]^j_a [\sigma][\sigma]$$

Here, $i = 1, ..., n_y, a, b = 1, ..., n_x$, while $j = 1, ..., n_x$. We obtained two systems of equations, where the unknowns are given by $[g_{xx}]^i_{ab}, [g_{x\sigma}]^i_a, [g_{\sigma x}]^i_a, [g_{\sigma\sigma}]^i, [h_{xx}]^j_{ab}, [h_{x\sigma}]^j_a, [h_{\sigma x}]^j_a, [h_{\sigma\sigma}]^j$. They can be solved for using the same strategy, as for the first order approximation, i.e. taking, this time, the second order derivatives F with respect to x, σ and computing their value at $(x, \sigma) = (\bar{x}, 0)$. Again, these derivatives are equal to zero, since the same arguments hold as for the first order approximation. Based on $F_{xx}(\bar{x}, 0)$, we can identify both $g_{xx}(\bar{x}, 0)$ and $h_{xx}(\bar{x}, 0)$, as follows:

$$
\begin{aligned}
[F_{xx}(\bar{x}, 0)]^i_{jk} = &([f_{y'y'}]^i_{\alpha\gamma}[g_x]^\gamma_\delta[h_x]^\delta_k + [f_{y'y'}]^i_{\alpha\gamma}[g_x]^\gamma_k \\
&+[f_{y'x'}]^i_{\alpha\delta}[h_x]^\delta_k + [f_{y'x}]^i_{\alpha k})[g_x]^\alpha_\beta[h_x]^{\beta j} \\
&+[f_{y'}]^i_\alpha[g_{xx}]^\alpha_{\beta\delta}[h_x]^\delta_k[h_x]^\beta_j \\
&+[f_{y'}]^i_\alpha[g_x]^\alpha_\beta[h_{xx}]^\delta_{jk} \\
&+([f_{yy'}]^i_{\alpha\gamma}[g_x]^\gamma_\delta[h_x]^\delta_k + [f_{yy}]^i_{\alpha\gamma}[g_x]^\gamma_k + [f_{yx'}]^i_{\alpha\delta}[h_x]^\delta_k + [f_{yx}]^i_{\alpha k})[g_x]^\alpha_j \\
&+[f_y]^i_\alpha[g_{xx}]^\alpha_{jk} \\
&+([f_{x'y'}]^i_{\beta\gamma}[g_x]^\gamma_\delta[h_x]^\delta_k + [f_{x'y}]^i_{\beta\gamma}[g_x]^\gamma_k + [f_{x'x'}]^i_{\beta\delta}[h_x]^\delta_k + [f_{x'x}]^i_{\beta k})[h_x]^\beta_j \\
&+[f_{x'}]^i_\beta[h_{xx}]^\beta_{jk} \\
&+[f_{xy'}]^i_{j\gamma}[g_x]^\gamma_\delta[h_x]^\delta_k + [f_{xy}]^i_{j\gamma}[g_x]^\gamma_k + [f_{xx'}]^i_{j\delta}[h_x]^\delta_k + [f_{xx}]^i_{jk}
\end{aligned}
\tag{5.25}
$$

What we got is a system $n \times n_x \times n_x$ equations in $n \times n_x \times n_x$ unknowns which are represented by the elements in g_{xx} and h_{xx}. This is due to the fact that the derivatives of f, g and h with respect to $(y', y, x'x) = (\bar{y}, \bar{y}, \bar{x}, \bar{x})$ are known.

To determine the coefficients $g_{\sigma\sigma}, h_{\sigma\sigma}$, we use the derivative of $F_{\sigma\sigma}(\bar{x}, 0) = 0$. The following system of equations results:

$$
\begin{aligned}
[F_{\sigma\sigma}(\bar{x}, 0)]^i = &([f_{y'}]^i_\alpha[g_x]^\alpha_\beta[h_{\sigma\sigma}]^\beta \\
&+[f_{y'y'}]^i_{\alpha\gamma}[g_x]^\gamma_\delta[\eta]^\delta_\xi[g_x]^\alpha_\beta[\eta]^\beta_\phi[I]^\phi_\xi \\
&+[f_{y'x'}]^i_{\alpha\delta}[\eta]^\delta_\xi[[g_x]^\alpha_\beta[\eta]^\beta_\phi[I]^\phi_\xi \\
&+[f_{y'}]^i_\alpha[g_{xx}]^\alpha_{\beta\delta}[\eta]^\delta_\xi[\eta]^\beta_\phi[I]^\phi_\xi \\
&+[f_{y'}]^i_\alpha[g_{\sigma\sigma}]^\alpha \\
&+[f_y]^i_\alpha[g_{\sigma\sigma}]^\alpha \\
&+[f_{x'}]^i_\alpha[h_{\sigma\sigma}]^\beta \\
&+[f_{x'y'}]^i_{\beta\gamma}[g_x]^\gamma_\delta[\eta]^\delta_\xi[\eta]^\beta_\phi[I]^\phi_\xi \\
&+[f_{x'x'}]^i_{\beta\delta}[\eta]^\delta_\xi[\eta]^\beta_\phi[I]^\phi_\xi \\
&= 0
\end{aligned}
\tag{5.26}
$$

Here, $i = 1, ..n, \alpha, \gamma = 1, .., n_y, \beta, \delta = 1, ..., n_x$, while $\phi, \xi = 1, ..., n_\epsilon$. The above system of equations consists in n linear equations and n unknowns, where the unknowns are given by the elements of $g_{\sigma\sigma}$ and $h_{\sigma\sigma}$.

It can also be shown that the cross-derivatives $g_{x\sigma}$, and $h_{x\sigma}$, when we evaluate them at $(\bar{x}, 0)$, are also zero. We can write $F_{\sigma x}(\bar{x}, 0)$ as follows:

$$
[F_{\sigma x}(\bar{x}, 0)]^i_j = [f_{y'}]^i_\alpha[g_x]^\alpha_\beta[h_{\sigma x}]^\beta_j + [f_{y'}]^i_\alpha[g_{\sigma x}]^\alpha_\gamma[h_x]^\gamma_j + [f_y]^i_\alpha[g_{\sigma x}]^\alpha_j + [f_{x'}]^i_\beta[h_{\sigma x}]^\beta_j = 0
\tag{5.27}
$$

Here, setting $F_{\sigma x}(\bar{x}, 0)$ to zero leads to a system of equations of dimensions $n \times n_x$, with the unknowns being $g_{\sigma x}$ and $h_{\sigma x}$. Since the system is homogeneous, if a unique solution exists, then it can be obtained from the following equations:

$$
\begin{aligned}
g_{\sigma x} &= 0 \\
h_{\sigma x} &= 0
\end{aligned}
\tag{5.28}
$$

The equations above imply that, up to second order approximation, the policy functions coefficients for the terms linear in the state vector de not depend on the variance of the shocks. The following theorem gathers the main theoretical results we obtained so far:

Theorem 5.2: Let us assume a model represented as in Eq. (5.11) whose solution is given by Eqs. (5.13) and (5.14). Then, it holds that:

$$g_\sigma(\bar{x}, 0) = 0$$
$$h_\sigma(\bar{x}, 0) = 0$$
$$g_{x\sigma}(\bar{x}, 0) = 0$$
$$h_{x\sigma}(\bar{x}, 0) = 0$$

(5.29)

The main implication of this theorem is that a second order approximation of the policy function of a stochastic model which can be represented as in (5.11) differs from non-stochastic version by a constant term $(1/2)g_{\sigma\sigma}\sigma^2$ for the control variable, and by the first $n_x - n_\epsilon$ elements of $(1/2)h_{\sigma\sigma}\sigma^2$ for the state variable.

At the same time, the first two equations imply that, in a first order approximation, one does not need to take into account the constant term in the approximation of the policy function with the size of the variance of the shocks.

5.2.3 Applications in Julia

5.2.3.1 Optimal Growth Model

As a first application, I consider implementing a second order approximation of the optimal growth, which is also extensively covered in both [4] and [3]. The model has already been discussed in previous chapters (in the context of solving DSGE models or when presenting dynamic programming). This is why I focus here on presenting the first order condition of the model. The presentation and the implementation follow [3]. The optimal condition from household's optimization problem is given by:

$$\beta E_t[(c_{t+1}^{-\sigma})(\alpha exp(a_{t+1})k_{t+1}^{\alpha-1} + 1 - \delta) - c_t^{-\sigma}] = 0$$

(5.30)

The capital stock follows:

$$k_{t+1} = exp(a_t)k_t^\alpha - c_t + (1 - \delta)k_t$$

(5.31)

We aim at solving the two equations above, by finding the functions $g(\cdot)$ and $h(\cdot)$ such that the following hold:

$$c_t = g(k_t, a_t)$$

(5.32)

$$k_{t+1} = h(k_t, a_t) = exp(a_t)k_t^\alpha - c_t + (1 - \delta)k_t$$

(5.33)

However, once we solve for $g(k_t, a_t)$, we also get a solution for $h(k_t, a_t)$. This means that the original representation of the DSGE model in (5.11) can be written as:

$$E_t[G(c_{t+1}, k_{t+1}, a_{t+1}, c_t)] = 0$$

(5.34)

which is solved by the function $g(k_t, a_t)$. At the same time, we can use $c_{t+1} = g(k_{t+1}, a_{t+1}) = g(h(k_t, a_t), a_{t+1}) = f(k_t, a_t, \epsilon_{t+1})$, such that we write the model as:

$$E_t[G(f(k_t, a_t, \sigma), h(k_t, a_t), \rho a_{t+1} + (1 - \rho)\bar{a} + \sigma\epsilon_{t+1}, g(k_t, a_t)] = 0$$

(5.35)

This is equivalent to the more compact form:

$$E_t[F(k_t, a_t, \sigma)] = 0$$

(5.36)

A second order Taylor expansion of (5.36) around the steady state $(\bar{k}, \bar{a}, 0)$ would be written as follows:

$$E_t[F(\bar{k}, \bar{a}, 0) + F_k(\bar{k}, \bar{a}, 0)\tilde{k}_t + F_a(\bar{k}, \bar{a}, 0)\tilde{a}_t + F_\sigma(\bar{k}, \bar{a}, 0)\tilde{\sigma}$$
$$+ 1/2F_{kk}(\bar{k}, \bar{a}, 0)\tilde{k}_t^2 + 1/2F_{aa}(\bar{k}, \bar{a}, 0)\tilde{a}_t^2 + 1/2F_{\sigma\sigma}(\bar{k}, \bar{a}, 0)\tilde{\sigma}^2$$
$$+ F_{ka}(\bar{k}, \bar{a}, 0)\tilde{k}_t\tilde{a}_t + F_{k\sigma}(\bar{k}, \bar{a}, 0)\tilde{k}_t\tilde{\sigma} + F_{a\sigma}(\bar{k}, \bar{a}, 0)\tilde{a}_t\tilde{\sigma}] = 0$$

(5.37)

We might note that at the moment the decision are made by the representative consumer, both k_t, a_t are known such that the expectations operator can be dropped, and the above equation becomes:

$$F(\bar{k}, \bar{a}, 0) + F_k(\bar{k}, \bar{a}, 0)\tilde{k}_t + F_a(\bar{k}, \bar{a}, 0)\tilde{a}_t + F_\sigma(\bar{k}, \bar{a}, 0)\tilde{\sigma}$$
$$+1/2F_{kk}(\bar{k}, \bar{a}, 0)\tilde{k}_t^2 + 1/2F_{aa}(\bar{k}, \bar{a}, 0)\tilde{a}_t^2 + 1/2F_{\sigma\sigma}(\bar{k}, \bar{a}, 0)\tilde{\sigma}^2 \qquad (5.38)$$
$$+F_{ka}(\bar{k}, \bar{a}, 0)\tilde{k}_t\tilde{a}_t + F_{k\sigma}(\bar{k}, \bar{a}, 0)\tilde{k}_t\tilde{\sigma} + F_{a\sigma}(\bar{k}, \bar{a}, 0)\tilde{a}_t\tilde{\sigma} = 0$$

At the same time, we similarly approximate g using:

$$g(k_t, a_t, \sigma) \cong g(\bar{k}, \bar{a}, 0) + g_k(\bar{k}, \bar{a}, 0)\tilde{k}_t + g_a(\bar{k}, \bar{a}, 0)\tilde{a}_t + g_\sigma(\bar{k}, \bar{a}, 0)\tilde{\sigma}$$
$$+1/2g_{kk}(\bar{k}, \bar{a}, 0)\tilde{k}_t^2 + 1/2g_{aa}(\bar{k}, \bar{a}, 0)\tilde{a}_t^2 + 1/2g_{\sigma\sigma}(\bar{k}, \bar{a}, 0)\tilde{\sigma}^2 \qquad (5.39)$$
$$+g_{ka}(\bar{k}, \bar{a}, 0)\tilde{k}_t\tilde{a}_t + g_{k\sigma}(\bar{k}, \bar{a}, 0)\tilde{k}_t\tilde{\sigma} + g_{a\sigma}(\bar{k}, \bar{a}, 0)\tilde{a}_t\tilde{\sigma}$$

We already know that $g_\sigma(\bar{k}, \bar{a}, 0)$, $g_{k\sigma}(\bar{k}, \bar{a}, 0)$ and $g_{a\sigma}(\bar{k}, \bar{a}, 0)$ are zero. To find the remaining terms, we solve the following system of equations:

$$F(\bar{k}, \bar{a}, 0) = 0$$
$$F_k(\bar{k}, \bar{a}, 0) = 0$$
$$F_a(\bar{k}, \bar{a}, 0) = 0$$
$$F_{kk}(\bar{k}, \bar{a}, 0) = 0 \qquad (5.40)$$
$$F_{aa}(\bar{k}, \bar{a}, 0) = 0$$
$$F_{\sigma\sigma}(\bar{k}, \bar{a}, 0) = 0$$
$$F_{ka}(\bar{k}, \bar{a}, 0) = 0$$

The first equation is already solved for since it is actually the steady state of the model.

I implement a second order approximation of the optimal growth model in Julia following the implementation in [3]. The calibration used in applying the perturbation method and then simulation is rather standard. The capital share is set at $\alpha = 0.3$, the depreciation rate $\delta = 0.1$, the discount factor $\beta = 0.95$. For the productivity shocks, we use an autocorrelation of $\rho = 0.9$ and a volatility of 0.1. Finally, we also set $\sigma = 2.5$.

```
#Setup the model
# number of backward, forward looking variables and shocks
nx = 2; # backward variables
ny = 1; # forward and static variables
ne = 1; # shocks

# calibration
alpha = 0.3;
sigma = 1.5;
beta  = 0.95;
delta = 0.1;
as    = 0;
rhoa  = 0.9;
eta1  = 0.01;
ETA   = [0;eta1];
s2    = 1;

#steady state
ksy=alpha*beta/(1-beta*(1-delta));
ysk=(1-beta*(1-delta))/(alpha*beta);
ys=ksy^(alpha/(1-alpha));
```

```
ks=ksy*ys;
cs=ys*(1-delta*ksy);

# vector of parameters
param=[beta sigma alpha delta rhoa as]

# vector of steady state
xs=[ks as cs ks as cs];
xs=vec(xs);

#compute Jacobian and Hessian matrices
using Calculus

#define the model
# k' a' c' k a c
# 1  2  3  4 5 6
#eq(1)= kp-exp(a)*k^alpha+c-(1-delta)*k;
#eq(2)= ap-ra*a-(1-ra)*ab;
# Forward variables
#eq(3)= c^(-sigma)-beta*(cp^(-sigma))*(alpha*exp(ap)*(kp^(alpha-1))+1-delta);

#Jacobian
gr1 = Calculus.gradient(x -> x[1]-exp(x[5])*x[4]^alpha+x[6]-(1-delta)*x[4], xs);
gr2 = Calculus.gradient(x -> x[2]-rhoa*x[5]-(1-rhoa)*as, xs);
gr3 = Calculus.gradient(x -> x[6]^(-sigma)-beta*(x[3]^(-sigma))*(alpha*exp(x[2])*(x[1]^(alpha-1))+1-delta), xs);
#define the Jacobian
J = [gr1'; gr2'; gr3']

#Hessian
h1 = hessian(x -> x[1]-exp(x[5])*x[4]^alpha+x[6]-(1-delta)*x[4], xs);
h2 = hessian(x -> x[2]-rhoa*x[5]-(1-rhoa)*as, xs);
h3 = hessian(x -> x[6]^(-sigma)-beta*(x[3]^(-sigma))*(alpha*exp(x[2])*(x[1]^(alpha-1))+1-delta), xs);

h1=vec(h1);
h2=vec(h2);
h3=vec(h3);
#define the Hessian
H = [h1 h2 h3]

function solve(xs,J,H,ETA,nx,ny,ne);

Hs=xs[1:nx];
Gs=xs[nx+1:nx+ny];

# Order 1
J0=J[:,1:nx+ny];
J1=-J[:,nx+ny+1:end];

r = schurfact(J0,J1)
s = r[:S]
t = r[:T]
q = r[:Q]'   # So now q*a*z = s and q*b*z = t
z = r[:Z]

s,t,q,z=reorder(s,t,q,z)

z21 = z[nx+1:end,1:nx];
z11 = z[1:nx,1:nx];
```

```
if rank(z11)<nx;
error("Invertibility condition violated")
end

z11i = \(z11,eye(nx));
s11 = s[1:nx,1:nx];
t11 = t[1:nx,1:nx];

#if abs(t[nx,nx])>abs(s[nx,nx]) | abs(t[nx+1,nx+1])<abs(s[nx+1,nx+1]);
#warning("Wrong number of stable eigenvalues");
#end

#compute Gx and Hx
dyn = \(s11,t11);
Gx = z21*z11i;
Hx = z11*dyn*z11i;

tol=1e-6;
if maximum(maximum(imag(Gx)))<tol;
Gx=real(Gx);
end
if maximum(maximum(imag(Gx)))<tol;
Hx=real(Hx);
end;


# Computes Gxx and Hxx
Zx = [Hx;Gx*Hx;eye(nx);Gx];
Jxp= J[:,1:nx];
Jyp= J[:,nx+1:nx+ny];
Jx = J[:,nx+ny+1:2*nx+ny];
Jy = J[:,2*nx+ny+1:2*(nx+ny)];
XX1 = [kron((Jxp+Jyp*Gx),eye(nx*nx)) kron(Jyp,kron(Hx',Hx'))+kron(Jy,eye(nx*nx))];
XX0 = -kron(Zx',Zx')*H;
XX0 = vec(XX0);
HGXX= \(XX1,XX0);
Hxx = HGXX[1:nx*nx*nx];
if maximum(maximum(imag(Hxx)))<tol
Hxx=real(Hxx);
end
Gxx = HGXX[nx*nx*nx+1:end];
if maximum(maximum(imag(Gxx)))<tol
Gxx=real(Gxx);
end;

# Computes Gss and Hss
SS0= 0;
for i=1:ne;
Zs    =[ETA[:,i];Gx*ETA[:,i];zeros(nx,1);zeros(ny,1)];
TEMP0 = -kron(Zs',Zs')*H;
TEMP0 = vec(TEMP0);
TEMP1 = -Jyp*kron(eye(ny),kron(ETA[:,i]',ETA[:,i]'))*Gxx;
TEMP1 = vec(TEMP1);
SS0   = SS0+TEMP0+TEMP1;
end

SS1  = [Jxp+Jyp*Gx (Jyp+Jy)];
HGSS = \(SS1,SS0);
Hss  = HGSS[1:nx];
```

```
Gss  = HGSS[nx+1:nx+ny];
if maximum(maximum(imag(Hss)))<tol
Hss=real(Hss);
end
if maximum(maximum(imag(Gss)))<tol
Gss=real(Gss);
end

Hxx = reshape(Hxx,nx*nx,nx)';
Gxx = reshape(Gxx,nx*nx,ny)';

return Gs,Hs,Gx,Hx,Gxx,Hxx,Gss,Hss;
end;


function reorder(s,t,q,z);
nsize = size(s,1);
i = 1;
while i<=nsize-1;
if 1+abs(t[i,i]*s[i+1,i+1])>1+abs(s[i,i]*t[i+1,i+1]);
A=s; B=t; Q=q; Z=z;
s,t,q,z = qzswitch(i,A,B,Q,Z);

i=i+1;
end;
end;
return s,t,q,z;
end;

function qzswitch(i,A,B,Q,Z);
a = A[i,i]; d = B[i,i]; b =A[i,i+1]; e = B[i,i+1]; c = A[i+1,i+1]; f = B[i+1,i+1];

wz = [c*e-f*b, (c*d-f*a)'];
xy = [(b*d-e*a)', (c*d-f*a)'];
n = sqrt(wz'*wz);
m = sqrt(xy'*xy);

if n == 0
return
else
wz = \(n,wz);
xy = \(m,xy);
wz = [wz[1] wz[2]; -wz[2] wz[1]]
xy = [xy[1] xy[2]; -xy[2] xy[1]]
A[i:i+1,:] = xy*A[i:i+1,:];
B[i:i+1,:] = xy*B[i:i+1,:];
A[:,i:i+1] = A[:,i:i+1]*wz;
B[:,i:i+1] = B[:,i:i+1]*wz;
Z[:,i:i+1] = Z[:,i:i+1]*wz;
Q[i:i+1,:] = xy*Q[i:i+1,:];
end;

if ~(i==1);i = i-2;end
return A,B,Q,Z;
end;

#the solution
Gs,Hs,Gx,Hx,Gxx,Hxx,Gss,Hss = solve(xs,J,H,ETA,nx,ny,ne);
```

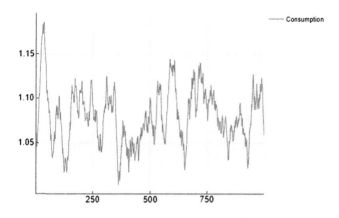

FIGURE 5.1   Consumption.

```
# compute the variables
long  = 1000;
tronc = 100;
slong = long+tronc;
T     = tronc+1:slong;
e     = randn(ne,slong)*sqrt(s2);

S1=zeros(nx,slong);
S2=zeros(nx,slong);
X1=zeros(ny,slong);
X2=zeros(ny,slong);

S1[:,1]=ETA*e[:,1]';
S2[:,1]=ETA*e[:,1]';
tmp=S2[:,1]*S2[:,1]';
tmp=vec(tmp);
X1[:,1]=Gx*S1[:,1];
X2[:,1]=X1[:,1]+0.5*Gxx*tmp[:];
for i=2:slong
S1[:,i]=Hx*S1[:,i-1]+ETA*e[:,i]';
X1[:,i]=Gx*S1[:,i];
S2[:,i]=S1[:,i]+0.5*Hxx*tmp+0.5*Hss*s2;
tmp2=S2[:,i]*S2[:,i]';
tmp2=vec(tmp2);
X2[:,i]=Gs+0.5*Gss*s2+X1[:,i]+0.5*Gxx*tmp2;
X1[:,i]=Gs+X1[:,i];
end;
```

I can plot the consumption simulated path as shown in Fig. 5.1:

```
#plot series
using Plots
plotly() # Choose the Plotly.jl backend for web interactivity
plot(X2[1,:],linewidth=1,label="Consumption")
```

5.2.3.2   An Asset Pricing Model

The Model

I present now a basic asset pricing model, following the simple version in [11], based on the earlier contribution by [12]. The presentation draws from [3] and [4].

The environment of the economy is frictionless and the economy is of pure exchange type. There is a single perishable good. The representative household maximizes the expected lifetime discounted life time utility:

$$E_t \sum_{t=0}^{\infty} \beta^t \frac{c_t^{\theta}}{\theta} \tag{5.41}$$

Here, $\theta \in (-\infty, 0) \cup (0, 1]$ and $\beta \in (0, 1)$ is the discount factor. The household faces the following budget constraint:

$$p_t e_{t+1} + c_t = (p_t + d_t) e_t \tag{5.42}$$

c_t is the consumption, p_t the asset price while e_t stands for the holdings of assets by the representative household. d_t are the dividends per tree. It is further assumed that the dividends follow the process:

$$d_t = exp(x_t) d_{t-1} \tag{5.43}$$

Here, x_t is the growth rate of dividends which is assumed to follow an AR(1) process:

$$x_t = (1 - \rho)\bar{x} + \rho x_{t-1} + \epsilon_t \tag{5.44}$$

We impose on the innovations to the growth of dividends x_t that they are i.i.d. and drawn from a normal distribution $N(0, \sigma^2)$. Denoting by y_t the price-dividend ratio, $y_t = p_t / d_t$, we write the optimal condition for the household as:

$$y_t = E_t[exp(\theta x_{t+1})(1 + y_{t+1})] \tag{5.45}$$

Following [11], it can be shown that this model has an analytical solution. The solution can be written as:

$$y_t = \sum_{i=1}^{\infty} \beta^i exp[a_i + b_i(x_t - \bar{x})] \tag{5.46}$$

Here, the coefficients a_i, b_i are given by:

$$a_i = \theta \bar{x} i + \frac{\theta^2 \sigma^2}{2(1-\rho)^2}[i - \frac{2\rho(1-\rho^i)}{1-\rho} + \frac{\rho^2(1-\rho^{2i})}{1-\rho^2}] \tag{5.47}$$

$$b_i = \frac{\theta \rho (1 - \rho^i)}{1 - \rho} \tag{5.48}$$

To solve the model using the perturbation method we rewrite first the two equations which characterize the model as follows:

$$\begin{aligned} y_t &= E_t[exp(\theta x_{t+1})(1 + y_{t+1})] \\ x_t &= (1 - \rho)\bar{x} + \rho x_{t-1} + \sigma \epsilon_t \end{aligned} \tag{5.49}$$

Using the above description of the model, the model solution can be written (as for the optimal growth model) using the policy functions $g()$ and $h()$ as follows:

$$\begin{aligned} x_{t+1} &= h(x_t, \sigma) \\ y_t &= E_t[f(y_{t+1}, x_{t+1})] \end{aligned} \tag{5.50}$$

The perturbation approach, at a second order, is then applied similarly as in the case of the optimal growth model. I use the calibration in [12]. The steady state dividend growth is set at $\bar{x} = 0.0179$. The persistence of the growth in dividend is set at $\rho = -0.139$, while the volatility of innovations at $\sigma = 0.0348$. The discount factor is set at $\beta = 0.95$, while we use a standard value for θ at -1.5.

The Julia implementation is presented below. I don't include the code for the functions for solving the model or ordering the eigenvalues, which remain the same.

```
#calibrate
nx   = 1;    # backward variables
ny   = 1;    # static variables
ne   = 1;    # shocks
rhox = -0.139;
eta  = 0.0348;
sx   = eta/sqrt(1-rhox*rhox);


beta  = 0.950;
theta = -1.500;
xb    = 0.0179;
rhox  = -0.139;
eta   = 0.0348;
ETA   = [eta];
s2    = 1;
sx    = eta/sqrt(1-rhox*rhox);
ys    = beta*exp(theta*xb)/(1-beta*exp(theta*xb));
param = [beta theta rhox xb];


# steady state
devx  = 5;
nbx   = 200;
xmin  = xb-devx*sx;
xmax  = xb+devx*sx;
xgrid = collect(linspace(xmin,xmax,nbx))


xs=[xb ys xb ys];
xs=vec(xs)


#compute Jacobian and Hessian matrices
using Calculus
#define the model
# variables (leads and lags)
#xp = xx(1);
#yp = xx(2);
#x  = xx(3);
#y  = xx(4);


#Jacobian
gr1 = Calculus.gradient(x -> x[1]-rhox*x[3]-(1-rhox)*xb, xs);
gr2 = Calculus.gradient(x -> x[4]-beta*exp(theta*x[1])*(1+x[2]), xs);


#define the Jacobian
J = [gr1'; gr2'];


#Hessian
h1 = hessian(x -> x[1]-rhox*x[3]-(1-rhox)*xb, xs);
h2 = hessian(x -> x[4]-beta*exp(theta*x[1])*(1+x[2]), xs);


h1=vec(h1);
h2=vec(h2);
#define the Hessian
H = [h1 h2]


Gs,Hs,Gx,Hx,Gxx,Hxx,Gss,Hss = solve(xs,J,H,ETA,nx,ny,ne);
```

5.2.3.3 Comparing the Accuracy of Approximations

A key aspect of doing approximations is to get a solution as closed as possible to the analytical solution. I study here the accuracy of the perturbation approximation for the asset pricing model and compare it to the analytical solution. I start from a basic calibration, the benchmark, and consider then a few variations in the calibration. The benchmark calibration corresponds to the calibration from the previous section. The Julia code is shown below:

```julia
nx  = 1;   # backward variables
ny  = 1;   # static variables
ne  = 1;   # shocks
rhoxx = -0.139;
etax  = 0.0348;
sxx   = etax/sqrt(1-rhoxx*rhoxx);
EP=[
0.950 -1.500 0.0348 -0.139;
0.500 -1.500 0.0348 -0.139;
0.990 -1.500 0.0348 -0.139;
0.950 -10.00 0.0348 -0.139;
0.950  0.100 0.0348 -0.139;
0.950  0.500 0.0348 -0.139;
0.950 -1.500 0.0010 -0.139;
0.950 -1.500 0.1000 -0.139;
0.950 -1.500 sxx       0;
0.950 -1.500 sxx*sqrt(0.75) 0.5;
0.950 -1.500 sxx*sqrt(0.19) 0.9];

#define vectors
E1 = zeros(size(EP,1),3);
Ei = zeros(size(EP,1),3);
#iterate
#k=10
for k=1:size(EP,1);
beta  = EP[k,1];
theta = EP[k,2];
xb    = 0.0179;
rhox  = EP[k,4];
eta   = EP[k,3];
ETA   = [eta];
s2    = 1;
sx    = eta/sqrt(1-rhox*rhox);
ys    = beta*exp.(theta*xb)/(1-beta*exp.(theta*xb));
param =[beta theta rhox xb];

# steady state
devx  = 5;
nbx   = 200;
xmin  = xb-devx*sx;
xmax  = xb+devx*sx;
xgrid = collect(linspace(xmin,xmax,nbx));

xs    = [xb ys xb ys];
xs    = vec(xs)

# True rule
nb=1000;
ri=rhox;
ri2=rhox;
ai= theta*xb+(theta*theta*eta*eta)/2;
bi= theta*rhox;
bti=beta;
tsol=bti*exp.(ai+bi*(xgrid-xb));
for i=2:nb;
ri  = rhox*ri;
ri2 = rhox*rhox*ri2;
ai  = theta*xb*i+(theta*theta*eta*eta)*(i-2*rhox*(1-ri)/(1-rhox)+rhox*rhox*(1-ri2)/(1-rhox*rhox))/(2*(1-rhox)*(1-rhox));
bi  = theta*rhox*(1-ri)/(1-rhox);
bti = bti*beta;
tsol = tsol+bti*exp.(ai+bi*(xgrid-xb));
end

# Jacobian matrix
using Calculus
#define the model
# variables (leads and lags)
#xp = xx(1);
```

TABLE 5.1 Accuracy check

	Linear		Quadratic (CE)		Quadratic	
	E_1	E_∞	E_1	E_∞	E_1	E_∞
Benchmark	1.4414	1.4774	1.4239	1.4241	0.0269	0.0642
$\beta = 0.5$	0.2537	0.2944	0.2338	0.2343	0.0041	0.0087
$\beta = 0.99$	2.9414	2.9765	2.9243	2.9244	0.0833	0.1737
$\theta = -10$	23.7719	25.3774	23.1348	23.1764	4.5777	8.3880
$\theta = 0.1$	0.0098	0.01002	0.0097	0.0097	1.05973e-5	2.16478e-5
$\theta = 0.5$	0.2865	0.2904	0.2845	0.2845	0.0016	2.2265
$\sigma = 0.001$	0.0012	0.0012	0.0012	0.0012	0.0000	0.0000
$\sigma = 0.1$	11.8200	12.1078	11.6901	11.6901	1.2835	2.2265
$\rho = 0.0$	1.8469	1.8469	1.8469	1.8469	0.0329	0.0329
$\rho = 0.5$	5.9148	8.2770	4.9136	5.2081	0.7100	1.5640
$\rho = 0.9$	57.5112	226.203	31.8128	146.6219	36.8337	193.1591

Source: Own computations and [3]

```
#yp = xx(2);
#x  = xx(3);
#y  = xx(4);

#Jacobian
gr1 = Calculus.gradient(x -> x[1]-rhox*x[3]-(1-rhox)*xb, xs);
gr2 = Calculus.gradient(x -> x[4]-beta*exp.(theta*x[1])*(1+x[2]), xs);
#define the Jacobian
J =  [gr1'; gr2']

# Hessian
h1 = hessian(x -> x[1]-rhox*x[3]-(1-rhox)*xb, xs);
h2 = hessian(x -> x[4]-beta*exp.(theta*x[1])*(1+x[2]), xs);
h1=vec(h1);
h2=vec(h2);
#define the Hessian
H =  [h1 h2]

Gs,Hs,Gx,Hx,Gxx,Hxx,Gss,Hss = solve(xs,J,H,ETA,nx,ny,ne);
asol1 =Gs.+(Gx.*(xgrid-xb));
asol2 =Gs.+0.5*Gss.+Gx.*(xgrid-xb)+0.5*Gxx.*(xgrid-xb).*(xgrid-xb);
asoleq=Gs.+Gx.*(xgrid-xb)+0.5*Gxx.*(xgrid-xb).*(xgrid-xb);

Err1=abs.((tsol-asol1)./tsol);
Err2=abs.((tsol-asol2)./tsol);
Erreq=abs.((tsol-asoleq)./tsol);

E1[k,:]=100*mean([Err1 Erreq Err2],1)
Ei[k,:]=100*maximum([Err1 Erreq Err2],1);
end;
```

I summarize the results in Table 5.1. I present the approximation errors for the various calibrations used, starting with the basic calibration, the benchmark. There are three types of approximation, linear (first-order approximation), Quadratic CE (certainty equivalent quadratic approximation, with the correction implied by volatility ignored), and Quadratic, with the correction included.

Table 5.1 shows the accuracy errors for the benchmark case and different values for the parameters, with variations in the discount factor (agents are more or less patient), a bigger volatility, higher persistence in the growth of dividends as well as a bigger curvature in the utility function. The results are pretty interesting as they indicate that the linear approximation works well only for standard calibration and small volatility. For increased volatility or persistence in the dividend growth, both the linear and quadratic CE do not work well.

5.3 PARAMETERIZED EXPECTATIONS ALGORITHM

In this section, I focus on the parameterized expectations algorithm (PEA, hereafter). The main idea behind this algorithm is to focus on approximating the expectations functions, in contrast with other approaches that deal with the decision rules. The PEA can also be seen as a generalized method of undetermined coefficients, with agents learning the decision rule in each iteration of the algorithm.

5.3.1 The Theory

The PEA approach can be traced back to the contribution by [6]. Good presentations of the subject can be found in [1] or [3]. In this section, I detail the theory behind PEA following [3].

PEA is used to solve models that can be written using the following representation:

$$F(E_t(\mathcal{E}(y_{t+1}, x_{t+1}, y_t, x_t)), y_t, x_t, \epsilon_t) = 0 \tag{5.51}$$

Here, the function $F : \mathbb{R}^m \times \mathbb{R}^{n_y} \times \mathbb{R}^{n_x} \times \mathbb{R}^{n_e} \to \mathbb{R}^{n_x + n_y}$ corresponds to the model. The function $\mathcal{E} : \mathbb{R}^{n_y} \times \mathbb{R}^{n_x} \times \mathbb{R}^{n_y} \times \mathbb{R}^{n_x} \to \mathbb{R}^m$ stands for the transformed variables on which the expectations operator is applied. E_t is the conventional expectations operator while ϵ_t are the innovations in structural shocks on the economy.

To build some intuition, I describe first the optimal growth model and then cast the PEA algorithm so as to solve this model. The solution to the optimal growth model can be written as follows:

$$\lambda_t - \beta E_t[\lambda_{t+1}(\alpha z_{t+1} k_{t+1}^{\alpha-1} + 1 - \delta)] = 0 \tag{5.52}$$

$$c_t^{-\sigma} - \lambda_t = 0 \tag{5.53}$$

$$k_{t+1} - z_t k_t^{\alpha} + c_t - (1 - \delta)k_t = 0 \tag{5.54}$$

$$z_{t+1} - \rho z_t - \epsilon_{t+1} = 0 \tag{5.55}$$

Here, we group the variables as follows. The vector y_t comprises the control variables such that $y_t = \{c_t, \lambda_t\}$, the vector x_t comprises the state variables, and we write $x_t = \{k_t, z_t\}$. Finally, ϵ_t are the shocks. Based on the representation above, the model can also be written using the function F and $\mathcal{E}$ as follows:

$$\mathcal{E}(\{c, \lambda\}_{t+1}, \{k, z\}_{t+1}, \{c, \lambda\}_t, \{k, z\}_t) = \lambda_{t+1}(\alpha z_{t+1} k_{t+1}^{\alpha-1} + 1 - \delta) \tag{5.56}$$

$$F(\cdot) = \begin{cases} \lambda_t - \beta E_t[\mathcal{E}(\{c, \lambda\}_{t+1}, \{k, z\}_{t+1}, \{c, \lambda\}_t, \{k, z\}_t)] \\ c_t^{-\sigma} - \lambda_t \\ k_{t+1} - z_t k_t^{\alpha} + c_t - (1 - \delta)k_t \\ z_{t+1} - \rho z_t - \epsilon_t \end{cases} \tag{5.57}$$

As already underlined in the introduction to this method, PEA focuses not on approximating decision rules, but on approximating the expectation functions. In this particular case, PEA will provide an approximation of $\mathcal{E}(x_{t+1}, y_{t+1}, x_t, y_t)$, using a polynomial approximation written as $\Phi(x, \theta)$, where x stands for the variables, while θ for the parameters. The approximation verifies the following condition:

$$F(\Phi(x_t, \theta), y_t, x_t, \epsilon_t) = 0 \tag{5.58}$$

In terms of optimization there are several ways to write the problem. First, the problem can be written such that the vector θ is chosen while ensuring that the rational expectations hypothesis is verified:

$$\text{argmin}_{\theta \in \Phi} ||\Phi(x_t, \theta) - E_t(\mathcal{E}(y_{t+1}, x_{t+1}, y_t, x_t))||^2 \tag{5.59}$$

This optimization problem relies on using the squared norm. Alternatively, the optimization can be recasted into a general method of moments framework by writing:

$$\text{argmin}_{\theta \in \Phi} \mathcal{R}(x_t, \theta)' \Omega \mathcal{R}(x_t, \theta) \tag{5.60}$$

Here, $\mathcal{R}(x_t, \theta) = \Phi(x_t, \theta) - E_t(\mathcal{E}(y_{t+1}, x_{t+1}, y_t, x_t))$, while Ω is a weighting matrix.

We can now formally present the algorithm as follows:

1. Initialize θ and set a guess value for the function $\Phi(x_t, \theta)$. Set a stopping criterion (denoted by η), a sample size for draws as well as draw a sequence of shocks $\{\epsilon_t\}_{t=0}^{T}$.
2. Denote each iteration by i and at each i, given a value of the parameters at this iteration denoted by θ^i, we simulate $\{y_t(\theta^i)\}_{t=0}^{T}$ and $\{x_t(\theta^i)\}_{t=0}^{T}$.
3. Using the default setup of the optimization problem based on the quadratic norm, we solve for $G(\theta^i)$ such that:

$$\hat{\theta} \in \text{argmin}_{\theta \in \Phi} \frac{1}{T} \sum_{t=0}^{T} ||\mathcal{E}(y_{t+1}(\theta), x_{t+1}(\theta), y_t(\theta), x_t(\theta)) - \Phi(x_t(\theta), \theta)||^2 \tag{5.61}$$

4. We update the vector of parameters in the next period $i+1$ by using the following recursive equation: $\theta^{i+1} = \gamma \hat{\theta^i} + (1 - \gamma)\theta^i$. Here γ is a preset parameter that controls the degree or smoothness of updating the vector of parameters.
5. Check the convergence by using $|\theta^{i+1} - \theta^i| < \eta$ and if the convergence has not been achieved yet, get back to step 2.

We should note that, usually, the smoothing parameter γ can be usually set as close to 1, except for highly nonlinear models. A lower value generally helps at achieving the convergence, at the cost however of a higher computationally burden.

5.3.2 An Example in Julia

I apply the standard PEA approach to the optimal growth model following [3]. Let us first write down the key equations of the optimal growth model to ease the presentation:

$$\lambda_t - \beta E_t[\lambda_{t+1}(\alpha z_{t+1} k_{t+1}^{\alpha-1} + 1 - \delta)] = 0 \tag{5.62}$$

$$c_t^{-\sigma} - \lambda_t = 0 \tag{5.63}$$

$$k_{t+1} - z_t k_t^{\alpha} + c_t - (1 - \delta)k_t = 0 \tag{5.64}$$

$$log(z_{t+1}) - \rho log(z_t) - \epsilon_{t+1} = 0 \tag{5.65}$$

As already mentioned, PEA focuses on approximating not decision rules but expectation functions. Here, we need to approximate the expectation function in Eq. (5.62), i.e. $\beta E_t[\lambda_{t+1}(\alpha z_{t+1} k_{t+1}^{\alpha-1} + 1 - \delta)]$. The standard PEA approach relies on a simply polynomial approximation. Since this expectation function involves two state variables, namely k_t and z_t, we rely on the following polynomial as a guess:

$$\Phi(k_t, z_t; \theta) = exp(\theta_0 + \theta_1 log(k_t) + \theta_2 log(z_t) + \theta_3 log(k_t)^2 +$$
$$\theta_4 log(z_t)^2 + \theta_5 log(k_t) log(z_t)) \tag{5.66}$$

Where $\theta = \{\theta_0, \theta_1, \theta_2, \theta_3, \theta_4, \theta_5\}$ is a vector of unknown parameters.

Given this vector θ, Eq. (5.62) will allow us to a compute a value for λ as a function of θ vector, i.e. $\lambda(\theta) = \Phi(k_t(\theta), z_t(\theta); \theta)$. We use then the second equation in the model, i.e. (5.63) to compute the value of consumption conditional on the value of θ vector:

$$c_t(\theta) = \lambda_t(\theta)^{-1/\sigma} \tag{5.67}$$

This further allows to compute the next period capital stock k_{t+1} conditional on the θ vector as:

$$k_{t+1}(\theta) = z_t k_t(\theta)^{\alpha} - c_t(\theta) + (1 - \delta)k_t(\theta) \tag{5.68}$$

It is possible now to compute the full sequences $\{k_t(\theta)_{t=0}^{T}\}$, $\{z_t(\theta)_{t=0}^{T}\}$, $\{c_t(\theta)_{t=0}^{T}\}$ and $\{\lambda_t(\theta)_{t=0}^{T}\}$. We can compute now the next period value of the expectation function with the help of the first variable as:

$$\varphi_{t+1}(\theta) = \lambda_{t+1}(\theta)(\alpha z_{t+1} k_{t+1}(\theta)^{\alpha-1} + 1 - \delta) \tag{5.69}$$

To get an approximation value for the vector θ, i.e. to compute $\hat{\theta}$, we can run the following exponential regression:

$$\varphi(k_t, z_t; \theta) = \theta_0 + \theta_1 log(k_t(\theta)) + \theta_2 log(z_t) + \theta_3 log(k_t(\theta))^2 +$$
$$\theta_4 log(z_t)^2 + \theta_5 log(k_t(\theta)) log(z_t) \tag{5.70}$$

This estimated value $\hat{\theta}$ is used in the updating equation from Step 4 of the algorithm and we rerun the algorithm until we reach convergence.

The algorithm is implemented below. To check the results against those in [3], I use the same shocks. Alternatively, I could draw a different set of shocks, but the results would differ a bit.

```
# set algorithm parameters
long  = 200;
init  = 50;
slong = init+long;
T     = init+1:slong-1;
T1    = init+2:slong;
tol   = 1e-6;
crit  = 1;

#set model parameters
gam   = 1;
sigma = 1;
delta = 0.1;
beta  = 0.95;
alpha = 0.3;
ab    = 0;
rho   = 0.9;
se    = 0.01;

#steady state
ksy =(alpha*beta)/(1-beta*(1-delta));
yss = ksy^(alpha/(1-alpha));
kss = yss^(1/alpha);
iss = delta*kss;
css = yss-iss;
csy = css/yss;
lss = css^(-sigma);

#generate shocks
srand(1)
e   = se*randn(slong,1);

#or load shocks from Collard(2015)
e=readdlm("e1_noise.csv");

#productivity series a
a   = zeros(slong,1);
a[1]= ab+e[1];
for i=2:slong;
a[i]=rho*a[i-1]+(1-rho)*ab+e[i];
end

#initial solution
ncont  = 3;              # of static equations
nbend  = 1;              # endogenous predetermined variables
nshoc  = 1;              # of shocks
nback  = nbend+nshoc;    # of state variables
nforw  = 1;              # of costate variables
nstat  = nback+nforw;    # of state and costate variables
Mcc    = zeros(ncont,ncont);
Mcs    = zeros(ncont,nstat);
Mss0   = zeros(nstat,nstat);
Mss1   = zeros(nstat,nstat);
Msc0   = zeros(nstat,ncont);
```

```
Msc1    = zeros(nstat,ncont);
Mse     = zeros(nstat,nshoc);

#setup the matrices
# Output
Mcc[1,1] = 1;
Mcs[1,1] = alpha;
Mcs[1,2] = 1;

# investment
Mcc[2,1] = 1;
Mcc[2,2] = -iss/yss;
Mcc[2,3] = -css/yss;

# consumption
Mcc[3,3] = -sigma;
Mcs[3,3] = 1;

# capital
Mss0[1,1] = 1;
Mss1[1,1] = delta-1;
Msc1[1,2] = delta;

# technology shock
Mss0[2,2] = 1;
Mss1[2,2] = -rho;
Mse[2,1]  = 1;

# Euler
Mss0[3,1] = (1-beta*(1-delta));
Mss0[3,3] = -1;
Mss1[3,3] = 1;
Msc0[3,1] = (1-beta*(1-delta));

# Solving the system
M0=inv(Mss0-Msc0*inv(Mcc)*Mcs);
M1=(Mss1-Msc1*inv(Mcc)*Mcs);
W=-M0*M1;

# MU -> eigenvalues, P -> eigenvectors
v,w = eig(W)
r=[abs.(v) w']
vsize=size(v,1)

for i = 1:vsize
for j = i+1:vsize
if  real(r[i,1])> real(r[j,1])
tmp = r[i,:];
r[i,:]=r[j,:];
r[j,:]=tmp;
elseif real(r[i,1])== real(r[j,1])
if imag(r[i,1])> imag(r[j,1])
tmp = r[i,:];
r[i,:]=r[j,:];
r[j,:]=tmp;
end;
end;
end;
end;
```

```
lam= r[:,1];
P=r[:,2:4]';

Q=inv(P);
lam=diagm(lam);

#Direct solution

Gamma=-inv(Q[nback+1:nstat,nback+1:nstat])*Q[nback+1:nstat,1:nback];
MSS=W[1:nback,1:nback]+W[1:nback,nback+1:nstat]*Gamma;
PI=inv(Mcc)*(Mcs[:,1:nback]+Mcs[:,nback+1:nstat]*Gamma);
MSE=[zeros(nbend,nshoc);eye(nshoc)];

S  = zeros(nback,long+init);
S[:,1]= MSE*e[1];
for i = 2:long+init;
S[:,i]= MSS*S[:,i-1]+MSE*e[i];
end;

lb = Gamma*S;
lb = lss*exp.(lb);
lbv= vec(lb);
k   = log(kss)+S[1,:];
kv = vec(k);
ek = exp.(kv);
a   = S[2,:];
av = vec(a);
ea = exp.(av);
T   = init+1:init+long-1;
T1 = init+2:init+long;
XX  = [ones(long-1,1) kv[T] av[T] kv[T].*kv[T] av[T].*av[T] kv[T].*av[T]];
yy  = log.(beta*lb[T1].*(alpha*ea[T1].*ek[T1].^(alpha-1)+1-delta));
b0 = \(XX,yy)

#Main Loop
iter=1;
crit=1;
while crit>tol
k   = zeros(slong+1,1);
lb = zeros(slong,1);
X   = zeros(slong,length(b0));
k[1]= kss;
for i= 1:slong;
X[i,:]= [1 log.(k[i]) a[i] log(k[i])*log(k[i]) a[i]*a[i] log(k[i])*a[i]];
lb[i]  = exp.(X[i,:]'*b0);
k[i+1] = exp.(a[i])*k[i]^alpha+(1-delta)*k[i]-lb[i]^(-1/sigma);
end
y     = beta*lb[T1].*(alpha*exp.(a[T1]).*k[T1].^(alpha-1)+1-delta);
bt    = X[T,:]\log.(y);
b     = copy(gam*bt+(1-gam)*b0);
crit = maximum(abs.(b-b0));
b0    = copy(b);
println("solution",b0)
iter=iter+1;
end;
```

The decision rules are given in Table 5.2.

TABLE 5.2 Decision rules

	θ_0	θ_1	θ_2	θ_3	θ_4	θ_5
Initial	1.36	−2.43	1.43	0.98	1.37	−2.01
Final	2.01	−3.77	1.21	1.66	1.63	−1.78

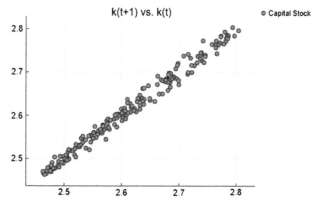

FIGURE 5.2 Expected capital stock vs current capital stock.

The results in terms of expected capital stock k_{t+1} versus current capital stock k_t are plotted in Fig. 5.2:

```
using Plots
plotly() # Choose the Plotly.jl backend for web interactivity
scatter(k[T],k[T1],label="Capital Stock",title="k(t+1) vs. k(t)")
33333999922
```

5.4   PROJECTION METHODS

The first application of projection method (or the minimum weighted residual method) in the context of solving economic models is due to [7]. As it will become apparent later, the previously discussed algorithm, PEA, and the projection method (PM), have something in common. In short, they both can be understood using the generalized method of moments framework. While the PEA approach relies on approximating the expectation function with a parametric function, in the PM, we approximate either the decision rule, as in [7], or, alternatively, the expectation function, as in the later refinement by [8].

5.4.1   The Theory

To introduce the method, I start from a basic example due to [9]. I move then to present the general approach, following largely [3].

A Basic Example

Let us start from a basic first-order differential equation. Assume the following equation:

$$d'(x) + d(x) = 0 \tag{5.71}$$

Here, the initial point $d(0)$ is assumed as known. Furthermore, it also holds that $x \in [0, \bar{x}]$. Solving this problem leads to the following solution: $d(x) = exp(-x)$. To facilitate the more general presentation below, we can also write this in terms of a function equation as follows:

$$F(d)(x) = d'(x) + d(x) = 0 \tag{5.72}$$

We can propose a simplified solution consisting in polynomials of the form: x^i, with $i = 1, ...n$. In this particular case, we can approximate $d(x)$ by using the following polynomial:

$$d^n(x; \theta) = 1 + \theta_1 x + \theta_2 x^2 + ... + \theta_n x^n \tag{5.73}$$

This representation implicitly assumes that the first element of the basis functions is equal to one, i.e. $\psi_0(x) = 1$, such that the boundary condition for $x = 0$ is satisfied. Doing the approximation implies finding the θ_i coefficients, with $i = 1, ...n$. To find the coefficients we can apply a weighted residual method and solving for θ the linear system of equations, $A\theta = b$.

The General Approach

I describe here the general framework for the Projection Method following [3]. The minimum weighted residual method can be applied to dynamic general equilibrium models that can be represented as follows:

$$E_t F(y_{t+1}, x_{t+1}, y_t, x_t, \epsilon_{t+1}) = 0 \tag{5.74}$$

Here, the system of equations of the model is described by $F : \mathbb{R}^{n_y} \times \mathbb{R}^{n_x} \times \mathbb{R}^{n_y} \times \mathbb{R}^{n_x} \times \mathbb{R}^{n_\epsilon} \to \mathbb{R}^{n_y+n_x}$. The vector ϵ comprises the shocks in the model.

Solving the model consists in finding the decision rules given by the following equation:

$$y_t = g(x_t; \theta) \tag{5.75}$$

While the next periods state variables might be written as:

$$x_{t+1} = h(x_t, y_t, \epsilon_{t+1}) = h(x_t, g(x_t, \theta), \epsilon_{t+1}) \tag{5.76}$$

Then, the model can be written in the following form:

$$E_t R(x_t, \epsilon_{t+1}; g, \theta) = 0 \tag{5.77}$$

The Projection Method aims at replacing the decision rule by an approximation function $\phi(x_t; \theta)$ based on the current value of the state variable x_t and a vector of parameters θ. The vector of parameters θ has to chosen in such a way that the initial equation $E_t F(x_t, \epsilon_{t+1}; g, \theta)$ is minimized.

Formally, the Projection Method aims at finding the vector of parameters θ such that, assuming a weight function $\omega_i(x)$, the following equation holds:

$$||E_t R_t(x_t, \epsilon_{t+1}; g, \{\theta\}_{i=0}^n)||_\omega = 0 \tag{5.78}$$

This can be equivalently expressed as:

$$\int_\chi E_t R_t(x_t, \epsilon_{t+1}; g, \theta)\omega_i(x)dx = 0 \tag{5.79}$$

Here, $i = 0, ..., n$.

Implementing the Projection Method

The implementation of the Projection Method relies on a few assumptions regarding three key modeling issues:

1. The approximation functions
2. The weighting function
3. The approximation method for the integral

The Approximation Functions: There are two distinct approaches in the literature with respect to dealing with setting the family of approximation functions. On one hand, we can use the finite elements methods, on the other hand we can rely on spectral methods.

The *Finite elements method* is a piece-wise approach to approximating a function. This approach relies on dividing the state space on disjoint intervals, and fit lower order polynomials for each of these sub-intervals. Thus, the initial function is approximated through a collection of small-dimensional polynomials which are called finite elements. The finite element approach in the context of weighted residual method has been introduced to macroeconomics following the contributions by [9].

The alternative approach, the spectral method, relies on using approximations based on higher order polynomials that are done over the whole initial interval. This implies that the resulting approximation function is both continuous and differentiable, a property which does not characterize the former approach. In this particular approach, assuming that the order of approximation is p, we might write the approximation of the decision function as:

$$y_t = \sum_{i=0}^{p} \theta_i \psi_i(x_i) \tag{5.80}$$

Here $\{\psi_i(\cdot)\}_{i=0}^{n}$ is a family of orthogonal polynomials.

Both methods are discussed within the larger context of function approximation in Chapter 2 on Basic Numerical Techniques, Section 2.4.

The Weighting Function: Another critical choice is that of the weight function. Since the choice of the weight function affects the way the residual function is evaluated, this is also an essential step in designing the different methods to implement the minimum weighted residual approach. There are three such basic ways to choose the weighting function, as described below:

1. The Least Square method: This amounts to setting the weighting function as:

$$\omega_i = \frac{\partial R(x_t, \epsilon_{t+1}; g, \theta)}{\partial \theta_i} \tag{5.81}$$

under the condition that the vector of parameters $\hat{\theta}$ chosen satisfies:

$$\hat{\theta} \in \operatorname{argmin}_\theta \int_\chi E_t R(x_t, \epsilon_{t+1}; \theta)^2 dx_t \tag{5.82}$$

2. The collocation method: This sets the weighting function using the Dirac function. Formally, we write the weights as:

$$\omega(x) = \delta(x - x_i) = \begin{cases} 1 & \text{if, } x = x_i \\ 0 & \text{if, } x \neq x_i \end{cases} \tag{5.83}$$

In words, this technique implies setting the residuals to zero for the nodes $x_1, ..., x_n$.

3. The Galerkin method

In this approach, the weighting function are set using the basis functions, see again Chapter 2 on Basic Numerical Techniques, Section 2.4, for a more detailed presentation of basis functions. In other words, when assuming an approximation based on Chebychev polynomials, of order 0 up to order p, the weighting function will also be set using Chebychev polynomials of order 0 up to p. We would write then:

$$\omega_i = \psi_t(x) \tag{5.84}$$

The Approximation Method for the Integral: There are two issues at hand here. One is the assumption used with respect to the specification of the shock process. Assuming the simpler case of Markov chains would ease a lot the approximation of the integral through a simple sum. On the other hand, for the case of a continuous support for shocks, assuming Gaussian shocks, we would rely on a Gauss-Hermite quadrature method to approximate it.

The second problem is that of computing the inner product resulting from the error function. In this case, the solution method depends on the weights set, see the previous point. For the specific case of collocation, since the residuals are set to zero, no integration is used. For the Least square method, one usually prefers the Legendre quadrature, while for the Galerkin method, a Chebychev quadrature can be applied.

The topic of Numerical Integration, including the various methods described above, is discussed at length in Chapter 2, Section 2.6 on Numerical Integration.

5.4.2 The Projection Method Algorithms and Applications

In this section I present and implement in Julia two of the most widely used minimum weighted residual methods, the collocation and the Galerkin approaches. In each case, I start by present the general algorithm, then discuss the practical implementation of the algorithm for the optimal growth model. The presentation follows [3].

Both implementations are part of the class of spectral methods (see the earlier discussion on the approximation functions) and they rely on the Chebychev polynomials.

5.4.2.1 The Collocation Approach

We start by considering the solution of DSGE model that can be written using the following representation:

$$E_t R(x_{t+1}, \epsilon_{t+1}; g, \theta) = 0 \tag{5.85}$$

Solving this model requires to approximate the decision rule $g(x_t)$ on the domain $[\underline{x}, \bar{x}]$. We propose the following representation of the approximation:

$$\Phi(x_t, \theta) = \sum_{i=0}^{n} \theta_i T_i(\varphi(x_t)) \tag{5.86}$$

Here $T_i(\cdot)$ stands for the Chebychev polynomial of order i with $i = 0, ..., n$. Under these assumptions, the problem becomes finding the vector θ such that the following condition is verified:

$$E_t R(x_i, \epsilon_{t+1}; \Phi, \theta) = 0 \tag{5.87}$$

For $i = 0, ...n$. To simplify the presentation, the algorithm for the univariate case might be written as shown below:

1. We set an approximation order which we denote by n. We then determine the n+1 roots for the Chebychev polynomial of order n+1 using:

$$z_i = cos(\frac{(2i-1)\pi}{2(n+1)}) \tag{5.88}$$

We also set an initial value for the θ.

2. Using the roots, we compute the values x_i using:

$$x_i = \underline{x} + (z_i + 1)\frac{\bar{x} - \underline{x}}{2} \tag{5.89}$$

For $i = 1, ..., n+1$. This also ensures that $x_i \in [\underline{x}, \bar{x}]$.

3. We can calculate now:

$$E_t R(x_i, \epsilon_{t+1}; g, \theta) \tag{5.90}$$

for $i = 1, ..., n+1$.

4. If the above expression is approximately zero, the algorithm stops and we can determine the approximated decision rule using:

$$\Phi(x_t, \theta) = \sum_{i=0}^{n} \theta_i T_i(\varphi(x_t)) \tag{5.91}$$

If this not the case, then we update the value of θ using a nonlinear solver and go back to step 3.

Following [3], I consider two alternative implementations of the stochastic growth model, depending on the assumptions regarding the stochastic process, that is the stochastic process is a Markov chain or an AR(1) process.

The Markov Chain Implementation

We assume a Cobb Douglas production function with k_t the capital stock and a_t the total factor productivity. We write it as: $y_t = exp(a_t)k_t^{\alpha}$. It is assumed that TFP follows a Markov chain that takes two values, $\underline{a}$ or $\bar{a}$. The transition matrix is given by:

$$\begin{bmatrix} p & 1-p \\ 1-p & p \end{bmatrix} \tag{5.92}$$

It is assumed that the capital stock follows a standard dynamic:

$$k_{t+1} = exp(a_t)k_t^{\alpha} - c_t + (1-\delta)k_t \tag{5.93}$$

The Euler equation is written as:

$$c_t^{-\sigma} - E_t[c_{t+1}^{-\sigma}(\alpha exp(a_{t+1})k_{t+1}^{\alpha-1} + 1 - \delta)] = 0 \tag{5.94}$$

Since the TFP process can take two values, $\underline{a}$ and $\bar{a}$, we may explicitly write the Euler equation as follows (the same applies for the capital stock equation):

$$c_t(\underline{a})^{-\sigma} - \beta p[c_{t+1}(\underline{a})^{-\sigma}(\alpha exp((\underline{a}))k_{t+1}(\underline{a})^{\alpha-1} + 1 - \delta)]$$
$$-\beta(1-p)[c_{t+1}(\underline{a})^{-\sigma}(\alpha exp((\underline{a}))k_{t+1}(\underline{a})^{\alpha-1} + 1 - \delta)] = 0 \tag{5.95}$$

$$c_t(\bar{a})^{-\sigma} - \beta(1-p)[c_{t+1}(\bar{a})^{-\sigma}(\alpha exp((\bar{a}))k_{t+1}(\bar{a})^{\alpha-1} + 1 - \delta)]$$
$$-\beta p[c_{t+1}(\bar{a})^{-\sigma}(\alpha exp((\bar{a}))k_{t+1}(\bar{a})^{\alpha-1} + 1 - \delta)] = 0 \tag{5.96}$$

The Projection Method thus will provide approximations for the two corresponding decision rule (for realization of the shock, $\underline{a}$, $\bar{a}$). They can be written as follows:

$$c_t(\underline{a}) \simeq \Phi(k_t, \theta(\underline{a})) = \sum_{j=0}^{n} \theta_j(\underline{a})T_j(\varphi(log(k_t))) \tag{5.97}$$

$$c_t(\bar{a}) \simeq \Phi(k_t, \theta(\bar{a})) = \sum_{j=0}^{n} \theta_j(\bar{a})T_j(\varphi(log(k_t))) \tag{5.98}$$

Using these notations, we may rewrite the algorithm as follows:

1. We set an approximation order denoted by n. We determine next the n+1 roots for the Chebychev polynomial of order n+1 using:

$$z_i = cos(\frac{(2i-1)\pi}{2(n+1)}) \tag{5.99}$$

We also propose initial guesses for $\theta(\underline{a})$ and $\theta(\bar{a})$.

2. Based on the roots, we compute the values k_i using:

$$k_i = exp(log(\underline{k}) + (z_i + 1)\frac{log(\bar{k}) - log(\underline{k})}{2}) \tag{5.100}$$

For $i = 1, ..., n + 1$. This approach ensures that $k_i \in [\underline{k}, \bar{k}]$.

3. We can determine now the two decision rules using:

$$c_t(\underline{a}) \simeq \Phi(k_t, \theta(\underline{a})) = \sum_{j=0}^{n} \theta_j(\underline{a})T_j(\varphi(log(k_i))) \tag{5.101}$$

$$c_t(\bar{a}) \simeq \Phi(k_t, \theta(\bar{a})) = \sum_{j=0}^{n} \theta_j(\bar{a})T_j(\varphi(log(k_i))) \tag{5.102}$$

for each node k_i and $i = 1, ..., n + 1$. At the same time, we write the dynamics of capital stock for the two realizations of the stochastic process as:

$$k_{t+1}(k_i, \underline{a}) = exp(\underline{a})k_i^{\alpha} - \Phi(k_i, \theta(\underline{a})) + (1 - \delta)k_i \tag{5.103}$$

$$k_{t+1}(k_i, \bar{a}) = exp(\bar{a})k_i^{\alpha} - \Phi(k_i, \theta(\bar{a})) + (1 - \delta)k_i \tag{5.104}$$

4. We also must compute the future levels of consumption. They depend on the possible combinations of the current and future realizations of stochastic processes, i.e. a_t and a_{t+1}, which are four, namely $(\underline{a}, \underline{a})$, and so on. For example, to estimate the future level of consumption for $a_t = \underline{a}$ and $a_{t+1} = \underline{a}$, we use:

$$\Phi(k_{t+1}(k_i, \underline{a}), \theta(\underline{a})) = \sum_{j=0}^{n} \theta_j(\underline{a})T_j(\varphi(k_{t+1}(k_i, \underline{a}))) \tag{5.105}$$

5. We evaluate now the residuals for the two realizations of the stochastic shocks:

$$R(k_i, \underline{a}; \theta) = \Phi(k_i, \theta(\underline{a}))^{-\sigma} - \beta p \Psi(k_i, \underline{a}, \underline{a}) - \beta(1 - p)\psi(k_i, \underline{a}, \bar{a}) \tag{5.106}$$

$$R(k_i, \bar{a}; \theta) = \Phi(k_i, \theta(\bar{a}))^{-\sigma} - \beta(1 - p)\Psi(k_i, \bar{a}, \underline{a}) - \beta p \psi(k_i, \bar{a}, \bar{a}) \tag{5.107}$$

Here, the function Ψ is defined as:

$$\Psi(k_i, a_t, a_{t+1}) = \Phi(k_{t+1}(k_i, a_t), \theta(a_{t+1}))^{-\sigma}(\alpha exp(a_{t+1})k_{t+1}(k_i, a_t)^{\alpha-1} + 1 - \delta) \tag{5.108}$$

with $i = 1, ..., n$.

If the residuals are not approximately zero, then the value of θ is updated using a Newton type algorithm and we go back to step 3.

The approach is implemented below in Julia:

```julia
# The Optimal Growth Model
# Collocation method (Markov Chain case)
global kmin, ksup, XX, kt;
global nstate, nbk, ncoef, XX, XT, PI;

# Parameters
nbk    = 4;    # Degree of polynomials (capital)
nodes = nbk + 1;    # Nodes
nstate= 2;
ncoef = nbk +1 ; # of coefficients

# Structural Parameters
delta  = 0.1;
beta   = 0.95;
alpha  = 0.3;
sigma  = 1.5;
ysk    =(1-beta*(1-delta))/(alpha*beta);
ksy    = 1/ysk;
ys     = ksy^(alpha/(1-alpha));
ks     = ys^(1/alpha);
is     = delta*ks;
cs     = ys-is;
ab     = 0;

function hernodes(nstate)
TOL    = sqrt(2.2204e-16);
MAXIT  = 30;
PIM4   = pi^(-1/4);
n  = nstate;
m  = (n+1)/2;
m  = convert(Int64, floor(m));
x  = zeros(n,1);
w  = zeros(n,1);
z  = 0;
z1 = 0;
pp = 0;
for i= 1:m
# Initialize the first four roots
if i == 1;
z= sqrt(2*n+1) - 1.85575 * (2*n+1)^(-1/6);
elseif i== 2;
z= z - 1.14 * (n^.426)/z;
elseif i== 3;
```

```
z= 1.86 * z - .86 * x[1];
elseif i== 4;
z= 1.91 * z - .91 * x[2];
else;
z= 2 * z - x[i-2];
end;
for its= 1:MAXIT
p1 = PIM4;
p2 = 0;
for j  = 1:n
p3 = p2;
p2 = p1;
p1 = z*sqrt(2/j)*p2 - sqrt((j-1)/j)*p3;
end;
pp = p2 * sqrt(2*n);
z1 = z;
z  = z1 - p1/pp;
if abs(z-z1) < TOL; break; end;
end;
x[i]    = z;
x[n+1-i]= -z;
w[i]= 2/(pp*pp);
w[n+1-i]= w[i];
end;
return x,w
end;

function transprob(ym,wm,m,r,s)
# this function computes the transition matrix
# Variables:
# ym is the vector of quadrature points
# wm is the vector of weights
# m is the mean of the process
# r is the rho of the process
# s is the conditional std.dev. of the process

n,n0=size(ym) ;        # get the number of quadrature points n
xx =  ones(n,1);
xx=round.(Int64,vec(xx)); #make it integer: indices value in Julia must be integer
x=ym[:,xx] ;           # get x, nxn matrix, whose ji element is consumption
# growth in state j - so x is the value of
# consumption growth at time t, if the state is
# j at time t and i at time t+1 (notice it's
# constant across i)

y=x' ;                 # also an nxn matrix whose ji element is
# consumption growth in state i - so y is the
# value of consumption growth at time t+1, if
# the state is j at time t and i at time t+1
# (notice it's constant across j)

w=wm[:,xx]' ;     # converts the weight vector to a nxn matrix
# whose ji element is w(i) for all j

f=(y-m*(1-r)-x*r) ;
c1=exp.(-(f.*f)./(2.0*s*s))./(sqrt(2.0*pi)*s) ;


f=(y-m*(1-r)-m*r) ;
```

```
c2=exp.(-(f.*f)./(2.0*s*s))./(sqrt(2.0*pi)*s) ;

p=(c1.*w)./c2 ;           # builds the transition matrix with elements
# p(j,i)=f[y(i)|x(j)]w(i)/f[y(i)|mu]

sm=sum(p',1)' ;           # creates column vector with elements
# s(j)=sum(i) p(j,i)

p=p./sm[:,xx];

return p;
end;

# Markov Chain technological process
rho  = 0.8;
se   = 0.2;
ma   - 0;
agrid,wmat=hernodes(nstate);
agrid=agrid*sqrt(2)*se;
PI=transprob(agrid,wmat,0,rho,se)
at=agrid+ma;

#define functions rcheb transfo itransfo
function rcheb(nn);
mod=nn-floor(nn/2)*2;
n1=floor(nn/2);
k=collect(1:n1).';
r1=cos.((2*k-1)*pi/(2*nn));
r1=[r1 -r1];
if mod==1;
r1=[r1 0];
end;
r1=vec(r1);
rr=real(sort!(r1));
return rr
end;

function transfo(x,xmin,xmax);
z=(2*(x-xmin)/(xmax-xmin))-1;
return z
end;

function itransfo(x,xmin,xmax);
z=0.5*(x+1)*(xmax-xmin)+xmin;
return z
end;

function cheb(xx,nn);
cc=real(cos.(kron(acos.(complex(xx)),nn)))
return cc
end;

# grid for the capital stock
kmin  = log(1.2);
ksup  = log(6);
rk    = rcheb(nodes);            #roots
kt    = exp.(itransfo(rk,kmin,ksup)) #grid
vnbk  = collect(0:nbk).';
XX    = cheb(rk,vnbk);
```

```
#initial conditions
a0=repmat([-0.2 0.65 0.04 0 0]',nstate,1);
a0=vec(a0);
param=[alpha beta delta sigma]';

# function makepoly
function makepoly(XA,XW);
nba   = size(XA,2);
nba1  = size(XA,1);
nbw   = size(XW,2);
nmax  = max(nba,nbw);
XX    = Float64[]  ;
for i=1:nbw
for j=1:nba
XX=[XX; kron(XW[:,i],XA[:,j])];
end
end
return XX
end;


f   = function(theta);
RHS=Float64[];
LHS=Float64[];
resid=Float64[];
ct = 0.0;
c1 = 0.0;
lt = length(theta);
lt = round.(Int64,lt/nstate);
theta = reshape(theta,lt,nstate);
for i   = 1:nstate
ct   = exp.(XX*theta[:,i]);
k1   = exp.(at[i])*kt.^alpha+(1-delta)*kt-ct;
rk1  = transfo(log.(k1),kmin,ksup);
vnbk = collect(0:nbk).';
xk1  = cheb(complex(rk1),vnbk);
aux  = 0;
for j=1:nstate;
c1   = exp.(xk1*theta[:,j]);
aux  = aux+PI[i,j]*beta*(alpha*exp.(at[j])*k1.^(alpha-1)+1-delta).*c1.^(-sigma);
end;
RHS  = [RHS;-sigma*log.(ct)];
LHS  = [LHS;log.(aux)];
end;
resid      = LHS-RHS;
return vec(resid);
end;

#solve for decision rules and print them
#using NLsolve;
sol  = nlsolve(not_in_place(f),a0);
fsol = reshape(sol.zero,ncoef,nstate);
println("Display final rule:",fsol)

#simulate the variables
lt  = length(sol.zero);
nb  = 1000;
kt  = collect(kmin:(ksup-kmin)/(nb-1):ksup);
rk  = transfo(kt,kmin,ksup);
```

TABLE 5.3 Decision rules

θ_0	θ_1	θ_2	θ_3	θ_4
0.161955	0.343494	0.00949691	4.27686e-5	−1.06076e-5
0.0163026	0.383178	0.0084339	−7.84181e-5	−1.22279e-63

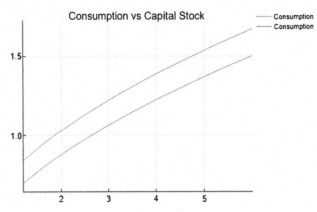

FIGURE 5.3 Decision rules: consumption.

```
rk  = vec(rk);
XX  = cheb(rk,vnbk);
kt  = exp.(kt);
ct=[];k1=[];ii=[];
for i=1:nstate
ct  = cat(i,ct, exp.(XX*fsol[:,i]));
k1  = cat(i, k1, exp.(at[i])*kt.^alpha+(1-delta)*kt-ct[:,i]);
ii  = cat(i,ii, exp.(at[i])*kt.^alpha-ct[:,i]);
end;
```

The decision rules are presented in Table 5.3.

I can plot the results using a surface plot as follows (see Fig. 5.3):

```
using Plots
plotly()
plot(kt,ct, linewidth=1,title="Consumption vs Capital Stock", label="Consumption")
```

The AR(1) Implementation

In this section, I present the Collocation method using the assumption of an AR(1) process for the technology process. This is written as:

$$a_{t+1} = \rho * a_t + \epsilon_{t+1} \tag{5.109}$$

Here, ρ is the degree of persistence, while it assumed that the shocks are normally distributed with $\epsilon\ N(0, \sigma_\epsilon^2)$.

In this case, the Euler equation is written as:

$$c_t^{-\sigma} - E_t[c_{t+1}^{-\sigma}(\alpha exp(a_{t+1})k_{t+1}^{\alpha-1} + 1 - \delta)] = 0 \tag{5.110}$$

The capital stock follows:

$$k_{t+1} = exp(a_t)k_t^\alpha - c_t + (1 - \delta)k_t \tag{5.111}$$

The Euler equation can be further written as follows (after taking into account the specification of the AR(1) process):

$$c_t^{-\sigma} - \frac{1}{\sqrt{2\pi\sigma_\epsilon^2}} \int_\infty^{-\infty} [c_{t+1}^{-\sigma}(\alpha exp(\rho a_t + \epsilon_{t+1})k_{t+1}^{\alpha-1} + 1 - \delta)]exp(-\frac{\epsilon_{t+1}^2}{2\sigma_\epsilon^2})d\epsilon_{t+1} = 0 \tag{5.112}$$

We can exploit the Gaussian nature of the shock and use the following change of variable in the integral within the Euler equation: $z = \epsilon / \sqrt{2\sigma_\epsilon}$:

$$c_t^{-\sigma} - \frac{1}{\sqrt{\pi}} \int_{\infty}^{-\infty} [c_{t+1}^{-\sigma}(\alpha exp(\rho a_t + z\sqrt{2\sigma_\epsilon})k_{t+1}^{\alpha-1} + 1 - \delta)]exp(-z^2)dz = 0 \tag{5.113}$$

The Gaussian nature of the shocks allows using a Gauss-Hermite quadrature approach (see Section 2.6.4 on approximating integrals using Gaussian Quadrature Methods in Chapter 2 on Basic Numerical Techniques). Assuming the weights are given by ω_i, the approximation of the Euler equation can be formulated as follows:

$$c_t^{-\sigma} - \frac{1}{\sqrt{\pi}} \sum_{j=1}^{q} \omega_j [c_{t+1}^{-\sigma}(\alpha exp(\rho a_t + z_j\sqrt{2\sigma_\epsilon})k_{t+1}^{\alpha-1} + 1 - \delta)] = 0 \tag{5.114}$$

To approximate the decision rule for consumption, we can use the following guess:

$$c_t \simeq \Phi(k_t, a_t, \theta)) = exp(\sum_{j_k=0}^{n_k} \sum_{j_a=0}^{n_a} \theta_{j_k j_a} T_{j_k}(\varphi(log(k_t))) T_{j_a}(\varphi(a_t))) \tag{5.115}$$

The decision rule takes into account the values of the technology shocks. As it is specific to the collocation method, the number of nodes equals the number of coefficients.

The algorithm can be explicitly written as follows:

1. We set the approximation order as n_k and n_a for the two dimensions. We determine next the $n_k + 1$ and $n_a + 1$ roots for the two Chebychev polynomials:

$$z_k^i = cos(\frac{(2i-1)\pi}{2(n+1)}) \tag{5.116}$$

For $i = 1, ..., n_k + 1$.

$$z_a^j = cos(\frac{(2j-1)\pi}{2(n+1)}) \tag{5.117}$$

For $j = 1, ..., n_a + 1$. We also make an initial guess for θ.

2. Based on the roots z_k^i and a_k^i, we compute the values k_i and a_i using:

$$k_i = exp(log(\underline{k}) + (z_k^i + 1)\frac{log(\bar{k}) - log(\underline{k})}{2}) \tag{5.118}$$

$$a_j = log(\underline{a}) + (z_a^j + 1)\frac{\bar{a} - \underline{a}}{2} \tag{5.119}$$

For $i = 1, ..., n_k + 1$ and $j = 1, ..., n_a + 1$ respectively. This implies that $k_i \in [\underline{k}, \bar{k}]$, while $a_j \in [\underline{a}, \bar{a}]$.

3. We can determine now the Euler equation and the law of motion for the capital stock:

$$c_t \simeq \Phi(k_i, a_j, \theta) = exp(\sum_{j_k=0}^{n_k} \sum_{j_a=0}^{n_a} \theta_{j_k j_a} T_{j_k}(\varphi(log(k_i))) T_{j_a}(\varphi(a_j))) \tag{5.120}$$

$$k_{t+1}(k_i, a_j) = exp(a_j)k_i^\alpha - \Phi(k_i, a_j, \theta) + (1 - \delta)k_i \tag{5.121}$$

for each node (k_i, a_j) with $i = 1, ..., n_k + 1$ and $j = 1, ..., n_a + 1$.

4. For each node (k_i, a_j) we can compute now the future level of consumption:

$$c_{t+1} \simeq \Phi(k_{t+1}(k_i, a_j), \rho a_j + z_l\sqrt{2\sigma_\epsilon}, \theta) \simeq$$

$$exp(\sum_{j_k=0}^{n_k} \sum_{j_a=0}^{n_a} \theta_{j_k j_a} T_{j_k}(\varphi(log(k_{t+1}(k_i, a_j)))) T_{j_a}(\varphi(\rho a_j + z_l\sqrt{2\sigma_\epsilon}))) \tag{5.122}$$

5. We evaluate now the residuals using:

$$R(k_i, a_j; \theta) = \Phi(k_i, a_j, \theta)^{-\sigma} - \frac{\beta}{\sqrt{\pi}} \sum_{l=1}^{q} \omega_l \Psi(k_i, a_j, z_l; \theta) \qquad (5.123)$$

Here, the function Ψ is defined as:

$$\Psi(k_i, a_j, z_l; \theta) = \Phi(k_{t+1}(k_i, a_j), \rho a_j + z_l \sqrt{2\sigma\epsilon})^{-\sigma} (\alpha exp(\rho a_j + z_l) k_{t+1}(k_i, a_j)^{\alpha-1} + 1 - \delta) \qquad (5.124)$$

with $i = 1, ..., n_k + 1$ and $j = 1, ..., n_a + 1$.

Again, if the residuals are not approximately zero, then the value of θ is updated using a Newton type algorithm and we go back to step 3.

The code in Julia is presented below:

```
# The Optimal Growth Model
# Collocation method (AR(1) case)
global nbk, kmin, ksup, XK, kt;
global nba, amin, asup, XA, at;
global nstate, nodea, nodek, wmat, wgrid;

# Parameters
nbk   = 4;   # Degree of polynomials (capital)
nba   = 2;   # Degree of polynomials (technology shock)
ncoef = (nbk+1)*(nba+1); # # of coefficients
nodek = nbk+1; # # of Nodes
nodea = nba+1; # # of Nodes
nstate= 12;

# Structural Parameters
delta = 0.1;
beta  = 0.95;
alpha = 0.3;
sigma = 1.5;
ysk   =(1-beta*(1-delta))/(alpha*beta);
ksy   = 1/ysk;
ys    = ksy^(alpha/(1-alpha));
ks    = ys^(1/alpha);
is    = delta*ks;
cs    = ys-is;
ab    = 0;

# Technology shock process
rho   = 0.8;
se    = 0.2;
ma    = 0;

function hernodes(nstate)
TOL   = sqrt(2.2204e-16);
MAXIT = 30;
PIM4  = pi^(-1/4);
n = nstate;
m = (n+1)/2;
m = convert(Int64, floor(m));
x = zeros(n,1);
w = zeros(n,1);
z = 0;
z1 = 0;
pp = 0;
```

```
for i= 1:m
# Initialize the first four roots
if i == 1;
z= sqrt(2*n+1) - 1.85575 * (2*n+1)^(-1/6);
elseif i== 2;
z= z - 1.14 * (n^.426)/z;
elseif i== 3;
z= 1.86 * z - .86 * x[1];
elseif i== 4;
z= 1.91 * z - .91 * x[2];
else;
z= 2 * z - x[i-2];
end;

for its= 1:MAXIT
p1 = PIM4;
p2 = 0;
for j  = 1:n
p3 = p2;
p2 = p1;
p1 = z*sqrt(2/j)*p2 - sqrt((j-1)/j)*p3;
end;

pp = p2 * sqrt(2*n);
z1 = z;
z  = z1 - p1/pp;
if abs(z-z1) < TOL; break; end;
end;
x[i]    = z;
x[n+1-i]= -z;
w[i]= 2/(pp*pp);
w[n+1-i]= w[i];
end;
return x,w
end;

wgrid,wmat=hernodes(nstate);
wgrid=wgrid*sqrt(2)*se;

#define functions rcheb transfo itransfo
function rcheb(nn);
mod=nn-floor(nn/2)*2;
n1=floor(nn/2);
k=collect(1:n1).';
r1=cos.((2*k-1)*pi/(2*nn));
r1=[r1 -r1];
if mod==1;
r1=[r1 0];
end;
r1=vec(r1);
rr=real(sort!(r1));
return rr
end;

function transfo(x,xmin,xmax);
z=(2*(x-xmin)/(xmax-xmin))-1;
return z
end;
```

```
function itransfo(x,xmin,xmax);
z=0.5*(x+1)*(xmax-xmin)+xmin;
return z
end;

function cheb(xx,nn);
cc=real(cos.(kron(acos.(complex(xx)),nn)))
return cc
end;

# grid for the income
amin=(ma+wgrid[nstate]);
asup=(ma+wgrid[1]);
ra=rcheb(nodea);              #roots
at=itransfo(ra,amin,asup); #grid
vnba = collect(0:nba).';
XA=cheb(ra,vnba)        # Polynomials

# grid for the capital stock
kmin  = log(1.2);
ksup  = log(6);
rk    = rcheb(nodek);                #roots
kt    = exp.(itransfo(rk,kmin,ksup)) #grid
vrbk  = collect(0:nbk).';
XK    = cheb(rk,vrbk)

#initial conditions
a0=[ -0.23759592487257;
0.60814488103911;
0.03677400318790;
0.69025680170443;
-0.21654209984197;
0.00551243342828;
0.03499834613714;
-0.00341171507904;
-0.00449139656933;
0.00085302605779;
0.00285737302122;
-0.00002348542016;
-0.00011606672164;
-0.00003323351559;
0.00018045618825];
param=[alpha beta delta sigma ma rho]';

# function makepoly
function makepoly(XA,XW);
nba   = size(XA,2);
nba1  = size(XA,1);
nbw   = size(XW,2);
nmax  = max(nba,nbw);
XX    = Float64[]  ;
for i=1:nbw
for j=1:nba
XX=[XX; kron(XW[:,i],XA[:,j])];
end
end
return XX
end;
```

```
f   =function(theta);
RHS=Float64[];
LHS=Float64[];
XX =Float64[];
ct = 0.0;
c1 = 0.0;
for i   = 1:nodek
for j=1:nodea
XX0  = makepoly(XA[j,:],XK[i,:]);
ct   = exp.(dot(XX0,theta));
XX   = [XX;XX0];
k1   = exp.(at[j])*kt[i].^alpha+(1-delta)*kt[i]-ct;
rk1  = transfo(log.(k1),kmin,ksup);
#if abs(rk1)>1;disp('problem k(t+1)');end
vrbk = collect(0:nbk).';
xk1  = cheb(complex(rk1),vrbk);
a1   = rho*at[j]+(1-rho)*ma+wgrid;
ra1  = transfo(a1,amin,asup);          # grid
#if abs(ra1)>1;disp('problem a(t+1)');end
XA1  = cheb(complex(ra1),vnba);                # Polynomials
XX1  = makepoly(XA1,xk1);
XX1  = reshape(XX1,size(XA1,1), size(XA1,2)*size(xk1,2))
c1   = exp.(XX1*theta);
aux  = wmat'*(beta*(alpha*exp.(a1)*k1.^(alpha-1)+1-delta).*c1.^(-sigma))/sqrt(pi);
RHS  = [RHS;log.(aux)];
LHS  = [LHS;log.(ct.^(-sigma))];
end;
end;
resid      = LHS-RHS;
return vec(resid);
end;

#solve the model using NLsolve
#Pkg.add("NLsolve");
using NLsolve;
sol = nlsolve(not_in_place(f),a0);
println("Display final rule:",sol.zero)

lt  = length(sol.zero);
nk  = 20;
na  = 10;
kt  = collect(kmin:(ksup-kmin)/(nk-1):ksup);
at  = collect(amin:(asup-amin)/(na-1):asup);
rk  = transfo(kt,kmin,ksup);
rk  = vec(rk);
ra  = transfo(at,kmin,asup);
ra  = vec(ra);
vrbk= collect(0:nbk).';
XT  = cheb(rk,vrbk);
vnba= collect(0:nba).';
XA  = cheb(ra,vnba);
kt  = exp.(kt);
ct  = zeros(nk,na);
k1  = zeros(nk,na);
ii=[];
for i=1:nk
for j=1:na;
XX0  = makepoly(XA[j,:],XT[i,:]);
ct[i,j] = exp(dot(XX0,sol.zero));
```

TABLE 5.4 Decision rules

	θ_0	θ_1	θ_2	θ_3	θ_4
$T_0(a_t)$	0.117961	0.361884	0.00831576	3.45746e-5	−4.07343e-6
$T_1(a_t)$	0.493804	−0.104603	0.00119796	0.00026351	−1.03949e-5
$T_2(a_t)$	0.0406254	−0.001996	−0.0009009	5.36035e-5	3.20045e-6

Next period capital stock

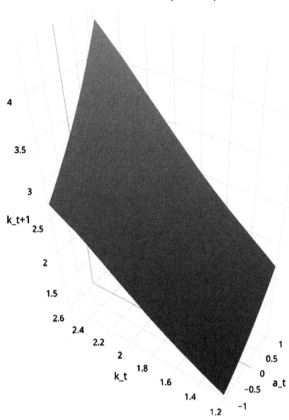

FIGURE 5.4 Next period capital stock.

```
k1[i,j] = exp(at[j])*kt[i].^alpha+(1-delta)*kt[i]-ct[i,j];
end;
end;
```

The algorithm leads to the decision rules that are given in Table 5.4.
I can plot the results using a surface plot as follows (see Fig. 5.4):

```
import PlotlyJS
PlotlyJS.plot([PlotlyJS.surface(x=at,y=kt,z=k1)])
```

5.4.2.2 The Galerkin Approach

In this section I focus on the Galerkin approach. Again, after presenting the general algorithm, I move to the implementation of the algorithm for the optimal growth model. I consider, as in the previous section, two ways in which the shocks can be modeled, i.e. as an AR(1) process or as a Markov chain.

I focus on models that can be represented using the following specification:

$$E_t R(x_t, \epsilon_{t+1}; g, \theta) = 0 \tag{5.125}$$

Again, the objective is to find an approximation to the decision rule $g(x_t)$. For the approximation function the following specification is used:

$$\Phi(x_t, \theta) = \sum_{i=0}^{n} \theta_i T_i(\varphi(x_t)) \tag{5.126}$$

The decision rule is approximated over the domain $[\underline{x}, \bar{x}]$. In the equation above, $T_i(\cdot)$ are Chebychev polynomials with $i = 0, ..., n$ standing for the order of the polynomial. The approximation problem will consist in finding the vector θ that satisfies the following equation:

$$\int_{1}^{-1} E_t R(x, \epsilon_{t+1}; \Phi, \{\theta_i\}_{i=0}^{n}) \omega_i(\varphi(x)) d\varphi(x) = 0 \tag{5.127}$$

Where $i = 0, ..., n$. Here the weights ω_i are given by:

$$\omega_i(x) = \frac{T_i(\varphi(x))}{\sqrt{1 - \varphi(x)^2}} \tag{5.128}$$

This integral can be approximated using a Gauss-Chebychev quadrature (see Chapter 2 on Basic Numerical Techniques, Section 2.6.4) for which the weights are equal. Therefore, we can write:

$$\sum_{j=1}^{m} E_t R(x_j, \epsilon_{t+1}; \Phi, \{\theta_i\}_{i=0}^{n}) T_i(\varphi(x_j)) = 0 \tag{5.129}$$

This can be equivalently represented as:

$$\mathcal{T}(\varphi(x)) R(x, \epsilon_{t+1}; \Phi, \theta) = 0 \tag{5.130}$$

Here, $\mathcal{T}(x)$ stands for:

$$\mathcal{T} = \begin{bmatrix} T_0(\varphi(x_1)) & .... & T_0(\varphi(x_m)) \\ ... & .... & ... \\ T_n(\varphi(x_1)) & .... & T_n(\varphi(x_m)) \end{bmatrix} \tag{5.131}$$

The general form of the Galerkin approach might be written as follows (using a uni-dimensional representation to simplify things):

1. We set first an approximation order, denoted by n. We compute first the m roots of the Chebychev polynomial, where $m > n$ using:

$$z_i = \cos\left(\frac{(2i - 1)\pi}{2m}\right) \tag{5.132}$$

Here, $i = 0, ..., m$. We also propose an initial value for θ.

2. Using the nodes computed above, we determine the matrix $\mathcal{T}(x)$ which is written as:

$$\mathcal{T} = \begin{bmatrix} T_0(z_1) & .... & T_0(z_m) \\ ... & .... & ... \\ T_n(z_1) & .... & T_n(z_m) \end{bmatrix} \tag{5.133}$$

3. We compute the values for x_i using the same approach as for the Collocation method:

$$x_i = \underline{x} + (z_i + 1)\frac{\bar{x} - \underline{x}}{2} \tag{5.134}$$

For $i = 1, ..., m$. This equation implies that $x_i \in [\underline{x}, \bar{x}]$.

4. We can compute now $E_t R(x_i, \epsilon_{t+1}; g, \theta)$ such that we can check now whether $T(\varphi(x)) R(x, \epsilon_{t+1}; g, \theta)$ is approximately equal to zero given a tolerance.

5. If the above expression is approximately zero, we can evaluate now:

$$\Phi(x_t, \theta) = \sum_{i=0}^{n} \theta_i T_i(\varphi(x_t)) \tag{5.135}$$

If this is not the case, θ is updated using a Newton type approach and we go back to step 3.

I move now the applying the algorithm to the case of the optimal growth model. As for the case of the collocation method, there are two ways to treat the stochastic process. Since the modifications in the algorithms are rather secondary, and follow closely the collocation method, I present them in a succinct manner.

I start first with the model used. I employ the same specification for the optimal growth model. Namely, the production function is given by:

$$y_t = exp(a_t) k_t^\alpha \tag{5.136}$$

Here, the process for total factor productivity a_t is specified later as a Markov chain or as an AR(1) process.
The Euler equation is given by:

$$c_t^{-\sigma} - E_t[c_{t+1}^{-\sigma}(\alpha exp(a_{t+1})k_{t+1}^{\alpha-1} + 1 - \delta)] = 0 \tag{5.137}$$

I assume the same process for the capital stock:

$$k_{t+1} = exp(a_t)k_t^\alpha - c_t + (1 - \delta)k_t \tag{5.138}$$

Markov Chain

Assuming a Markov chain process for the technological process, then a_t can take too values, $\underline{a}$ or $\bar{a}$. The transition matrix is written as:

$$\begin{bmatrix} p & 1-p \\ 1-p & p \end{bmatrix} \tag{5.139}$$

There are two basic differences relative to the collocation implementation based on the Markov chain. First, instead of $n + 1$ nodes, we use $m > n$ nodes for approximation. We do not set the residuals to zero (since we need to compute the integral), but the following two equations (depending on the realization of the stochastic shock):

$$\mathcal{T}(z)R(k, \underline{a}; \theta) = 0$$
$$\mathcal{T}(z)R(k, \bar{a}; \theta) = 0 \tag{5.140}$$

A larger number of nodes is used in the implementation in Julia.

AR(1) Process

When an AR(1) process is assumed for the technology, then we write:

$$a_{t+1} = \rho * a_t + \epsilon_{t+1} \tag{5.141}$$

The Julia implementation for this case differs from the collocation approach only by considering a larger number of nodes, as well as by the use of complete basis instead of a tensor basis (see Chapter 2 for the theory behind).

An implementation of the Galerkin method in Julia (for which the shocks are assumed to follow an AR(1) process) is shown below:

```
# The Optimal Growth Model
# Galerkin method (AR(1) case)
```

```
global nbk, kmin, ksup, XK, kt;
global nba, amin, asup, XA, at;
global nstate, nodea, nodek, wmat, wgrid;

# Parameters
nbk   = 4;     # Degree of polynomials (capital)
nba   = 2;     # Degree of polynomials (technology shock)
ncoef = (nbk+1); # # of coefficients
nodek = 20;    # # of Nodes
nodea = 10;# # of Nodes
nstate= 12;

# Structural Parameters
delta  = 0.1;
beta   = 0.95;
alpha  = 0.3;
sigma  = 1.5;
ysk    =(1-beta*(1-delta))/(alpha*beta);
ksy    = 1/ysk;
ys     = ksy^(alpha/(1-alpha));
ks     = ys^(1/alpha);
is     = delta*ks;
cs     = ys-is;
ab     = 0;

function hernodes(nstate)

TOL    = sqrt(2.2204e-16);
MAXIT  = 30;
PIM4   = pi^(-1/4);

n  = nstate;
m  = (n+1)/2;
m  =  convert(Int64, floor(m));
x  = zeros(n,1);
w  = zeros(n,1);

z  = 0;
z1 = 0;
pp = 0;
for i= 1:m

# Initialize the first four roots
if i == 1;
z= sqrt(2*n+1) - 1.85575 * (2*n+1)^(-1/6);
elseif i== 2;
z= z - 1.14 * (n^.426)/z;
elseif i== 3;
z= 1.86 * z - .86 * x[1];
elseif i== 4;
z= 1.91 * z - .91 * x[2];
else;
z= 2 * z - x[i-2];
end;

for its= 1:MAXIT
p1 = PIM4;
p2 = 0;
for j  = 1:n
```

```
p3 = p2;
p2 = p1;
p1 = z*sqrt(2/j)*p2 - sqrt((j-1)/j)*p3;
end;

pp = p2 * sqrt(2*n);
z1 = z;
z  = z1 - p1/pp;
if abs(z-z1) < TOL; break; end;
end;

x[i]     = z;
x[n+1-i]= -z;
w[i]= 2/(pp*pp);
w[n+1-i]= w[i];
end;

return x,w
end;

# Technology shock process
rho     = 0.8;
se      = 0.2;
ma      = 0;
wgrid,wmat=hernodes(nstate);
wgrid=wgrid*sqrt(2)*se;

# grid for the income
amin=(ma+wgrid[nstate]);
asup=(ma+wgrid[1]);
ra=rcheb(nodea);                #roots
at=itransfo(ra,amin,asup); #grid
vnba = collect(0:nba).';
XA=cheb(ra,vnba);        # Polynomials

# grid for the capital stock
kmin  = log(1.2);
ksup  = log(6);
rk    = rcheb(nodek);                 #roots
kt    = exp.(itransfo(rk,kmin,ksup)) #grid
vrbk = collect(0:nbk).';
XK     = cheb(rk,vrbk);

#initial conditions
a0=[
-0.23759592487257;
0.60814488103911;
0.03677400318790;
0.69025680170443;
-0.21654209984197;
0.00551243342828;
0.03499834613714;
-0.00341171507904;
-0.00449139656933;
0.00285737302122;
-0.00002348542016;
-0.00011606672164;
];
param=[alpha beta delta sigma ma rho]';
```

```
f   =function(theta);
RHS=Float64[];
LHS=Float64[];
XX =Float64[];
XX0=Float64[];
ct = 0.0;
c1 = 0.0;
for i   = 1:nodek
for j=1:nodea
XX0  = makepoly(XA[j,:]',XK[i,:]');
ct   = exp.(dot(XX0,theta));
XX   = [XX;XX0];
k1   = exp.(at[j])*kt[i].^alpha+(1-delta)*kt[i]-ct;
rk1  = transfo(log.(k1),kmin,ksup);
#if abs(rk1)>1;disp('problem k(t+1)');end
vrbk = collect(0:nbk).';
xk1  = cheb(complex(rk1),vrbk);
a1   = rho*at[j]+(1-rho)*ma+wgrid;
ra1  = transfo(a1,amin,asup);             # grid
#if abs(ra1)>1;disp('problem a(t+1)');end
XA1  = cheb(complex(ra1),vnba);                    # Polynomials
XX1  = makepoly(XA1,xk1);
XX1  = reshape(XX1,size(XA1,1), size(XA1,2)*size(xk1,2)-3)
c1   = exp.(XX1*theta);
aux  = wmat'*(beta*(alpha*exp.(a1)*k1.^(alpha-1)+1-delta).*c1.^(-sigma))/sqrt(pi);
RHS  = [RHS;log.(aux)];
LHS  = [LHS;log.(ct.^(-sigma))];
end;
end;
XX   = reshape(XX,size(XX0,1), nodek*nodea)
resid    = XX*(LHS-RHS);
return vec(resid);
end;

#Pkg.add("NLsolve");
using NLsolve;
sol = nlsolve(not_in_place(f),a0);
println("Display final rule:",sol.zero)

#final
lt  = length(sol.zero);
nb  = 100;
kt  = collect(kmin:(ksup-kmin)/(nb-1):ksup);
rk  = transfo(kt,kmin,ksup);
rk  = vec(rk);
vnbk= collect(0:nbk).';
XT  = cheb(rk,vnbk);
kt  = exp.(kt);
c=[];k1=[];ii=[];
XX0=[];

for i=1:nodea
XX0 = makepoly(XA[i,:]',XT)
XX0 = reshape(XX0,size(XT,1), size(XA,2)*size(XT,2)-3)
c   = [c; exp.(XX0*sol.zero)];
end;
c = reshape(c,100, nodea)
for i=1:nodea
```

TABLE 5.5 Decision rules

	θ_0	θ_1	θ_2	θ_3	θ_4
$T_0(a_t)$	0.117961	0.361884	0.00831576	3.45746e-5	−4.07343e-6
$T_1(a_t)$	0.493804	−0.104603	0.00119796	0.00026351	−1.03949e-5
$T_2(a_t)$	0.0406254	−0.001996	−0.0009009	5.36035e-5	3.20045e-6

```
k1 = [k1; exp.(at[i])*kt.^alpha+(1-delta)*kt.-c[:,i]];
ii = [ii; exp.(at[i])*kt.^alpha-c[:,i]];
end;
k1 = reshape(k1,100, nodea);
ii = reshape(ii,100, nodea);
```

The decision rules are presented in Table 5.5.

REFERENCES

[1] K. Judd, Numerical Methods in Economics, MIT Press, 1998.

[2] J. Miao, Economic Dynamics in Discrete Time, MIT Press, 2014.

[3] F. Collard, Notes on numerical methods, Mimeo, 2015.

[4] S. Schmitt-Grohe, M. Uribe, Solving dynamic general equilibrium models using a second-order approximation to the policy function, Journal of Economic Dynamics and Control 28 (2004) 755–775.

[5] F. Collard, M. Juillard, Accuracy of stochastic perturbation methods: the case of asset pricing models, Journal of Economic Dynamics and Control 25 (2001) 979–999.

[6] A. Marcet, Solving nonlinear stochastic models by parametrizing expectations, Mimeo, Carnegie-Mellon University, 1988.

[7] K. Judd, Projection methods for solving aggregate growth models, Journal of Economic Theory 58 (1992) 410–452.

[8] L. Christiano, J. Fisher, Algorithms for solving dynamic models with occasionally binding constraints, Journal of Economic Dynamics and Control 24 (2000) 1179–1232.

[9] E. McGrattan, Application of weighted residual method to dynamic economic models, Mimeo, Federal Reserve Bank of Minneapolis, 1998.

[10] J. Fernandez-Villaverde, J.F. Rubio-Ramirez, F. Schorfheide, Solution and estimation methods for DSGE models, in: J.B. Taylor, H. Uhlig (Eds.), Handbook of Macroeconomics, vol. 2, 2016, pp. 527–724, Supplement C.

[11] Craig Burnside, Solving asset pricing models with Gaussian shocks, Journal of Economic Dynamics and Control 22 (1998) 329–340.

[12] Rajnish Mehra, Edward Prescott, The equity premium: a puzzle, Journal of Monetary Economics 15 (1985) 145–161.

Chapter 6

Heterogeneous Agents Models

Contents

6.1 INTRODUCTION

In this chapter I further extend the presentation of the quantitative techniques from modern macroeconomics by considering heterogeneous agents models. Despite the real advances made by the representative agent framework, there are clear cases when one should neglect the actual fact that individuals are different (in skills, endowments, education, age, etc.).

While the are plenty of materials that present standard or more advanced computational techniques that deal with representative agent framework, the materials covering the heterogeneous agents framework are just a few. My theoretical presentation relies on general macroeconomics textbooks like the one by [1], [2], and on the excellent work by [3]. An additional excellent material is the set of lecture notes by [4].

6.2 COMPUTING THE STATIONARY DISTRIBUTION

I start by discussing the computation of stationary distribution of the state variables in the heterogeneous agents framework. I start by presenting a baseline model and algorithms to compute the stationary distribution for it.

6.2.1 The Baseline Model

I start from a baseline model following [3]. The model assumes aggregate certainty. We assume a continuum of agents with a total mass equal to one. Each agent corresponds to a household. An agent maximizes its lifetime utility given by:

$$E_0 \sum_{t=0}^{\infty} \beta^t u(c_t) \tag{6.1}$$

Here, β is the discount factor, while E_0 is the standard expectations operator which implies that expectations are conditioned on the available information at time zero. The preferences of an agent are represented through the following utility function:

$$u(c_t) = \frac{c_t^{1-\eta}}{1-\eta} \tag{6.2}$$

Here, the parameters η is the coefficient of relative risk aversion and it is assumed that $\eta > 1$. The households differ through their assets endowment as well as employment status, while c_t stands for consumption. The following convention is assumed: lowercase letters stand for individual variables while uppercase letter for aggregate variables.

It is further assumed that each agent has one unit of time each period. The agent can either work and earn a wage w_t or be unemployed and receive unemployment benefits represented by b_t. Assuming that the level of income tax is τ, then we impose that $(1 - \tau)w_t > b_t$, such that the net earnings exceed the unemployment benefits. The unemployment is taken as exogenous in this model. The employment state of a given individual follows a first-order Markov chain, with the transition

Introduction to Quantitative Macroeconomics Using Julia. https://doi.org/10.1016/B978-0-12-812219-8.00013-6

matrix given by:

$$\pi(\epsilon'|\epsilon) = Prob\{\epsilon_{t+1} = \epsilon|\epsilon_t = \epsilon\} = \begin{bmatrix} p_{uu} & p_{ue} \\ p_{eu} & p_{ee} \end{bmatrix} \tag{6.3}$$

In this matrix, the element $p_{eu} = Prob\{\epsilon_{t+1} = u|\epsilon_t = e\}$ is the probability that an individual is unemployed in $t+1$ conditional on being employed in the current period t.

Conditioned on the employment status, the budget constraint can be written as follows:

$$a_{t+1} = \begin{cases} (1 + (1-\tau)r_t)a_t + (1-\tau)w_t - c_t, \text{ if } \epsilon = e \\ (1 + (1-\tau)r_t)a_t + b_t - c_t, \text{ if } \epsilon = u \end{cases} \tag{6.4}$$

The specification used for the budget constraint implies that both the wage income and the interest rate income (with r_t is interest rate in period t), are taxed with the same rate τ. a_t stands for assets and when the agent is unemployment, the assets are depleted. This leads to heterogeneity in asset holdings.

Given the objective function in Eq. (6.1) and the budget constraint in Eq. (6.4), the Lagrangian of the problem might be written as:

$$\mathcal{L} = E_0 \sum_{t=0}^{\infty}\{\beta^t[u(c_t) + \lambda_t(1_{\epsilon_t=u}b_t + (1 + (1-\tau)r_t)a_t + \tag{6.5}$$

$$1_{\epsilon_t=e}(1-\tau)w_t - a_{t+1} - c_t)]\}$$

Here, the functions $1_{\epsilon_t=e}$ and $1_{\epsilon_t=u}$ are indicator functions. The household optimally chooses c_t and a_{t+1}. Solving for the optimal solution, we get the following first order condition:

$$\frac{u'(c_t)}{\beta} = E_t[u'(c_{t+1}(1 + (1-\tau)r_{t+1}))] \tag{6.6}$$

Eq. (6.6) implies that we get a policy function that depends on the employment status and on the asset holdings, i.e. $c(\epsilon_t, a_t)$. This policy function along Eq. (6.4) also provide us the next period assets. We may write: $a_{t+1} = a'(\epsilon_t, a_t)$.

On the firms' side, we assume a representative firm whose production function is modeled through a Cobb-Douglas production function. We write it in terms of aggregate variables (uppercase letters):

$$F(K_t, N_t) = K_t^{\alpha} N_t^{1-\alpha} \tag{6.7}$$

Here, K_t is the aggregate capital stock, N_t stands for the labor, while α is the capital share for which $\alpha \in (0, 1)$. The market is competitive, such that the factors, i.e. the interest rate and the real wage, are given by:

$$r_t = \alpha(\frac{N_t}{K_t})^{1-\alpha} - \delta$$

$$w_t = (1-\alpha)(\frac{N_t}{K_t})^{\alpha} \tag{6.8}$$

Here, r_t is the interest rate, w_t is the real wage, while δ is the depreciation rate of capital stock.

Finally, the government expenditures, i.e. the expenditures on unemployment benefits, denoted by B_t, at the aggregate level, equal the aggregate taxes, denoted by T_t: $B_T = T_t$.

6.2.2 The Stationary Equilibrium

We deal in this section with a stationary equilibrium, where the aggregate variables and the factor prices are constant in time. The distribution of assets is also constant in time irrespective to the employment status.

We compute the two resulting distributions of asset holdings, i.e. for employed and unemployed agents. They are denoted by $F(e, a)$ and $F(u, a)$, respectively, with the corresponding density functions denoted by $f(e, a)$ and $f(u, a)$, respectively. The state space consists in the sets $(\epsilon, a) \in \chi = \{e, u\} \times [a_{min}, \infty)$.

To present the stationary equilibrium, I follow [3] notation and approach and use a rather simpler framework based on simple probability and statistics (no measure theory involved). The solution relies on a recursive representation of the household's problem, but this is already familiar from the chapter on dynamic programming (see Chapter 4). We define $V(\epsilon, a)$ as the value function corresponding to the objective function of a household that has an employment status ϵ and asset holdings denoted by a. Given the budget constraint in Eq. (6.4), the government policy described by $\{b, \tau\}$ and the employment status described by Eq. (6.3), we may formally write:

$$V(\epsilon, a) = \max_{c,a'}[u(c) + \beta E\{V(\epsilon', a')|\epsilon\}] \tag{6.9}$$

Then, a stationary equilibrium, given a set of policy parameters b, τ, is given by a value function $V(\epsilon, a)$, policy rules for consumption $c(\epsilon, a)$ and next-period asset holdings $a'(\epsilon, a)$, a constant density of the state variable $x = (a, \epsilon) \in \chi$, the density functions $f(e, a)$ and $f(u, a)$, constant factor retributions $\{w, r\}$ and constant aggregate variables K, N, C, T, B such that the following hold:

1. We can compute the factors, consumption, tax revenues and unemployment benefits by aggregating with respect over households:

$$K = \sum_{\epsilon \in \{e,u\}} \int_{a_{min}}^{\infty} a f(\epsilon, a) da \tag{6.10}$$

$$N = \int_{a_{min}}^{\infty} f(\epsilon, a) da \tag{6.11}$$

$$C = \sum_{\epsilon \in \{e,u\}} \int_{a_{min}}^{\infty} c(\epsilon, a) f(\epsilon, a) da \tag{6.12}$$

$$T = \tau(wN + rK) \tag{6.13}$$

$$B = (1 - N)b \tag{6.14}$$

2. The policy rules $c(\epsilon, a)$ and $a'(\epsilon, a)$ correspond to the optimal solution of the household decision program;
3. Factor prices r, w are given by their marginal productivity as in Eq. (6.8);
4. The goods market is in equilibrium:

$$F(K, L) + (1 - \delta)K = C + K' = C + K \tag{6.15}$$

5. The government budget is in equilibrium, i.e. $T = B$;
6. The distribution of the individual state variable (ϵ, a) is stationary, i.e.:

$$F(\epsilon', a') = \sum_{\epsilon \in \{u,e\}} \pi(\epsilon'|\epsilon) F(\epsilon, a'^{-1}(a', \epsilon)) \tag{6.16}$$

6.2.3 A General Algorithm

There are many computational methods to solve models like the one outlined above. In this section, I discuss a general algorithm to numerically compute the solution of the above model. This basically involves two steps. In the first step, using the previously developed techniques in Chapter 4 and 5, we can solve for the optimal conditions of the individual households, and determine the policy functions $c(\epsilon, a)$ and $a'(\epsilon, a)$ conditional on given aggregate variables K, N and the tax rate τ. Second, we compute the distribution of the individual state variables and aggregate the state variables conditioned on the aggregate constraints holding.

A general version of the algorithm can be written as follows:

1. We first determine the stationary level of employment N. This is easily determinable using the fact that it depends on the already known level of employment in the previous period. Then we can compute the current period employment using the following equation:

$$N_t = p_{ue}(1 - N_{t-1}) + p_{ee} N_{t-1} \tag{6.17}$$

2. Propose an initial value for the capital stock K at aggregate level and the tax rate τ.

3. Determine the factor prices w and r.
4. Solve for the optimal solution of the households' problem.
5. Determine the implied distributions of assets for both the employed and unemployed agents.
6. Determine the aggregate values for K as well as the tax rate τ that verify the aggregate constraints and the government budget respectively.
7. Update the values for K, as well as τ and return to step 2 if the errors are still large.

In the above algorithm, at step 5, we must derive the stationary distribution of the assets in the economy. There are different approaches that can be undertaken to achieve this. I describe below three such methods following [3]

Discretization of the Distribution Function

The state space is characterized by two dimensions, the employment state ϵ and the wealth level a. Fortunately, the employment status can take only two values such that it is sufficient to discretize only the wealth variable a. The discretization method has already been met in the context of dynamic programming. We define a grid of m points on the asset space $\{a_1, ..., a_m\}$. In this case, the state variable (ϵ, a) will take only $2 \cdot m$ values. The distribution function is denoted by $F(\epsilon, a)$.

We fix a piecewise distribution function with $F_0(\epsilon = e, a)$ and $F_0 = (\epsilon = u, a)$ over this grid. We also derive the inverse of the decision rule $a'(\epsilon, a)$. We can iterate now on $F_{i+1}(\epsilon', a')$ until we obtain the convergence using the following iteration rule:

$$F_{i+1}(\epsilon', a') = \sum_{\epsilon=e,u} \pi(\epsilon', \epsilon) F(a^{t-1}(\epsilon, a), \epsilon) \tag{6.18}$$

Monte Carlo Simulation

Since this is based on simulation, it requires selecting a large number of households (a few thousands). We start from setting a large number N of households that will be traced during the simulation. For each household, we fix the initial assets a_0^i and initial employment status ϵ_0^i. We can iterate on this sample and determine for each household the next period wealth level $a'(\epsilon^i, a^i)$. We can compute a few statistics for each sample (mean, standard deviation). The iteration continues until these statistics converge.

Function Approximation

The topic of function approximation has been already discussed at length in Chapter 2, in the section on Function Approximation. Since the distribution is itself a function, we can approximate it using the same techniques detailed there. Following [8], the n-th order approximation of the distribution function of the holdings of assets for the agents with employment status given by $\epsilon \in \{e, u\}$ can be done with exponential functions:

$$F(\epsilon, a) = 0, \text{ if } a < a_{min}$$

$$F(\epsilon, a) = \rho_0^\epsilon \int_{-\infty}^a e^{\rho_1^\epsilon x + ... + \rho_1^\epsilon x} dx, \text{ if } a \geq a_{min} \tag{6.19}$$

6.2.4 Examples in Julia

I consider in this section basic applications in Julia. The application features the reference models in this field by [6] and [7].

6.2.4.1 Aiyagari Model

The motivation behind the Aiyagari's paper lies in the following two reasons. First, data on individual consumption or assets holdings does not correspond to predictions of complete markets models within the representative agent framework. Second, it has been found that heterogeneous agent models can be used with success to address issues from monetary policy to business cycles. Aiyagari extended the standard growth model to account for endogenous heterogeneity and borrowing constraints.

The contribution had two goals: to provide a model in which the aggregate behavior results from the interaction of many agents which face idiosyncratic shocks and to use this model to study whether individual risk matters for aggregate saving.

The proper framework to understand such models is to start from the individual's income fluctuation problem, see [2], [6]. The problem of the individual is to maximize the discounted lifetime utility function:

$$E_0 \sum_{t=0}^{\infty} \beta^t U(c_t) \tag{6.20}$$

Here, c_t is the utility function, E_0 is the expectation operator which we already met, β is the discount factor while U is the utility function. The individual face the following constraint:

$$c_t + a_{t+1} = w l_t + (1+r) a_t \tag{6.21}$$

The variable a_t stands for the assets, w, r are factor prices, i.e. the wage and the return on assets, while l_t is the labor endowment. The consumption is constrained to be nonnegative, i.e. $c_t \geq 0$. There is also a limit on borrowing (which results from nonnegative consumption, see [6] for an argument), such that $a_t \geq -b$ almost surely (a.s.) with $b > 0$ the limit on borrowing. However, when $b > w l_{min}/r$ almost surely (a.s.), b does not bind, and the borrowing limit becomes $w l_{min}/r$. We may then write:

$$a_t \geq -\phi \tag{6.22}$$
$$\phi = min\{b, w l_{min}/r\}, \text{ for } r > 0 \tag{6.23}$$

We can now introduce two new variables, $\hat{a}_t$ and z_t and define them as:

$$\hat{a}_t = a_t + \phi \tag{6.24}$$
$$z_t = w l_t + (1+r)\hat{a}_t - r\phi \tag{6.25}$$

where z_t can be interpreted as the total resources that are available to an agent at time t. We can rewrite Eq. (6.21) as:

$$c_t + \hat{a}_{t+1} = z_t, \text{ if } c_t \geq 0, \hat{a} \geq 0 \tag{6.26}$$
$$z_{t+1} = w l_{t+1} + (1+r)\hat{a}_{t+1} - r\phi \tag{6.27}$$

The two equation above can be further written in a recursive manner using the approach already outlined in Chapter 4. Let us define the optimal value function for the agent with total resources z_t as $V(z_t, b, w, r)$. This is the unique solution to the following dynamic programming problem:

$$V(z_t, b, w, r) = max\{U(z_t - \hat{a}_{t+1}) + \beta \int V(z_{t+1}, b, w, r) dF(l_{t+1})\} \tag{6.28}$$

The dynamic programming problem consists in choosing $\hat{a}_{t+1}$ such that the RHS of above equation is maximized, given the constraints in equations (6.26)–(6.27). [1] showed that, if the condition $\beta(1+r) < 1$ holds, then z_t has a unique invariant measure $\lambda*$. This can be generalized to Markov chains with two states.

Following [1] the recursive problem can be written as:

$$V(a_t, l_t) = \max_{a_{t+1} \geq -\phi} \{U(c_t) + \beta \int V(a_{t+1}, l_{t+1}) Q(D l_{t+1}, l_t) \tag{6.29}$$

with the constraints given by Eqs. (6.21) and (6.22)–(6.23). Using primes to replace next-period value, the result of the optimization problem is a policy function denoted by $a' = g(a, l)$. The state space of (a, l) is S. This follows a Markov process whose transition function is:

$$P(A \times B, (a, l)) = 1_{g(a,l) \in A} Q(B, l) \tag{6.30}$$

Here $A \times B$ is a Borel set on the space S. The transition function above results in a sequence of distributions given by:

$$\lambda_{t+1}(A \times B) = \int P(A \times B, (a, l)) d\lambda(a, l) \tag{6.31}$$

If this converges in a weak sense to an invariant distribution denoted by $\lambda^*(a, l)$, then we can compute the average assets using: $E[a(r, w)] = \int g(a, l)d\lambda^*(a, l)$.

The Aiyagari model also features a standard production sector. A representative firm produces a final good employing capital K and labor l. The production function is given by:

$$Y_t = F(K_t, L_t) \tag{6.32}$$

The profit maximization leads to the typical first-order conditions:

$$F_K(K, L) = r + \delta$$
$$F_L(K, L) = w \tag{6.33}$$

As in [1], the stationary recursive equilibrium can be written as follows.

Definition 6.1: A stationary recursive equilibrium for the problem defined above consists in a value function $V : S \to \mathcal{R}$, policy functions for households $g : S \to \mathcal{R}$ and $c : S \to \mathcal{R}_+$, the choice of the representative firm in terms of capital stock K and labor L, factor prices w and r as well as a stationary measure λ^* on S such that the following hold:

1. For a given set of prices (r, w), the policy functions (g, c) determine the optimal solution of the household problem while V is the corresponding value function.
2. For a given set of prices (r, w), the representative firm chooses optimally the inputs K and L.
3. Factor prices r, w equal their marginal productivity as in Eq. (6.33).
4. The labor market is in equilibrium: $L = \int l d\lambda^*(a, l)$.
5. The asset market is in equilibrium: $K = \int g(a, l)d\lambda^*(a, l)$.
6. The economy's resource constraint is verified:

$$\int c(a, l)d\lambda^*(a, l) + \delta K = F(K, L) \tag{6.34}$$

7. For all Borel sets $A \times B$ on S, the distribution λ^* is stationary:

$$\lambda^*(A \times B) = \int 1_{g(a,l) \in A} Q(B, l)d\lambda^*(a, l)) \tag{6.35}$$

The implementation is Julia is presented below. The implementation is based on the Matlab version due to [11]:

```
#  set parameter values
sigma  = 1.50;          # risk aversion
beta   = 0.98;          # subjective discount factor
prob   = [ .8 .2; .5 .5]; # prob(i,j) = probability (s(t+1)=sj | s(t) = si)
delta  = 0.97;          # 1 - depreciation
A      = 1.00;          # production technology
alpha  = 0.25;          # capital's share of income
theta  = 0.05;          # non-rental income if unemployed is theta*wage
Kstart = 10.0;          # initial value for aggregate capital stock
g      = 0.20;          # relaxation parameter
#   form capital grid
maxkap = 20;                      # maximum value of capital grid
inckap = 0.025;                   # size of capital grid increments
nkap   = trunc(Int,maxkap/inckap+1);  # number of grid points: make it integer - Julia indexes must be integer
#global variables
decis  = zeros(nkap,2);
lambda = zeros(nkap,2);
probk  = zeros(nkap,1);
#   calculate aggregate labor supply
D = [0.0 0.0; 0.0 0.0];
ed,ev = eig(prob);
```

```
#    make a matrix from the eigenvalues
edm   = diagm(ed)
(emax,inmax) = findmax(edm)
D[inmax,inmax] = emax;
pinf = ev*D*inv(ev);
pempl = pinf[inmax,inmax];
N = 1.0*pempl + theta*(1-pempl);


liter   = 1;
maxiter = 50;
toler   = 0.001;
metric  = 10.0;
K = Kstart;
Kold= K;
wage=1.0;
rent=1.0;
println("ITERATING ON K");
println("");
println("Iter    metric                    meanK                    Kold");


#    loop to find fixed point for agregate capital stock
while  (metric[1] > toler) & (liter <= maxiter);


# calculate rental rate of capital and wage
#
wage = (1-alpha) * A * K^(alpha)   * N^(-alpha);
rent = (alpha)   * A * K^(alpha-1) * N^(1-alpha);
#
# tabulate the utility function such that for zero or negative
# consumption utility remains a large negative number so that
# such values will never be chosen as utility maximizing
#
util1=-10000*ones(nkap,nkap);  # utility when employed
util2=-10000*ones(nkap,nkap);  # utility when unemployed
for i=1:nkap;
kap=(i-1)*inckap;
for j=1:nkap;
kapp = (j-1)*inckap;
cons1 = wage + (rent + delta)*kap - kapp;
if cons1 > .0;
util1[j,i]=(cons1)^(1-sigma)/(1-sigma);
end;
cons2 = theta*wage + (rent + delta)*kap - kapp;
if cons2 > .0;
util2[j,i]=(cons2)^(1-sigma)/(1-sigma);
end;
end;
end;
#
# initialize some variables
#
v       = zeros(nkap,2);
tdecis1 = zeros(nkap,2);
tdecis2 = zeros(nkap,2);

test    = 10;
rs,cs = size(util1)
```

```
r1=zeros(cs,cs);
r2=zeros(cs,cs);

#
#  iterate on Bellman's equation and get the decision
#  rules and the value function at the optimum


while test != 0;
for i=1:cs;
r1[:,i]=util1[:,i]+beta*(prob[1,1]*v[:,1]+ prob[1,2]*v[:,2]);
r2[:,i]=util2[:,i]+beta*(prob[2,1]*v[:,1]+ prob[2,2]*v[:,2]);
end;
(tv1,inds1)=findmax(r1,1);
tdecis1   =map(x->ind2sub(r1, x)[1], inds1)    #to find the relative position of the max in a column
(tv2,inds2)=findmax(r2,1);
tdecis2   =map(x->ind2sub(r2, x)[1], inds2)

tdecis=[tdecis1' tdecis2'];
tv=[tv1' tv2'];

test=maximum((tdecis-decis));
copy!(v, tv);
copy!(decis, tdecis);
end;

decis=(decis-1)*inckap;

#   form transition matrix
#   trans is the transition matrix from state at t (row)
#   to the state at t+1 (column)
#   The eigenvector associated with the unit eigenvalue
#   of trans' is  the stationary distribution.

g2=spzeros(cs,cs);
g1=spzeros(cs,cs);
for i=1:cs
g1[i,tdecis1[i]]=1;
g2[i,tdecis2[i]]=1;
end
trans=[ prob[1,1]*g1 prob[1,2]*g1; prob[2,1]*g2 prob[2,2]*g2];
trans=trans';
probst = (1/(2*nkap))*ones(2*nkap,1);
test=1;
while test > 10.0^(-8);
probst1 = trans*probst;
test = maximum(abs.(probst1-probst));
copy!(probst, probst1);
end;

#   vectorize the decision rule to be conformable with probst
#   calculate new aggregate capital stock   meanK

kk=vec(decis);
meanK=probst'*kk;

# calculate measure over (k,s) pairs
# lambda has same dimensions as decis
lambda=reshape(probst, cs,2)
```

```
#   calculate stationary distribution of k
d1,v1=eig(prob');
d1m  = diagm(d1)
dmax,imax=findmax(diag(d1m))

probst1=v1[:,imax];
ss=sum(probst1);
probst1=probst1./ss;
probk=sum(lambda',1)'
#   form metric and update K
Kold= K;
Knew= g*meanK[1] + (1-g)*Kold;
metric = abs.((Kold-meanK)./Kold);
K = Knew;
println(liter,"        ", metric[1],"          ",meanK[1],"           ",Kold);
liter = liter+1;
end;
```

The solution of the model is displayed below.

```
#print  results
println("PARAMETER VALUES");
println("");
println("sigma     beta     delta      A      alpha     theta");
println(sigma,"        ",beta, "        ",delta," ", A, "  ",alpha,"   ",theta);
println("");
println("EQUILIBRIUM RESULTS ");
println();
println("K               N            wage          rent");
println(round(Kold,4),"           ", round(N,4), "          ",round(wage,4),"         ", round(rent,4) );
```

```
PARAMETER VALUES

sigma     beta     delta      A      alpha     theta
1.5       0.98     0.97     1.0    0.25    0.05

EQUILIBRIUM RESULTS

K               N            wage          rent
7.0115          0.7286       1.321       0.0458
```

I also perform a simulation. First, I present first a function that simulates a Markov model before showing the code for the actual simulation.

```
function markov(T,n,s0,V);
r,c  = size(T);
v1,v2 = size(V);

#rand('uniform');
#using Distributions
X=rand(Uniform(0,1), n-1,1)
state=zeros(2,99);
chain=[];
s=zeros(r,1);
s[s0]=1
cum=T*triu(ones(size(T)));
ppi  =[];
```

```
state[:,1]=s
for k=1:length(X);
#k=1
state[:,k]=s;
ppi =[0 s'*cum];
ss1= convert(Array{Float64},((X[k].<=ppi[2:r+1])))
ss2= convert(Array{Float64},(X[k].>ppi[1:r]))
s=(ss1.*ss2)
s=reshape(s,2,1)
end

chain=V*state
return state,chain
end
```

The code for simulating the model is displayed below:

```
using Distributions

println("SIMULATING LIFE HISTORY");
k = Kold;                 # initial level of capital
n = 100;                  # number of periods to simulate
s0 = 1;                   # initial state
hist = zeros(n-1,2);
cons = zeros(n-1,1);
invest = zeros(n-1,1);

grid  = collect(0:inckap:maxkap);
r,c   = size(prob);
T     = prob;
V     = collect(1:r)';

state, chain= markov(prob,n,s0,V)

chain=convert(Array{Int64,2},chain);
state=convert(Array{Int64,2},state);

for i = 1:n-1;
hist[i,:] = [ k chain[i] ];
I1 = trunc(Int,k/inckap) ;
I2 = trunc(Int,k/inckap) + 1;
if I1 == 0;
I1=1;
println("N.B.  I1 = 0");
end;
if I2 > nkap;
I2 = nkap;
println("N.B.  I2 > nkap");
end;
weight = (grid[I2,1] - k)/inckap;
kprime = weight*(decis[I1,chain[i]]) +  (1-weight)*(decis[I2,chain[i]]);
if chain[i] == 1;
cons[i] = wage + (rent + delta)*k - kprime;
elseif chain[i] == 2;
cons[i] = wage*theta + (rent + delta)*k - kprime;
else;
println("something is wrong with chain");
chain
```

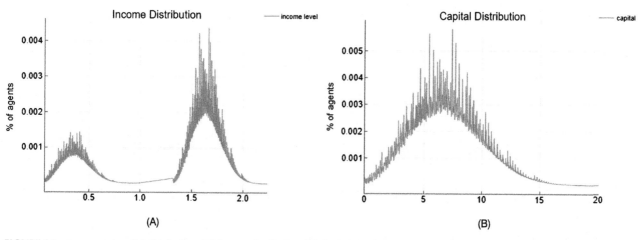

FIGURE 6.1   Income and capital distribution. (A) Income distribution. (B) Capital distribution.

```
end;
k = kprime;
invest[i] = kprime;
end;}
```

Using the simulation results, I also show two figures with the distribution of income and capital among the agents (see Fig. 6.1).

6.2.4.2   Huggett Model

I model a heterogeneous-agent economy where there is no production. This is a so-called endowment economy. The model is due to [5] and it was used to explain the low risk-free interest rate. Each period, the agents receive an endowment consisting in the only good from the economy. The endowment can take two values, depending on the employment status of the agent, such that the endowment set is $\mathcal{E} = \{e_h, e_l\}$, where e_h is the high endowment and it stands for the earnings when an agent is employed, and e_l are the low endowments when an agent is unemployed.

We model again the endowment process (and, implicitly the employment process too) as follows a Markov chain of order 1, with a transition probability given by:

$$\pi(\epsilon'|\epsilon) = Prob\{\epsilon_{t+1} = e'|\epsilon_t = e\} \tag{6.36}$$

Here, $e', e \in \mathcal{E}$.

Each agent maximizes its expected discounted lifetime utility modeled as:

$$E_0 \sum_{t=0}^{\infty} \beta^t \frac{c_t^{1-\eta}}{1-\eta} \tag{6.37}$$

Here, the parameter β is the discount factor, while E_t is the standard expectations operator. The parameter $1 - \eta$ is the coefficient of relative risk aversion.

The focus of the model lies on the credit supply and demand. Each agent holds a single asset. Denote by q the price of a' goods next period. If an agent takes a credit of value a then it can buy a units of consumption this period, while taking a credit of a' goods next period, he pays for them $a'q$ goods in the current period. The model also imposes a credit constraint which says that the credit balance cannot be lower than $\underline{a} < 0$.

Given these assumptions and notations, we may write the budget constraint of each agent as follows:

$$c + a'q \leq a + e \tag{6.38}$$

Here, it is assumed that $a' \geq \underline{a}$ and that $c \geq 0$.

Following [6], I introduce some notations to ease the presentation of the recursive problem. We use a vector $x \in X$ to describe the position of an agent at a moment t in time, with $x = (a, e)$, where the credit balance is a and the employment status e. The individual state space is described by $X = A \times \mathcal{E}$. Here we define $A = [\underline{a}, \infty)$ and $\mathcal{E} = \{e_h, e_l\}$ for which it holds that $e_h > e_l$. We also denote by $q > 0$ the constant value of price credit balances.

The problem of the individual agent may also be written recursively as follows:

$$V(x, q) = \max_{x \in \Gamma(x;q)} [U(c) + \beta \sum_{e'} V(a', e'; q)\pi(e'|e)] \tag{6.39}$$

With the budget constraint given by Eq. (6.38). Here Γ is a correspondence (see Chapter 4 on dynamic programming) and it is given by:

$$\Gamma(x; q) = \{(c, a') : c + a'q \leq a + e; c \geq 0; a' \geq \underline{a}\} \tag{6.40}$$

The price of the next-period credit balances is related to the interest rate through the following equation: $r = 1/q - 1$.

We can formulate now a stationary equilibrium of the model for which the price q of next-period credit balance a' is constant, while the distribution of individuals' holdings of asset given by $f(e, a)$ is invariant.

As in [1], the stationary recursive equilibrium can be written as follows.

Definition 6.2: A stationary recursive equilibrium for the problem defined above in equations consists in a value function $V : S \rightarrow \mathcal{R}$, a policy function for households' accumulation of assets $g : S \rightarrow \mathcal{R}$, an interest rate r that is risk-free as well as a stationary measure λ^* on S such that the following hold:

1. For a given risk-free rate r, the policy function (g) is an optimal solution of the household problem while V is the corresponding value function.
2. The asset market is in equilibrium: $\int g(a, e)d\lambda^*(a, e) = 0$.
3. For all Borel sets $A \times B$, the distribution λ^* is stationary:

$$\lambda_{t+1}(A \times B) = \int 1_A g(a, e) Q(B, e) d\lambda^*(a, e)) \tag{6.41}$$

I present now the implementation is Julia (which is also based on Matlab code in [11]):

```
#   set parameter values
sigma  = 1.50;           # risk aversion
beta   = 0.98;           # subjective discount factor
prob   = [ .8 .2; .5 .5]; # prob(i,j) = probability (s(t+1)=sj | s(t) = si)
theta  = 0.05;           # non-interest income if unemployed
wage   = 1.00;           # non-interest income if employed
Rstart = 1.021;          # initial gross interest rate
F      = -2.0;           # borrowing constraint parameter
g      = 0.60;           # relaxation parameter

#initialize variables
A      = 1.0;
Aold   = 1.0;
Anew   = 1.0;
meanA  = 1.0;

#form asset grid
maxast = 8;              # maximum value of asset grid
minast = -5;             # minimum value of asset grid
incast = 0.5;            # size of asset grid increments
nasset = trunc(Int,((maxast-minast)/incast+1)); # number of grid points
assetp = 1.0;

#global variables
decis  = zeros(nasset,2);
tdecis = zeros(nasset,2);
lambda = zeros(nasset,2);

# loop to find R such that sum(lambda*A) = 0
```

```
liter   = 1;
maxiter = 50;
toler   = 0.0001;
step    = 0.05;
R = Rstart;
flag = 1;

println("ITERATING ON R");
println("");
println("Iter        R                                    A                                    newstep");
while  (flag != 0) && (liter <= maxiter);

#tabulate the utility function such that for zero or negative
#consumption utility remains a large negative number so that
#such values will never be chosen as utility maximizing

util1=-10000*ones(nasset,nasset);  # utility when employed
util2=-10000*ones(nasset,nasset);  # utility when unemployed

for i=1:nasset
asset=(i-1)*incast + minast;
for j=1:nasset
assetp = (j-1)*incast + minast;
cons = wage + R*asset - assetp;
if assetp >= F && cons > 0;
util1[j,i]=(cons)^(1-sigma)/(1-sigma);
end;
end
for j=1:nasset
assetp = (j-1)*incast + minast;
cons = theta*wage + R*asset - assetp;
if assetp>= F && cons > 0;
util2[j,i]=(cons)^(1-sigma)/(1-sigma);
end;
end;
end;

#  initialize some variables
v       = zeros(nasset,2);
tdecis1 = zeros(nasset,2);
tdecis2 = zeros(nasset,2);

decis   = zeros(nasset,2);
tdecis  = zeros(nasset,2);

test1   = 10;
test2   = 10;
rs,cs   = size(util1);
r1=zeros(nasset,nasset);
r2=zeros(nasset,nasset);

#  iterate on Bellman's equation and get the decision
#  rules and the value function at the optimum

while (test1 != 0) || (test2 > .1);
for i=1:cs;
r1[:,i]=util1[:,i]+beta*(prob[1,1]*v[:,1]+ prob[1,2]*v[:,2]);
r2[:,i]=util2[:,i]+beta*(prob[2,1]*v[:,1]+ prob[2,2]*v[:,2]);
end;
```

```
(tv1,inds1)=findmax(r1,1);
tdecis1    =map(x->ind2sub(r1, x)[1], inds1)    #to find the relative position of the max in a column
(tv2,inds2)=findmax(r2,1);
tdecis2    =map(x->ind2sub(r2, x)[1], inds2)

tdecis=[tdecis1' tdecis2'];
tv=[tv1' tv2'];

test1=maximum((tdecis-decis));
test2=maximum(abs.(tv-v));
copy!(v, tv);
copy!(decis, tdecis);
end;
decis=(decis-1)*incast + minast;

#    form transition matrix
#    trans is the transition matrix from state at t (row)
#    to the state at t+1 (column)

g2=spzeros(cs,cs);
g1=spzeros(cs,cs);
for i=1:cs
g1[i,tdecis1[i]]=1;
g2[i,tdecis2[i]]=1;
end
trans=[ prob[1,1]*g1 prob[1,2]*g1; prob[2,1]*g2 prob[2,2]*g2];
trans=trans';
probst = (1/(2*nasset))*ones(2*nasset,1);
test = 1;
while test > 10.0^(-8);
probst1 = trans*probst;
test = maximum(abs.(probst1-probst));
copy!(probst, probst1);
end;

#    vectorize the decision rule to be conformable with probst
#    calculate new aggregate asset meanA
aa=vec(decis);
meanA=(probst'*aa)[1];

# calculate measure over (k,s) pairs
# lambda has same dimensions as decis
lambda=reshape(probst, cs,2)


#    calculate stationary distribution of k
lambda=reshape(probst, cs,2)
probk=sum(lambda',1);      # stationary distribution of capital - sum by each column
probk=probk'


if liter == 1;
A=copy(meanA);;
if meanA > 0.0;
step=copy(-step);
end;
end;
```

```
Aold = copy(A);
Anew = copy(meanA);

if sign(Aold) != sign(Anew)
step = copy(-.5*step);
end;
println(liter,"        ",R,"                                        ",meanA,"                        ",step);
if abs.(step) >= toler;
R=copy(R+step);
else;
flag = 0;
end;
A=copy(Anew);
liter = liter+1;

end;
```

The solution of the model is presented in the following:

```
display solution
#   calculate consumption and expected utility
grid = collect(minast:incast:maxast) ;
congood = wage*(ones(nasset,1)) + R*grid - grid[tdecis[:,1]];
conbad  = theta*wage*(ones(nasset,1)) + R*grid - grid[tdecis[:,2]];
consum  = [congood conbad ];
cons2   = [congood.^2 conbad.^2];
meancon = sum(diag(lambda'*consum));
meancon2  = sum(diag(lambda'*cons2));
varcon = ( meancon2 - meancon^2 );
UTILITY = ((complex(consum)).^(1-sigma))./(1-sigma);
UCEU2 = sum(diag(lambda'*UTILITY));

#   print out results
println("PARAMETER VALUES");
println("");
println("sigma      beta      F        theta");
println(sigma,"        ",beta,"      ",F,"        ", theta);
println("");
println("EQUILIBRIUM RESULTS");
println("");
println("R              A            UCEU    meancon        varcon");
println(round(R,4),"        ",round(meanA,4),"        ",real(round(UCEU2,4)),"        ",round(meancon,4),"        ",round(varcon,4));
```

```
PARAMETER VALUES

sigma      beta      F        theta
1.5        0.98      -2.0        0.05


EQUILIBRIUM RESULTS

R              A            UCEU    meancon        varcon
0.9788        -0.4287      -2.5003    0.7377      0.0634
```

6.3 DYNAMICS OF THE DISTRIBUTION FUNCTION

In this section, I extend the results in the previous section and I focus on methods to compute the dynamics of a model with heterogeneous agents. The presentation is largely based on [3] and [7]. I start by a simple extension of the general algorithm to compute the stationary distribution of the baseline model in Section 6.2.1. I consider then an economy with aggregate uncertainty and present an algorithm to solve this model.

6.3.1 Introducing Dynamics in a Model Economy With Heterogeneous Agents

In this section, we consider a basic extension to the stationary model presented earlier in Section 6.2.1. There are many papers that proposed solutions methods to heterogeneous agents models featuring aggregate uncertainty, see [8] for a recent collection of this topic. In the following, I focus on the baseline model introduced in [3]. Consider again that households maximize their lifetime discounted utility. We write:

$$E_0 \sum_{t=0}^{\infty} \beta^t u(c_t) \tag{6.42}$$

The notation is preserved such that β is the discount factor, while E_t is the standard expectations operator which implies that expectations are conditioned on the available information at time zero. The following preferences are assumed:

$$u(c_t) = \frac{c_t^{1-\eta}}{1-\eta} \tag{6.43}$$

Here, c_t is the consumption in period t. The parameter η stands for the coefficient of relative risk aversion (again, it is assumed that $\eta > 1$). The households differ through both the endowment in terms of assets and the employment status.

In terms of budget constraint, given the dependency on the employment status, the budget constraint is written as follows:

$$a_{t+1} = \begin{cases} (1 + (1 - \tau_t)r_t)a_t + (1 - \tau_t)w_t - c_t, \text{ if } \epsilon_t = e \\ (1 + (1 - \tau_t)r_t)a_t + b_t - c_t, \text{ if } \epsilon_t = u \end{cases} \tag{6.44}$$

The transition matrix for employment status is given by:

$$\pi(\epsilon'|\epsilon) = Prob\{\epsilon_{t+1} = \epsilon'|\epsilon_t = \epsilon\} = \begin{bmatrix} p_{uu} & p_{ue} \\ p_{eu} & p_{ee} \end{bmatrix} \tag{6.45}$$

Where the elements of the matrix are interpreted in a similar manner as in Section 6.2.1. We also continue to differentiate between individual variables (denoted by small letters) and aggregate variables (denoted by uppercase letters). We can write then the aggregate capital stock as:

$$K_t = \sum_{\epsilon_t \in \{e,u\}} \int_{a_{min}}^{\infty} a_t f_t(\epsilon_t, a_t) da_t \tag{6.46}$$

The novel element in the dynamic model is the presence of an equation for the dynamics of the distribution function:

$$F_{t+1}(\epsilon_{t+1}, a_{t+1}) = \sum_{\epsilon_t \in \{e,u\}} \pi(\epsilon_{t+1}|\epsilon_t) F_t(\epsilon_t, a_{t+1}^{-1}(\epsilon_t, a_{t+1})) = G(F_t) \tag{6.47}$$

Here, $a_{t+1}^{-1}(\epsilon_t, a_{t+1})$ is interpreted similarly as the inverse of the policy function $a_{t+1}(\epsilon_t, a_t)$ relative to the current holdings of assets a_t. Since the model is dynamic, the aggregate capital stock K_t the aggregate consumption C_t, as well as the factor prices are not constant. They are given by:

$$\begin{aligned} r_t &= r(K_t, N_t) \\ w_t &= w(K_t, N_t) \end{aligned} \tag{6.48}$$

With the mention that for the specific case of aggregate certainty, N_t is constant.

Furthermore, the first order consumption is identical to the one for the basic model:

$$\frac{u'(c_t)}{\beta} = E_t[u'(c_{t+1}(1 + (1 - \tau_{t+1})r_{t+1}))] \tag{6.49}$$

While in the case of the stationary model, the policy function depends only on the arguments ϵ_t, a_t such that we write $a'(\epsilon_t, a_t)$, in this case the policy function depends on the distribution of assets too and the optimal policy function is written as $a'(\epsilon_t, a_t, F_t)$. To understand why we need to include the distribution function, we can notice first that the equation above implies that the solution depends on r_t which is not constant and it varies with K_t as in (6.48). However, we could not include directly K_t in the optimal policy function $a_{t+1} = a'(\cdot)$ since the individual agent does not know the next period aggregate capital stock (necessary in order to compute the next period interest rate r_{t+1}). Thus, for a household to find the next period aggregate capital stock, and hence next period interest rate and solve (6.48), it is assumed that he knows the distribution of individual states $F(\epsilon_t, a_t)$.

We formulate again the model in terms of a recursive representation and eliminate the time notation. The households maximize their value function and we can write this as:

$$V(\epsilon, a, F) = \max_{c,a'}[u(c) + \beta E\{V(\epsilon', a', F')|\epsilon, F\}] \tag{6.50}$$

Here, the budget constraint in (6.44) is assumed, the government policy given by $\{b, \tau\}$, the employment status as in (6.45), the distribution dynamics in (6.47). We might notice here that the value function depends on the assets a and employment status ϵ as in the stationary case, but it also depends on the distribution $F(\cdot)$. The model can now be written as follows (after dropping the time subscript, although, as underscored, the factor prices w_t, r_t and the taxation rate τ do vary):

1. The household maximizes the value function:

$$V(\epsilon, a, F) = \max_{c,a'}[u(c) + \beta E\{V(\epsilon', a', F')|\epsilon, F\}] \tag{6.51}$$

Under the constraints provided by the budget constraint, Eq. (6.44), government policy $\{b, \tau\}$, the employment status as in (6.45), the dynamics of the distribution function and the condition that $a \geq a_{min}$;

2. Factor prices r, w result from firm's optimization problem in Eq. (6.48):

$$\begin{aligned} r &= w(K, N) \\ w &= r(K, N) \end{aligned} \tag{6.52}$$

3. Furthermore, the dynamics of the distribution function is given by:

$$F'(\epsilon', a') = \sum_{\epsilon_t \in e, u} \pi(\epsilon'|\epsilon) f_t(\epsilon, a'^{-1}(\epsilon_t, a', F)) \tag{6.53}$$

4. We obtain the capital stock, employment, consumption, tax revenues and unemployment benefits by aggregating over households:

$$K = \sum_{\epsilon \in \{e,u\}} \int_{a_{min}}^{\infty} a f(\epsilon, a) da \tag{6.54}$$

$$N = \int_{a_{min}}^{\infty} f(\epsilon, a) da \tag{6.55}$$

$$C = \sum_{\epsilon \in \{e,u\}} \int_{a_{min}}^{\infty} c f(\epsilon, a) da \tag{6.56}$$

$$T = \tau(wN + rK) \tag{6.57}$$

$$B = \int_{a_{min}}^{\infty} b f(u, a) da \tag{6.58}$$

The key part of simulating such a model is to approximate the dynamics of the distribution as given in Eq. (6.53). There are basically two ways that were proposed in the literature: partial information and the shooting method.

Partial Information

This method is due to [7] and [9]. The key assumption in this approach is that the agents do not rely on the whole information about F (i.e., the whole distribution), but rather on a restricted number of statistics. This simplifies the infinite dimensional problem of estimating the dynamic of F to a finite-dimensional problem.

There are different ways to approximate the distribution function. One can use an exponential function, or rely on the moments of the distribution. Here, as in [3] who follow [7], I use the moments of the distribution functions to simplify the characterization of the distribution function. Let us assume that the agents use I statistics to characterize $F' = G(f)$. We write the set of I statistics as $m = (m_1, ..., m_I)$. To further simplify the problem, assume that the agents use only the first moment to approximate the distribution function (Krussel and Smith demonstrate that the use of higher order moments is not necessary). In this case, the law of motion for m can be written as:

$$m' = H_I(m) \tag{6.59}$$

Once we know the current and the next period for m, we can solve for the households' optimization problem using the recursive representation. To simplify, the time index is dropped in the following:

$$V(\epsilon, a, m) = \max_{c, a'}[u(c) + \beta E\{V(\epsilon', a', m')|\epsilon, m\}] \tag{6.60}$$

Under the constraints provided by the budget constraint, Eq. (6.44), government policy $\{b, \tau\}$, the employment status as in (6.45) and the distribution dynamics in (6.47).

The current capital stock can be computed using the approximation proposed, i.e. the first moment of the distribution function:

$$K = m_1 \tag{6.61}$$

Once the capital stock K is known, we can also compute the factor prices, using $w = w(K, N)$ and $r = r(K, N)$. We can compute now the income tax rate τ and the unemployment benefit b from:

$$T = \tau K^\alpha N^{1-\alpha} = B = (1 - N)b$$
$$b = \zeta(1 - \tau)w = \zeta(1 - \tau)(1 - \alpha)\left(\frac{K}{N}\right)^{-\alpha} \tag{6.62}$$

Finally, we approximate the next period capital stock by relying on the following parametric specification, as in Krussel and Smith (1998):

$$\ln K' = \gamma_0 + \gamma_1 \ln K \tag{6.63}$$

The next algorithm, suggested by [3], can be written as follows (based on the assumption of using only the first moment to approximate the distribution):

1. Start from an initial distribution of assets F_0 with capital stock K_0;
2. Propose a functional form and parametrization for the H_1 and guess their initial values of the parameters;
3. Solve consumer's problem and compute the value function $V(\epsilon, a, m)$;
4. Perform a simulation for the dynamics of the distribution;
5. Estimate a law of motion for the selected moments m;
6. Check whether convergence has been achieved in terms of parameters of H_I; if not, get back to Step 2 and change the functional form and/or the parametrization for H_I.

Shooting Method

Despite its advantages, partial information method can lead to a heavy computational cost when additional endogenous variables are considered. An alternative approach, the shooting method, proposes the computation of the value function based on individual variables and not relying on the aggregate capital stock as in the partial information approach. The algorithm below, due to [10], suggests a solution to the implementation of the shooting method. This approach however applies to deterministic models.

1. Set T, the number of transition periods;
2. Compute the stationary distribution $\bar{F}$ and the set the first-period value for the distribution function F_1;
3. Starting from the first period value $t = 1$, as implied by the initial distribution, compute the values for factor prices r, w, income tax rate τ, and unemployment benefits b. Compute a guess path for these variables. The last period values $t = T$ for r, w, τ, b are obtained from the stationary distribution $\bar{F}$.

4. Iterating backwards, with $t = T - 1, ..., 1$, compute the optimal decision functions using the guess values for r, w, τ, b;
5. Using the derived optimal policy functions and initial value of the distribution function, simulate the distribution function for $t = 1, ..., T$;
6. Derive the factor prices r, w the income tax rate τ and the unemployment benefits b, get back to step 3 if it is the case;
7. Check whether the simulated distribution F_T is close enough to the stationary distribution $\bar{F}$; if not, increase the number of periods T.

6.3.2 Dynamic Heterogeneous Agents Models With Aggregate Uncertainty

In this section, I further extend the analysis based on heterogeneous agents. While the previous sections were based on the risk present only at individual level (idiosyncratic), I introduce here uncertainty at the aggregate level too. This is not new, since, for example, the baseline DSGE model introduces uncertainty via a stochastic process for technology level. This is how aggregate uncertainty is introduced here too.

To be more concrete, assume a Markov process for the technology process. The transition matrix is given by $\Gamma_Z(Z'|Z)$, where Z' is the next period productivity level. We now write the production function as follows:

$$F(K_t, N_t) = Z_t K_t^\alpha N_t^{1-\alpha} \tag{6.64}$$

The factor prices depend on the stochastic technology too, and we write:

$$r_t = Z_t \alpha K_t^{\alpha-1} N_t^{1-\alpha} - \delta$$
$$w_t = Z_t (1 - \alpha) K_t^\alpha N_t^{-\alpha} \tag{6.65}$$

There are now two sources of uncertainty in the model: the productivity Z_t at the aggregate level, which switches between a higher level in good times Z_g and a lower level in bad times Z_b. We can write the joint process for the shocks using a Markov process written as $\Gamma(Z', \epsilon'|, Z, \epsilon)$. Since we assumed only two states for the technology process Z_g, Z_g and two states for employment e, u, we obtain a joint Markov process (Z, ϵ) with 4 states. The transition matrix elements are of the form $p_{Z\epsilon Z'\epsilon'}$ and they are interpreted as indicating the probability of the transition from (Z, ϵ) to (Z', ϵ').

We can describe now the model with heterogeneity at households level and aggregate uncertainty as follows.

1. The household maximizes the value function:

$$V(\epsilon, a, Z, F) = \max_{c,a'}[U(c) + \beta E\{V(\epsilon', a', Z', F')|\epsilon, Z, F\}] \tag{6.66}$$

2. The constraints are similar to the previous cases, namely, the budget constraint as in

$$a' = \begin{cases} (1 + (1 - \tau)r_t)a + (1 - \tau)w - c, & \text{if } \epsilon = e \\ (1 + (1 - \tau)r_t)a + b - c, & \text{if } \epsilon = u \end{cases} \tag{6.67}$$

the stochastic joint process which becomes now:

$$\Gamma(Z', \epsilon'|Z, \epsilon) = Prob\{Z_{t+1} = Z', \epsilon_{t+1} = \epsilon'|Z_t = Z, \epsilon_t = \epsilon\} =$$

$$\begin{bmatrix} p_{Z_g e Z_g e} & p_{Z_g e Z_g u} & p_{Z_g e Z_b e} & p_{Z_g e Z_b u} \\ p_{Z_g u Z_g e} & p_{Z_g u Z_g u} & p_{Z_g u Z_b e} & p_{Z_g u Z_b u} \\ p_{Z_b e Z_g e} & p_{Z_b e Z_g u} & p_{Z_b e Z_b e} & p_{Z_b e Z_b u} \\ p_{Z_b u Z_g e} & p_{Z_b u Z_g u} & p_{Z_b u Z_b e} & p_{Z_b u Z_b u} \end{bmatrix} \tag{6.68}$$

the equation $a \geq a_{min}$ holds and the government policy conditions are given by:

$$\zeta = \frac{b}{1 - \tau} w$$
$$T = B \tag{6.69}$$

3. The dynamics of the distribution is denoted now by $F(\epsilon, a; Z, K)$:

$$F'(\epsilon', a'; Z', K') = \sum_\epsilon \Gamma(Z', \epsilon'|Z, \epsilon) F(\epsilon, a; Z, K) \tag{6.70}$$

4. Factor prices r, w are those given by the optimal conditions in Eq. (6.65):

$$r = \alpha Z (\frac{N}{K})^{1-\alpha} - \delta$$

$$w = (1 - \alpha) Z (\frac{K}{N})^{\alpha} \tag{6.71}$$

5. We also obtain the capital stock, employment, consumption, tax revenues and unemployment benefits by aggregating over households:

$$K = \sum_{\epsilon} \int_a^{\infty} a f(\epsilon, a; Z, K) da \tag{6.72}$$

$$N = \int_a^{\infty} f(\epsilon, a; Z, K) da \tag{6.73}$$

$$C = \sum_{\epsilon} \int_a^{\infty} c(\epsilon, a) f(\epsilon, a; Z, K) da \tag{6.74}$$

$$T = \tau(wN + rK) \tag{6.75}$$

$$B = \int_a^{\infty} b f(\epsilon, a; Z, K) da \tag{6.76}$$

Along the lines suggested by [3], we turn to a simplified version of the model in [7].

Employment

In such a model the state variable would consist in $\{\epsilon, a, Z, f, N\}$. The reason is that the current employment probabilities at individual level depend on both the current productivity, and the current employment status. Thus, aggregate employment becomes itself a state variable.

Assuming that the unemployment rate takes only two values, u_g in good times and u_b in bad times, such that $u_b > u_g$. The following restriction is imposed on the transition matrix Γ:

$$u_z \frac{p_{Z_u Z_u'}}{p_{ZZ'}} + (1 - u_Z) \frac{p_{Z_e Z_u'}}{p_{ZZ'}} = u_{Z'} \tag{6.77}$$

Here, the $Z, Z' \in \{Z_g, Z_b\}$. This implies that whenever $Z' = Z_g$, unemployment is u_g and whenever $Z' = Z_b$, unemployment becomes u_b. It also implies that the employment is not anymore a state variable since N' is predetermined by Z'.

The Distribution of Capital

In this model, the distribution of capital stock is not stationary due to the presence of aggregate uncertainty. The main reason for this fact is that the income and savings of an individual household vary over time, resulting in a varying distribution of capital stock.

The perceived law of motion of aggregate capital stock takes into account now the productivity level and it is written as follows:

$$m' = H_I(m, Z) \tag{6.78}$$

Since Z takes two possible values $\{Z_g, Z_b\}$, we can write the dynamics for next period capital stock using the first moment as follows:

$$\ln K' = \begin{cases} \gamma_{0_g} + \gamma_{1_g} \ln K, \text{ if } Z = Z_g \\ \gamma_{0_b} + \gamma_{1_b} \ln K, \text{ if } Z = Z_b \end{cases} \tag{6.79}$$

I present now an algorithm to simulate the model with household heterogeneity and aggregate uncertainty, following [3]:

1. Set T, the number of transition periods;
2. Given the current realization of productivity Z, compute aggregate employment using $N = N(Z)$;
3. Set the order I for the approximation moments m;
4. Propose a parameterized form for H_I and set the initial parameters;
5. Obtain a solution to consumers' optimization problem and determine the value function $V(\epsilon, a, Z, m)$;
6. Perform a simulation for the distribution function dynamics;
7. Given the obtained time path of the distribution, estimate the law of motion for the moments m;
8. Iterate to get the convergence for the parameters of H_I;
9. Check the goodness of fit for H_I using relevant statistics and stop if the fit is good enough, or, if not, go back to Step 4 and change the functional form for H_I (or increase I).

REFERENCES

[1] J. Miao, Economic Dynamics in Discrete Time, MIT Press, 2014.

[2] L. Ljungqvist, Th. Sargent, Recursive Macroeconomic Theory, 3rd edition, MIT Press, 2012.

[3] B. Heer, A. Maussner, Dynamic General Equilibrium Modelling, Computational Methods and Applications, 2nd edition, Springer, 2008.

[4] W. Den Haan, Teaching notes, Mimeo, London School of Economics, 2015.

[5] M. Huggett, The risk-free rate in heterogeneous-agent incomplete-insurance economies, Journal of Economic Dynamics and Control 17 (1993) 953–969.

[6] S.R. Aiyagari, Uninsured idiosyncratic risk and aggregate saving, The Quarterly Journal of Economics 24 (1994) 659–684.

[7] P. Krussel, A. Smith, Income and wealth heterogeneity in the macroeconomy, Journal of Political Economy 106 (1998) 867–896.

[8] W. Den Haan, K. Judd, M. Juillard, Computational suite of models with heterogeneous agents: incomplete markets and aggregate uncertainty, Journal of Economic Dynamics and Control 34 (2010) 1–3.

[9] W. Den Haan, Solving dynamic models with aggregate shocks and heterogeneous agents, Macroeconomic Dynamics 1 (1997) 335–386.

[10] J.V. Rios-Rull, Computation of equilibria in heterogeneous-agent models, in: R. Marimon, A. Scott (Eds.), Computational Methods for the Study of Dynamic Economies, 2001, pp. 238–264.

[11] G. Hall, Lecture notes on advanced macroeconomics, Mimeo, Brandeis University, 2006.

Index

Printed in the United States
By Bookmasters